Gendered Pasts

Gendered Pasts:

Historical Essays in Femininity and Masculinity in Canada

edited by
Kathryn McPherson, Cecilia Morgan,
and Nancy M. Forestell

UNIVERSITY OF TORONTO PRESS
Toronto   Buffalo   London

Originally published by
© Oxford University Press Canada 1999
© University of Toronto Press Incorporated 2003
Toronto Buffalo London
Printed in Canada

ISBN 0-8020-8690-X (paper)

∞

Printed on acid-free paper

National Library of Canada Cataloguing in Publication

Gendered pasts : historical essays in feminity and masculinity in Canada /
edited by Kathryn McPherson, Cecilia Morgan and Nancy M. Forestell.

(The Canadian social history series)

Includes bibliographical references and index.
ISBN 0-8020-8690-X
1. Sex role – Canada – History – 19th century. 2. Sex role – Canada – History –
20th century. 3. Feminity – Canada – History – 19th century. 4. Masculinity –
Canada – History –20th century. 5. Sex differences (Psychology) – Canada –
History – 19th century. 6. Sex differences (Psychology) – Canada – History –
20th century. I. McPherson, Kathryn M.   II. Morgan, Cecilia Louise, 1958–
III. Forestell, Nancy M. (Nancy Margaret), 1960– IV. Series: Canadian
social history series.

HQ1075.5.C3G453 2003   305.3′0971′09034   C2003-906471-9

University of Toronto Press acknowledges the financial assistance to its publishing program of the Canada Council for the Arts and the Ontario Arts
Council.

University of Toronto Press acknowledges the financial support for its
publishing activities of the Government of Canada through the Book Publishing Industry Development Program (BPIDP)

Contents

Acknowledgements

For many of us, this collection of essays represents more than a decade of political and intellectual engagement with feminist historical scholarship in Canada and internationally. *Gendered Pasts* was born out of a socialist-feminist reading group we established in the early 1990s to help us work through our shared struggles with historical theory and research. Over time, we widened our intellectual circle, establishing links with colleagues across the country who were facing similar questions and debates, though in very different temporal and chronological domains. Although we came together in search of intellectual challenge and shared academic interests, we have forged important and lasting friendships in the process. We would like to acknowledge in particular Lykke de la Cour, one of the original members of the reading group, who decided not to contribute an article, but whose ideas, research, and friendship none the less influenced greatly the shaping of this volume.

To Greg Kealey we owe thanks for his sustained support through the publication process. Over the years, and in many capacities, Greg has served as a mentor and friend, an academic who demonstrates that scholarly rigour and challenge need not preclude compassion and good humour. We continue to appreciate the skill and hard work of our colleagues at Oxford University Press. We would like to thank in particular Ric Kitowski, Phyllis Wilson, and Laura Macleod, as well as our copy-editor, Richard Tallman. We benefited from the comments of the anonymous appraisers who challenged us to sharpen our claims.

Feminist scholars have insisted that the concept of 'separate spheres' never captured the reality of women's and men's lives in the past, that the 'public' and the 'private' were always inextricably linked. Our families would probably respond 'no kidding'. For all the holidays, rented movies, and dinner hours that were interrupted by meetings or phone calls about this book, we're sorry. For all the jokes you made about us, that's okay. For continuing to acknowledge that the personal is political, thank you.

Contributors

KAREN DUBINSKY is a member of the Department of History at Queen's University. She is the author of *Improper Advances: Rape and Heterosexual Conflict in Ontario, 1880–1929* (1993), and is now preparing a manuscript on gender, tourism, and Niagara Falls.

NANCY FORESTELL teaches history and women's studies at Nova Scotia's St Francis Xavier University. She is currently completing a manuscript entitled 'Gendered Terrains: Work, Family, and Community Life in a Northern Ontario Mining Community, 1909–1950'.

ADAM GIVERTZ's contribution to this volume is part of his doctoral dissertation research on the history of incest. A founding editor of *Left History: an interdisciplinary journal of historical enquiry and debate*, Adam is enrolled in York University's Osgoode Law School.

FRANCA IACOVETTA is author of the award-winning book, *Such Hard Working People: Italian Immigrants in Postwar Toronto* (1992), and teaches history at the University of Toronto. One of Canada's leading scholars in immigration and ethnic history, Franca is currently completing a new monograph, 'Making New Citizens in Cold War Canada'.

MARGARET LITTLE teaches women's studies and political science at Queen's University and is the author of *No Car, No Radio, No Liquor Permit: The Moral Regulation of Single Mothers in Ontario, 1920–1997* (1998).

JOHN LUTZ, recently appointed to the History Department at the University of Victoria, researches the history of Aboriginal/non-Aboriginal relations on the Pacific coast of Canada and in the American Pacific

Northwest. His doctoral dissertation from the University of Ottawa, 'Work, Wages and Welfare in Aboriginal-Non-Aboriginal Relations, British Columbia 1843–1979', won the John Bullen thesis prize.

LYNNE MARKS is the author of *Revivals and Roller Rinks: Religion, Leisure and Identity in Late Nineteenth-Century Small-Town Ontario* (1996), which won the Chalmers Award. Her new project analyses the relationship between gender and religion in nineteenth-century Canada. Lynne teaches history at the University of Victoria.

KATHRYN McPHERSON is the author of *Bedside Matters: The Transformation of Canadian Nursing, 1900–1990* (1996). Her current research focuses on women in the prairie West. She is a member of the History Department at York University.

CECILIA MORGAN is author of *Public Men and Virtuous Women: The Gendered Languages of Religion and Politics in Upper Canada, 1791–1850* (1996) and has co-edited the document collection, *Material Memory: Documents in Pre-Confederation History* (1998). Cecilia teaches history at OISE at the University of Toronto.

SUZANNE MORTON has published widely in Atlantic Canadian history. She is author of *Ideal Surroundings: Domestic Life in a Working-Class Suburb in the 1920s* (1995) and co-editor of *Separate Spheres: Women's Worlds in the 19th Century Maritimes* (1994). Suzanne teaches history at McGill University.

MARY ANN POUTANEN is a member of the Montreal History Group and a research historian. Her contribution to this volume is drawn from her Ph.D. dissertation from the Université de Montréal, entitled 'To Indulge Their Carnal Appetites': Prostitution in Early Nineteenth Century Montreal, 1810–1842'.

ERIC SETLIFF has an MA in History from the University of Toronto. He is currently completing a degree in the history of design at the Bard Graduate Center in New York.

Introduction:

Conceptualizing Canada's

Gendered Pasts

Kathryn McPherson, Cecilia Morgan, and Nancy M. Forestell

Not so long ago, it seems, historians who placed the question of gender at the centre of their research did so from the margins of academic scholarship. But in more recent times, the analysis of how femininity and masculinity shaped and were shaped by specific historical contexts fuels the research of a wide range of scholars, using diverse theoretical and methodological approaches. The proliferation of articles, books, and even journals devoted to gender history reflects the new intellectual and international importance given to gender as a 'category of analysis'.[1]

The dramatic growth in the field has not occurred without controversy. As traditional areas of historical scholarship and publication made grudging, if any, room for gender analyses, substantial debate erupted among feminists over the relationship between the study of women and that of gender. Some consider gender history the logical progression from women's history, a much-needed application of feminist insights to all dimensions of the past: in Gisela Bock's words, women's history is gender history *par excellence*.[2] Others view the emergence of this new field with a great deal more scepticism, claiming that it shifts attention away from real women and dulls our sensitivity to the full force of patriarchal power. Sceptics claim that the use of the term 'gender' reflects the vitiation of the women's movement and a retreat to a more respectable, less threatening nomenclature, itself the result of the professionalization of feminist scholarship and its divorce from its activist roots. In response, advocates point to the theoretical sophistication that has driven research in gender history, celebrating the critique of an 'essential' or universalized femininity (or masculinity) that gender historians have mounted and the possibilities for social change that such a critique offers.[3]

These debates, especially acute in North America,[4] have proved critical in opening up new theoretical and evidential questions. At the same time, the tendency to view women's and gender history as antithetical has often ignored the complexity of analysis undertaken by 'traditional' women's history and has underestimated the diversity of scholarship that characterizes 'new' gender history.[5] In assembling this collection, we have been struck by the links between the two; their relationship has often appeared much more symbiotic than the fundamental opposition sometimes suggested. As the contributors to this volume exemplify, many researchers comfortably cohabit the categories of 'women's' and 'gender' history, while those trained in other subfields of history have undertaken gendered analyses and in so doing tell us much about understudied groups of women.

Yet it would be disingenuous to claim that the feminist debates over women's and gender history are so slight as to be of no political, epistemological, or methodological consequence. Those debates have fundamentally shaped the field, and have paralleled theoretical discussions taking place within historical scholarship more generally. And researchers from a range of subspecialties have found in gender analysis theoretical perspectives that have transformed their own area of research. Four questions in particular—the biological and social bases of gender categories, the methodological importance of language and literary analysis, the conceptualization of power, and the study of masculinity—have dominated the dialogues among feminists and have made gender history a dynamic and challenging field of study.

It is now commonplace to state that gender (like race and sexuality) is 'socially constructed'. By this, scholars mean that there is no 'natural' or 'essential' sex difference. Biological definitions of male and female are, and were, argue theorists, human constructions like any other—scientific efforts to explain the cultural or social attributes or expectations imposed on human bodies. Gender categories must thus be analysed as historically constituted and open to change, not static or fixed. Accordingly, women's historians have been criticized for assuming that the category 'women' in the past was similar to what it is in the present, or that it even could be immediately recognizable to contemporary observers. In Mariana Valverde's words, women's historians 'presupposed the object of their inquiry'.[6]

This current disavowal of biological 'sex' does constitute a significant analytic turn for women's historians, many of whom had adhered to an understanding of sex/gender systems—with sex being the biological or physical 'reality' and gender being the culturally imposed traits that gave meaning and power to one sex over the other. Of course, not all scholars have given the same analytic weight to the two halves of the sex/gender system. Socialist-feminist historians and historians of ethnic or racialized minorities have long acknowledged that the category 'woman' meant different things to different members of the 'sex'. For instance, throughout the 1970s and 1980s feminist scholars studying the Canadian working class emphasized the fundamental differences that divided working-class women from their counterparts in the bourgeoisie. But those scholars also agreed that the common (if never universal) physical experience of being born 'female' constituted the possibility for shared gender identity across class, racial, and ethnic divisions. Biological sex was thus theorized both as a source of oppression but also as a potent force of collective action and resistance. Feminist scholars are now thus divided over whether to build on the popular understanding of biological difference as a mechanism to unite women against gender oppression, or to deconstruct gendered structures and traditions so as to expose the fallacy of 'maleness' and 'femaleness' that shores up patriarchal power—if there is no 'real' gender, there is no 'real' basis for systemic oppression or discrimination.

As they deconstruct the 'real', some researchers have moved away from analysing the material conditions of women's (or men's) lives to focus on linguistic or 'discursive' constructions of gender. Using the tools of literary criticism and post-structuralist philosophy, these gender historians focus on the ways masculinity and femininity have been constituted through 'language', especially through the process of naming one thing in opposition to its 'other'. Such scholars focus on the relational dimensions of social categories—how femininity and masculinity are defined in relation to one another—but also on the margins or borders of those categories, where evidence of deviance, defiance, or alternative constructions are more easily seen. Most importantly, the insistence by gender historians that 'gender' was a fundamental social force even when 'real' women were absent has prompted sophisticated analyses detailing how gender is, in Joan Scott's words, a 'primary way of signifying power'. In realms such as the political and military, the absence of women was often a crucial dimension of organizing and maintaining hierarchical relationships.[7]

Feminist theorist Michele Barrett has coined this new interest in language as a shift from 'things to words' wherein social scientific research has been superseded by cultural analysis of 'symbolization and representation . . . and attempts to develop a better understanding of subjectivity, the psyche, and the self'.[8] Yet, many scholars resist the trend away from studying the gendered *experiences* of specific women or men. This concept of experience was a critical tool for feminists seeking to validate women's own stories and female-specific life-course events in the face of patriarchal traditions that had defined what was 'normal' and what was 'important' in decidedly masculine terms.[9] Equally important, feminist historians saw in the concept of experience a way to theorize women's social identity. Building on E.P. Thompson's use of the term to signify the formation of class identity, feminist historians asserted that women understood their social location not only through ideological prescriptions—or through language—but also through the material and physical lessons learned as a consequence of childbirth, sexual violence, hunger, poverty, and work.[10] For this reason, feminist scholars such as Christine Stansell have recognized the importance of studying language—what she calls 'rhetoric'—but maintain that identity or consciousness is formed as much through material forces as through discourses.[11]

A third issue that has provoked debate among researchers has been the nature of social power. Historians influenced by theorists such as Michel Foucault have conceptualized power as decentred, a fundamental aspect of all human relationships, and embedded in multiple locations and sites. Power is therefore neither monolithic nor a discrete entity, but rather the result of human relations.[12] It is also fragmented and diffuse. They observe that ordinary women and men regularly exercise power, though not always or only in response to forms of oppression (such as patriarchy or capitalism) but over their children, or neighbours, or servants. By contrast, earlier scholarship in women's history emphasized the concentration of patriarchal power, its resilience and dominance. Socialist feminists complicated the paradigm substantially in their articulations of how patriarchy intersected with capitalism (as either dual or separate systems of power) and where women or the working class or minority groups wielded power as resistance or agency.[13]

Rethinking the locations of power has become particularly important when the experiences of racial, ethnic, and sexual minorities are considered. Arguments over the primacy of one set of relationships or identities have begun to give way to a more nuanced investigation of the complex ways in which gender, race, and class relations intersect with, overlap, and at times contradict each other. The empirical and theoretical insights produced by this kind of historical investigation should not, however, be attributed solely to gender historians. Since its inception, the work of African-American historians, for example, has demonstrated that femininity and masculinity have not held the same meanings for women and men of African descent.[14] Nor do certain historical processes, such as imperialism or colonization, produce the same kinds of gender relations for women and men from subaltern groups as they do for women and men of the imperial power.[15] Some gender historians have taken the project of decentring and deconstructing even further in their attempts to understand how 'White womanhood', often the norm underpinning much feminist history and theory, has been actively, historically constructed as a category encapsulating both racial and gender identity.[16] This new approach shifts historians' focus away from the universal category of 'woman' and emphasizes, instead, the fundamental differences that divide gendered subjects as well as the historically specific processes that unite people into a shared gendered consciousness.

The analytic emphasis on contradictions among categories and fragmentation or multiplicity of identity has prompted a decline in attention paid to historical models, such as modernization or the Marxian stages of economic history. While some feminist scholars continue to work within large-scale paradigms of social changes, others see no necessary or predictable outcome of these historically specific deployments of power, no metanarrative into which struggles must be written.[17]

A final area of theorizing within gender history revolves around a critical analysis of masculinity, in which researchers have investigated how masculinity, like femininity, has been socially constructed. In fairness, early women's historians recognized that what counted as 'history' was in fact the history of men and thus purposefully ignored chronicling the overstudied half of humanity, but an unintended result of this approach was that men's gendered behaviour was treated as 'natural' and therefore left invisible. Problematizing and historicizing hold out the promise of dislodging or decentring the ungendered, universalized male subject. In addition, this new attention to men's gendered experiences allows historians to probe the relational dimensions of gender formation: how femininity was formed in relation to masculinity, and vice versa.[18]

Writing 'men' into the historical narrative has proven no less controversial than was the case for women. For instance, some of the earliest published works on masculinity seemed to celebrate, however subtly, middle-class men and their involvement in fraternal orders, organized religion, educational institutions, and business enterprises without confronting the tremendous social power those men wielded over women and other men.[19] Labour historians, examining the meanings of 'manhood' for working-class men, have been more attentive to questions of social power, though the contradictions inherent in working-class men's subordination in the workplace versus their superordination at home demands still greater analysis.[20] Scholarship in gay history has advanced the issue of sexual power most directly, underscoring the differences among men and emphasizing that masculinity is, and was, far from monolithic.[21] Within gay and lesbian history, a substantial debate (parallel to that occurring among feminists) has developed over the relative significance of 'essential' (homo)sexuality versus socially constructed sexual identities. Here, historians have made important contributions, documenting the many traditions of non-heterosexual behaviours and pinpointing when the social categories of 'straight' and 'gay' have emerged and overlapped.[22]

Within these various approaches to the study of men, whether middle class, working class, or homosexual, ethnicity and race require substantially more attention. Such research would highlight further diversity in how masculinity was defined, but would also facilitate our knowledge of how racial privilege enhanced the gendered status of some men over others. This point is cogently argued by Gail Bederman, who writes: 'As middle class men actively worked to reinforce male power, their race became a factor which was crucial to their gender. In ways which have been well understood, whiteness was a palpable fact and a manly ideal for these men.'[23] Like studies that focus on femininity, analyses of masculinity challenge researchers to interrogate the multiple identities of gender, sexuality, class, ethnicity, and race, as well as those such as age, religion, and nation, that might well coalesce or compete in any specific historical moment.

These debates around rethinking masculinity, power, identity, and social categories have been instrumental in shaping the field of gender history, as the essays presented in this volume reveal. But the essays here also reflect the fact that as historians have used new theoretical and methodological approaches to construct research projects and interpret evidence, their engagement with conceptual debates rarely falls neatly on one side of an issue or another. For instance, in this collection the essays are roughly equally distributed among those that focus on femininity, on masculinity, and on the relations between the two. Eric Setliff in Chapter 9 and Cecilia Morgan in Chapter 1 pay almost exclusive attention to language, while John Lutz in

Chapter 4 and Nancy Forestell in Chapter 8 are interested in the material conditions from which social categories flow. In Chapter 7 Margaret Little emphasizes the fragmented nature of power within rural communities, compared to Mary Anne Poutanen's documentation in Chapter 2 of the growing power of the state. Some contributions explore competing versions of femininity or masculinity, others chart the consolidation of dominant gender roles and identities. All the chapters reflect the larger goal of gender history to locate femininities and masculinities in their specific historical contexts.

This volume explores specific gendered dimensions of nineteenth- and twentieth-century Canadian history. While we make no claims to be completely representative, we have been able to include essays that cover a range of geographic, chronological, and thematic areas. This collection brings together researchers from various academic interests, many from women's history, but others from Native history, gay history, and working-class history. The contributions here focus on the history of politics, religion, urban space, sexuality, the welfare state, the labour movement, First Nations people, and race and ethnicity in Canada. While roughly half the authors consider some element of Ontario history—a fact that reflects, in part, the concentration of doctoral programs and access to archival sources in central Canada—other contributors locate their studies in Nova Scotia, Quebec, Manitoba, and British Columbia, while rural and northern locales, as well as urban ones, are examined. Initially conceived while many of the authors were beginning their research careers, this collection unites scholars who now have established publication records in the field of gender history with others who are in the process of doing so. The authors share a collective commitment to the intellectual and political contribution critical, feminist scholarship offers Canadian society.

Gendered Pasts begins with the early 1800s, a period of tremendous economic and social change. In the first decades of the nineteenth century British colonial rule was firmly established, even as local agitation for responsible government challenged that rule. New immigrants from Great Britain and the United States participated in the expansion of the staples economies and fostered the growth of towns and cities that provided services and were home to rudimentary manufacturing centres.

Historians of women have begun the process of documenting the gendered dimensions of life in British North America. They have shown how the assertion of British legal traditions served to disenfranchise female property holders and to limit women's chances of inheritance.[24] British authorities made it clear that however much

Loyalist women suffered and sacrificed for the Crown, their status depended on that of their husbands or fathers.[25] Certain economic opportunities did exist for popular-class women, especially as tavern keepers, small merchants, authors, proprietors of small local schools, and, of course, domestic servants, while women of the élite class wielded considerable social authority through their family connections or family economic enterprises.[26] Most women, though, were defined by their dependent status, subordinate to the male head of household, and this status was inscribed in advice literature and common law.[27]

Building on this portrait of a patriarchal colonial society, Cecilia Morgan in Chapter 1 offers an analysis of the gendered political language of manliness employed by political reformers and conservatives. As political commentators debated the nature of the Canadian state, they defined political participation in decidedly male terms, using feminine imagery to signify the weaknesses in their opponents' political vision. In Chapter 2 Mary Anne Poutanen identifies a comparable intensification of gender divisions in her examination of an understudied dimension of early nineteenth-century life, that of emerging urban society. In Montreal, urban growth spawned new efforts to control who used the streets and for what purposes. These efforts had particular meaning for the popular-class women targeted for vagrancy and prostitution. Lynne Marks, in Chapter 3, shifts the focus away from the authority of the state to assess the mechanisms of moral and sexual regulation imposed by Ontario's Protestant churches. In her study of the church courts, Marks shows how these denominations tried to establish a single sexual and moral code for women and men, replacing the double standard embedded in British law. Together, these essays suggest that gender roles were being reshaped by wider social changes—neither masculinity nor patriarchal colonial society was a fixed, constant entity—and that in evangelical religion, political discourse, and the streets it was possible to contest or rewrite gendered paradigms.

By the end of the nineteenth century, colonial society was supplanted by an industrial one. During the 1880–1920 years, the Canadian federal state was established as a national entity and, with it, the final colonization of Native peoples occurred. The Canadian industrial revolution and the attendant increases in immigration and urbanization made Canada a 'nation', complete with social dislocation and dramatic class conflict.

Many historians have charted the gendered dimensions of Canada's path to modernity, initially emphasizing women's struggles to win political enfranchisement. The suffrage campaign, and the massive mobilization that constituted Canada's first women's movement, drew scholarly attention to the many middle-class female reformers who laboured to solve the problems of the newly emerging urban industrial order.[28] At the same time, historians of working women traced the emergence of a gender-divided world of paid labour in which women worked in blue- and white-collar female 'ghettos' characterized by lower pay, a high turnover, and limited union representation.[29] Yet it was not their exploitation at the workplace that attracted the attention of social reformers. Rather, reformers viewed the presence of young, single women, living outside the control of home and family, as part and parcel of the 'moral decay' of urban Canada. Much recent scholarship has analysed how unconstrained female sexuality came to signify a broader range of social problems plaguing the nation.[30]

But as Karen Dubinsky and Adam Givertz demonstrate in Chapter 4, male sexuality could also signify social danger. Their comparative analysis of sexual and racialized 'villains' in southern Ontario and British Columbia suggests fruitful new avenues for deconstructing male heterosexual power (or lack thereof). Their conclusion, that gender and race intersected in highly localized ways, is substantiated in Chapter 5 by John Lutz's research on a west coast First Nations community. Tracing the relations of Lekwammen women and men to the state and the economy, Lutz argues that the process of colonization inverted 'White' gender relations, offering Lekwammen women relatively greater economic authority than their male kinfolk or Euro-Canadian counterparts. Colonization, Lutz shows, was gendered, just as gender roles were transformed by colonization. Suzanne Morton, in Chapter 6, shifts the focus to the east coast, where, in the wake of the Halifax explosion, local authorities responded to inquiries about adopting children orphaned by the explosion. Mining this rich collection of letters written to the Halifax Relief Commission, Morton demonstrates the existence of a continent-wide consensus over the qualities that determined a 'good mother' and a 'good father', as well as a good child. Normative definitions of femininity and masculinity were not only imposed from above, but were created and reinforced as ordinary citizens forged family relations.

By the 1920s, the emerging welfare state in Canada was developing mechanisms to formalize such definitions of proper parenting. The last five chapters in this volume consider the gendered elements of modern Canadian society, from 1920 to the 1960s. A period characterized by the formation of a continental economy and heavily influenced by (American) consumer culture, the decades since World War I witnessed the emergence of a welfare state apparatus, the dislocation caused by the Depression and World War II, massive immigration (from Europe, but also from Asia, Africa, and the Caribbean), and, more recently, the development of popular movements: Native rights, gay and lesbian rights, and 'second-wave' feminism.

The influence of gender in these more recent decades is only now receiving systematic analysis. Substantial attention has been paid to the ways that gender, race, and class have intersected in federal immigration policies and public health initiatives.[31] Socialist feminists have continued the task of analysing women, work, and family, ranging from the domestic labours of housewives in Flin Flon to the industrial work performed by the women of Peterborough.[32] And sexuality has emerged as an important subject of study for authors studying the discourses of social anxiety over gender roles, as well as for scholars excavating nascent lesbian and gay communities.[33]

The authors in our collection contribute to this new scholarship in the history of sexuality, although in different ways. Margaret Little, in Chapter 7, demonstrates that, from its earliest incarnation, the welfare state was preoccupied with gender, sexuality, and morality. The single mothers she studies found their welfare support threatened when state investigators (or nosy neighbours) suspected any violation of dominant moral codes. By contrast, the tabloid *Hush Free Press* fed on the transgression of these moral codes. In Chapter 9, Eric Setliff analyses the post-World War II urban gay community depicted on the pages of *Hush*. He argues that mocking gay men was stock-in-trade for *Hush* columnists but the stereotypes they created were of the 'swish' and not the 'sex fiend', a sexual transgressor, not a sexual villain. Whereas *Hush* portrayed gay men as 'performing' their gender 'wrong', nurses have been constrained to fulfil a proscribed definition of gender. Kathryn McPherson, in Chapter 10, uses Judith Butler's theory of gender as performance to demonstrate how an occupationally specific definition of appropriate femininity and heterosexuality was constructed through the rituals and repetitions of performing female sexuality 'right' within the nursing profession. McPherson argues for the continued significance of investigating the links between gender and sexuality, and of locating such investigations in specific political economies.

The importance of analysing the intersection of gender and work is underscored in Chapters 8 and 11, by Nancy Forestell and Franca Iacovetta, respectively. Forestell's analysis of the 'miner's wife' in Timmins reveals the very real material and ideological limitations faced by married working-class women in a single-industry town. The place-specific gender category helped create a gendered hierarchy of needs within the working-class community but also contained the possibility for social validation of women's unpaid labour. The question of social validation is also addressed in Iacovetta's study of strikes in Toronto's construction industry during the early 1960s. Immigrant working-class men based their claims to class justice on manly honour, a discourse that evoked men's respected status as breadwinners (even when their wives' wages put bread on the table) and legitimized immigrants' place as citizens: the language of gender slid easily into that of race and class and nation.

Clearly, then, popular perceptions of appropriate masculinity and femininity have proved central, both to the lives of women and men and to large social processes, such as responsible government, colonization, and the union movement. The essays in *Gendered Pasts* confirm the importance of understanding specific historical contexts if we are to know precisely how gender roles and definitions have been deployed, and by whom. As these essays suggest, historians using a wide range of evidence and methodologies have shown that there is no single 'gender history', no single history of Canada with gender 'written in'.

However diverse the approach or conclusions of gender history, it is imperative that historians not lose sight of the power relations that constitute, and are constituted by, gender. It is not sufficient for scholars to observe benignly, as does one editor in a recent publication in the field, that 'gender is one of the key determinants of life.'[34] It is gender asymmetry—the social power that one obtains by conforming (or not conforming) to gendered norms—that garners some members of society greater authority and control over others. In this regard, gender historians have much to learn from their colleagues in women's history, and this is perhaps where the real connection between women's history and gender history lies. As Natalie Davis has recently observed, the traditions of feminist scholarship on women and on 'what we used to call the relations between the sexes' have demonstrated the value of nurturing the links between feminist gender history and women's history.[35] Indeed, it is perhaps less important what the subject of historical research is: women or men, gendered language or gendered experience, but rather the sensitivity to where social power was located and how it was used by whom and on whom. The feminist lessons of women's history remain critical as historians seek to map out Canada's gendered pasts.

1

'When Bad Men Conspire, Good Men Must Unite!': Gender and Political Discourses in Upper Canada, 1820s–1830s

Cecilia Morgan

One of the most studied episodes in Canadian history is the Upper Canadian Rebellion of 1837. Conflict between the established 'conservative' élite (who answered to the British Crown) and political reformers (who demanded responsible government) escalated into armed rebellion and repression, but had been brewing for several decades as a war of words in the local press. As that public debate made clear, conservatives and reformers alike laid claim to the cornerstones of the British political structure: neither law nor constitution, as historians of Upper Canadian political and legal history have pointed out, held identical meanings for the political groupings of reform and conservative.[1]

But what historians have not examined is the gendered nature of Upper Canada's political contest. In colonial society of the 1820s and 1830s, debates over political reform were grounded in conceptions of public and private and were couched in language suffused with gendered imagery and symbols. These symbols relied heavily on claims of 'true manhood' to validate and legitimate claims to political power, while using images of woman and the feminine to undermine their opponents' positions.

At present, little scholarly research has been undertaken on masculinity and institutional politics in either international or Canadian history[2]. This absence is curious because, after all, political institutions were exclusively male throughout the nineteenth century. Furthermore, they were the loci of struggles between groups of men openly competing for power, the place where many of the lessons learned in other, all-male institutions (such as the British public school) supposedly were put to use. Fortunately, feminist historians have examined women's participation in the American and French Revolutions and British radicalism, as well as the different meanings that political changes held for women and the ways in which political discourse was gendered.[3] Building on these insights, this chapter analyses the language of manliness that infused the rhetoric of conservatives and reformers in the turbulent years of the Upper Canadian Rebellion. Such language asserted particular versions of masculinity, but also used female symbolism negatively to signify inappropriate political behaviour. The chapter concludes by considering the implications of gendered language for women who entered the political sphere.

Employing recent feminist theory allows us to uncover the heretofore unseen dimension of masculinity in colonial political discourses and the influence of conceptions of political power on the formation of ideals of masculinity. By examining language, we find both past struggles to fix meanings to masculinity and the power relations embedded in the concept, for 'gender is one of the recurrent references by which political power has been conceived, legitimated, and criticised.'[4] Moreover, as American historian Carroll Smith-Rosenberg has argued, in order for historians to understand the links between politics and culture, they must start examining not just constitutions but also 'the *constitution* of new political subjects . . . we must move from political theory to cultural theory, from the history of political ideas to the history of political *rhetoric*.' And, she adds, in doing so scholars will become 'doubly visioned', enriching 'one form of analysis with the insights of another'.[5] In shifting our focus from electoral returns of 'high' political theory to political rhetoric and debate and to the forum of insult and invective common to the colonial press, we may begin probing the complex processes in which political subjectivities were publicly and collectively moulded in this period.

The Context

A British colony officially established by the Constitutional Act of 1791, Upper Canada fell between the Ottawa River in the north and east, the St Clair River in the west, and Lakes Erie and Ontario in the south. The 1791 Act established a political structure similar to that of the imperial government: a bicameral legislature made up of a seven-member, appointed legislative council and an elected assembly of at least 16 members. The council members held their seats for life and in Upper Canada were appointed by the lieutenant-governor. The council's function was that of an advisory body, answerable to the governor and not to the legislature. The assembly was composed of White men who, while not necessarily property-holders themselves, were elected for four-year terms. Their constituents were either landowners with rural freeholds worth at least 40 shillings per year or urban property valued at five pounds or tenants who paid a minimum of 10 pounds rent per year. The lieutenant-governor's powers were quite broad and included the right to call, prorogue, and dissolve the legislature and withhold royal assent from bills passed by both branches of the legislature. During the early nineteenth century, dissatisfaction with the council and lieutenant-governor's control led to the formation of reform movements in both Lower and Upper Canada. By 1837, reformers' frustration culminated in an armed rebellion in both provinces.[6]

Upper Canadian politics had never been completely peaceful, but political debate intensified in the years after the War of 1812. In the decade before the war, controversies had erupted over the operation of the constitution, the relationship between the legislature and the executive, and the role of the judiciary. These kinds of conflicts, often based in York (now Toronto) and Kingston, found their way into the pages of the local newspapers, along with disputes over electoral candidates' fitness for public office.[7] However, the growth of newspapers in the colony after the war (from one in 1813 to seven in 1824, 30 in 1833, and 114 in 1853) meant that participants in political discourse not only grew in numbers but also began to vary the kinds of political languages used. From the early 1820s on, colonial newspapers were the sites of vigorous discussions about the domestic issues of importance to Upper Canadians; the press provided coverage of political debates both inside and outside the legislature, as well as editorial comments, letters, pieces of political satire, and other articles on colonial politics. The smaller body of pamphlet and sermon literature written in Upper Canada also contributed to political discourses.[8]

Linked to the growth of the colonial press was the growing tide of British immigration to the colony in the years after the Napoleonic Wars. Although it did not reach its height until the 1840s, the arrival of emigrants from England, Scotland, and Ireland provided a new cast of participants for the political arena, helping to create sharper divisions between conservatives and reformers and, as part of this process, supplying the colony with a small, yet extremely vocal, reform press. Not all the new arrivals, of course, were reform supporters, nor did all reformers reach unanimity on the meaning of reform itself. Francis Collins, for example, the editor of the *Canadian Freeman*, was an advocate of press freedom and was arrested and jailed in 1828 under the Sedition Act. Nevertheless, he disagreed violently with reformer William Lyon Mackenzie over his political tactics.[9] Yet, as a number of historians of Upper Canadian politics have pointed out, by the 1820s the Upper Canadian press had become an extremely significant force in the colony's political culture.[10]

As the colonial press proliferated, so, too, did political discourses rely more and more on concepts of gender, the family, and differing views of public and private. The articles, editorials, and letters that made up the texts of public political discourses were encoded with notions of morality, virtue, and manhood.[11] Political discourses were not 'just about' gender and the family, nor were they 'just about' Burkean versus Lockean theories of government; one set of constructs informed the other.

The Conservatives

Conservative political writing contained a number of themes, but one of its most striking motifs was that of self-restraint and control: the political man as a rational, civilized creature, one governed by reason. Sometimes, conservative actors and principles were represented directly as men and their opponents as women. In the *Upper Canada Gazette*'s 'Front Page Exchange' of 25 January 1823, the story 'One Hundred Miles from the Metropolis' depicted Mrs Slipslop, 'an old gossiping politician', discussing the throne speech with Mr Canada, 'a plain, sensible, well-informed man'. The conversation focused on ministerial attitudes towards union with Lower Canada, which Mrs Slipslop declared to be 'ambiguous' because the government had brought the issue forward but had no 'interest' in union. By dint of a superior command of both language and political sensibility, Mr Canada led her on ingenuously to declare her faith in 'one who is labouring so hard by night and by day, for your benefit; with a view to open your eyes to the enormities of folks in power'. Having thus exposed her simplistic grasp of such terms in the political arena as interest and ambiguity, Mr Canada had the final word, lecturing Mrs Slipslop on the use of criticism: 'a dangerous weapon in the hands of an ignorant and an illiterate person'.

Gender relations, of course, are apparent in this story. Feminine foolishness and flightiness are juxtaposed with solid, reasoned male judgement, and in the process criticism of government policy is dismissed as ephemeral. This binary opposition of male and female was also used to parcel up a number of other cultural traits. Mr Canada was able to control their discussion and invoke its closure not only because of his rational nature but also because of his learning, using his knowledge of Samuel Johnson's dictionary to point to Mrs Slipslop's faulty understanding of her own terms.[12] In contrast with his self-control, she was 'all of a titter (shaking hysterically)' and needed, in his words, 'the little bottle which you keep in your closet'.[13]

In this piece of political satire, the target was not women *per se*, although there was a lesson to learn about female participation in political life. This and other articles used either the figure of a woman or characteristics that, in the cultural lexicon of eighteenth- and early nineteenth-century Britain, had become identified with femininity. Excess of emotion leading to hysteria, the abandonment of rational, logical thinking, and the encroachment of previously inviolate boundaries: all were pressed into the service of political insult and the denigration of a particular political perspective.[14]

Conservatives frequently painted themselves as sensible, honest men combating forces that either were innately hysterical or would lead to the release of emotions threatening political and moral stability. This aspect of conservative discourse was, of course, not new or unique to Upper Canada, but its *gendered* nature has received little attention from historians.[15] Identifying their opponents with the forces of hysteria and excessive emotion shored up conservative claims to be men of honour, respectability, and morality. As political debate intensified throughout the 1820s, so did the frequency of these insults.[16]

The behaviour and persona of the journalist and reform politician, William Lyon Mackenzie, attracted the greatest number of political attacks. Mackenzie, according to 'John Bull' in the *Niagara Spectator*, pitched his 'editorial drivelings to the worst passions of the worst classes of the community in order to gain that foetid popularity which steams from the political brothel of a prostituted press.'[17] When Mackenzie was expelled from the Legislative Assembly in 1833, the *Patriot and Farmers' Monitor*, a vocally anti-reform and anti-Methodist paper, described his behaviour as that of a 'madman' who 'stamped and raved with all the fury of a maniac'.[18] Even when the explicit target was not an irrational woman or hysterical femininity, satirists implied that a man who lost control of his mental or emotional or sexual faculties could no longer claim the status of 'manliness' and the social and political privileges that flowed from such a position.[19]

Excessive displays of emotion, the inability to maintain self-control, and immorality (reformers were also accused of attempting to 'seduce' Upper Canadians) were all gendered insults used to construct reform as a political maelstrom of feminized and debauched evil. To be sure, reformers were generally not accused of actual sexual immorality. Although he had fathered an illegitimate child in Scotland, neither Mackenzie nor any of his supporters were depicted as following in the footsteps of the eighteenth-century radical and sexual libertine, John Wilkes.[20] But in a society in which the *symbol* of unleashed feminine sexuality could trigger great fears about social and political stability, accusations that linked reformers to femininity and instability were important weapons.[21] In the eyes of the political élite, reformers were bent on the destruction of the moral fabric of colonial society, men who threw off all ties to society and worked merely for their own selfish, individualistic ends.

Conservative discourse in the 1820s and 1830s emphasized the destruction of family ties that reform would bring, using 'family' either in the immediate, more literal sense or as a metaphor for the 'family' of the Empire. Much was made of the 'rights of Englishmen' or the 'sturdy yeoman', terms that reformers also favoured. Yet the concept of 'family' was tied to these terms and was brought into political discourse to underscore and legitimate them. The family was besieged, needlessly made anxious about the future, by unscrupulous men.[22] Using the concept of 'family' in a slightly different manner, in the pages of the *Kingston Chronicle* 'John Barleycorn' characterized Barnabus Bidwell, an American-born member of the Legislative Assembly, as hypocritical and treacherous: 'The country and Government under which we have been brought up are naturally dear to us; as a child loves his parent, so a good subject reveres his country and his King. . . . Was it not the vivid light of allegiance that shewed to a Nelson the paths of glory, through the deep; and that now plays over his tomb, to guide our sons to the same honourable career?'[23] 'Barleycorn' linked Upper Canadian loyalty and opposition to incipient American republicanism in terms that united both British and patriarchal authority. Reformers' subversion of the two was usually depicted metaphorically as a challenge to the filial, paternal tie that bound Upper Canadians to their royal father.

Occasionally they were accused of a more direct usurpation of paternal authority. In a letter to the editor of the *Kingston Spectator*, Roberts Jeffers complained that his underaged son had been induced to sign a reform petition without Jeffers's consent. Arguing that his child was his property, especially with regard to the 'exercise of his bodily or mental powers', Jeffers called for the passage of a law that would 'inflict heavy fines' on acts that undermined paternal control. And, concerned lest female political activity would further erode his authority, Jeffers advocated that the law protecting children from political involvement should be extended to women. 'Ladies should not become *masculine*—should not have their attention diverted away from those maternal offices—those tender assiduities which qualify them to infuse the drop of comfort into man's bitter cup.' The editor agreed with Jeffers and, pleased that he spoke out against the petition, hoped 'that all fathers of families in the Province will take advantage of a hint so opportunely and forcibly given.'[24] Although Jeffers's was a lone voice, his jeremiad raises some tantalizing questions—both about the sexual and familial politics of petitioning and about the role of political differences in the households of Upper Canada. Were women solicited as petitioners or did some women actively support reformers at the local level? Their absence from the petitions published in the press should not lead us to assume that they were not interested in political affairs. More likely, women were excluded from certain public records of political discourse. The editorial support given to Jeffers itself suggests that day-to-day family harmony was threatened by these issues.

Conservatives, moreover, were fond of pointing out that none was safe from the reformers' personal libels and slanders, especially Mackenzie's. In the altercation between Samuel Jarvis, son of the prominent York conservative family, and Mackenzie in 1826—over Jarvis's killing of Thomas Ridout in their 1817 duel—Jarvis insisted that reformers had subjected respectable citizens to personal attacks. In his *Statement of Facts, Relating to the Trespass, on the Printing Press, in the Possession of Mr. William Lyon Mackenzie, in June 1826*, Jarvis depicted York as a peaceful town before their arrivals, a town where:

> many of our Townsmen had here, as in all other countries, risen to independence and to respectability in character and circumstances, by their own exertions, without having drawn upon them, by their prosperity, the envy of malignant spirits—without having their wives and mothers, their daughters and sisters, and even their grandmothers, insulted and spoken of, with coarse and unfeeling influence, in newspapers industriously circulated throughout the province.[25]

That wounded women of York were being directly insulted by reformers was a recurring theme throughout this pamphlet. Indeed, even when complaining about Mackenzie's abuse of himself, Jarvis insisted the most painful part was the effect on his wife and children: the 'wound' and 'pain' they would suffer from hearing their husband

and father attacked.[26] Invoking their female relatives and other 'townswomen' allowed conservatives such as Jarvis to attribute their own behaviour to a code of manly protectiveness, one similar to that used in patriotic discourse. Proclamations of manly protectiveness also reinforced women's fragility and dependence on male relatives to defend their honour.[27] According to Jarvis, throwing Mackenzie's printing press into the York harbour, the 'Types Riot', was not the act of vandalism that his reform critics claimed it to be. Instead, he and his companions were only making the public spaces of York fit for their female relatives.

To conservatives, though, any attack on an individual was *ad hominem* and potentially libellous. Yet it was their definition of manhood in political life, one that saw men as bound into their society as members of families in various ways, that brought the private into the so-called public. Reformers' critiques of the intermingling of the two, especially in the distribution of patronage, was part of the reform attempt to impose more rigid distinctions between the private and the public, something that, it seems, conservatives could never fully understand. To those such as Jarvis, family was sacrosanct: it ought never be defamed and it was the cornerstone of colonial society.

The Reformers

Reformers were eager to use the language of the 'True', 'Honest', or 'Old Whigs' to describe themselves. They opposed 'placemen' (patronage appointments) in parliament, disliked standing armies, and distrusted the extension of government agencies, spending, and centralization. 'True Whigs' celebrated an opposition of honest, independent, and freeborn men, those who were truly loyal to the constitution and their country and who would represent the wishes of 'the people' free from the malevolent and corrupting influences of royal authority—the court.[28]

With the arrival of the *Colonial Advocate* in 1824, Upper Canadian reformers had a forum and voice for their views. 'When Bad Men Conspire, Good Men Must Unite!' proclaimed Mackenzie, the paper's editor, to his readers on 7 May 1829. The 'bad men' of Mackenzie's title were, as those familiar with Upper Canadian history might expect, the lieutenant-governor of Upper Canada, Sir John Colborne, and members of his administration, John Strachan, John Beverley Robinson, Henry Boulton, Christopher Hagerman, and John Macauley. They 'and their sort as [Colborne's] divan', warned Mackenzie, 'will be made use of to induce the next session of parliament to consent to severe and arbitrary militia and other laws, new and oppressive taxes, and other such strong measures as the present system requires.' Such 'bad men' and their wicked deeds, Mackenzie argued, must be opposed by the 'good men' of Upper Canada, those who possessed enough manliness and political virtue to stand alone and resist the 'divan's' inducements and manipulations.[29]

To be sure, Mackenzie hoped that new ways of discussing politics might be attempted. In his editorial address in the first issue of the *Advocate*, 18 May 1824, he told his readers that 'we are perfectly exempt from all unfriendly personal feelings, and if we speak of men, it will solely be in references to their public acts.' Moreover, he proclaimed, 'we are far from saying . . . that the nobleman now at the head of the Colonial Government in North America is other than an able, and a prudent ruler. It is the system we condemn.'[30] True, Mackenzie and other reform writers went on to describe their rulers in precisely the opposite manner—as incompetent fools, at the very least. In spite of their repeated attempts to find a new way of discussing politics, the reformers fell back constantly on men, not just institutions or systems. However unsuccessful in shifting the discourse from the private to the public, reform rhetoric did point to a different way of conceiving the public. Reformers saw a crucial difference in the private behaviour and characters of politicians—'public men'—and their public personae. One did not, they asserted, lead to the other, a separation of men from their personae that would appear to mark reformers as classic nineteenth-century liberals. When Mackenzie attacked the family backgrounds of the Robinsons and their peers, it was because he believed that the latter had cited their exalted ancestry to justify political control—a use of the 'private' that Mackenzie and other reformers believed was inexcusable. Indeed, throughout reform discourse, the nature of a man's *public* character was even more important in determining whether he possessed enough masculine virtue for public life. When reformers attacked their opponents' manhood, it was in precisely those terms of reference, not as private men.[31]

More than anything else, the reformers studied here based their claim to virtuous political manhood on independence. Here the spectre of the 'Commonwealthman' arises: he who cannot be bought by place or pension. One such paragon was Charles Fothergill, the King's printer from 1823 to 1826 and a reform member of the Legislative Assembly from 1825 to 1830. Although Mackenzie initially was opposed to Fothergill, the latter's championing of religious and civil liberty won Mackenzie's admiration.[32] In 1825, Mackenzie confessed that he had been mistaken about Fothergill. 'As long as he shall persevere in the manly, independent, upright course hitherto pursued by him in parliament,' he declared, 'he shall have my sincere wishes for his, and his family's prosperity.' As representative of the people, Fothergill had acted in 'the most honourable manner, as became A FREEBORN ENGLISHMAN.'[33]

Yet it was not just Fothergill who might be called on to exercise such manly fortitude. 'Up, then, and be doing', Mackenzie urged 'the electors of Upper Canada' on 8 July 1824. 'Stir yourselves, like men, and strike at the roots of corruption, in the persons of our late corrupt representatives.'[34] Throughout the 1820s and 1830s, Mackenzie's calls on the mechanics, labourers, and farmers of Upper Canada appealed to their 'manly virtue', '[m]anly independence of character', and their 'free, manly independent spirit'.[35] Such a determined and consistent appeal to his supporters' masculinity was not merely a personal quirk of Mackenzie's; they, in turn, asserted their own manly independence, either directly or by questioning that of their opponents. A 'Friend of Liberty' who wrote to the *Colonial Advocate* in 1833 declared that 'free men' entitled to 'rights and privileges' were the catalysts of the 'moral and physical change' needed in Upper Canadian politics.[36] Manliness became a significant symbol in reform discourse—an element that would transcend the old regime's corruption and immorality. In turn, only those possessing true manliness qualified for political citizenship.

The reformers' assertion of their masculinity was shaped not only by their claim to be independent men, but also by the denigration of their opponents' public characters. To have a full understanding of what the reformers declared they were, as men, we must also appreciate what they declared they were not—and often these were qualities associated with femininity. Certainly other groups in the colony were beginning to argue that women's dependence and reliance on male protection were the hallmark of 'virtuous womanhood'. And in conservative discourse, the image of femininity reliant on male protection was crucial to the meaning of patriotic activity in Upper Canada.[37]

But for men in the reformers' discourse, dependence of any kind was the antithesis of manliness. It smacked of the court, of corruption, luxury, and sycophancy. In one of Mackenzie's many warnings to the electorate, he prophesied, 'if ye will, as heretofore, choose collectors and king's advocates, ambassadors, parasites, and sycophants, to manage your affairs, you will dearly rue it.' Had not Spain, Greece, and revolutionary France made these mistakes and paid for them dearly, queried Mackenzie. And, even though 'the errors were in the princes in the end, [they] sprang from an effeminacy in the people in the beginning.'[38] 'Pampered placemen', who by accepting public office or pension through royal patronage had 'prostituted' their manly independence, figured prominently in many reformers' writing. Growing fat and idle on the honest toil of the people, these 'parasites and drones' were kept in a compromised yet luxurious condition until Upper Canadian political institutions resembled a 'vast network of brothels'.[39] Dependence equalled not just effeminacy but sexually corrupted effeminacy.

Moreover, gendered dependency had a class dimension. Men with aristocratic pretension, who in Mackenzie's words wanted 'to be dictated to by a despicable faction—all such as are willing to kiss the slipper of those in a little brief authority', had given up their claim to honest manhood.[40] Such men might be classified with 'well corseted dandies . . . a person who struts about in *frock-coat* and *corsets* and who looks down with disdain upon the vulgar herd below, who labour for a living; one whose chief pretensions to superiority arises from the emptiness of his skull and who has the good fortune to share a small part of a public purse.'[41] Worse still, the 'domineering faction' monopolized local office while the people, the 'genuine source' of aristocratic power and wealth, 'are vilified and traduced by them and their parasites, the base, corrupt, and mercenary hirelings of a prostituted press, with every disgraceful epithet that malice can invent, or ribaldry supply.'[42] It was not just that the men who dominated political life were, as Mackenzie believed, effeminate, fond of 'frippery', and prone to petty tyranny; through their ill-gotten power, prostituting themselves to the governing élite, they perverted and degraded the whole political process.

Dependence and a subsequent loss of manliness were thus endemic to a political system that relied on patronage, a system with tentacles that encircled and poisoned all that it touched. Moreover, the reformers' critique of the York élite's structure reveals yet another aspect of masculinity and reform. The phrase 'Family Compact'— used to describe Upper Canada's kin-related political élite—has an unexplored relationship to the reformers' critique of masculinity. Their stress on manly independence from all ties, links, and bonds other than those to 'the people' suggests that 'family' stood for more than just the Robinsons, Hagermans, Boultons, and Jarvises. In the reformers' discourse, it symbolized a web of intrigue. 'The triple bonds of relationships, intermarriages, a common private *interest* directly opposed to that of the country' was Mackenzie's definition of the Compact's structure.[43] It was 'a few families' who 'usurped' all the patronage of the province, 'who bestow it lavishly on their own kindred, however humble their merit, and parsimoniously only on the needy aspirants to the crumbs that fall from their corrupt tables.' As a result, 'parasites and old women' received the public revenues.[44]

The most notorious of such invectives were the *Colonial Advocate*'s 'Patrick Swift' commentaries. In these columns, Mackenzie launched a full-fledged attack on his opponents. His topics ranged from the Bank of Upper Canada and customs duties to the effects of nepotism on the colonial legal structure, but also targeted the familial origins of the local élite, poking fun at those who justified their power and prestige by citing their supposedly exalted backgrounds. Challenging the respectability of the Robinsons' Virginian descent, Mackenzie reminded his readers that the Virginia colony was the 'Botany Bay of the British Kingdom, the unhallowed recepticle of thieves, rogues, prostitutes, and incorrigible vagabonds'. Families such as the Robinsons descended from

> mothers who came there to try their luck and were purchased by their sires with tobacco at prices according to the quality and soundness of that article. And it is from such a source that we may look for the tyranny engendered, nursed, and practised by those whose blood has been vitiated and syphilized by the accursed slavery of centuries.[45]

Here, it was clear, sexual improprieties appeared to be precisely the issue: the legacy of prostitution and its corollary, an incurable sexual disease (one that might also result in madness), made it impossible for such families to rule colonial society legitimately. Women who were sexually enslaved, 'purchased by their sires with tobacco at prices according to the quality and soundness of that article', 'nursed' and 'engendered' future generations whose bodies and minds were enslaved by incurable disease and who themselves produced a political system engendering further slavery. At stake in such verbal assaults was not only John Beverley Robinson's female and sexual ancestry. In his vicious critique, Mackenzie rejected that the conservatives' élite background made them morally superior or justified their claims to political power, and he maintained that men's private lives should not enter the public realm. While sexual symbols, sexuality as a metaphor, and a literal use of sexual insults were threaded through reform critiques, the image of the family as a source of vice and of its ability to pervert the public realm was used most frequently. Despite the trouble his attack on Robinson's lineage created, the link between family and tyranny was not a theme Mackenzie was willing to relinquish.[46]

Unlike the discourses of republicanism in the American and French Revolutions, in which the family was *at times* seen as the bedrock of the state and in which women's roles were thus given some attention, 'family' in Upper Canadian reform discourse symbolized everything the reformers opposed.[47] Only occasionally were men reminded as fathers and husbands to exercise their rights 'and consolidate [their] freedom'.[48] Reformers were far more likely to couch their appeal to men by reminding them of their independence, their obligation to themselves as men to act freely and without the constraint of any ties. Family, in the reformers' script of political life and the state, was rewritten as brotherhood, to signify a supposed universality. 'A nice conjuring trick', in political theorist Carol Pateman's words, was performed, whereby the patriarchal authority beloved by conservatives *theoretically* disappeared.[49] Yet even this appeal to a transcendental fellowship was cast in terms that, while not necessarily and essentially masculine, relied heavily on an ideal of masculine virtue and morality.

Furthermore, the reformers' reluctance to discuss the private realm left them without a clear position on the family's relationship to the state or its role in achieving political change. Discussions of boycotted goods in the mid-1830s, for example, paid little attention to women's contribution as managers of the domestic economy.[50] Such discussions that had taken place in America during the Revolution and the post-Revolutionary period saw the formation of an ideology of republican motherhood that, while problematic for women, at least brought them into political discourses.[51] Contemporary British radicalism had a number of women members, either in mixed-sex or all-women groups, and the organizational strategies of Chartism (such as schools and Sunday schools) brought whole families into the movement.[52]

No parallel existed in Upper Canadian political discourse. Possibly the more confined and narrower program of the Upper Canadian reformers, in comparison with their counterparts in France, America, and Lower Canada, made it less likely (and necessary) that a wide range of social realms such as the family or women's contribution to a new sociopolitical order would come under scrutiny. Upper Canadian reformers, by and large, were not interested in a Jacobinic reordering of society and the creation of new forms of political and social structures. Instead, they were preoccupied with rooting out the corruption of a colonial élite that was perverting existing institutions.[53] Family would eventually figure in the reformers' writings, but as a focus of attack on the colonial government.

Upper Canadian reform owed as much to its British antecedents and perhaps to a conception of British republicanism as it did to American or French influences. For the most part, Upper Canadian reform was indebted to British constitutional history inspiring Mackenzie and his colleagues to question their opponents' appropriation of the symbols and images that would legitimate their actions as 'true honest British men'.[54] While such discursive strategies did not close political discourse completely to those who might not have been British or men, they did help to set the boundaries and fix the terms in which political participation was discussed. But by 1836, these terms had begun to change. A growing dissatisfaction with the Colonial Office and affairs in the colony led some reformers away from Britain and the Commonwealth tradition to a greater embrace of American republicanism. This process was intensified by the failure of the Rebellion and the official repression in its wake. As reformers' discursive ground shifted, so did their use of gendered imagery within the political realm.

The 'Woman' in Politics

Throughout the late summer and fall of 1837 the *Constitution* and *Colonial Advocate* displayed a growing impatience with Britain, not just the province's élite and the lieutenant-governor.[55] With this new impatience came greater use of political metaphors based on either actual or symbolic women.[56] One woman in particular was targeted for her rank, gender, age, and, at times, physical appearance. The young Queen Victoria became the symbol of the reformers' anger at Britain, as she did in Lower Canada, where she was attacked with greater virulence and vitriol.[57]

Calling for meetings, political unions, and the expression of grievances in August of 1837, the editor of the *St Thomas Liberal* warned reformers that neither Lord Glenlg nor London's House of Commons would listen. 'Nor can your cries ever be permitted to disturb the frills or the frolics of that young damsel that sits as Queen, and flirts her fan over the empire.'[58] In November, Mackenzie published an editorial discussing the relationship between the Queen, newly appointed lieutenant-governor Sir Francis Bond Head, and the people of Upper Canada. Although Victoria might be called 'the mother of the people . . . it is a strange manifestation of maternal love to avow hatred to her children.' Managing to take a poke at both the monarch and her representative, Mackenzie declared that 'Sir Francis cannot be said to represent her majesty's feminine nature, for in that case he would dress in petticoats.' (In other articles Mackenzie had described Head as vain, puffed up, and a fop.) Rather, Head represented her 'royal prerogative, her royal feelings and pleasure'.[59] Because this power and these emotions had been used in 1837 to crush reformers in what the defeated believed to be a cruel and capricious manner—the logical outcome when femininity was allied with monarchical power—neither Victoria nor her representative could personify either true maternal caring or honest 'manly' justice.

Attacks on the Queen intensified after the Rebellion. The actions of British troops and the Upper Canadian government were attributed to her personal whims and desires. 'The Queen, by her officers seized upon the late Colonel Lount's property, and took every thing, she did not even leave his unfortunate family their wearing apparel. So much for royal gentleness in America.'[60] In 'What is a Queen?', a scurrilous poem published in *Mackenzie's Gazette*, 4 August 1838, the anonymous author described a woman who is distinguished from other mortals only by the 'diadem, and gay attire,/that witlings crave and fools admire.'[61] And, the *Gazette* declared, the Rebellion had left Victoria with a seraglio of men rotting in her jails—a far cry indeed from the conservative press's accolades to the young and virtuous Queen.[62]

To some extent the Queen was a logical target, and the mere fact of these attacks illustrates the extent of the reformers' bitterness and disillusionment. However, in the past such assaults had been reserved for lieutenant-governors and (primarily) members of the Executive Council; reformers usually had treated the monarch with respect. In the pages of the *Gazette*, Victoria, the traditional symbol of legitimate authority, was transformed into an ignorant, unattractive, childish, and at times libidinous tyrant, thereby undermining British moral authority and her claim to colonial dominion.[63]

If Victoria represented the antithesis of the upright, honest, and virtuous man the reformers had chosen as their symbol, other configurations of woman and the private, domestic realm existed. Until the Rebellion, reformers had said little about their families, but the executions of rebels Samuel Lount and Peter Mathews combined with the government seizures of rebels' property brought the plight of rebels' families into the pages of the *Gazette*. This unusual set of references to the private lives of reformers again served to challenge the legitimacy of Britain and the Upper Canadian government; the private was used to expose the immorality of actions taken by the public authorities. Articles recounting meetings between the prisoners' families and Head's successor, Sir George Arthur, described in moving detail the families' unsuccessful appeals for clemency. Such pleas were rebuffed by 'the sanguinary monster who spurned these interesting mourners from his presence, with a cold and cautious look, adding "He [Lount] must die!" O, how they sobbed.'[64] The 'Van-Demon Arthur' compounded his unnatural and tyrannical behaviour by refusing to give Elizabeth Lount 'her murdered husband's' body.[65]

Elizabeth Lount's letter to John Beverley Robinson, one of the few pieces written by a woman that appeared in the Upper Canadian reform press, exemplified this denial of the government's claim to represent the Upper Canadian people. Her husband's execution, her loss 'of home and all that could make that home pleasant', the 'egregious outrages upon private property, and even life itself', must, she declared, become public knowledge. Although woman 'should not lead the way' to redress the wrongs of even 'an oppressed, enslaved, and insulted people' (a position that rightly belonged to the 'lion heart and eagle eye' of the male sex), Robinson had abdicated his claim as a man to assist Upper Canada. Observing that 'every man has his price', she inferred that Robinson had sold his manhood. The 'series of hardships brought upon me and my orphan children by you, and others of the tory party in Canada . . . would call a full grown tear to manly eyes.' Lount's widow thus intervened in the public debate but spoke from her place in the private realm, one that the government's actions had destroyed.

Rather than stand as a female intervention into the public political realm, Elizabeth Lount's critique served to underscore reformers' gendered vision and division of political labour. She insisted that Robinson's refusal to let the public see the 'manly corpses of Lount and Mathews' stemmed from his fear that 'the generous sympathies of a noble people . . . might rise.'[66] Their bodies symbolized virtuous Upper Canadian manhood betrayed by the tyranny, despotism, and immorality of the authorities. The government's treatment of reformers' families unequivocally exposed its lack of manliness and invalidated its right to rule. The state's claim to authority was based on nothing more than military might and the bullying of defenceless women and children.[67] Women's voices thus were heard and the private realm was discussed in the post-Rebellion period, but as strategic devices that allowed reformers to continue their political critique of public authority and also evoke sympathy. The letters and articles in the *Gazette* did not indicate that reformers' conceptions of masculinity and gender relations had changed inasmuch as they signalled a willingness to employ gender in a variety of ways as a fundamental part of political discourse.[68]

Conclusion

A number of questions arise from the arguments made above. What, for example, are we to make of the reformers' constant use of the phrase 'the people', which posited universality in the midst of arguments focused on and addressed to the enfranchised adult British man? As literary critics have reminded us, language is a slippery medium and symbols are often multidimensional. 'The people' as a discursive tactic legitimated and enlarged the basis for the reformers' support, promising a mirror for all members of society, while obscuring the hierarchies and barriers inherent in the reform notion of political citizenship.[69] Yet 'the people' also might serve as an important symbolic weapon for those who wished to establish a claim to that citizenship from which they had been excluded. In Upper Canada there appears to have been no direct, organized, and sustained challenges by women to their exclusion from political language, no public attempts to challenge the discourses of either manly fraternity or political hierarchy.[70]

Both reform and conservative writers relied on images of the feminine, but the particular use to which it was put did little to open up political discourse to women. The valorization of the patriarchal family, on the one hand, and the high price placed on manly independence, on the other, could not speak to the concept of women's participation as political actors. The first glorified a structure and relationships in which women were subordinate; the second neglected to address the problem of those who were not clearly defined as independent in Upper Canadian society.

Women's corporeal absence from formal political structures does not alter the fact that gender relations were deeply embedded in colonial political discourses, manifested most clearly as competing notions of manliness. Moreover, while institutions such as the home, the school, and the workplace have been integral to discussions of changes in gender in the nineteenth century, we must also consider politics as part of this spectrum. Debating who was, and was not, fit to define the colonial 'body politic' of the early nineteenth century helped define whose 'bodies' would have greatest representation and power in the British North American state.

The Homeless, the Whore, the Drunkard, and the Disorderly: Contours of Female Vagrancy in the Montreal Courts, 1810–1842

Mary Anne Poutanen

One late summer day in September 1836 Constable Henry Hébert spotted Catherine McDonald, Betsey Allcart, Eleonor Galarneau, and Harriet Hamelle inebriated and lying in a street near the Quebec Barracks in the old city. They were reputed to be lewd, idle, and disorderly women, common vagabonds, and prostitutes who frequented the red-light district, so Hébert apprehended them for vagrancy.[1] Five years later, Rachel Young was arrested for the same misdemeanour when a policeman discovered her wandering about the city streets attired in male clothing. For this penchant to cross-dress, the justice of the peace sentenced her to two months' imprisonment.[2] That same year, police charged Fanny Douglass with vagrancy after she broke a pane of glass while in a drunken state. Accompanied by Mrs Lane, who was also intoxicated, Douglass allegedly used 'the most shocking language'.[3]

These accounts of vagrancy challenge two major themes that have dominated the historiography of vagrancy. First, scholarly works have, in general, centred on men.[4] By focusing on male vagrants or tramps, historians have created the impression that only men, rather than women, too, perambulated the pre-industrial and industrial streets of urban centres. Consequently, misdemeanours such as drunkenness, disturbing the public peace, and homelessness were construed as male crimes by virtue of their very public nature.[5] Women, on the other hand, were assumed to be elsewhere: in the home, the schoolhouse, and the brothel. More recent studies by feminists such as Christine Stansell, Mary Ryan, Penelope Corfield, and Marilynn Wood Hill, which chronicle women's everyday experiences, have returned them to the streets and public spaces of urban neighbour-hoods.[6] Popular-class women lived large parts of their lives working and socializing in the streets, and here public space was shared because the distinction between male and female spheres was blurred. Second, contemporary researchers often uncritically reproduce the opinion of nineteenth-century social reformers that all women vagrants were street prostitutes. Although historians of prostitution have shown how vagrancy laws were used by police and the courts to crack down on street prostitution and while it was also true that the majority of Montreal women apprehended for vagrancy were work-ing in the sex trade, these ordinances were applied to a plethora of public behaviours. Hence, vagrancy laws came to incorporate a host of infractions that affected a large group of people, including even those suspected of committing a felony. Vagrant women were described as being loose, idle and disorderly, inebriated, unable to give a satisfactory account of themselves, as having no honest employment, as keeping 'bad' company, and as being insane, physi-cally and verbally aggressive, and petty larcenists. Therefore, not all vagrants were men and those who were women were not always pros-titutes; however, they were doing something in a public place that was considered sufficiently improper to attract the attention of the police.

This chapter will focus on those women who appeared before a justice of the peace accused of vagrancy. Although the efforts to regu-late public space were bringing larger numbers of men and women into conflict with authorities, this considers how vagrancy laws tar-geted specific female behaviour and held particular meaning for pop-ular-class women trying to survive in an era of tremendous change. Montreal in this period was a city in economic, social, and demo-graphic transformation and flux, accompanied by heightened anxiety due to the uncertainty of the times and exacerbated by the armed insurrection of 1837 and 1838. The rise of a male bourgeoisie that gained control over the levers of power, growing acceptance of new meanings of respectability, and encroaching capitalist relations in the workplace with its related changes in work discipline are some fea-tures that had particular ramifications on the public life of Montreal-ers, and on women in particular. The police's definition of what constituted a vagrant, with its ethnic, class, and gender implications, meant that many female activities were construed as illicit and sub-ject to state intervention. It was in the public sphere that the power of the state was asserted, contested, and resisted. Thus, any attempt on the part of the state to curtail or redefine public behaviour increas-ingly encroached on women's use of the street.

Evidence about vagrancy comes from the records of Montreal's lower criminal court.[7] These documents serve as a window through which to view women's activity on the streets and in green spaces in and around the city. All of the cases involving women who were charged with vagrancy, being loose, idle, and disorderly, and being common prostitutes between 1810 and 1842 have been examined. Imbedded in these court dossiers are fragments of women's lives that illuminate aspects of their relationships with their families, their communities, and the criminal justice system. These court records and police ledgers, prison registers, and local newspapers reveal some of the ways that Montreal women used the streets for leisure and for work. Thus, both the public and private arenas were inextricably linked and gendered.

Demographic Features of the Women

Between 1810 and 1842, at least 2,528 incidents of vagrancy were committed by women. Most of these episodes involved women who were non-Francophone, arrested only once, and single.[8] Only 207 women were identified in the depositions as married and 39 as widowed. Overall, numbers show that non-Francophone women constituted nearly three-quarters (71 per cent) of this group; Francophone women made up the remaining 29 per cent.[9] Irish women dominated the non-Francophone group. When the demographic characteristics are examined over the period, the changing composition of ethnicity becomes apparent. Between 1810 and 1829 the numbers of Francophone and non-Francophone women accused of vagrancy were almost evenly divided. By the second period, 1830–7, fewer Francophone women were charged with vagrancy. Their numbers continued to drop consistently, so that between 1838 and 1842 non-Francophones composed over three-quarters of the vagrants. These changing configurations of ethnicity mirrored certain demographic transformations taking place in the city. Not only had the population of the city almost doubled between 1822 and 1844, but the dominant ethnic proportions of Montrealers shifted. By 1825 a third of the population was made up of immigrants from Britain, the United States, and elsewhere, and by 1832 Anglophones comprised the majority in the city.[10]

Most of the Montreal women accused of vagrancy were arrested only one or two times, and these account for only a third (32 per cent) of the total female arrests. Faced with bleak employment opportunities upon their arrival in British North America, some women resorted to the street, where they did whatever they could—including working in the sex trade—to deal with the immediate needs of food and shelter. This struggle for daily survival is perhaps best portrayed by 25-year-old Mary Smith, a widow from Guernsey. She told one watchman that since arriving in Quebec five weeks earlier she had been unable to find more than three days of work. She survived by 'receiving small gifts from others' but had no place to live or food to eat.[11] When new opportunities arose, most of the women disappeared from the criminal justice system.

A smaller number of women (233, or 24 per cent) were repeatedly arrested for vagrancy-related offenses. These women accounted for two-thirds of the arrests (1,724 incidents, or 68 per cent).[12] The demographic features of the recidivist group and all female vagrants were similar. Most were non-Francophone and single, and about one-tenth were married or widowed. Some of these women had turned to street prostitution to provide for themselves and their children, and in so doing they garnered multiple arrests over a short period of time. Take, for example, the poignant history of Jane Hicks. In January 1831 she was accused of stealing clothing from the house of Martin Duval. She offered to sell the wearing apparel to Josephte McFarlane, saying, *'elle demandait à emprunter, disant qu'elle n'avait pas de quoi manger et qu'elle avait besoin d'acheter quelque chose pour ses enfants.'*[13] By the end of the month, she faced her first in a series of nine arrests for street prostitution between 1831 and 1833. Her decision to work in the sex trade was in all probability the consequence of her poverty, which prevented her from adequately caring for her children. Some recidivist vagrants suffered from chronic alcoholism. According to Julie Archange Daigneau's husband, Jean Dérouin, she had abandoned him and their four daughters for the streets.[14] Between 1829 and 1835, Daigneau accumulated at least seven arrests for vagrancy and two for larceny and assault and battery. The most extreme recidivist was Mary Ann Green. A well-known Montreal street prostitute and occasional petty larcenist, Green had been apprehended at least 32 times over an eight-year period. Incarcerated most of 1841 and 1842, she was sent to prison 18 times in this interval, with sentences ranging from three days to two months. More than likely her involvement in the city's sex trade made her vulnerable to arrest.

Élite Discourse and the Vibrancy of Montreal Street Life

For most Montrealers daily life had a decidedly public face in the years 1810 to 1842. The city's streets teemed with life and activity.

Men and women spent a great deal of their time in the public spaces around the city, conducting business, socializing, and loitering.[15] The narrow and winding roadways within the old fortifications[16] bustled with people of all social groups.[17] Travellers wrote of elegant ladies strolling in these streets dressed in gowns made of satin, silk, lace, or muslin, wearing gauze bonnets trimmed with feathers, ribbons, or flowers, and carrying parasols.[18] Mohawk women attired in moccasins, hats, and blankets sold basket products and moccasins in these same thoroughfares.[19] Popular-class women of different ethnic backgrounds travelled the byways of the walled city conducting their daily business. Beggars solicited alms from pedestrians or inhabitants in their homes throughout the period. Even as late as the 1860s, William Atherton likened Montreal to a 'primitive village', where elderly men sat at their doorsteps 'to gossip with passing friends and often the family would be found there of an evening.'[20] Montrealers patronized public buildings as well as houses of entertainment. Some people continued to use the river for public bathing, in spite of a regulation prohibiting this practice.[21] In Penelope Corfield's words, all manner of events happened in public spaces: men and women worked, played, loved, and died there.[22]

The separation of private and public spheres was clearly not part of the everyday experience of most women in early nineteenth-century Montreal. Rather, the domestic space of labouring women spread out past the physical demarcation of their lodgings to the neighbourhood streets. The extension of popular-class Montreal household activity into the public arena was similar to that in New York City. Christine Stansell's study of New York popular-class women shows that women performed certain crucial domestic duties in the streets, such as 'pinching and saving, of cleaning and borrowing and lending, of taking—and of being taken'.[23] In the streets they helped each other, raised their children, and voiced their pleasures and grievances.[24] Property-less New Yorkers in the 1820s and 1830s used the streets to make a living by 'peddling, prostitution, foraging, gambling, and theft'.[25]

Montreal's élites—businessmen, philanthropists, physicians, lawyers, and landowners, who were preoccupied with popular-class morality—criticized the public nature of everyday life, which rebutted bourgeois notions of respectability. Since prostitutes, vagrants, beggars, and drunkards were associated with immorality, idleness, crime, and intemperance, which stood in opposition to morality, industry, discipline, and sobriety, they were seen as part of a disreputable, unregulated public that posed a general threat to the authorities' attempt to control public space and a particular threat to their ability to govern a city in the throes of armed insurgency. Élites denounced urban street life and meeting places such as brothels, tippling houses, and taverns and demanded better regulation of the public.[26] Fearful of moral contagion and the corrosive effect of drink, they condemned the use of the city streets as a receptacle of the idle, the drunk and disorderly, and the indecent. It was no coincidence that temperance organizations appeared for the first time in Montreal in the late 1820s and gained momentum through the 1830s and 1840s. With a decidedly religious bent, temperance campaigners associated drink with poverty, crime, and disease.[27] Thus, sobriety was seen as the solution to social problems that the élite believed were rampant in the city. In addition, new definitions of what constituted the deserving or undeserving poor served to separate what reformers referred to as the morally contagious from the pure.[28] Similarly, criminals were also targeted. City notables were preoccupied with criminal women, particularly recidivist prostitutes and vagrants, and demanded that they be segregated from other imprisoned females according to type of crime and history of criminal activity.[29] In that way vagrant women would not contaminate those with whom they came in contact.

The Policing of the Public

It was the responsibility of watchmen and constables to patrol the city streets, to arrest vagrants and streetwalkers whom they confronted in the public spaces of Montreal, and to preserve the peace. In other words, policing public order occupied a large part of the watchmen's and policemen's time.[30] Vagrancy ordinances used to regulate the public changed throughout the early nineteenth century in relation to the increasingly vocal demands of reformers to maintain social order.[31] The legal definition of what constituted a vagrant person incorporated a growing number of behaviours over the period, moving from the general to the specific. At the same time, the vagueness of the law of the early period,[32] as well as the broader, more extensive definition after 1837,[33] allowed city constables and watchmen flexibility in applying the vagrancy statutes. Some historians contend that vagrancy laws were a catch-all category for social undesirables, facilitating the policing of the poor.[34] According to Judith Walkowitz, intervention in the lives of street prostitutes allowed police to scrutinize poor neighbourhoods; consequently, in London in the 1820s, vagrants were increasingly subjected to new forms of policing.[35] In Montreal, vagrant women were perceived as an impediment to a well-ordered society. Female vagrants, by virtue of their sex and public behaviour, symbolized the decline of morality and the disintegration of the family on which society was based.

Montreal women were often accused of vagrancy, street prostitution, or being loose, idle, and disorderly by the police, and occasionally by neighbours and family members. They were customarily arrested in the public streets by a constable or watchman and conveyed to the watch house, police station, Common Gaol, or House of Correction, where they were confined. Depositions were later drafted by the arresting officer. Thus, constables and watchmen acted as both prosecutors and as police. That is not to say that they always exercised this power without some charity towards vagrant women. When Mary Henderson and Ann McCann were brought to the watch house as vagrants one evening in November 1836, they were released after promising to behave. Six hours later they were rearrested by the same watchmen after they received two complaints about Henderson and McCann's comportment: Théophile Bruneau argued that they had been 'lurking' about Mr Perrault's wood yard and Joseph Rodgers denounced them for disturbing the peace in St Dominique Street when they knocked at the door of his neighbour, Mrs Doran. They were confined overnight and then released.[36] The fact that they were released shortly after being picked up, and subsequently kept overnight after being rearrested, suggests some flexibility on the part of the authorities.

Occasionally, neighbours and relatives complained to the police about vagrants they knew. Neighbours, for example, made charges, warrants were issued against the accused, and the police made the arrests, as in the case of Eliza Holiday. Described as a 'loose, idle, and disorderly woman from Laprairie', she was apprehended on a warrant and charged with vagrancy.[37] In some cases relatives swore out depositions against family members, whom they accused of being vagrants and prostitutes. In 1815, Nathaniel Goodwin denounced his daughters, Angélique and Elizabeth, as prostitutes after failing in his efforts to persuade them not to lead such a life.[38]

The system of police surveillance was fundamental to the policeman's ability to maintain public order.[39] Before 1823 in Montreal there were no fixed patrols in the city except for market constables.[40] Uniformed watchmen, however, provided some form of surveillance by keeping vigil in the old city from eight o'clock in the evening until five o'clock in the morning. In addition, since watchmen were responsible for lighting street lamps, early patrols were in all likelihood associated with this task. Lanterns existed in the old city as early as 1822 in sections of St Paul and Notre Dame streets. Presumably, patrols were established outside the old city when the suburbs were illuminated much later. This geography of police patrols determined the arrest patterns of vagrant women. Police apprehended the bulk of these women within the fortifications of the old city. Thus, when peace officer John Prenoveau picked up Angélique Bourdeau near the old market in St Paul Street after he observed her intoxicated, throwing stones at pedestrians, and breaking a pane of glass in a nearby shop, he was simply maintaining the public peace in the neighbourhood where he worked.[41] Once the arrest took place, the prisoner was usually escorted by the watchman or constable to the police office. In this case, since Angélique Bourdeau was too intoxicated to walk with John Prenoveau to the police office, he had her transported by cart to the House of Correction. When patrols were extended to the suburbs after 1830, greater numbers of women were arrested in the streets and green spaces of the suburbs. For instance, Constable Henry Blake arrested Margaret Wilson in a field near the Canal bridge on Wellington Street after he discovered her indecently exposing herself to a sailor.[42]

In looking to the policing agencies to ameliorate the regulation of public space, city notables insisted that more constables be hired, that the method of patrolling be transformed, and that a system similar to Peel's new London police be established.[43] In the wake of the Rebellions and the subsequent suspension of democratic government in Lower Canada, the Special Council reorganized the police force. This council, made up of loyal male citizens with unfettered control to make laws, replaced the police structure with one that reformers had been demanding before the armed conflict. Uniformed police officers were assigned to beats they patrolled around the clock.

The most obvious effect of this enlarged police force was an increase in the surveillance of public space and behaviour.[44] Figure 1 illustrates that after 1837 the number of women arrested for being loose, idle, and disorderly rose significantly. In part, this was due to the enlarged definition of what constituted a vagrant person, as well as to an increase in policing in the immediate post-Rebellion period. Figure 1 also shows that a significant rise in the arrest levels of female vagrants occurred earlier in the same decade. Because the 1830s were characterized by more poverty in the city in conjunction with a growing population, the struggle faced by poor women, especially new immigrants, to find food and shelter must be underscored. It is also striking that the elevated rate of arrests began in 1832, the same year that an outbreak of cholera struck the city. Perhaps the police targeted homeless women in an attempt to contain the disease.

Figure 1
Number of Female Vagrants Arrested in Montreal, 1810–1842

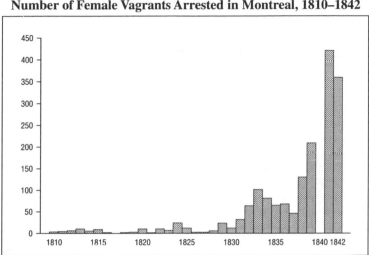

NOTE: Numbers are based only on court records. The 1817 records show no arrests for prostitution that year, nor do they indicate why the year was anomalous. The absence of data for 1840 is a consequence of not being able to locate depositions at the Quebec Ministry of Justice's Centre des Pré-Archivages.

The law was a powerful vehicle for constructing sexual identity, defining deviance, and asserting control over women, as Philippa Levine argues.[45] An incident in 1840 suggests that once a woman was charged with vagrancy, she was inevitably viewed as a vagrant and in essence became the offence. In September of that year, when a city policeman failed to identify a vagrant previously arrested for this misdemeanour, the Inspector of Police ordered the chief constables to parade all vagrants arrested the previous day in front of the policemen before they were dismissed from duty. Anyone who could not recognize these vagrants in future would be discharged from the force.[46] The proper identification of vagrants and subsequent removal from the public were central to the constabulary's successful regulation of public space. Since Montreal police equated the woman on the street with some sort of illicit activity, be it prostitution, homelessness, drunkenness, loitering, or larceny, their expanding surveillance of a range of women's activities affected a diverse group of women. This incident also serves as a reminder of how difficult it had become to distinguish vagrants in a rapidly growing urban population.

The Imprint of Vagrancy on the Urban Landscape

Women charged with vagrancy were usually apprehended in city streets throughout the urban landscape. They were also picked up at the markets, at the military stables and barracks, in sentinel boxes, in abandoned houses, at the beach, and in a variety of outbuildings. For instance, when Chief Constable Smith discovered Ellen Dowde and May Brass in a shed, he charged them with vagrancy.[47] The location of arrests can tell us something about the relationship that vagrant women had to public space. Those who were homeless sought refuge wherever they could find it, in abandoned houses and barns, in outbuildings around the city, and at the watch and police stations. Many of the women who provided sexual services to men did so in a variety of public places: in green spaces, in the streets, or in public buildings. One watchman discovered Ann Taylor sleeping on a bench in the New Market at midnight after having *'forniquer [sic] avec un soldat'*.[48] Other women who were apprehended had sought out men for drink, food, companionship, and money on the farms that surrounded the city. Finally, some women were accused of vagrancy while they carried out activities of daily life, often not far from their homes. A servant by the name of Mary complained in a letter to the *Montreal Transcript* that she had been stopped by a policeman one evening while running an errand for her mistress. This policeman accused her of being out on some 'bad intention', which necessitated her removal to the watch house. The intervention of some gentlemen prevented Mary's arrest. Instead, she was escorted back to her mistress's house, where her story was verified.[49]

Before 1830 most of the arrests occurred within the fortifications of the old city, where police patrols had already been established. The red-light district[50] around the Quebec Barracks in the old city[51] was one such area. A popular place for streetwalkers seeking clients, women and men were attracted to the numerous drinking establishments, public buildings, and brothels in the vicinity. Sarah Smith and Mary Ann Knight were charged with vagrancy when Constables O'Neil and Colombe observed them loitering about the Barracks yard at 11 o'clock one May evening.[52] After 1830, when police surveillance extended into the suburbs, vagrants were apprehended in all of the suburbs and in the green spaces in and around the city. Some homeless women preferred the fields and orchards where they could find shelter, fruit and vegetables to eat, and even milk to drink. Five women were arrested for vagrancy after Constable O'Neil and a number of policemen found them loitering and milking cows at St Gabriel's Farm.[53] Another farmer complained to the authorities that 'improper girls' habitually trespassed in his orchard, where they stole apples and damaged his fruit trees.[54] Towards the end of the period under study, women were arrested just for loitering in these areas.

Women's Activities at the Time of Arrest

Court records reveal that women charged with vagrancy were in fact involved in a wide variety of activities. While there was no stereotypical female vagrant, street prostitutes were the most likely to face arrest. Of the 2,528 incidents involving vagrancy, approximately two-thirds probably involved women who were working in the city's sex trade, caught soliciting or providing sexual services. The remaining third were apprehended for such behaviours as cross-dressing, larceny, loitering in the streets and green spaces, using obscene language, making threats and assaults, homelessness, and drunkenness. A few days following the New Year revelry in 1831, policeman Patrick Ryan detained Margaret Colborne for being intoxicated and disturbing the peace.[55] Thus, some Montrealers were charged with vagrancy for an occasional or isolated incident of drunken, raucous behaviour. Even women with physical handicaps were charged with vagrancy. High Constable Benjamin Delisle arrested Mary Quinn as a vagrant 'in such a state as to be unable to walk the streets being a cripple' and loitering about the city streets 'almost in a state of nudity'.[56] Homeless women who lived on the streets were accused of vagrancy for begging and loitering, and even for being insane.[57] Some women, in carrying out activities of daily living, got caught up in incidents that led to charges of vagrancy. Helen Gilbert apparently assaulted Mary Rogers by calling her a 'bitch and whore' and throwing a basin full of water in her face when she had passed in front of Gilbert's door while searching for her daughter in the neighbourhood street.[58] As these episodes reveal, the older pattern of publicly settling accounts with neighbours might now bring Montrealers into direct contact with the law.

Similarly, street prostitutes were arrested and charged with vagrancy for a range of offences, including settling their differences by fighting in public places, as Margaret McGinnis and Margaret Carr discovered. They were charged with vagrancy after Constable Louis Malo caught them drunk and fighting together in a field behind the *champs de mars.*[59] The vast majority of streetwalkers were arrested in groups, sometimes accompanied by men, and usually in the streets or fields around the city. They may have been simply loitering in public spaces or actually soliciting customers, as in the case of four women pursuing men in Papineau Road. Peggy Dollar, Mary Rice, Catherine Korker, and Eliza Harvey were apprehended for following after Francis Grant, Pierre Lemoine, and Jean Baptiste Laviolette.[60] Sometimes a woman was charged with vagrancy after being observed in the company of people of ill fame or if she was reputed to live in a house of prostitution. Catherine Murphy was arrested by Théophile Charretier as a vagrant when she caused a disturbance in the street by swearing and shouting. Charretier complained that she resided in a common bawdy house, which suggests that her reputation contributed significantly to her arrest.[61] Legal historian Constance Backhouse argues that disorderly behaviour, which might have been overlooked in other women, resulted in prosecution when committed by a prostitute.[62] Jeffrey Adler notes that while police raids on brothels served to establish a certain standard of behaviour, streetwalkers seemed uncontrollable. Madams oversaw women who worked for them, husbands and fathers restrained family members, but nobody could control the woman alone.[63] Although the authorities clearly worried about prostitution, and their preoccupation with women's sexual behaviour was reflected in arrest and incarceration patterns, women were sanctioned for other conduct as well. Thus, the history of vagrancy was more complex than the existing historiography suggests. Some of the streetwalkers were actually discovered providing sexual services in a public space. Many of them were also alcoholics, sometimes turning to prostitution to pay for alcohol, food, and lodging.

Women without any apparent connection to prostitution but who were intoxicated were also accused of vagrancy for disturbing the peace, impeding the sidewalks, or causing a crowd to gather. Samuel Goodwin accused Sarah Lucy Clarke of vagrancy when, in a drunken state, she disturbed the peace and broke a window at the confectionery shop of David Wilson Crater where he worked as a clerk.[64] Beggars, too, were targeted, as in the case of Celeste Moreau. Policeman Poitrin apprehended her at 11 o'clock in the morning in April 1840 for begging in the street.[65] Others who could have been arrested and charged with crimes such as assaulting a constable, enticing soldiers to desert, threatening to break windows, and petty larceny were charged under the vagrancy law instead. One such woman, Jennet l'Huissier, was charged with vagrancy for concealing an accused felon in her home, assisting him in various acts of frauds, and keeping a large sum of money for him. Apparently Charles Mitchell confessed that 'she and others had his fate in their hands and that she was much attached to him'.[66] The vagrancy statutes equipped policemen with the tools to arrest women in any 'compromised' position. An incident in March 1837 demonstrates at what point watchmen and constables might employ vagrancy ordinances and the rationale behind their intervention. After city watchmen transported a woman by the name of McDonald to the watch house for riotous behaviour, she passed the night incarcerated and making a 'most desperate racket' and disturbing the 'repose of the men'. The next morning one watchman recommended that the next time she appeared at the watch house, she be committed to jail as a vagrant.[67]

The Seasonal Pattern of Vagrancy

Vagrant women were more likely to be arrested in Montreal when they were most visible on the streets. Arrests started to climb in the spring (22 per cent or 544), peaked in the summer (33 per cent or 838), and began to decline in the autumn (25 per cent or 631), reaching its lowest levels in the winter (20 per cent or 515). Jim Phillips found that vagrancy rates in Victorian Halifax at mid-century, as in Montreal, increased in the summer months, from May to September, when streetwalking was more visible, and decreased during the winter and early spring months. Halifax vagrants arrested in the fall would receive sentences that they served over the winter. Moreover, some of these vagrants used the local prison as a winter refuge, a sign of the degradation of their lives.[68] Similarly, homeless repeat offenders in Montreal turned to the criminal justice system for refuge, food, medical treatment, and as a final retreat to die.

When women needed refuge, officials of the criminal justice system complied. Police often dealt with female vagrancy in a paternalistic manner, by providing overnight lodging at the watch house or station house and by apprehending many of these women during the winter months when they were most susceptible to cold and hunger. This paternalism suggests some sort of tacit understanding of the economic realities that female vagrants faced. Nicholas Rogers, in his study of eighteenth-century London vagrancy, argues that the recognition of women's vulnerable economic circumstances led magistrates to retain wide discretionary powers in dealing with vagrancy while resisting more systematic incarceration.[69] Although Montreal justices of the peace also used imprisonment in a paternalistic manner to deal with vagrancy, they were more likely to sentence women to varying terms in the local prison than were their British counterparts. This dependence on incarceration was most likely related to certain environmental features of Montreal: the cold, long winter and vulnerability to hypothermia without adequate shelter, and a limited number of charities to which vagrant women could turn for assistance. That some of these women were indigent is clearly evident in the case of five female prisoners who were committed to the House of Correction in 1822. In order to be released from jail, they were supposed to appear before the magistrate at the court house. Because of their inappropriate demeanour, being in an 'almost naked state', the women needed an order from the court to be discharged.[70]

Some women even petitioned for an extension of their jail sentences. In January 1825, 'several female culprits' who probably feared being discharged from the House of Correction during the winter requested that the justices of the peace delay their release. Sometimes magistrates extended imprisonment over the harshest winter months, and the jailer occasionally recommended that female prisoners undergoing medical intervention have their length of confinement extended in order to complete the treatment. And for those who spent their dying days in prison, some kindness could be extended. For instance, Lydia Corneille, a chronic alcoholic and well-known vagrant, received wine and beer at the infirmary of the Common Gaol just before her death.[71]

Throughout the period under study, Montreal watchmen and constables arrested vagrant women in danger of perishing from cold and hunger due to lack of food and lodging. High Constable Jacob Marsten apprehended Mary Weeks in February 1820 out of concern that she 'will perish in the public streets' unless incarcerated.[72] Similarly, in early spring of 1835, Sophie St Onge was charged with vagrancy after she asked Constable Antoine Bergeron to be imprisoned. Bergeron described her as an 'unfortunate vagrant suffering from want of house and home, and apparel' who would benefit from incarceration since her 'habits are worthless and detrimental to society'.[73] These examples reveal that the debates in the historiography pertaining to the principal role the police performed in a society—whether they provided a social service or social control—are too simplistic.[74] At the same time that the police furnished social welfare to homeless vagrants, they regulated public space and, as studies have shown, some were directly involved in illicit activities such as public drunkenness while on duty, extortion, and prostitution.[75] Thus, the role of the police force was multifaceted, involving activities that were both legal and illegal. Moreover, not all vagrant women were treated in this paternalistic manner; policemen did not provide social welfare to all who needed it, as some historians have suggested. There were numerous examples of Montreal women who died after being released from prison.[76]

Many vagrant women in Montreal used imprisonment during the winter months as a survival strategy either by requesting detention themselves or by committing petty crimes in order to be arrested. Eleonore Galarneau, Catherine Corkan, Mary Boyle, and Sarah Kennedy threatened to break the windows at the Palais de Justice if their request for imprisonment was denied. The police claimed in an 1836 affidavit that these women risked perishing from cold and hunger if they were not incarcerated.[77] A female prisoner in the Common Gaol[78] admitted to members of an 1836 grand jury that she had pleaded guilty to crimes she had not committed to prevent her demise in the streets.[79] Concern about the use by some women of the prison as shelter and not as an effective means of punishment was expressed by one grand jury; members argued that its inadequacy could not possibly lead to crime prevention because, for many prisoners, confinement was not felt as a punishment.[80] Rather, in their eyes, the prison served as a refuge for the homeless, the poor, the insane, pregnant women, and children, as well as those accused and convicted of misdemeanours and felonies. Whatever rehabilitative or deterrence goals the city's élites might have had in mind were subverted; imprisonment could not serve as a deterrence for many of the women who had nowhere else to go.

The Strong Arm of the Law: Incarceration as Punishment

However benevolent the authorities might have been on some occasions, it is important to remember that incarceration remained primarily a tool of punishment. In those cases (65 per cent) in which sentences were recorded by the court clerk on the depositions in the registers of the court of quarter sessions and police court, or were published in local newspapers, vagrant women were treated quite harshly by the criminal justice system. Figure 2 shows that in the first period, 1810–29, over three-quarters of the women received prison sentences of two or more months. While there was variation in the length of sentences, some women were confined to prison for very long periods of time. Marguerite Beauchamp, Rosalie Desjardin, Thérèse Desjardin, and Betsey Stevens are cases in point. In April 1812 they were imprisoned in the House of Correction for 12 months at hard labour.[81] Occasionally, magistrates rendered other sorts of

Figure 2
Sentences of Women Convicted of Vagrancy

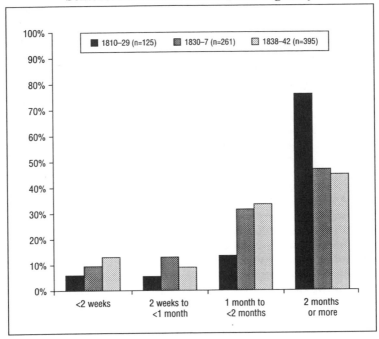

judgements. A justice of the peace discharged Geneviève Ducharme from the House of Correction upon her promising to quit town.[82] Some magistrates allowed a recognizance for good behaviour, as in the case of eight women committed to the House of Correction for six months as incorrigible vagabonds. Their imprisonment would be terminated if they could give security for good behaviour for six months.[83]

In the second and third periods, magistrates were imprisoning women for shorter periods. This was particularly so in the third period, during and immediately following the Rebellions. True, some vagrant women continued to receive lengthy sentences even though prisons were overcrowded with political prisoners. Moreover, although brothel-keepers were being discharged from prison to make room for these *patriots*, streetwalkers and vagrant women were not released early. Viewed by the state as a threat to a regulated public, certain vagrant women endured the full force of the law. Yet, we must be careful not to overlook the increasing number of women who were receiving prison terms of less than a week. As a wider assortment of refractory behaviour fell under the rubric of vagrancy, justices of the peace were using shorter sentences for certain types of offences and longer ones for others.

If a woman was charged with being disorderly, she was more likely to receive a short sentence. For instance, a police magistrate committed Mary Cullins to three days for drunkenness, disturbing the peace, breaking windows, and causing a crowd to gather in front of a house.[84] Ellen Lang was imprisoned for 24 hours after she was arrested and found guilty of disturbing the peace, using insulting language, and breaking Mr Doherty's windows.[85] Streetwalkers, like Magdeleine Couture, were more likely to receive longer sentences, of one to two months. Described as a 'whore on the streets', she was jailed for two months.[86] Women with a history of recidivism were also more likely to receive longer sentences. For instance, Elizabeth McDonald was committed to prison for one month, having several times before been apprehended by the police as a vagrant.[87]

Notwithstanding the benevolent use of incarceration towards some vagrants, the treatment of Montreal vagrant women at the hands of the criminal justice system illustrates the growing coercive nature of the state. Over the period under study, increasing numbers of women exhibiting a wide range of behaviours were being charged with vagrancy and sentenced to briefer sojourns in prison at the same time that street prostitutes received lengthier sentences despite the fact that they were charged with the same offence. The austere form of punishment towards streetwalkers, in conjunction with the concerted effort by mid-century reformers and police to repress street prostitution, may account for historians' and nineteenth-century reformers' unproblematic equation of female vagrancy with prostitution. However, as public space became increasingly regulated, it was not just women's sexual behaviour that was being contested but a whole range of popular-class female activities.

Conclusion

By using a variety of legal documents, this examination of Montreal female vagrancy between 1810 and 1842 illustrates the ways that gender influenced the changing nature of policing as well as the changing use of urban space. In this period, city élites expressed anxiety about their perception of a rising crime rate, of the inappropriate public nature of popular-class life, and of the disorder associated with an unregulated public cluttered with beggars and vagrants, and thus demanded that the police oversee public space more effectively. The élites also insisted on the establishment of a variety of institutions, such as hospitals, houses of correction, refuges, and prisons, to treat and regulate wayward members of society. These institutions could intervene directly in the lives of certain members of the population, usually the poor, by inculcating them with emerging bourgeois notions of sobriety, discipline, cleanliness, and hard work. The gendered nature of such social change was made evident when poor women, in particular vagrants, were targeted. Although magistrates relied on other methods of punishment, such as recognizances to keep the peace or requesting pledges to leave town, in the vast majority of cases vagrants spent long intervals incarcerated in harsh prison conditions. By the late 1830s, magistrates imposed much shorter prison sentences on all vagrant women in general, but streetwalkers were still more harshly punished when compared to the overall group.

The charge of vagrancy served as a broad category that allowed the net of the criminal justice system to be cast over a large number of women who could be arrested for a variety of reasons. Montreal women were charged with vagrancy for disturbing the peace, drunkenness, mental illness, loitering in the streets, exhibiting no visible means of support, and prostitution. The definition of what constituted a vagrant and its application expanded over the period to include greater numbers of women—not only prostitutes but also the homeless, drunk, disorderly, and idle. Women were apprehended for vagrancy in the streets, in green spaces in and around the city, and in red-light districts throughout the city. They were stopped in their pursuit of work as street prostitutes and of leisure. Destitute women were policed for having no visible means of support, even on the suspicion of being on the verge of turning to prostitution. The broad definition of vagrancy enabled the police, the courts, family members, and neighbours to curb the activities of women in public.

This investigation of vagrancy also sheds light on the complex range of activities that women engaged in on the streets of early nineteenth-century Montreal. For women with few social or economic resources the streets offered some means of survival, whether through peddling, theft, bartering with neighbours, or selling sex. The streets also served as extensions of popular-class households, as sites of leisure, and as domains to elude overzealous parental surveillance, and in particular, as an alternative to staying at home with overbearing fathers. By using the streets in these ways, women shared similar experiences with their male counterparts, but some elements of those experiences were clearly gendered. Most importantly, the increasing regulation of street life affected women. As policing structures were reorganized to impose more effectively bourgeois notions of what was 'appropriate' activity in Montreal streets, they reshaped women's and men's street behaviour differentially. Although police tried to impede female and male vagrancy, women's affiliation with prostitution led the authorities to be particularly strident in their efforts to rid the streets of prostitutes. At the same time, no alternative form of street behaviour, such as walking to and from places of work or eking out a living, was made available to women. The streets, and urban public space generally, became an increasingly male domain—a process that contributed to the apparently sharp divide between 'public' and 'private' that would emerge as the century progressed.

3

No Double Standard?:

Leisure, Sex, and Sin in Upper Canadian

Church Discipline Records, 1800–1860

Lynne Marks

Like many Presbyterians across Ontario during the first half of the
nineteenth century, William A. of Bond Head was confronted in
September 1836 by the leaders of his church, who had heard rumours
that he had had 'illicit antenuptial intercourse with his wife'. William
A. acknowledged that he had in fact had sex with his wife prior to
marriage, but he clearly did not think that he had committed a major
sin. He argued that 'his having married the woman ought to be considered as sufficient reparation'. The church elders, who expected
both men and women to express deep contrition for sexual 'misbehaviour', strongly disagreed with him. In response to their require-
ment that he express repentance for his actions, William A. 'gave
utterance to a number of exclamations against ecclesiastical tyranny
and abruptly left the house'.[1]

In early Ontario certain churches regulated spheres of life that we
would today consider far beyond the purview of religious control.
Family life, leisure activities, business practices, sexuality, slander,
and private quarrels could all come under church scrutiny. Some of
these behaviours were regulated in relatively similar ways by the
churches and the developing legal system of the colony: theft, fraud,
and debt were censured by the churches, as by the secular law,
although penalties obviously differed. Both church law and secular
law were reluctant to undermine male authority within the family,
although both would occasionally intervene to enforce male financial
support for dependants or to prevent the worst excesses of wife
assault.[2] In other areas, most particularly leisure and sexuality, certain

churches went far beyond the realm of the secular law in regulating the behaviour of church members, in spite of the fact that the church courts did not operate with state sanction as they had in earlier centuries in New England, Scotland, and elsewhere. Certain churches were willing to define as sinful, and thus proscribe, a much broader range of sexual and leisure activities than the state sought to regulate through the legal system.

Certainly within Upper Canada religious and secular gender ideologies had much in common: male dominance was accepted by both, as was a gendered division of labour and, to some extent, a gendered division of leisure. But in the realm of sexual behaviour gendered standards diverged significantly. The churches were not less vigilant in regulating women's sexual behaviour than was the state. Indeed, the churches censured a much broader range of sexual behaviour than did the secular legal system. However, in so doing, certain Upper Canadian churches made a much greater effort to ensure that both women and men adhered to a single standard of sexual behaviour than either the secular courts or the less formal court of public opinion. At the same time, attempts to impose a 'genderless' sexual standard were constrained by divergent norms of masculine and feminine behaviour within the larger society. Many evangelical men clearly recognized and resented the fact that the churches asserted more control over their behaviour than did the secular legal system or the realm of public opinion, both of which were more accepting of a sexual double standard. Women's greater willingness to accept church regulation reflected the more powerful restrictions they faced within the secular world as well as a recognition that women gained certain benefits from church efforts to regulate male behaviour.

While both American and British social historians have found church discipline to be a valuable source for exploring a range of issues from sexuality to attitudes towards authority, this chapter represents one of the first efforts to look at church discipline in Upper Canada as a window into larger social beliefs and practices.[3] In this way this work contributes to the social and religious history of Upper Canada, as well as to the as yet largely unwritten gender history of the colony. The few existing examinations of Upper Canadian church discipline have focused on this practice in the narrow context of church history. Gender has not been a significant variable in such work.[4] Within Upper Canadian history more broadly, while a few scholars have explored aspects of women's experience, Cecilia Morgan's work on the gendered nature of political and religious discourse broke new ground by examining attitudes towards both masculinity and femininity in the Upper Canadian context.[5] This chapter builds on Morgan's work by examining how the gendered Christian discourse she explores was applied in concrete cases of church discipline, and how Christian Upper Canadians actually responded to such discipline. I argue here that we cannot fully understand church discipline without studying its gendered nature and how, in the actual practice of church discipline, the gender ideology of the evangelical churches intersected with, and was undermined by, the rather different gendered values of the larger society.

Church Discipline and Gender in the Early Nineteenth Century

We still know very little about Upper Canadian social life in the first half of the nineteenth century, but we do know that this was a period of major social, economic, and political change. Over the course of this half-century First Nations inhabitants were increasingly marginalized by large numbers of British and American settlers. By the 1840s much of the colony had moved from the period of pioneer subsistence farming to a more settled and established society. This decade saw the emergence of a significant middle class, particularly in the growing towns and villages. Increasingly, Upper Canadians worshipped in their own churches, rather than occasionally hearing an itinerant minister in a local barn or private home. At the political level, frequently bitter struggles led to an increasing separation of church and state, with the Baptists, Methodists, and certain branches of the Presbyterian Church being particularly wedded to voluntarist principles. At the same time the first half of the century also saw the gradual establishment of state institutions, such as legal and educational systems. While such systems were in place by 1850 they had not yet attained the level of legitimacy and power they were to acquire over the course of the century, leaving room for alternative forms of control and regulation, such as informal community actions or church discipline.[6]

The three major evangelical Protestant denominations of Upper Canada, the Methodists, Baptists, and Presbyterians, all subjected church members to the close supervision of personal behaviour. Each denomination had its own mechanisms for enforcing discipline. Among the Methodists, members received mutual support and supervision in small groups or classes. Among Presbyterians, the behaviour of members was overseen exclusively by the minister and church elders (the Session), who had the power to demand public confession or to excommunicate erring members. While Baptist deacons and ministers also had particular power in enforcing discipline, discipline cases were discussed at monthly covenant meetings attended by the entire congregation.

Since no records were kept of Methodist class meetings, our knowledge of early church discipline comes exclusively from the Session minutes of Presbyterian elders and the church minutes of Baptist congregations. Together, the Baptists and Presbyterians made up about a quarter of all Upper Canadians in the first half of the century.[7] Among both groups church discipline was part of what it meant to be a member of the church. By joining the church and declaring their faith in Jesus, individuals agreed to live according to what their denomination defined as biblically ordained Christian behaviour and, if they strayed from such behaviour, to submit to church discipline. In subjecting each other to 'fraternal correction', church members believed they were adhering to the rules of the early Christian church.[8] Church members were expected to be part of distinct communities of believers, or in the words of one historian, 'islands of holiness', in a surrounding world of sin.[9] Decisions to be subject to church discipline were thus in some ways individual decisions, based on one's spiritual state. However, given the close-knit nature of many religious communities, such decisions were not a simple matter of voluntary choice.

Members of Presbyterian or Baptist church communities knew that rumours of any deviation from church norms could lead to a summons to appear before the Session or to a visit from a committee of church members. Those who had sinned were expected to confess before the Session, or in some cases in front of the entire congregation. While behaviour that was considered too heinous or too frequently repeated could result in either temporary suspension or permanent expulsion, in most cases evidence of sincere contrition allowed the member to be retained in, or restored to, full membership. Serious Christians could not simply evade church supervision by leaving town. Any Baptist or Presbyterian church member who wished to join a church in a new community had to present a letter or 'certificate' from his or her home church, certifying that the individual was a member in good standing.

Any study of church discipline must start with a recognition that within the institutions imposing this discipline the distribution of power was firmly gendered. In both denominations only men could be ministers. Male control was more absolute among the Presbyterians. Male members of the congregation nominated other men to be elders. The elders then sat as members of the Session deciding on cases of church discipline. Women had somewhat more power within Baptist congregations. They attended the monthly covenant meetings at which discipline cases were discussed, and at least occasionally they spoke out regarding such cases. Women were also among those appointed to visit erring church members, and in the absence of sufficient male church members they could sometimes hold church office.[10] None the less, men retained much of the formal power within both Baptist and Presbyterian congregations.

The fact that men held such formal power did not mean that their behaviour was less subject to scrutiny than that of women. One area of church discipline, that regarding business matters, was almost exclusively concerned with the regulation of male behaviour. While women made essential economic contributions to their families in this period, it was the formal 'public' business sphere that the church regulated, censuring and often excommunicating men for fraud, theft, debt, and other business irregularities.[11]

Leisure Activities

While the legal system also sought to regulate male business behaviour, in other realms the churches extended the regulation of male behaviour far beyond that of the secular legal system. The Presbyterian and Baptist churches defined as sinful many leisure activities that were ignored by the secular law. Many such worldly distractions were activities most commonly enjoyed by men. Horse-racing, a popular male pursuit, was subject to censure and possible excommunication, at least among Baptists. The Boston Baptist Church lumped horse-racing together with other particularly male leisure activities in declaring that 'we disapprove of Brothers amusing themselves with the world by jumping, hopping, horseracing and every evil design.'[12]

Other leisure activities were popular among both men and women and were proscribed for both. For example, Baptist churches clearly frowned on members attending 'bees', a major form of entertainment for both women and men in rural areas in early nineteenth-century Ontario. Play-acting in any form was also unacceptable. In 1843 the Vittoria Baptist Church decided that the 'exhibitions performed of late in some of the school houses by the youth of our country and by some of our members are very detrimental to the peace and progress of religion in the human heart.' As a result, any member 'performing or attending any of the above exhibitions will be considered guilty of committing capital crime against the church'.[13] Some Baptist churches were particularly zealous in policing attendance at plays. For example, in 1825 the Oxford Baptist Church excommunicated Sister G. for 'joining with the world and giddy multitude in plays and sham marrying'. Two years later the same church censured Brother C. for 'joining in plays and feasting with the world's people'.[14]

Despite such examples the policing of a range of leisure activities, from attending plays to horse-races, was sporadic at best among the Baptists and can rarely be found in Presbyterian Session minutes. This suggests that the policing of leisure activities was more zealously undertaken in some congregations than in others. While it is possible that in most churches members remained fully committed to complete separation from all leisure activities of 'the world', it seems more likely that some churches were not willing or able to censure every lapse. However, some leisure activities were regularly subject to regulation. Dancing, for example, was censured by many Baptist churches. For example, in 1809 the Boston Baptist Church excommunicated Joseph L. for 'trying to dance'.[15] While some men were censured for trying or succeeding at dancing, the churches focused more attention on dancing among women. Some women were not willing to give up this pastime even to remain members of a Christian community. For example, the Wicklow Baptist Church had particular difficulty with Rachel M., who as the church minutes noted sadly, had 'been previously laboured with for the sin of dancing'.[16]

Drinking and Church Censure

Some church members who attended dances compounded their sin by also drinking alcohol at these events. Overindulgence in alcohol was the leisure activity most commonly censured in both Presbyterian and Baptist church records. As far as the church records were concerned, such overindulgence was primarily a male sin. Out of the 77 cases of censure for drinking found among the Presbyterian records, only eight involved women. Among the Baptists, 87 per cent of those censured for drinking were men.[17] Both men and women who were disciplined for drinking were not challenged for drinking at all—they were censured for drinking too much and losing control of themselves. A common charge in the church records was of 'drinking to excess'. For example, Boston Presbyterian Church suspended Peter M. for having 'been openly seen grossly drunk to the injury of his own reputation and scandal of the church'. On the other hand, Andrew H., who was charged with drunkenness, claimed that he had 'not drank more ardent spirits than necessary' and had his case dismissed with a warning.[18]

Given the prevalence of drinking in Upper Canadian culture, it was clearly difficult for male church members to remain aloof from those they worked and lived among, for whom drinking 'to excess' appears to have been a common part of life. Those cited for drunkenness by the church often penitently regretted having given in to the entreaties of companions to go drinking. For example, in early 1846 when John M., an elder of Dundas Presbyterian Church, was charged with having been 'seen intoxicated in public', he came before the Session and 'acknowledged the truth of the charges made against him . . . and expressed his sorrow that he had so far forgotten his duty and his character as an Elder as to allow himself to be led astray . . . by too easy a compliance with the invitations of others.'[19] John M. was not the only elder to have so 'forgotten his duty'. The records of both Baptist and Presbyterian churches commonly include references to elders, deacons, and other church officers who had been seen drunk. Such cases point to the prevalence of drinking in Upper Canadian society, despite the efforts of the churches and of a range of more secular temperance organizations.

The fact that the churches were much more likely to censure men for alcohol use suggests that drinking, or at least drinking in public, either was primarily a male activity or was constructed as such. Still, the discipline records reveal that at least some women also drank in public at this time. For example, in 1847 a Mrs H. of Dundas Baptist Church denied the charge of 'drinking too much spiritous Liquors', although one member of the congregation claimed to have seen her 'go to a Tavern and call for a glass of Liquor and drink it', while others claimed to have seen her 'under the influence of too much liquor'.[20] Other women, like many men, also appear to have had trouble defining the point at which one had drunk 'too much liquor'. For example, in October of 1819 Sister C. told the Wicklow Baptist congregation that 'she thought it would not be possible that she had been intoxicated and therefore denied it.' Other church members clearly felt differently, and Sister C. decided that after 'hearing the minds of others' she was 'willing to submit and hopes they will forgive her.'[21]

A minority of women, then, clearly crossed the line beyond which drinking was acceptable to early nineteenth-century evangelical Christians. What is striking about the reports of female drinking, however, is not that some women were drinking, but that the tone in which their behaviour was reported was very similar to that found in reports of male drinking. There is no evidence in the records of a particular sense of shock or repugnance over women's drinking. By the late nineteenth century, images of women as particularly moral and pure, when combined with the identification of drinking as an exclusively male vice, meant that women who drank were seen as completely beyond the pale of appropriate femininity. In fact, as Cheryl Krasnick Warsh has noted, by the late nineteenth century alcoholic women were no longer considered real women, but instead were associated with a 'bastardized masculinity'.[22]

The lack of any particular horror over female drinking in early nineteenth-century church records suggests an absence of higher standards for women, combined with an unwillingness to identify drinking as a particularly male sin. While social practice made it more common and easier for men to succumb to the temptation of 'drinking to excess', the churches viewed drinking as a sin that all Christians were to avoid. The church records suggest an effort to take a similar 'genderless' approach to sexual sins. However, imposing a single standard of sexual morality on both men and women was a more pronounced break with the dominant gender ideology than the effort to censure male and female drinkers on similar terms. While there is some evidence in the historical record of drinking being particularly associated with male sin, there is a long history of women's particular association with sexual sin.

Seeking a Single Standard for Sexual Behaviour

A great deal more work remains to be done on the subject of the secular law in Upper Canada. None the less, the sexual double standard in which women are blamed and punished far more for sexual 'irregularity' than men does appear to have been dominant. Both divorce law (in which a man could gain a divorce for his wife's adultery but a woman had to prove that her husband had not only been adulterous but had in addition committed other serious crimes) and rape trials (in which a woman's sexual reputation was on trial at least as much as was the man she had accused) reveal a clear sexual double standard.[23]

The churches extended the regulation of sexuality well beyond the realm of the secular law. In seeking to uphold what they defined as appropriate Christian standards of sexual behaviour the evangelical churches condemned any form of sexual behaviour beyond sexual intercourse within monogamous heterosexual marriage. The churches did not just define the area of sexual regulation much more broadly than did the courts, they were also much more proactive in policing sexuality. Any rumours regarding illicit sexual behaviour of church members were subject to investigation by the appropriate church body. Both men and women were expected to be chaste before marriage and faithful within it. While both men and women would have found their sexual options stringently constrained by such expectations, many men would have found such constraints particularly unfamiliar.

Men who appeared before church bodies on charges of sexual misbehaviour could not rely on the double standard to lessen their guilt. Unlike the secular courts, women's past sexual behaviour or character never appears to have provided an excuse that allowed men to escape censure. Most men seemed to recognize the behaviour that the churches would expect of them as committed Christians. On rare occasions men like William A. who were charged with antenuptial fornication might claim that they had married the woman, and so should not be subject to censure. More commonly, when charged with antenuptial fornication, fornication, or adultery, men either expressed sincere contrition or refused to appear at all. There were no examples in the almost 200 cases of sexual misbehaviour found in the records of a man claiming that the woman involved had previously been unchaste, or that she had tempted him by dressing or behaving provocatively, or any of the other examples of the double standard so common in secular courts both in the nineteenth century and today.[24] The silences in the records are eloquent. Men charged before the churches with sexual misconduct did not use such defences because they believed they would be held to the same standard of sexual behaviour as women. True Christian men were expected to be as 'pure' as women.

The punishment meted out to men and women charged with sexual misconduct also suggests that the churches took such conduct equally seriously, regardless of gender. Among Presbyterians those who confessed to sexual misconduct such as antenuptial fornication or fornication were at a minimum expected to express their penitence before the Session before being absolved of their sin. In many Presbyterian churches those confessing such sins had to come before the Session three times to express their penitence. A minority of churches, such as Franktown's congregation, expected those guilty of such behaviour to confess before the entire congregation and publicly 'submit to rebuke' by the minister before being absolved and restored to church privileges.[25] There is no evidence that women were treated more harshly in such cases than men. It does appear, though, that men were more likely simply to refuse to appear before the church, thus escaping public rebuke but also forfeiting church membership.

The fact that both men and women were absolved of sin after confession and expressions of penitence also differed from more secular treatment of sexual misconduct by women. The church sanctions do not conform to the prescription whereby once a woman had 'fallen' she was permanently stained and could not redeem herself. Of course, we cannot know whether or not a man and woman, walking out of a church on Sunday morning after being absolved of 'fornication', were then treated very differently by the larger community in which they lived. It is most probable that regardless of church policies, the community did treat female sexual misconduct more harshly than that of men. At least at the official level, however, the churches appear to have been more forgiving, even of women with particularly stained reputations. For example, in 1851 the Niagara-on-the-Lake Session minutes record the story of a Mrs H., who was abandoned by her husband and whose home then became a 'place of resort for soldiers', and who then married one of the soldiers, a man named William H. The Session decided, since Mrs H. had 'given every evidence of deep repentance for the errors of the past . . . [and had] given every evidence of being worthy of restoration [of] church privileges by her Christian deportment', that she be restored to church privileges. The church did agree to this with the proviso that 'her marriage with William H. be placed on footing recognized by Law so that at no future period there should arise any collision beween the civil law and any proceedings of our church courts.'[26] Clearly, the church was not sure that the law would be as forgiving as the church in this case.

While the Presbyterians might have been willing to forgive both men and women and restore them to the congregation, the Baptists were less forgiving of sexual transgressions. In most cases those found guilty of such offences, chiefly 'fornication' or adultery, were summarily excommunicated from the church. Like the Presbyterians, however, the Baptists appear to have been equally ready to excommunicate men for such sins as they were women. For example, in November 1844 the St Catharines Baptist Church found William H. guilty of fornication. Although he 'expressed contrition' the congregation decided that 'the honour of the Church and the glory of God' required that he be excluded from the church.[27] While both men and women may have been excluded for sexual misconduct, women perhaps suffered more in the larger community for such behaviour because they felt such excommunication more keenly than did men. For example, among the records of Yarmouth Baptist Church is found a heart-rending letter from a former member, Anna B., in which she confesses 'shamefully yield[ing]' to a seducer. She asks, 'Brethren, can you forgive me, you who once loved me, you with whom I have taken sweet council [sic], for charity's sake I implore your forgiveness though I feel that I deserve nothing but banishment from you.' The church did not report any action in this matter.[28]

Men and women were punished relatively equally by the Presbyterian Sessions and Baptist congregations, but the churches' close regulation of sex outside of marriage meant that they proved completely insensitive to women's particular vulnerability to sexual violence. The Oxford Baptist Church summarily excluded Lorina A. for 'sitting with a couple of rufins [sic—ruffians?] after [they?] violated her person.'[29] The Presbyterians could be equally insensitive to the difference between rape and fornication. For example, when Margaret M. appeared before the Session of Brockville's Presbyterian Church seeking admission to the church and stating that although she had had an illegitimate child, 'she is not guilty of any crime on this matter as it was against her will, the person charged with being the father of said child took her violently and violated her person', the Session did 'seriously consider the matter'. They concluded, however, that although they 'feel disposed to sympathize with Mrs. M. they would not be warranted in admitting anyone to the privileges of the church under such circumstances without a humble confession of guilt and evidence of sincere repentance.'[30] From their point of view sexual intercourse outside marriage was fornication, requiring repentance of sin, whether rape was involved or not.

While the churches did not acknowledge women's particular sexual vulnerability, they were capable of being harsh towards men whom they saw as frequently guilty of sexual misconduct. For example, while among Presbyterians most 'sinners' were restored to church privileges after expressing penitence, the Franktown Presbyterian Church took a harder line with Thomas F., a local schoolmaster. He was brought before the Session for twice seducing young women and for other 'immoral conduct' and lost his church privileges until 'by a course of consistent and good conduct he affords reasonable grounds of belief that he can value and improve [his conduct]'.[31]

Although men and women who actually came before the churches were treated relatively equally, the gender breakdown in the numbers of men and women charged with sexual offences suggests that the double standard was not completely absent here. Among the Baptists, two-thirds of those charged with sexual improprieties were women and only a third were men.[32] Among Presbyterians the situation was less clear-cut. Of church members who were charged individually with sexual sins, 61 per cent were female. However, when one looks at all cases of sexual misconduct among Presbyterians, almost 40 per cent involved both partners being charged together—usually for 'antenuptial fornication'.[33]

The fact remains, none the less, that in both denominations more women than men were charged with sexual misconduct. It may be that the informal community networks that often played a major role in such charges were more likely to notice women's sexual behaviour than that of men.[34] Women's overrepresentation also reflects the fact that over the nineteenth century women made up a majority of church members in most North American Protestant churches.[35] Among erring couples, the woman was thus more likely to be a church member than the man, and the churches made no effort to police the behaviour of non-church members. A further explanation can be found in men's greater mobility. In this period women had few options for survival outside the household. Men could more readily leave town in the face of an embarrassing charge of sexual misconduct from the local church. This meant that they would have to face some awkward questions if they applied for church membership in a new community, but the option of leaving town was more available to a man than to a woman, particularly if, as was often the case, she was pregnant. For example, in July of 1835 Jane B. appeared before Peterborough's Presbyterian Church and 'named Thomas M. . . . as the father of her child.' One of the elders noted that 'M. admitted the truth of this statement', but 'as he had gone to a distant part of the country no further satisfaction could now be obtained.'[36]

Even men who remained in the community were more likely than women to refuse to appear before the churches. These men knew that the churches' sexual codes were harsher towards men than were general community values. Indeed, women appear to have recognized this themselves, and on some occasions attempted to use confession before the church to force their partner to share their disgrace, and perhaps to marry them, if that was possible. Certainly in early to mid-nineteenth-century Upper Canada unmarried mothers who wished to pursue their former partners had little other official recourse. The secular law permitted the fathers of seduced daughters to sue the men involved. Women could not, however, take action in their own right in such cases.[37]

Certain churches did allow women to take such action. Among the Presbyterian records are 10 cases of women who appear to have come before the Session on their own account to force their partners to share their shame. For example, in March 1840 Margaret M. of Fergus appeared before the Session of her local Presbyterian church to confess that she had been 'delivered of a daughter born in fornication' and that a married man, Peter M., a distiller of Fergus, was the father. Margaret M. was 'admonished as to the sin and scandalous nature of her conduct', and had to appear before the Session three times before its members were 'satisfied as to her repentance and sorrow for the past' and absolved her of the 'scandal of her former guilty conduct'. The elders did not, however, only punish Margaret M. for her conduct, but also summoned Peter M. to 'acknowledge or disprove' Margaret's allegation. Peter M. appeared and confessed his behaviour. He, like Margaret, had to face several of the Session's admonitions before he was absolved of his sin.[38]

Other women were less successful in forcing their partners to face church censure. Another Fergus woman, Elizabeth N., also confessed to having been guilty of fornication. The man she named as the father of her daughter was George P., her former employer. George P., however, refused to appear before the church. The church did not give up easily, with the minister attempting to meet with him on several occasions and the Session issuing three summons for him to appear. When this failed, George P.'s behaviour was reported to a higher church court.[39] Most churches were not as vigilant as the Fergus Session in pursuing erring men, but those in Fergus were certainly not alone in finding that at least some male church members refused to come before the Session to answer charges of sexual misconduct.[40] The failure of such men to appear before the local Session points to their recognition that the church would be more likely to censure their behaviour than would the local community. Church efforts to impose a single standard of sexual behaviour could only be partially successful in the context of larger social mores that still gave men more latitude in sexual practice than they did women.

Gendered Responses to Church Discipline

Men's greater tendency to defy church efforts to regulate their sexuality can illuminate popular attitudes to male sexuality, but may also have other implications. Was male willingness to flout church strictures confined to sexual matters, or were men generally more willing than women to defy church authority? The church records certainly suggest that men were less likely to accept the church discipline than were women. While the majority of both men and women did accept church discipline rulings, four-fifths of Presbyterians who refused to accept their churches' rulings were men, as were three-quarters of Baptists.[41]

Many men clearly resented their churches' efforts to regulate their leisure habits. For example, Mr B. of Vittoria told a visiting committee of his Baptist brethren that 'he thought it was no persons business about his drinking as long as he paid for it'.[42] Similarly, Brother O. of Beamsville, when charged with dancing and other sins, responded that 'he did not think there was much harm in dancing and he took great delight in it and swearing and fighting'. Like other Baptist churches with similar problems, members of Beamsville Baptist Church had no recourse other than 'vot[ing] unanimously to withdraw fellowship from [Brother O.]'.[43]

While men were far more likely to challenge the authority of their churches, some women who refused to accept church discipline were as openly defiant as their male brethren. Certainly Sister B. of Woodstock was very clear in her attack on the church, telling them that 'they were all drunkards together and that she did not want to belong to such a set'.[44] Others, like Sister A. of Boston Baptist Church and Sister Violet Y. of Iona Station, were accused of rejecting the voice of the church and of railing against it.[45] Such women had not internalized the newly emerging ideas about femininine passivity and decorum. However, these women were a minority. Far fewer women than men rejected church regulation of their lives. Perhaps many had internalized the new ideas about woman's particular piety and morality. Or perhaps older ideas about womanly obedience remained powerful.

These women may have also obeyed the churches for their own reasons. The Baptist and Presbyterian churches certainly closely regulated and constrained women's leisure options and sexual behaviour. At the same time, though, they did offer something to women. For poor women, or those facing the possibility of destitution in old age and widowhood, the churches offered some minimal financial protection. In an era when state welfare was almost non-existent and private charity grudging and demeaning at best, many churches tried to provide some assistance to poorer members, usually widows.[46] As well as the possibility of material aid, the churches also advocated a code of appropriate sexual behaviour that was less hostile to women's interests than that of the larger society. Both Christian women and Christian men were to live up to a single standard of sexual purity. Neither Baptists nor Presbyterians quite managed to practise what they preached, but they did come closer than the secular courts. While more women came before the churches on charges of sexual misconduct than men, the men who did confess to sexual sins were punished as severely as their female partners. For 'wronged' women, then, the Baptist and particularly the Presbyterian churches provided a potential forum for seeking punishment for and possibly restitution from their sexual partners.

Clearly, the churches did offer something to women. What did they offer to men? Certainly they reinforced men's dominant social role. However, such dominance was enforced by a range of secular social and legal institutions. For many men the churches served more to constrain their options than to reinforce their privileges. For Upper Canadian men being a member of a Baptist or Presbyterian church meant that one's business, family, and sexual practices were much more firmly regulated than they would otherwise have been. Much 'normal' male leisure, such as drinking, gambling, and horse-racing, was forbidden or stringently regulated. Men who viewed themselves as serious Christians, and who were moving away from older, 'rougher' definitions of masculinity towards more gentle, mannered, and domestic ideals of manhood, may have been willing to accept much of this regulation.[47] Such newer ideals of manliness still appear to have had limited currency in Upper Canada, however, and would not in any event necessarily legitimize all forms of church regulation. Many Upper Canadian men doubtless chafed under church efforts to regulate their behaviour. Women were also constrained and regulated by church discipline. But women would have found their behaviour only slightly more limited within the churches than beyond them. And for women there were compensations, such as the potential of using the churches to constrain unacceptable male behaviour. By joining a Baptist or Presbyterian church men appear to have lost more and gained less than women.

Of course, people do not join religious institutions or remain within them solely on the basis of such instrumentalist calculations. The solace and spiritual and emotional power of faith and the comfort and security of community are central to decisions about belonging to religious groups. None the less, the men who defied church discipline clearly recognized, and resented, the particular constraints that church membership placed upon them. By the middle of the nineteenth century such constraints were gradually loosening, for men and women alike.

Conclusion

By the 1850s church minutes increasingly focus on doctrinal battles and concerns about financial matters. In most Baptist and Presbyterian churches efforts to oversee leisure and sexuality decline significantly over this decade.[48] By the 1880s references to such cases have almost disappeared from the church records, although the occasional notation of excessive drinking can still be found.[49] Most churches had retreated from efforts to regulate anything beyond the bounds of the 'sacred'.

In Ontario the period that saw the fading of church discipline also witnessed the growing presence and legitimacy of secular legal authority. The relationship between these changes remains a fascinating and largely unstudied area. While this relationship remains to be explained, scholars in both Canada and the US have turned to larger class and gender transformations to begin to explain the shift away from church discipline. The distinction made by a growing middle class between public and private life may have led to an increased reluctance to intrude into what were now seen as private matters. In an increasingly class-stratified society middle-class church members would also have been reluctant to have their private behaviour regulated by those they considered their social inferiors.[50] Curtis Johnson has also suggested a gender dimension here, arguing that middle- and upper-class American men were particularly reluctant to submit their business practices and personal behaviour to church regulation.[51] This seems to have been true in the Canadian context as well. In the 1850s Upper Canada saw the development of an increasingly prosperous urban middle class. The reluctance of men of this class to have their private and business lives subject to church regulation would not in itself explain the rapid decline in church discipline in this decade. But the restrictions the churches placed on men provide at least part of the answer.

As members of the Presbyterian and Baptist churches men were subject to church discipline, as were their 'sisters in Christ'. This did not mean that by joining these churches men were entering a world in which gender did not matter. Men retained much of the formal power within these communities. Certain sins, such as infractions within the business world, were gendered as male. Men were censured for failing to support their families, women for a lack of wifely obedience.[52] In regulating leisure and sexuality, however, gender differences appear to have been less significant. In the more secular world various leisure practices and sexual behaviour tended to be associated with either masculine or feminine vices. Sexual vices were certainly gendered as feminine, with women far more likely to be censured for sexual 'irregularities'. Gender does not disappear from the churches' regulation of leisure and sexuality. The regulation of leisure, in particular, had a gendered dimension, although we need to know far more about Upper Canadian leisure before assessing whether such patterns reflect the nature of actual leisure practices or of the churches' gendered concerns over such practices. The churches' regulation of sexuality reveals the clearest effort to impose a non-gendered definition of sin. Church attempts to impose a single standard of sexual behaviour were no doubt particularly galling to men accustomed to the greater sexual freedom accorded men in the larger society, and may help to explain their willingness to move away from the practice of church discipline. Without understanding the ideology and practice of gender both within and beyond the churches, then, we have at best only a partial understanding of the nature and meaning of church regulation, and of its gradual disappearance within nineteenth-century Ontario.

The abandonment of church discipline did not see the end of Christian efforts to impose a single standard of sexual behaviour. This single standard continued to be promulgated from pulpits, remaining the Christian ideal throughout the nineteenth century. Without the force of disciplinary mechanisms, however, the impact of such pious pronouncements was limited. By the end of the century church members, particularly women, became increasingly vocal about their unhappiness with the sexual double standard. The turn-of-the-century social purity movement reflected their efforts to impose a single standard of sexual purity, not simply within the Protestant churches but on an increasingly heterogeneous Canadian society.[53] The failure of this campaign did not spell the end of the Protestant contribution to the moral regulation of Canadians. Indeed, over the course of the twentieth century Christian moral assumptions have remained imbedded in the efforts of both state institutions and voluntary agencies to regulate a range of leisure and sexual behaviours.

4

'It Was Only a Matter of Passion': Masculinity and Sexual Danger

Karen Dubinsky and Adam Givertz

Much ink has been spilled in recent years coming to grips with the stunningly simple insight that 'gender' means 'men', too. Perhaps the most important historical contribution to this discussion was penned by British historians Michael Roper and John Tosh several years ago. Their argument that masculinity 'has been formed in relationship to male social power' has been kept central by too few historians of masculinity in general, particularly those studying the history of masculine sexuality.[1] It seems almost anachronistic to suggest that sexuality—and especially sexual conflict between women and men— also exerts considerable influence in shaping the contours of masculinity. Three decades of feminism have, one would think, taken us at least this far. Still, there have been few historical studies of masculine heterosexuality at all, which, in light of the recent explosion of coterminous interest in the history of sexuality, creates a curious deficiency. Thus, despite decades of activism and research on issues of heterosexual violence, we still know far more about how such conflicts affect women than men.[2]

Recent works in the history of sexuality, in several national contexts, have allowed us to glimpse the internal world of late nineteenth- and early twentieth-century courtship. If one is interested in rural, working-class, and immigrant communities, the records of state and 'state-like' agencies charged with supervising and shoring up lapses in sexual behaviour (such as the legal system and foundling hospitals) are a fruitful, though not uncomplicated source through which to reconstruct what American historian Christine Stansell has identified as the 'system of barter' between the sexes. A compelling portrait of the agonies, ecstasies, and fundamentally unequal status of women in the heterosexual barter system is emerging in the US, Britain, and Canada.[3] But where did men fit? What were the self-perceptions and public representations of the men who abandoned their pregnant girlfriends or were charged with assaulting their neighbours? Such men may well have escaped a set of onerous obligations, or even a jail term, but did they escape completely unscathed? Based on our combined research on the history of heterosexual conflict in Ontario between 1880 and 1929, and preliminary research into one particularly significant sex crime in British Columbia, this paper points to ways in which men explained their own sexual transgressions and how others explained their breaches of respectability. This may then suggest some of the ways that, historically, men have learned the rules, written the script, wielded power, and had power wielded over them in sexual relations with women.

Male Self-Perceptions and the Courts

Between 1880 and 1929, approximately 725 men were charged with sexual crimes against women in our sample of half the counties and districts of Ontario. When they were brought to trial, almost half of these men, 49 per cent, were judged not guilty by the courts.[4] There was no single surefire defence a man could invoke to make his version of events more believable, though we argue strongly that men who were able to harness any number of prevailing stereotypes about women's sexuality and morality had a greater chance of raising doubts about the character, and hence veracity, of the complainant's story.[5]

That the behaviour or character of the woman involved was scrutinized more intensively than the actions of men makes it that much more difficult to write men into the history of sexual assault. A turn-of-the-century rape trial revealed far more about the history, life circumstances, and specific behaviour of the female complainant than the male accused. Thus, this project immediately confronts a vexing political and methodological problem: what we call the irony of the invisible man. In a rape trial, the presumption of innocence of the accused included the assumption of consent by the woman, and therefore the trial was structured in such a way as to force the woman to prove her lack of consent. The more successful men charged with sexual crimes were (and remain) at deflecting attention to their female accusers, the more likely they were to walk away from both the courtroom and the historical record.

When men chose to explain their own actions in court, they told several different kinds of stories. Some issued outright denials. They claimed mistaken identity; they said they were too drunk (or, occasionally, sick) at the time to realize, or remember, their behaviour; they told inventive stories of walking into the wrong hotel room or water closet; they claimed they were being framed or 'put up' on a variety of personal conspiracies. In a handful of cases, outright admissions of culpability emerged; a few apologized. The vast majority of men, however, justified coercive sexual activity in terms of their right as men to 'take' women sexually. In Wentworth County, for example, in all but two of the 103 available cases men did not dispute that sexual contact of some sort had taken place.

The self-perceptions of men who claimed that their sexual involvements with women had not crossed the boundaries of the criminal law were by no means uniform. There was a wide spectrum of male responses to charges of sexual assault, which in turn suggests a variety of cultural frameworks that shaped understandings of masculine prerogatives within heterosexuality. As Karen Dubinsky's work on rape in Ontario during this period has shown, the sharply contrasting positions of power occupied by women and men within turn-of-the-century heterosexuality are often crystal clear.[6] Some men clearly believed that their more favoured position in the heterosexual barter system gave them a right to sexual conquest or ownership. In a similar vein, other men understood their behaviour as part of the 'spoils' of heterosexual competition. Those who claimed to have been 'just as seduced as she was' or who insisted that the woman was a prostitute obviously believed that they were acting properly within the boundaries of a contested sexual arrangement.

Others drew from the same cultural framework but admitted to a certain infraction of the rules, though not as serious an infraction as the criminal law suggested. Ross M. admitted in his 1922 trial that he got 'a little fresh' with 15-year-old Lila W. in his car as he was driving her home from a dance. 'I put my hands up her clothes, but did not pull down her drawers', he claimed. 'I laid up against her but did not have connection. She did not squawk, she only told me to stop.'[7] 'Women and men', notes British historian Françoise Barret-DuCrocq, 'met in a climate of mingled love and mistrust.'[8] There was no such thing as an absolute boundary line between respectability and deviance. How 'fresh' was too fresh? Such negotiations went on in countless back seats of countless vehicles, and just as women were ultimately expected to police the boundaries themselves, some men expected that they had the right to test, once or twice, to make sure the woman had drawn her line firmly. A fascinating set of explanations came forward from men who merged tales of masculine sexual privilege with biological imperatives. American historian Anthony Rotundo's argument that, by the late nineteenth century, male passion occupied a 'new and honoured place in the bourgeois definition of manhood' is well illustrated by the men who claimed passion as a legal defence.[9] 'My passion for women overcame me', claimed one man who raped two young girls at gunpoint in 1922.[10] Male passion was a potent force indeed, but many claimed that women bore some responsibility for inflaming it in the first place. Frederick L., who employed Vera B. as a domestic in his home in Oshawa, told police that he had sex with the 13-year-old because she was constantly 'fooling with him, and *he could not stand it.*'[11]

Men who explained their actions with reference to their passionate nature may have expressed either sorrow or defiance, but all tried to convey that this was a temporary lapse. Frederick L., for example, convinced his banker to testify to his high moral character, which helped reduce his sentence to a fine rather than a jail term. Others were able to convince judges that their actions displayed, as one judge put it, 'weakness, rather than wickedness'.[12] Passionate men failed to exhibit self-control *in the moment.* This was a character flaw, to be sure, and one that diminished—weakened—one's manhood. But this was not a condition that necessarily had lifelong consequences. It was a temporary falter, not equivalent to women's more dramatic 'fall'. The examples of relatively high-profile men who bounced back from sexual scandals suggests a certain elasticity to men's moral characters, which was rarely present for women.[13] 'Passionate men' were still, at the end of the day, 'normal men'.

'Fiends in Human Form': Monster Men and Normal Men

On 13 April 1883 a 10-year-old girl was sexually assaulted in Hamilton by Theodore F. The next day the story hit the newspaper with the headline: 'A horrible crime was committed and a beautiful girl was ravished by a drunken fiend in human form.' In 1925, another child molester was, because of 'his appearance rather than what he said', labelled subnormal by a medical expert on the witness stand. Such individuals, usually motivated by what the press declared 'inhuman lust', joined a group of men of this era who travelled quickly from the status of 'normal man' to 'monster man'.[14] The category of 'monster men' condemned certain kinds of behaviour (often, but not only, sex with children) by certain kinds of men (usually working-class men).

At the same time, of course, the category mystified the way in which these crimes both reflected and reinforced a system of sexual oppression of women and domination by men.

We are not suggesting that all 'normal' men raped their daughters, but rather that the lines between the normal and the abnormal, or deviant, were a subject of constant negotiation in a context in which men simply held more power than women. By placing such men outside the realm of 'normal' masculinity and classifying their actions as deviant, the legal system and the popular press saw to it that these men no longer reflected the relations of a masculine heterosexual order. Indeed, they were barely men at all, they were 'brutes', 'fiends', and 'animals'. Each crime was at the same time condemned and dismissed as an aberration. By locating sexual violence in the body of one man, or one type of man, everyone is relieved when the villain is found and removed from the larger body: the social.[15]

The creation of 'monster men' has a long history, for it continues, scarcely changed, to the present. For example, British feminist Wendy Holloway argues that debate over the motives of Peter Sutcliffe, England's 'Yorkshire Ripper'—whether he was 'mad' (clinically insane) or 'bad' (a warped product of his environment)—obscured 'garden variety' sexual violence. Thus, even when one man is found guilty, men in general are exonerated.[16] Canadians will likely also recognize the similarity to the case of Paul Bernardo, convicted in 1995 of a series of extremely high-profile rapes and murders in southern Ontario. Bernardo's arrest—and instant monsterization—in February 1993 brought enormous relief to the residents of Scarborough and St Catharines (two communities in which he committed his crimes), indicating that the eagerness to create and condemn one villain flourishes still. One can detect this process of monsterization of Bernardo even in his police and press-created nickname, 'The Scarborough Rapist'. By associating the crimes with a single individual and a distinct geographic location, the information gatekeepers heightened Bernardo's threat, and the actions of other rapists—in Scarborough as well as other communities—were subtly diminished.

Popular Sexual Villains

This process of naming or identifying the villain is also a process of locating villainy, of constructing distinct typologies of the sexual villain. Of all men who are seen as sexually threatening, none has an image more pervasively dangerous than the 'stranger'. Whatever the imagined location or the constructed scenario, the villain to be avoided is the stranger, lurking in the shadows, ready to pounce. In the past as in the present, this image of sexual violence looms much larger than its actual occurrence.[17]

Despite being a statistical minority, a number of types of dangerous strangers have been uncovered. Each had his own set of characteristics that made him particularly frightening. One such man was the taxi driver. In her 'exposé' of Canada's drug problem, Judge Emily Murphy, a leading Canadian feminist, suggested that taxi drivers were moral culprits twice over. The majority of these men, she claimed, were 'pedlars of drugs' as well as 'lascivious lechers'. Murphy even produced statistics to support her claim: of all occupational groups in Alberta, taxi drivers were most likely to have fathered illegitimate children.[18]

Another stranger, whose image was more ambiguous than that of the taxi driver, was the tramp. At times he could be seen charitably as a down-on-his-luck fellow, a harmless and lonely ragamuffin. Other times, the image of the eccentric tramp was itself enough to provoke suspicion and fear in women and men alike. Tramps, one police constable noted, were particularly suited to a life of crime since they 'tend to look alike and it is difficult to identify them.'[19] This association of tramps with crime and their status as outsiders often made tramps scapegoats in cases of sexual assault, especially in small communities, where they might be seen as malevolent infiltrators of rural harmony. The urban equivalent of the tramp was the 'street masher', that impolite boy or man who harassed women on the street. While serious physical abuse on the street did happen, such events were rare. Usually, street harassment in cities and towns involved men 'grabbing' women or making 'insolent' remarks. These 'everyday' events were not, however, ignored. In Ontario, the labour press as well as the commercial press took up a campaign against street mashers. Regulating male behaviour by chastising the rude and offering suggestions to the polite was a part of labour's program to foster a moral working-class masculinity.[20]

Moreover, as Dubinsky's work has also shown, events of street harassment were transformed into tales of depraved men and unsafe streets, in particular with the creation of the 'Jack the Hugger' character. Though Jack was a minor character, he was a well-travelled popular villain who roamed the streets of several Ontario communities between the years 1894 and 1916. These narratives about Jack and his wrongdoings contain four significant themes. First, they were urban stories: street harassment by strangers became a socially recognized problem whereas similar incidents in rural settings never engendered like panics. Second, the result of the Jack the Hugger scare was a perception that fear kept women off the street. As well, blame was not levied or moral aspersions cast on 'brazen' streetwalking women, as in so many other tales of urban sexual impropriety. Instead, the culprit was the street masher himself. Finally, Jack remained a villain only as long as he remained a *stranger*. The 'Jack-like' behaviour of a well-known character, such as a neighbourhood bully, was much less alarming.[21] Although Jack never displayed the absolute violence of his English cousin, the suggested relationship to Jack the Ripper seemed to both mock and mirror public fears.

The Aristocratic Libertine Meets the 'Heathen Chinese': Labour's Sexual Villain

The working class had its own cast of sexual villains. While both the labour press and the mainstream press tended to import their villains from England (after all, neither Jack the Ripper nor the aristocratic libertine were homegrown), labour's sexual villains were not simply reproductions of mainstream stereotypes but part of their critique of the relations of labour and capital. Their villains were constructed to counter the charge that urban workers were prone to vice. They argued that lascivious behaviour was one symptom of the disease of capitalism, prevalent among the ruling class but not within the ranks of modest working men. Hamilton's labour newspaper, the *Palladium of Labor*, for example, regularly castigated the social purity movement for failing to recognize that at the root of vice was the wage-labour system.[22]

We can observe a similar process in labour's discussion of the sexual dangers of Chinese men, in which the strands of masculinity, class identity, and ethnic/racial identity converged. The moral panic that used the image of the aristocratic libertine coincided with labour's anti-Asian campaign, which yielded a distinct sexual panic. One illustration will suffice: in October 1884 a *Palladium of Labor* writer, having glanced in the window of a Chinese laundry, reported seeing 'six or seven little girls' in their early teens frolicking with the 'Heathen Chinese'. The newspaper suggested that these girls were not at the laundry to pick up their 'washee' but had been plied with opium and taken advantage of. Along with a cautionary note to parents of girls 'to stay away from John Chinaman', the *Palladium* issued a not-so-subtle threat to 'Wah Lee' to 'give up coaxing little girls' or else.[23] This warning to beware of the exotic wily stranger was consistent with the generally racist campaign against Chinese immigration that dominated the pages of the Hamilton labour press.

The campaign to construct Chinese men as sexual villains involved the interaction of several historical processes, namely, the making and remaking of sexuality and the relatedness of gender, class, and race. The connection between these is illuminated in the fabrication of the Chinese man as simultaneously a degraded labourer and a debaucher of young White girls. Certainly working-class cognizance of the impact that Chinese immigration would have on the labour market must have played a part in the making of labourist racism. But working-class anti-Asian racism was not simply a manifestation of the insecurity of alienated labour. Though it could reflect labour market concerns, it was inconsistent in its application. Making 'Chineseness' a threat to young girls was a distinct typology, and Asian immigrants were regarded as especially threatening to the sexual and gender order.[24] This perceived economic and sexual threat was reflected in royal commissions on Asian immigration and in a series of exclusionary government immigration policies implemented between 1880 and 1923. The result was a predominantly male Chinese community, the presence of which, ironically, intensified the images of Chinese sexual immorality.[25]

Some may propose that the image of the lecherous Chinese male was invented by middle-class reformers and simply reproduced by working-class activists. But the notion of a dangerous sexuality inherent in Chinese men surfaced in the working-class position on immigration long before it became prominent in the discourse of middle-class moral reformers or, as Madge Pon has illustrated, in the pages of the Toronto press.[26] In both cases, the image of Chinese men entrapping White women was crucial to the formation of Anglo-Canadian male identity, and certainly also reinforced already existing concerns among White male labourers about economic competition. While many historians, most recently Gail Bederman, have noted how turn-of-the-century White men drew sustenance (and power) from their common-sense equation of 'whiteness' with civilization, this worked in class-specific ways.[27] Furthermore, as our next case will suggest, the boundary separating the civilized self from the dangerous, foreign other was not always understood with the precision that this binary opposition implies.

A British Columbia Panic: The Case of Jack Kong

The Chinese man was by no means the only or even necessarily the most 'dangerous' racialized sexual villain. Newspapers regularly commented on the ethnicity of southern and eastern European men charged with sexual crimes, but found other angles, such as alcohol or 'passion', when the men were British. Similarly, judges constantly offered stern rebukes about the 'lawlessness' of foreigners, turning 'obedience to the law' into a racial trait possessed by Anglos and lacking in all others. The dangerous foreigner was a villain thoroughly implanted in the Canadian mind. Yet the relationship between race and sexual villainy was not always so direct. In early twentieth-century British Columbia, a highly politicized atmosphere of racial conflict helped shape state and public responses to one particular crime. In this case, the possible sexual threat of the 'Chinaman' was rivalled by his economic and social threat, and mediated by his age.

One spring day in April 1914, Charles Millard, the chief ticket agent for the Canadian Pacific Railway, left his home in Vancouver for a business trip to nearby Victoria. Returning to his Pendrell Street home the next evening he was surprised to discover that his wife, 30-year-old Clara Millard, was not there waiting for him. When he failed to track her through family and friends the following day, he became worried and called the police. Within a couple of days, traces of human remains were discovered in the basement furnace. With this, all attention turned to Jack Kong, the family 'houseboy' who had been in their employ for three years. Kong was instantly taken in for questioning, and the *Vancouver Sun* explained what followed:

> The China boy, who is only 17 years of age, and who has been noted as the brightest scholar in the Lord Roberts school, sat in his stone cell, looking through the bars at his inquisitors and refused to say a word. Question after question was hurled at him by the officers, but the Oriental, who is so slight of frame as to appear almost girlish, simply stared with a sharp eyes at them and kept his lips tightly closed. His eyes, while unnaturally bright, had dark blue circles under them and he had the appearance of not having slept for several nights.[28]

Kong's 'girlish' frame instantly marked him as something other than a 'normal man'— a process of feminization noted by other historians of anti-Asian racism in Canada.[29] Indeed, as cultural critic Marjorie Garber has recently pointed out, there is a long history, in Western fantasies of 'the Orient', of emasculated, gender-blurred Asian maleness, of which David Hwang's play *M. Butterfly* is one recent example.[30] Yet, when an Asian man was rendered 'girlish', this did not necessarily make him safe, particularly when he was, as this quotation implies, also identified with the twin 'Oriental' evils of 'inscrutability' and drug use. After a day in police custody, and subject to continued questioning that included methods the newspapers straightforwardly termed 'the third degree', Kong confessed to the crime. He hit Mrs Millard accidentally during an argument over burnt porridge: he had burnt it, and she refused to eat it and demanded he cook more. He was late for school and refused, she reacted to his insolence by threatening him with a kitchen knife, and he threw a chair at her. She fell, hit her head, and was killed instantly, and, in panic, Kong hid the body in the furnace.[31]

In a region that had experienced enormous racial conflict, as Vancouver had for decades, the accusation of murder of an Anglo woman by an Asian man would hardly have escaped attention. Kong was certainly monsterized, but in particular ways. He slid, quite easily, into categories made available by decades of British Columbia racial politics: the economic threat, whose presence in the domestic economy became as contested as it had previously been in other industrial sectors, and the social threat, whose place in the school system was as worrisome as the presence of Asian shopkeepers or neighbours. What's missing here is sex, for, unlike other non-Anglo men who killed Anglo women in this era, Jack Kong's sexual habits never became part of the Kong/Millard narrative as it unfolded in British Columbia.[32]

This apparent anomaly can be understood in the context of the particular relationships between Anglos and Asians in turn-of-the-century British Columbia. The idea of Chineseness created by Europeans constructed Asians as lacking in both sanitation and morality.[33] The moral threat posed by Chinese men was more nebulous, but more far-reaching, than that posed by other 'dangerous' men. Behind Jack Kong's 'sharp eyes'—even if they were 'unnaturally brightened'—lurked a 'Celestial' mind, capable of feats of cunning far more dastardly than simple rape or murder; and 'none of us', reminded the *New Westminster News*, 'can fathom the workings of the eastern mind.'[34] In this political climate, the sexual dangers of Chinese men went beyond 'normal' sexual violence. Instead, they were feared for their ability to 'lure': they led women into opium smoking and prostitution, and children into untold vices. Prevailing racial discourses had dehumanized Asians in British Columbia; even the use of police brutality to extract a confession from Kong—the notorious 'third degree'—was defended in the press since 'any method by which can be used to extract the truth from the inscrutable Oriental is justifiable.'[35] It follows, therefore, that Chinese men, in some historical epochs, were not 'normal men' at all: they were 'Chinamen', and Kong, a 'China boy'.

Orientalizing the 'Celestial': Responses to Kong

Within days of Kong's arrest, several 'Chinamen' were stopped on the street and assaulted by White men. Chinese employment agents announced that at least 50 or 60 Chinese boys had been discharged from employment in hotels, restaurants, and private homes, and the call went out, from several quarters, for the complete segregation of the provincial school system.[36]

The campaigns against Chinese domestic servants and Chinese children in the school system fit an agenda of anti-Asian racism predating the actions of Jack Kong. The Trades and Labour Congress, for example, used the public clamour about the crime to repeat its request to the Vancouver Board of License Commissioners to bar 'Orientals' from working in hotels.[37] Some in the labour movement felt vindicated. According to the *BC Federationist*, newspaper of the British Columbia Federation of Labour, 'the organized labour movement did not have to see a woman murdered before taking pains to try and secure the exclusion not only of Chinese domestics, but of all kinds of Asiatic labour from Canada.'[38] In an earlier era, middle-class BC ladies regarded their 'China boys' as a precious commodity. Some White women, according to witnesses at the Royal Commission on Chinese Immigration in 1885, employed their 'Chinamen' to 'scrub them whilst in their baths.'[39] By the time of Kong's trial, however, debate raged about the dangers of domestic 'Celestials': to individual families, to unemployed White female domestics, and to the social and economic health of the province as a whole.

Anne McClintock has written provocatively of one of the paradoxes of Victorian culture, which zealously enforced the boundaries of middle-class self and degenerate other, while simultaneously gathering up thousands of those same others—working-class female domestic servants— into the family hearth. The result, she claims, at least for middle-class male children, was to re-create the contradictions of female sexuality literally from birth. Growing up with two (or more) starkly different mothers helped to dichotomize female sexuality 'distinctly along class lines'.[40] Furthermore, she suggests, Victorian discourse on degeneration served not only to dichotomize the sexuality of women in class terms, but to create racial distinctions as well. 'The more menial, paid work a woman did, the more she was manly and unsexed, the more she was a race apart.'[41]

If, by crossing the thresholds of private and public, home and market, working and middle class, the female domestic servant in England became 'the embodiment of a central contradiction within the modern industrial formation', let us consider the paradox of British Columbia.[42] In this context, one did not need to tax the imagination: neither age nor feminization could completely erase the fact that the Chinese houseboy was a masculine and 'foreign' presence in the domestic sphere. The furore created by the Kong story was thus attributable not only to the grisly death of Clara Millard but to the public exposure of one of the great 'threshold crossings' of turn-of-the-century British Columbia: public/private, male/female, Anglo/Chinese.

This exposure, however, was not limited to the domestic sphere, and here Kong's status as a schoolboy was as problematic as his role as houseboy. The demand to remove Chinese children from the school system had been raised in various levels of government since at least 1910—at which time fewer than 100 Chinese children attended Vancouver schools—and the Kong story gave this campaign fresh impetus. The day after Kong's arrest, the Vancouver city council debated a motion, which later got waylaid over legal technicalities, to separate Euro-Canadian and Asian children in schools. That Kong had spent several successful years in the Vancouver school system—and indeed, if his own confession was to be believed, that his reluctance to be late for school caused his disobedience to his employer—worked not to establish a character advantage for him, but rather to contaminate the entire public school system. The *Vancouver Sun*, for example, noted with dismay that Chinese boys were usually much older than their classmates; 17-year-old Jack Kong was a seat-mate of a 13-year-old White boy. Age difference, when combined with 'Oriental inscrutability', made for a dreadful combination:

> No one knows the moral standard of any Chinaman. A Chinaman's face as a rule is as expressive as a steam radiator. No one can tell by looking at him what is passing in his mind. What the result of contact of this youthful self confessed murderer may have had upon the minds of his more youthful contemporaries no one can tell. But this awful tragedy should teach the school board that their first duty is to segregate the Orientals from white children in all the schools.[43]

Age played a central role in delineating gender in this case. Combined with race, age initially helped to render Kong safe, a houseboy Mr Millard felt no qualms about bringing into the family hearth or leaving alone with his wife. After the crime, however, Kong's 'advanced' age, relative to his schoolmates, was portrayed as yet another source of danger.

Such were some of the ways in which Kong's villainy was framed. It is equally revealing, however, to consider what was not said. Kong was not, as he might easily have been, turned into a hypersexualized masculine object of peril to female employers, schoolteachers, or students. References to his 'girlishness' never triggered public speculation or innuendo about homosexuality or other 'lust-driven' diseases.[44] This raises interesting possibilities regarding regional and racial variations in the discourse of masculine sexuality. And this is even more apparent when we contrast the local reaction to the crime with reactions in other Canadian centres.

Clara Millard's murder received prominent press attention in Toronto, particularly when her southern Ontario roots were traced. A more sensational local connection, however, was that a bill to prohibit the employment of White women by 'Oriental' businessmen was being debated in the Ontario provincial legislature just as Kong was arrested for the crime. This heated up the debate considerably, and helped to reinforce pre-existing sexualized images of the Chinese man in Ontario. 'The people of the Orient do not consider human life by the same standards as we of the white race', declared the bill's sponsor, Dr Forbes Godfrey, MPP from West York. 'Witness the recent deplorable murder of a white women by a young Chinese in Vancouver.'[45]

The British Columbia example certainly added an impetus to the debate on this bill in the provincial legislature—a debate that resulted in the passage of the bill, conditional on the legality of similar legislation in Saskatchewan being contested before the Judicial Committee of the Privy Council.[46] But the Ontario debate had a distinctive flavour, captured in one Toronto newspaper headline: 'Chinese and Our Girls'.[47] There were, it was estimated, 120 'white girls' working for 'Chinamen' in Toronto, primarily in restaurants.[48] In 'socially purified' 1914 southern Ontario, however, these 120 girls had the same effect as the 98 Chinese children in Vancouver schools: they were a powerful metaphor for the dangers of racial mixing. The political discourse in southern Ontario, steeped as it was in the heavily racialized sexual anxieties of the social purity movement and the labour movement, determined that the debate would be framed in the familiar terms of the protection of 'White womanhood' from the 'degraded' Oriental male.

Gender identities, like racial identities, are created in the social world. We would not suggest that citizens of BC were 'more racist' in this era, or that those in southern Ontario were 'more sexually uptight'. Different communities, at different times, take up these issues in varying ways. The limitations of this comparison are obvious, and we can say little conclusively about the way racial and sexual panics came together in British Columbia based on one high-profile case. Further research in the history of sexual crime in British Columbia will help to determine whether the tenor of the reaction to Kong was representative of, or anomalous to, other men, Asian and non-Asian.[49] At this point, however, we would argue that these examples amplify Linda Gordon's contention that social definitions of violence and sexual antagonisms are products of political conflicts and struggles.[50] As the political home of the social purity movement and, before that, the Canadian stronghold of the Knights of Labor, early twentieth-century southern Ontario possessed a particular set of lenses through which to view racial and ethnic relations, which magnified the gendered and sexualized dimensions of non-Anglo 'others'. In this instance at least, the specifically feminist racist discourse of social purity did not resonate in BC in exactly the same fashion as Ontario, perhaps because of the way the 'frontier' muted Euro-Canadian women's political voices.[51] Jack Kong was monsterized in a manner that emerged from local conditions, particularly the long-standing provincial politics of economic and social exclusion of Asians. He did not become the hypersexualized masculine foreigner so familiar on the social landscape in other parts of the Victorian world.

The criminal justice system does not, as Angus McLaren has recently reminded us, 'simply rubber-stamp public prejudices'.[52] Nowhere is this more apparent than in Jack Kong's case. Agreeing with the defence's contention that Kong had hit Clara Millard accidentally and that she had died before dismemberment and cremation, the jury found him guilty of the lesser charge of manslaughter, rather than murder, for which the sentence would have been hanging. This was a tremendously unpopular verdict, which was only rectified somewhat by the imposition of the extraordinary sentence of 'natural life' in prison. This sentence, which could only be imposed for manslaughter where 'the character of the accused makes it appear that reform is not to be looked for', was used in this case for the first time in Canadian legal history.[53]

Conclusion

The fevered pitch of anti-Asian racism in early twentieth-century Canada is obviously well illustrated in the Jack Kong case. Moreover, and especially when compared to stories that could have been (but were not) regarded as similar in Ontario, it reinforces the way in which race, class, and region shape the contours of gender. Masculinity is not a property unto itself. In this case, Kong's 'Chineseness' and his status as a houseboy form the content of his masculine persona. This case also provides a useful example of the complex relationship of signifier (or event) and signification (or meaning). Chineseness could mean different things. It made Jack Kong a general public threat in British Columbia and, simultaneously, a specifically sexual threat in Ontario. It is also striking, as historian Constance Backhouse has pointed out, that while the apparently harmless, feminized Asian man was permitted into the households of middle-class Euro-Canadians, he became an exceedingly dangerous character if he employed White women in his own establishment. Two years before the Kong case Saskatchewan passed legislation to prohibit the employment of White women in Asian businesses and quickly convicted two Chinese restaurant owners for this offence.[54] That Jack Kong, Asian men, or men in general did not present a unified or solitary image, but had distinct regional characteristics, reinforces the point that the relationship between knower and known varies from place to place and subject to subject.

What is common, however, to all of these tales, is how communities could define the boundaries between insiders and outsiders: between harmless tramps, passionate if misguided lovers, or even innocent victims of vengeful females and those villains who were 'truly' deserving of legal or social condemnation—the monster men or the lecherous, deceitful Chinese 'Celestial'. As this comparative analysis of sexual and racialized villains in British Columbia and Ontario reveals, outsiders could be defined by their sexuality or by their 'race' or by both, but the particular interplay was neither predictable nor predetermined. The boundaries between normal men and monsters were shaped and reshaped within the class, racial, and sexual contexts of their time and place. The task of sorting out who was who makes historical inquiry into the history of male violence a challenging and complicated enterprise.

5

Gender and Work in Lekwammen Families, 1843–1970

John Lutz

Recent studies of the interaction between gender, race, and colonialism in North America and the Pacific are forcing a reorientation of Canadian history. In the light of this new work, the settlement of Canada is exposed as a 'colonial project' that involved the displacement and marginalization of one people by another. Even more important, it is becoming clear that while the words 'colonial project' or even 'colonialism' are convenient shorthands, they do not describe a single process. What we call colonialism was a constellation of factors that had distinct, even contradictory, impacts on different indigenous people. It is increasingly apparent that colonization was a gendered process with differential impacts on Aboriginal women and men, impacts that depended, in turn, on age and social status.[1] This chapter develops an understanding of the gendered effect of colonization in Canada by examining the interplay of one of its elements—the economy—with gender, age, and social position in an Aboriginal community, over a 130-year time-span. It offers a microhistory focusing on the experience of one Aboriginal community, the Lekwammen (Songhees)[2] people, whose ancestral territory is now occupied by Victoria, the capital city of British Columbia.

A start has already been made in exploring the gendered impact of colonialism on Canadian Aboriginal people, but the conclusions so far have painted a one-sided picture. A dramatic illustration is Karen Anderson's examination of gender relations among the Huron and Montagnais. Anderson shows that, within the relatively short period of 30 years, the impact of colonial society (primarily through the church) in New France was to reduce dramatically the power of Aboriginal women vis-à-vis Aboriginal men. Eleanor Leacock, Joanne Fiske, and Ron Bourgeault, examining the impact of colonialism on other Aboriginal groups at other times, came to similar conclusions.[3]

Important and thought-provoking as these studies are, it would be a mistake to generalize that the gendered impact of the colonial interchange was always to weaken the social power of all Aboriginal women. Given the vast range of gender relations in pre-contact Aboriginal societies, it is not surprising that in some, women were relatively powerful, while in others they were relatively powerless.[4] As well, European colonists came from different countries, represented different churches and different economic systems, and had different agendas in their dealings with Aboriginal people. Thus, the gendered outcome of individual colonial interchanges depended on the nature of both the particular European and Aboriginal societies involved and the circumstances of their meeting. Moreover, west coast Aboriginal societies, like the European societies they encountered, were stratified according to age and status. Given these pre-existing social divisions, it seems possible that even within the gender-divided groups of men and women, costs and benefits of colonization would be unevenly distributed. There is some evidence that upper-class Aboriginal women, for example, may have seen their positions eroded, while their female slaves may have found their post-colonial position enhanced.[5]

This is not an attempt to argue that the Lekwammen case is more typical than the Huron or Montagnais experiences described by others, but it does underscore that the impact of colonization on gender roles was complex and varied. Using a microhistorical method, we can focus precisely on the variety of ways metahistorical processes, like colonization, manifest themselves in different contexts.[6] By taking a single community and piecing together lives, and the interconnections between lives, from fragments, painstakingly extracted from the many different hiding places of historical memory—local newspapers, reminiscences, parish records, census records, Indian agents' reports, letters, photos—it is possible to get to know something about practically everyone who lived in that community. Organizing these reminders of lives, births, deaths, descendants, and, most important, relationships, into scrapbooks covering six or seven generations allows a close, nuanced look at the effect of colonialism on gender.

The Lekwammen felt the impact of European society late compared to many Canadian Aboriginal groups, but thereafter they experienced it with greater intensity. Their territory was selected as the site of Fort Victoria in 1843, and soon became the centre of European settlement in what is now British Columbia. When, in 1849, Vancouver Island became a British colony, Victoria became the capital and remained the most urban site in the colony, and later, in the province, until overtaken by Vancouver in the 1890s. With a city growing up in their midst, the Lekwammen felt all the administrative, religious, and social pressures of colonialism. But while Victoria's proximity had definite drawbacks, it also had possible benefits. Few Aboriginal groups were as well situated to take advantage of opportunities opened up by the new economy. Throughout the period covered here, economic relationships within Lekwammen society, and between the Lekwammen and immigrant society, reshaped gendered contributions to the household economy and gendered power more generally. By considering these changes over more than a century—beginning with contact, through the fur trade, establishment of the commercial fishery, global depression, world war, and post-World War II welfare state economy —this chapter analyses the shifting nature of gender roles and power within Lekwammen society. This approach also reveals the multiple and contradictory interactions between gender and the colonial and post-colonial economies.

The Ethnographic Moment

The Lekwammen had only recently come together as a group when James Douglas arrived in their territory on the steamship *Beaver* in 1843 to establish a trading establishment. Previously, the ancestors of the people now called Lekwammen lived in villages occupied during the winter months on the islands and bays along the coast of southeast Vancouver Island (see Map 1). In spring, summer, and fall they moved to seasonal campsites close to their fishing, hunting, or gathering grounds. Although they shared a common dialect, were neighbours with kin, and had ceremonial links to the others, these extended-family villages did not constitute a nation and did not act in concert in matters of peace or war. Due to depopulation from European-introduced disease, which first swept the coast in the 1770s, and increased raiding by European-armed northern Aboriginal groups, most of these winter villages were deserted in the late eighteenth century. As protection against the northern raiders, the 1,000–1,500 remaining Lekwammen congregated into two fortified villages, one in Esquimalt harbour and a larger village, Sungaya, in what is now called Cadboro Bay.[7]

Most of the knowledge we have of Lekwammen social life comes from the period that immediately brackets the arrival of Europeans in their territory. This is that 'ethnographic moment' that has come to be seen as 'since time immemorial'. Never mind that Aboriginal society, like all living societies, was continuously in flux, responding to new social and environmental pressures, including dramatic crises in the form of depopulation and concentration. This is the time when European observers found Aboriginal societies novel and recorded observations about them. When, beginning in the 1880s, ethnographers asked Aboriginal people to describe so-called 'traditional' lifestyles, they also heard a description of the time when most of the informants were raised, that is, the period surrounding the arrival of the fur traders.

Just as historic and ethnographic writing has privileged the contact era as 'time immemorial', it has put a gendered spin on social relations. Virtually all the Europeans who left comments about Aboriginal people—explorers and ethnographers—were males. What they observed and where they interconnected with Aboriginal society were arenas of male society or of mixed society, but never the private realms of women's society.[8] At the very least, this means that we have a much more detailed rendering of men's society than women's. It also alerts us that the descriptions might tend to exaggerate the importance of men's society and diminish that of women. Much of what we can know of women's and children's activities must come from 'listening to the silence' in the existing accounts.[9]

The Lekwammen had a distinctly gendered political and production system, but the first European immigrants in Lekwammen territory made little mention of it. In north-coast Aboriginal societies like the Tsimshian studied by Fiske and Cooper and the Tlingit examined by Klein, descent was reckoned matrilineally. In these societies women were prominent and Europeans frequently speculated about gender roles and the power of women. By contrast, the Lekwammen and other Coast Salish peoples, like Europeans, recognized descent bilaterally, from both paternal and maternal lines, with emphasis on the paternal. The Lekwammen's *siem*, heads of households that Europeans identified as 'chiefs', were all male. This position, along with its prerogatives and obligations, generally passed from a *siem*, on his death, to his eldest son, and if there were no sons, then to a brother and his sons. Because he controlled access to major resource sites, a *siem* controlled the wealth of the household and managed the major items of property as well as ceremonial privileges.[10] Within each household, less important items were either the joint property of families or owned by individuals. These included utensils of everyday use, wealth goods held in preparation for distribution, dogs, and

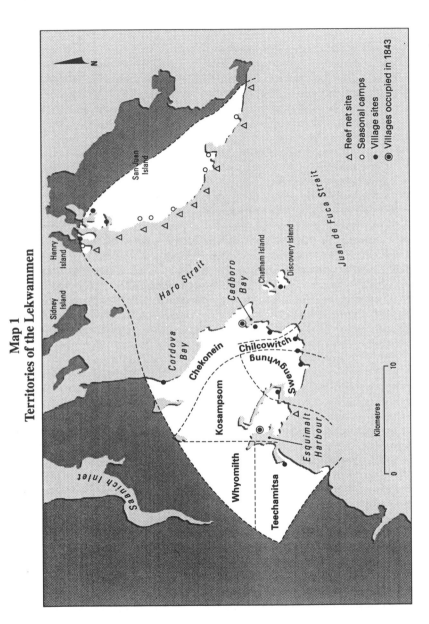

Map 1
Territories of the Lekwammen

△ Reef net site
○ Seasonal camps
● Village sites
◉ Villages occupied in 1843

spiritual knowledge derived from personal visions. Slaves were included among the private property of those who could afford them. Husbands and wives held their property separately; at death a husband's property would be transferred to his sons; a wife's property to her daughters.[11] Although not so highly stratified as north-coast Aboriginal societies, the Lekwammen were divided into three classes: 'Good People' or nobles, from which the *siem* would be drawn; 'Worthless People' or commoners; and slaves.[12] By 1839 slaves apparently outnumbered commoners and nobles combined.[13] Villages consisted of a number of extended families each occupying a large winter house. Paul Kane, in 1847, described their 'lodges' as 'the largest buildings of any description that I have met with among the Indians. They are divided in the interior into compartments [using rush mats], so as to accommodate eight to ten families.' One Lekwammen house (at the abandoned village on Garrison Island) was later measured to be 400 feet by 40 feet.[14] Households usually consisted of a male *siem*, his brothers, sons, and all their wives and children. It was also common to have unmarried sisters, widows, orphans, and perhaps nephews included in the household, as well as slaves. Although blood relationship was theoretically as strong on the maternal side as the paternal, wives usually lived with their husband's family.

Except for the fact that *siem* might have more than one wife, the newcomers could easily see him as an Aboriginal equivalent to an aristocratic patriarch—indeed they sometimes referred to important *siem* such as Chee-al-thuk of the Lekwammen as 'kings' and their wives as 'queens'.[15] None the less, the *siem*'s power lay strictly in his ability to persuade and reward. All decisions about collective action—when and whether to move to a seasonal camp, to hold a feast, to wage war—were made by the *siem* in consultation with family heads within households.[16]

In Lekwammen society men held the positions of economic and political power, but the practice of polygyny was, in part, a recognition of the importance of women as producers of goods and reproducers of labour. It was not uncommon for higher-ranking men to have more than one wife. Three seems to have been the maximum for all but the most prominent *siem*.[17] Since resources were generally abundant, the larger the family, the more labour available for accumulating surplus food and goods, and the higher the status a family could achieve. In addition to enlarging the household, polygyny had other practical purposes. Marriages among high-status families were often diplomatic unions, establishing a basis for friendly relationships between households, particularly households in different villages and different nations. This connection provided each set of in-laws with some access to the resources controlled by the other and some measure of 'safe passage' through the others' territories. It also established a gift-exchange cycle whereby one's in-laws would bring the rare and valuable commodities of their territory as gifts.

When it came to productive activities, men, women, children, and the elderly had distinctive roles. Males and females worked in separate but interdependent productive activities. The gendered division of labour was maintained, at least partly, by the belief that women, during menstruation and following childbirth, had properties that drove away the fish and animals depended on for food. If, at these times, a woman even touched fishing or hunting equipment it became unusable. If women, at either of these times, had intercourse with males, male hunting/fishing powers would be weakened or destroyed.

There is debate in the anthropological literature as to whether women were considered 'polluted' at these times or endowed with a special, uncontrollable power. Scholars who claim the latter argue that suggestions of women's 'pollution' come from male informants to male ethnologists. For the Lekwammen and their neighbours it is clear that the men, at least, saw women as polluted when menstruating and following childbirth. We have no surviving account from Lekwammen women, but the autobiography of Mourning Dove, an interior Salish woman culturally linked to the Lekwammen, accepts the term 'polluted' to describe menstruating women.[18]

As a result of these prohibitions, only men fished and hunted; however, women made the baskets and other vessels in which the food would be stored and preserved the catch so that food would be available throughout the year and for feasts. Men made the nets for catching fish, deer, or ducks, but from twine made by women. Men secured most of the protein in the Lekwammen diet; women produced the carbohydrates, starches, and other vegetables and fruits essential to their diet. Men were not prohibited from doing 'women's work', and for short periods, where time was of the essence, some tasks, like harvesting camas (a flowering plant with a starchy bulb that was a staple) or shellfish, might involve whole households.[19]

Although tasks of production were specifically gendered, among the Lekwammen gender was not necessarily determined by biological sex. Boas, in 1890, noted among the Lekwammen that 'sometimes men assume women's dress and occupations and vice versa.' He added that this custom was found all along the north Pacific coast.[20]

Food circulated in a 'subsistence economy' where individual gatherers and heads of families had some, but not total, control over its distribution. Other goods, including slaves owned by individuals and families, circulated in a 'wealth' or 'prestige economy'. The two economies functioned separately but were interconnected at various points.[21]

The most important reason for the production and accumulation of wealth goods in Salish society was the potlatch complex. 'Potlatch' is a Chinook jargon word for a variety of ceremonies among west-coast Aboriginal people that involve feasting, dancing, and, most importantly, the distribution of gifts. Although all the west-coast nations held potlatches, the occasions when they were held varied widely. For the Lekwammen and other Straits Salish, potlatches were held periodically to mark significant events, including marriage and the inheritance of rights such as those of the *siem*. Potlatches might also be held to clear away shame caused by oneself or one's family. Among the Lekwammen, a single potlatch was usually hosted by a number of families, each with its own event to memorialize. High-status recipients of potlatch gifts were expected to reciprocate with their own potlatches to maintain their relative social ranking.[22]

While subsistence production was shared relatively evenly between men and women, when it came to the production of prestige goods, women's contributions probably dominated. Men made a contribution through the acquisition of slaves in warfare and through manufacturing canoes, hunting implements, and regalia that might be given at a potlatch. None the less, the most important items in the potlatch economy were blankets made by women. Woven from cedar bark, wool, and occasionally other fibres, blankets had a prestige value far exceeding their utility. Because of their value, portability, and divisibility, blankets also functioned as a medium of exchange. These were the first and most valuable items the Lekwammen offered to exchange with Europeans.[23]

Women and children gathered and prepared cedar-bark fibres for the warp. The main source for the woof was from the Lekwammen's only domesticated animal—a dog specially bred for its wool. Dog wool was supplemented by mountain goat wool received in trade from the Squamish and Nooksack on the mainland. Wool-bearing dogs were the property of women who kept them segregated, often on small islands, to prevent cross-breeding with other dogs. Myron Eells, speaking of the southern Lekwammen's neighbours, recorded that 'a woman's wealth was often estimated by the number of such dogs she owned.' Women sheared these special dogs, spun their wool, and wove the blankets on large looms.[24] In addition to the blankets, women also made baskets and mats as trade and potlatch items, harvested and stored the camas that was exchanged for the products of other nations, and tanned hides that were occasionally items of exchange.

When Europeans arrived in Lekwammen territory they came to a society where political power was concentrated in the hands of elderly males, yet women had a measure of independence. Judith Brown has argued that women's power was commensurate with the value of and their control over the distribution of their own production.[25] Among the Lekwammen, women owned their own property and contributed the largest share of a household's wealth through the manufacture of important prestige items. They did not have much control over the distribution of these products.

The Colonial Moment

European colonization was less a matter of populating an empty land than of depopulating a full one. The missionary Bolduc estimated that he spoke to 1,200 people in the Lekwammen village of Sungaya in 1843. When James Douglas conducted his 1850 enumeration, he counted 700 Lekwammen. Their number had been reduced to 400 by 1859, to 285 by 1864, to 164 by 1891, and to a low of 117 in 1911.[26] The drastic population collapse is partly owing to the introduction of a dangerous form of home-brewed alcohol, but largely due to introduced diseases for which the Lekwammen had no immunity.

For those who survived, colonization brought a new economic system, based on wage labour, into their territory. The Lekwammen were surprisingly eager to participate—wages earned in a capitalist economy could be given away in the potlatch economy, thereby increasing workers' status in their own community. For their part, the immigrant Europeans were eager to employ the Lekwammen, but only in positions consistent with European ideas of racial hierarchy and appropriate gender roles. The Lekwammen—men, women, young and old—found that only certain jobs were open to 'Indians' according to racialized European beliefs that Aboriginal people were only suitable for menial work.[27]

The European arrival created some new opportunities and closed others, all of which affected Lekwammen gender relations. Lekwammen were hired primarily as labourers for construction, land-clearing, and ploughing and as paddlers for express-canoes. All these fell into the category of 'male work' in both the Lekwammen's and fur traders' world-view. The Lekwammen men who laboured for the fort were paid in factory-made blankets. Since blankets had been the main contribution of women to the Lekwammen economy, this new arrangement undermined women's economic importance. Moreover, the fur traders brought sheep to the island in 1849; after that, wool-bearing dogs, which had constituted the largest part of many women's personal wealth, lost their value and were left to interbreed with other dogs. By 1889 Franz Boas declared the special wool dogs 'extinct for some time'. None the less, a small part of the women's blanket-making skill remained useful in the immigrant economy: shearing the dogs had been a woman's job among the Lekwammen, so this may explain why sheep-shearing is the only labouring occupation at the fort where women are named as workers.[28]

In addition to paid labour, and probably even more important as a source of new income, the Lekwammen supplied food to the fort. In this arena as well, most of the provisions—fresh fish and game—were the products of male enterprise. Women contributed, to a lesser extent, through their control over potato crops (which the Lekwammen had been growing for several years by 1843) and in the harvest of clams and oysters for sale. In addition, women maintained their long-standing contributions to the subsistence economy.[29]

The immediate effect of the arrival of Euro-Canadians was to elevate the importance of Lekwammen men as producers of wealth relative to women. This might suggest that women's position ought to have been devalued as a result, but in fact this seems not have been the case. Colonial society was almost entirely male. In looking for short-term or long-term relationships the immigrant men courted Lekwammen women with some success. Charles Bayley, arriving in 1851, noted that outside the fort there were log shanties 'occupied by half breeds, Iroquois, French Canadian and Kanakas (Hawaiians) . . . most of them living with native women.'[30] The declining productive role of women was offset by the increasing demand for Lekwammen women as marriage and sexual partners.

Although there is an absence of direct accounts, it seems likely these unions in the 1850s were similar to those described in the 1860s. In a fusion of indigenous and immigrant practices, the fur trader would offer the father of a Native woman or the owner of a female slave a 'bridal gift'; a variety of reciprocal obligations were probably initiated, but it seems that in general the new 'husband' felt less obligation and had less incentive to maintain the lifelong cycle of ritual exchanges that normally accompanied Lekwammen marriages. If the arrangement ceased to be satisfactory for either party, or if the man moved, his 'country wife' often returned to her family. From the comments of Bayley and the experience in other parts of the Pacific Northwest it would seem that the overwhelming number of immigrant men, up to the 1858 gold rush at least, formed some kind of liaison with local Aboriginal women.[31] Given this extensive out-marriage on the part of the Lekwammen women, it is at first glance surprising that the gender balance of the local Aboriginal community continued to favour women by a small margin. Douglas's 1850 census of the Lekwammen showed 122 'men with beards', 134 women, 221 boys, and 223 girls, totalling 700. Subsequent censuses show that the male-female ratio remained relatively constant.[32]

The out-marriage of Lekwammen women to immigrant men was apparently made up by women from neighbouring nations marrying into the Lekwammen. Aboriginal accounts of Lekwammen men marrying Swinomish, Twana, Cowichan, and Saanich women survive from this period. The presence of the fort made the Lekwammen wealthy compared to their neighbours, and therefore desirable as marriage mates. It was also valuable for distant nations to have relatives in Victoria so they could trade unmolested at the fort and have a place to stay when they came. Moreover, the Lekwammen had a reputation for being unusually clever and for having powerful spirit-allies. [33]

While many Aboriginal women formed long-term liaisons with the immigrants, others sold sexual services. Contemporary observers described this as 'prostitution', but a closer look suggests the exchange of sex for payment, like other cross-cultural exchanges, had room for different interpretations on each side. Caroline Ralston argues in her study of Hawaiian women that 'the term "prostitution", with its undeniable sexist and moralistic connotations, is inapplicable as a description of the . . . casual sexual encounters in which money or material favours are exchanged.'[34] At Victoria it seems certain that some of what the Europeans called prostitution was the coerced 'rental' of women slaves. From the first appearance of Europeans on the coast, the hiring out of women slaves to the fur traders and sailors had been a sideline venture for slaveholders. With the gold rush, opportunities for selling sex increased, but so did the avenues for slaves to escape their owners and seek protection from missionaries or kin. As slavery dwindled in importance in the 1860s, the transactions became more complex. There are a number of accounts, both in Aboriginal stories and in accounts by non-Aboriginal observers, that some women of other groups, the Haida, Tsimshian, and Tlingit as well as the Kwakwaka'wakw, used what the Whites called prostitution to earn wealth independently of men in order to potlatch and enhance their personal status in their society.[35]

Overall, the first 20 years of the colonial encounter affected Lekwammen men and women differently depending on their location in Lekwammen society. Common women and men had, for the first time, the means to accumulate wealth and raise their status through their own potlatches. As a result, male and female members of the nobility found their relative status diminishing. With the decline of the patriarchal power system, common women probably experienced a relative increase in their political power. For slaves, the initial effect may have been to worsen their lot since male and females were rented out as manual labourers by their owners and female slaves were prostituted. But by the 1860s, the colonial encounter became a benefit to slaves. Missionaries and government officials offered refuge to runaways and the Royal Navy worked to suppress the institution of slavery.

The Industrial Moment

Opportunities for the economic independence of women and the cash contribution of children and the aged, which had increased with the gold rush, increased even further in the late 1870s and early 1880s with the establishment of a salmon-canning industry. Whereas in other places colonial pressure was pushing Aboriginal women out of the public sphere of wage work,[36] on the west coast the new fish-canning factories appropriated the gendered division of work from Aboriginal societies: Native men fished and women mended nets and processed fish. The infirm looked after the infants, while even young children had work cleaning cans. In peak seasons, every available person would be brought in and infants placed in a corner where they could be watched.[37] In addition to the Aboriginal gender division of labour, another element of the earlier economy, the separate personal property of husband and wife, continued into the industrial era. In the cash economy, the Lekwammen's Indian agent noted, 'among these Indians, the wife's purse is generally entirely separate from the husband's.' There was also continuity when it came to subsistence production. The Lekwammen people carried on their earlier gendered subsistence production and continued to pool their food resources. Food and wealth economies were kept separate.[38]

In the 1880s the canneries hired more Aboriginal men as fishers than they hired women as processors, but by the 1890s this ratio was reversed. Competition from European and Japanese fishermen eroded the demand for Aboriginal men, while a rapidly expanding canning industry and limits on Chinese immigration meant that demand for Aboriginal women workers continued to grow into the twentieth century.[39] This high demand for female cannery labour ensured that Native men with families were hired as fishermen. According to a prominent canner: 'The real reason that you want to have [cannery-owned boats] and get Indian fishermen is they bring their families around and you have Indian women and boys, and some of the men, not fishermen to work in the canneries.'[40]

Family-based production was also the norm for the Lekwammen's labour migration to the hop fields in the Fraser Valley and Puget Sound, which had begun demanding a large labour supply in the late 1870s. The hop-picking season closely followed the canning season, allowing families to participate in both. The Indian agent assigned to the Lekwammen noted that 'Indian women and children are always the most eager to go to the hop fields, where they always earn considerable sums of money.'[41] This new 'industrial' pattern was disrupted by the completion of the Canadian Pacific Railway in 1885, when some 6,000 laid-off Chinese labourers sought work in many of the industries where Aboriginal people dominated the labour force. At the canneries, Aboriginal women found that 'their places had been taken by Chinamen in cleaning and canning the fish.'[42] An Indian agent observed that even 'the poor Indian women and old men, their boys and girls, [who] used to make considerable money every summer picking berries', had been 'ruined' by 'large numbers of Chinamen'.[43] The availability of impoverished Chinese workers reduced, but did not eliminate, the demand for the labour of Aboriginal women and children.

In the meantime, the new economy and disease were having a dramatic effect on household structure. In the early 1880s, the nuclear family extolled by the missionaries became economically possible in a way that it had not been before. Previously, a large household ensured the labour force necessary to harvest resources like camas and salmon, which were plentiful only for short periods. Now, with access to seasonal wage labour a small household could earn enough to purchase a subsistence that was becoming less and less available from the land. Wage labour opportunities meant that even small families, with both parents and the elder children working, could accumulate sufficient wealth goods to hold their own potlatch, something that would have previously required the combined effort of a larger household. The Lekwammen responded to these economic and demographic forces by shrinking their household size. This is apparent in a comparison of Paul Kane's 1847 observation that households contained eight to ten families with Bishop Hills's

1860 comment that Chief Freezie's house contained only three small families. By 1910, the average Lekwammen household contained 2.3 people.[44]

The new economy and the shift to households built around nuclear families disadvantaged the elderly among the Lekwammen. Previously, the aged stood at the apex of Lekwammen society. The *siem* who controlled the most productive resources were often elderly men. The rituals and spiritual wealth of the community, on which the material wealth was thought to depend, were very much in the hands of the older members. As well, the practical experience of the elderly in everyday activities, ranging from gathering food to warfare, was of enormous importance to the household. The colonial encounter may have initially buttressed the importance of the elderly, so long as labour for the newcomers was organized by the *siem*, but the industrial order did not. According to the Indian agent assigned to the Lekwammen:

> The very old people who formerly lived entirely on fish, berries and roots, suffer a great deal through the settling up of the country. . . . With the younger men, the loss of these kinds of foods is more than compensated by the good wages that they earn, which supplement what they produce on their allotments; but this mode of life does away with their old customs of laying in a supply of dried meat, fish and berries for winter use, and thus the old people again suffer.[45]

Among the Lekwammen the disadvantaged elderly were most often widowed women.[46]

Changes in Lekwammen gender relations are also reflected in patterns of household formation. When the Europeans first arrived, marriages among the Lekwammen were arranged by parents with a view to making alliances. It was not uncommon for a *siem* to marry women much younger than himself. Although by 1891 no polygamous relationships show up in the census, males were, on average, four years older than their wives; several husbands were a decade older, and one was 35 years older than his wife. Two decades later, this situation had also reversed itself. In 1910 wives were, on average, a year older than their husbands and it was not uncommon for a wife to be more than five years older than her husband. The older age of wives compared to their husbands may reflect women's increasing ability to choose their own partners, frequently marrying out into the large pool of non-Aboriginal bachelors.[47]

Shrinking household size put additional pressure on the remaining members to contribute to the household economy. The annual reports of the British Columbia Indian Superintendent from 1902 to 1910 particularly focused on women's contribution:

> The Indian women, it may be remarked, are also money earners to no inconsiderable extent. During the canning season and at the hop fields they find profitable employment; they engage extensively in the manufacture of baskets, which they dispose of profitably to the tourists and others; they cure and dress deer and caribou skin, out of which they make gloves and moccasins, and they frequently find a market for dressed skins intact, they being useful for many purposes; mats from the inner bark of the cedar and rags are also made, some of which are of an attractive and superior quality; they make their own and their children's clothing, being much assisted in the latter by sewing and knitting machines; they also gather large quantities of berries, which in some cases they sell among the white people, a major portion is, however, dried for winter use; in doing chores and laundry work for white neighbours they also find considerable employment.[48]

The Superintendent was reflecting on the provincial scene, but Lekwammen women could be found engaged in every activity he mentioned. True, the dressing of hides, gathering and selling of berries, and making of mats and baskets were less and less important as the Lekwammen's access to resources diminished. Instead, Lekwammen women expanded their sewing and knitting.[49] Sometime prior to 1872 Aboriginal women adapted their long-standing knowledge of spinning wool and weaving decorative blankets to the preparing of knitted woollen items, having learned knitting from the immigrants. Knitting what came to be called 'Cowichan sweaters' by the Cowichan people and other Coast Salish, including Lekwammen, later grew into a major source of income for women.[50]

As the Lekwammen gradually added kitchen gardens, a practice noted in the annual reports of the early 1890s, and as chickens became part of the domestic economy, women's and children's roles in household production expanded to include these responsibilities. By 1910 most Lekwammen homes had a chicken shed attached. There were probably others like Mrs Williams (Discovery Island band), who was responsible for 60 chickens and 21 geese; her daughter had her own flocks.[51]

After two decades of declining employment there was a considerable improvement in paid work for the Lekwammen in 1905 when

J.H. Todd and Sons established the Empire Cannery on the nearby Esquimalt Indian reserve. Between 1907 and 1913, the new cannery and the labour shortages that accompanied a boom unprecedented since the gold rush guaranteed work for Lekwammen men and women.[52]

A detailed survey of the Lekwammen taken in November 1910 provides a clear picture of employment during the boom. The survey, done by the Indian agent, was part of an evaluation of band's ability to manage the large sum of money that would result from the sale and relocation of their reserve. Even though it is unlikely that this survey captured all paid work, it offers a more complete picture than the earlier censuses since it indicates the main jobs held by the band members through the year, not just at the time of the survey.[53] Among the 31 men over 16 years old, stevedoring/longshoring was now the biggest single source of work, employing 40 per cent (12) of the men full- or part-time. Other jobs included: general labourer (4), gardening (1), deckhand (1), logger or sawmill worker (2), laundry worker (1), construction worker (1), fish curer (1), and hunting/fishing guide (1). Of the 29 women over age 16, just over half were listed with occupations. Of these, four did domestic work, four cannery labour, four fishing/clamming (two on their own account and two with their husbands), two worked in a steam laundry, and one at fancy sewing work and hide tanning. Of those with no occupation listed, 11 were mentioned as housewives only and three were in school. The survey itself makes no mention of hop-picking, but the agent's correspondence makes it clear that 'nearly all' the Lekwammen migrated to Washington to pick hops for a few weeks each autumn leading up to 1910.

The industrial era had returned women to a place of importance and even dominance in producing wealth for Lekwammen households. While this had the potential to translate into a more significant political role for Lekwammen women, these changes occurred at the same time as the Canadian state intervened to restrict Aboriginal women's legal and political rights. The increasing economic independence of Lekwammen women in the 1880s was undermined by the application of the Indian Act of 1876, which dramatically weakened their legal and political position. According to the Act, women could not vote on matters concerning the band, nor could a woman serve as chief or councillor. In practice, this did not alter the political situation of Lekwammen women, who had not yet held political power, but it removed any flexibility for them to assume more power as productive relationships evolved.[54] More immediate in its impact was the Indian Act's stipulation that if an Aboriginal woman married a non-Indian or an Indian of a different band, she lost all rights to inherit her parents' house or land or to return to live with her birth family, even if her marriage ended in divorce or widowhood. Suddenly, Lekwammen women were much more dependent on their husbands.[55]

The state affected the Lekwammen economy in another way in 1885 when the Indian Act was revised to prohibit the potlatch. The intent of the anti-potlatch law was to hasten the assimilation of Aboriginal people by striking at the institution that tied their society together. Missionary Thomas Crosby had correctly concluded that 'the potlatch relates to all the life of the people, such as giving of names, the raising into social position, their marriages, births, deaths.' In prohibiting the potlatch the government was banning the whole prestige economy, as well as the hereditary ownership of the subsistence economy's key resource sites, which could only be validated through potlatching.[56] Women, who had only begun to have independent means to participate in the potlatch economy, also found this route to social advancement cut off.

The state had another major impact on the Lekwammen economy and gender relations in 1911 when negotiations with the Lekwammen resulted in the sale of their downtown reserve and relocation to the suburbs (see Map 2). The relocation suddenly placed the Lekwammen among the richest Aboriginal people in the province, though this wealth was not evenly distributed. As part of the settlement, the 41 heads of families received $10,000 in cash, plus the value of their 'improvements', including houses, barns, stables, fences, and fruit trees. The Lekwammen insisted that the money be paid to them directly, not, as was required by the Indian Act, held in trust for them by the Department of Indian Affairs. This condition of sale was so extraordinary the federal Parliament had to pass special legislation to permit it.[57] Moreover, the decision to pay heads of families meant that most of the money went to the Lekwammen men. Of the 41 groups considered families, 30 were headed by men, 11 by women. Two-thirds of the groups headed by men were married couples, some with children. Two instances where husbands gave their wives part of the settlement were explicitly mentioned in a report done by the Indian agent two years after the distribution. In one case the wife received 30 per cent of settlement and in the other, 15 per cent.[58] But while wives did not benefit as much as husbands from the settlement, the elderly benefited disproportionately. Since they were considered heads of households, the seven Lekwammen widows each received the full cash payment of $10,000, as did the few widowers. For the first time since the breakdown of extended families, the Lekwammen elderly had some financial security.

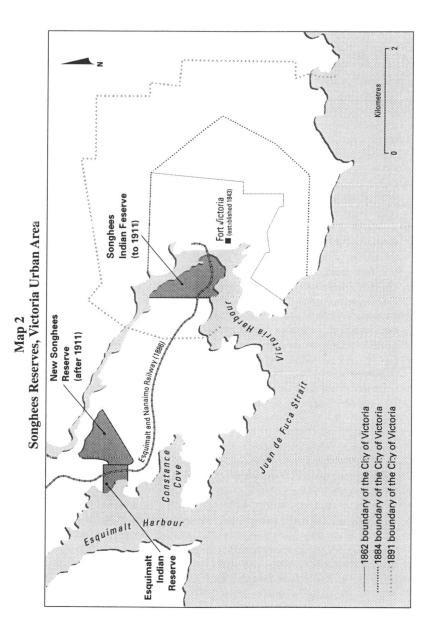

Map 2
Songhees Reserves, Victoria Urban Area

Depression and War

The 1929 onset of the Great Depression, like the previous 1892 and 1914 depressions, seemed to hit the Lekwammen harder than their non-Aboriginal neighbours, and income statistics confirm this. Four years into the Depression, when the average Canadian income from wages and salaries was 61 per cent of its 1929 level, the average for registered Indians was down to 37 per cent of the 1929 level. In explaining this the Department of Indian Affairs pointed to racism as the reason why Indians were in more need than others: 'The Indian was the first to be thrown out of work when the depression started and evidently will be the last to be again absorbed when the conditions improve.'[59]

When employment opportunities for Lekwammen men and women declined in the 1930s, they refocused on what remained of the subsistence economy as well as home manufactures, and then turned to relief payments for additional help. 'Relief' had first been given to the Lekwammen in 1888, when elderly members of the band received food that they were unable to gather from their declining subsistence base. Thereafter the state offered the destitute access to a new 'welfare economy'. By the 1930s, relief payments were paid 'in kind' to a value of $4 per month. This was less than one-quarter of the $16.50 non-Indians were getting in relief from the province and municipalities, as Mrs Dora Ross, a non-Aboriginal woman who became an 'Indian' through marriage, pointed out to the department. The agents, aware of the inadequate relief rates, encouraged Indians to return to subsistence activities or home manufactures as supplements. The importance of this non-wage income was highlighted by Mrs Ross: 'I can't possibly make out on the $4.00 [per month] grocery order. . . . The Indians here might make it do but they can do other jobs, also make sweaters etc. I have no means of adding anything to the allowance.'[60]

During the Depression, women's home production, particularly knitting, which had been a consistent supplement to employment income since the establishment of a cash economy, took on primary importance. Due to the home-based nature of the work, estimates of production are tenuous and hard to come by. One contemporary observer in the 1930s thought that Aboriginal women on southern Vancouver Island produced about 500 sweaters a year. Sweaters were traded to storekeepers for food, until supply outstripped demand. Susan Cooper wrote the agent in March 1933: 'I owe a great deal to the store which I will pay by making sweaters[,] but the store keeper will not let me trade with sweaters for groceries any more after I pay him all because he has to[o] many sweaters on hand right now so that is why I am asking you for some groceries.' Later in the year Elsie Kamia wrote the agent: 'I understand you are buying Indian sweaters[—]I have one made—the stores in town offer small money for them so I wondered if you could help us—many women in this reserve make them.' According to one knitter, a sweater in 1935 could bring in as much as $4.50; with wool costing only three cents a pound, the net payment to the knitter for each sweater would have been close to the $4.00 monthly grocery order available through relief.[61]

Knitting fit well with the other elements of the Aboriginal economy because it could be done in the evenings and seasons when there was little other work; it also allowed parents, particularly women, to work at home and provide their own child care, and it was an enterprise where most of the family could contribute. One knitter from southern Vancouver Island recalled about the early 1930s: 'I was eight years old when I started knitting with my mother. Our dad went fishing once in awhile but it was seasonal. My dad used to card the wool, my mom would spin and knit.' Another knitter, interviewed by Sylvia Olsen, recalled learning to knit from her mother before she was a teen: 'We were like contractors—we knit sleeves for mom—but we never got paid for it.'[62]

Another means of supplementing relief, pursued by both sexes, was clamming for food and for sale, but this required transportation. 'Everybody is digging clams except me', wrote Robbie Davis in 1934. 'I have no boat or canoe.' As a result, 'I wish you would give me relieve [sic] for it is about three weeks from the time I did went out of grocery . . . please hurry.'[63] Hop-picking continued through the 1930s but wages were so low that in 1932 many who went south did not even make enough to pay for their passage home, and so were stranded. Still, the Inspector of Indian Agencies, though he had previously tried to dissuade Indians from this annual migration, wished them well in 1933: 'Unfortunately there is nothing else for them in the way of employment in B.C., with the exception of those who may get work in the canneries.' Berry-picking, locally and in Washington state, took some off the relief roles for the summer, but they were back on again in the fall.[64]

The work situation started to change in 1939; by 1940 the relief list was down to 12 and in 1943 it was down to four 'old widows and invalids', according to Chief Percy Ross. Lekwammen men were all employed by 1942–3, many of them by the local shipyards trying to meet the wartime shipbuilding demand. Aboriginal women moved into new occupations, too, including wood processing and oil refining, as well as expanding their work in canneries, laundries, and garment manufacturing.[65]

Expanded wartime demand and the government's removal of Japanese Canadians from coastal areas combined to increase the need for Lekwammen labour in the fishing and canning industries. In 1944, the Empire Cannery added four herring canning lines to its three salmon lines, more than doubling its labour force. Herring canning also expanded the work season from the two summer months to include the four fall months. The annual payroll at the Empire Cannery jumped tenfold from its 1941–3 levels to $59,250 in 1944. The herring lines employed 40–80 Aboriginal women from September to December, in addition to the 15–20 who worked the summer on the salmon lines. The expanded demand drew Aboriginal women from all over southern Vancouver Island, as well as a few elderly Lekwammen men. The men who continued to fish made good incomes owing to high prices and absence of competition from ethnic Japanese.[66]

A couple of Lekwammen men enlisted in the military early in the war and a few others were drafted later on, making a total of six who did military service. Compared to a $4 monthly relief cheque, the pay of an enlisted man looked pretty good. Mrs Frank and Mrs Dick received $85–$93 per month, which included a portion of their husbands' military pay plus a wife's and child's allowance.[67]

Whereas the Depression had pushed the Lekwammen back to the subsistence economy and to home production, the war drew Aboriginal men, women, children, and the elderly back into the workforce in a way that had not been seen since 1919. The agent's report for 1946 noted that 'women and elderly people, as well as the older children worked in the canneries and berry and hop-fields, both in British Columbia and the State of Washington. . . . Conditions were good and work plentiful for Indians of all ages.' Berry-pickers earned an unprecedented 85¢ an hour and the hop companies paid pickers five cents a pound. 'Crops were good and the returns to the Indians were most satisfactory', reported the agent.[68] Whereas in the 1930s there was virtually no paid labour to be found and families reverted to an economy based on subsistence and women's home production, in the early 1940s men and women, young and old, had as much work as they wanted.

Welfare Colonialism

Several factors came together in the immediate postwar period and reshaped the Lekwammen economy once again. First, the return of demobilized servicemen and ethnic Japanese from detention camps alleviated the wartime labour shortage. Second, and even more important in the long run, was an overall slackening in the demand for low-skill seasonal labour, which since the late 1880s had been the mainstay of the Lekwammen economy. In the meantime, tighter fishing restrictions further limited the subsistence economy. Finally, the state began a dramatic expansion of welfare payments to Indians.

The first evidence of the expanded welfare economy was the Family Allowance program instituted for all Canadians in 1945. Although payments were made for each child, cheques were payable to their mothers. Like knitting, Family Allowance provided year-round income and so was particularly valuable in the seasonal economy. The cash contribution of Lekwammen women to the household probably peaked in the late 1940s when Family Allowances could be added to June-to-December income from the Empire Cannery and sales of sweaters knitted from December to June.[69]

The closure of the Empire Cannery in 1951–2 was a major blow to Lekwammen participation in the postwar economy. Like so many other canneries on the coast, Empire fell victim to financial consolidation and technological change. Improved refrigeration techniques meant fish harvested at the firm's traps in Sooke could be transported to a cannery on the Fraser River and processed more cheaply there than by maintaining a separate cannery in Esquimalt. With its closing, Lekwammen women lost their most regular source of employment. Instead of six months' work next door to their home, what remained was one, or at most, two months' employment in the hop yards of Washington state. But even the demand for hop-pickers was declining. The hop fields that remained were experimenting with mechanical harvesters and Mexican labourers, so that by 1960 even this option was largely closed to the Lekwammen.

While the cannery jobs were shrinking, Aboriginal fishermen were also under increasing pressure. The Lekwammen's Indian agent (now called Superintendent) remarked in 1954 that 'With the return of numerous Japanese fishermen to the Pacific Coast, Indians are again finding it difficult to negotiate contracts with the fish canners who prefer to deal with the Japanese because of their dependability in paying accounts. Poor fishing conditions last year also resulted in the majority of Indian fishermen being financially "broke" during the winter months.'[70]

The same year that Empire closed, the federal and provincial governments extended Old Age Security allowances to Indians. Twenty-eight years after it was extended to other Canadians, Indians over 70 received the full old-age pension. Destitute Indians between 65 and 70 could also qualify for a pension. Four Lekwammen over age 70 were eligible for the $40/month payment.[71] For the first time in 40 years, elderly Lekwammen could live independently, with a minimum level of comfort, or make a financial contribution if living with others.[72]

With the closure of work opportunities and the opening of social welfare programs to Aboriginal people, the importance of the wage economy fell. Families turned to an increasingly robust welfare economy and Lekwammen women returned to their knitting. In his December quarterly report for 1955, the Lekwammen's Indian agent noted that 'requests for relief assistance have been unusually heavy. . . . Fortunately,' he added, 'the Indian women of this agency derive a very considerable income from knitting sweaters.'[73] By 1950 sweater production had increased so that there were three major sweater dealers on southern Vancouver Island. One of these, Norman Lougheed, was buying 1,500 sweaters a year. A decade later, he bought 5,000 sweaters in a single year. One indication of the value of the industry is the 1959 estimate, from one of the three main sweater dealers, that he paid $185,000 that year to Aboriginal knitters in the Cowichan Indian Agency, which included the Lekwammen.[74]

Barbara Lane noted that although Indian men had earlier helped with the knitting, this practice was dying out by the 1940s 'due to the modern prejudice that it is women's work'. The knitting industry, she concluded, 'has had far reaching effects on . . . the status of women. The latter now have an independent year-round source of income, while the men are usually dependent on seasonal labour. The earning power of women has had repercussions in the marriage pattern and in family life generally', giving women more independence.[75] For single mothers, knitting was even more important. Left with eight children when her husband died in the mid-1950s, Priscilla, a Saanich woman living on a reserve just north of the Lekwammen, recalled:

> I was knitting about seven sweaters a week at that time. I stayed up most of the night. I would first pack wood up from the beach for the fire. Then I would knit all night. I always liked knitting. All the kids would go to sleep and I would knit. . . . The kids had to eat and we had to work where ever we could.[76]

Although knitting sustained families in tough times in the 1950s and 1960s, as it had in the 1930s, by 1970 the money available from knitting was also in relative decline. Rising costs of wool and reduced prices from mechanical competition meant that knitters were making less than one dollar an hour in 1972 in exchange for 'both physically hard work in washing the wool and monotony'.[77] That year, Kathleen Mooney found that 'even the knitting of Cowichan sweaters, long an important source of supplementary [income,] has become increasingly unprofitable. Although an Indian-owned and operated sweater store is located on the reserve, and people in ten of the 15 sample households used to knit regularly, only four continued to do so.'[78]

In 1954 the agent conducted a rough employment review and found the majority of Lekwammen men earned their living in unskilled intermittent jobs 'in neighbouring booming grounds and sawmills, and in various jobs in Victoria such as contracting, coalyards, etc.'[79] Aboriginal women's employment was evidently considered of such marginal importance that it was not counted. From the 1950s through to the 1970s, when non-Aboriginal women were increasingly attracted into retail, food and beverage, clerical, nursing, and teaching occupations, Aboriginal women were largely excluded from these jobs by a combination of inadequate academic preparation and racism.[80] Mooney's research shows that in stark contrast to earlier times, in these two decades Aboriginal women were much less likely to be employed than non-Aboriginal women. Mitchell's 1972 study of Aboriginal women in a Victoria-area reserve confirms Mooney's research, finding that for those few who had employment, 'the median income for the year was an absurd $183.' By comparison, Indian men who lived on the reserve earned a median of $1,900 and non-Indian women in the Victoria area earned an average $2,600. Mitchell estimated the median income from all sources, including social assistance, for Indian women was $975 per year, compared to $3,400 for Indian men.[81]

Complete relief records survive for the Cowichan Indian Agency, which included the Lekwammen, for the year 1 April 1960 to 31 March 1961. During the peak summer employment season a quarter of the Indians were receiving relief. Over the winter, when seasonal employment was scarce, just over 50 per cent were receiving relief.[82]

Comparing the late 1960s with the 1891 and 1910 censuses highlights the important transformations that had taken place in Lekwammen economic lives. The population of the Lekwammen band, 134 in 1890, was almost identical to the 131 in the band in 1967,[83] but the percentage of the population in the workforce had dropped dramatically. In 1891 the census showed 35 per cent of the Lekwammen with occupations, while a 1967 survey showed only 15 per cent had occupations.[84] Lekwammen men and, especially, Lekwammen women had become 'increasingly unemployed' in the twentieth century. Women were still able to participate to a small degree in the subsistence economy, but this had minuscule importance to the household economy compared to five and 10 decades earlier. By 1970 women's main contribution to the household economy was through their claims on state welfare payments.[85]

Conclusion

The microhistorical method of asking wide-ranging historical questions in very localized contexts reveals the ebb and flow of economic and power relationships between men and women in a way that historical studies using blunter tools and coarser filters cannot. Focusing on gender and work, this study suggests that the gendered economic power depended on local factors like labour supply and demand, technological change, and pre-existing gender ratios in both indigenous and immigrant populations, as well as more general factors such as racial attitudes and government policies. At some moments in the colonial and post-colonial eras, Lekwammen women, taken as a whole, had a more important economic role in Lekwammen society than they did in the immediate pre-colonial period. At other historical junctures they had less. And how women's economic contribution translated into other kinds of power in the household and community was also shaped by changes occurring in the broader political realm. When the Canadian state intervened in 1876 to exclude Aboriginal women from the official governing process on Indian reserves, it confirmed an earlier, pre-contact male control over this sphere. Given the complexity of changes, it is critical to realize that colonialism did not translate directly into a decline of the power of Aboriginal women vis-à-vis Aboriginal men.

Whereas Anderson and Leacock found that gender roles transformed rapidly and irrevocably after the arrival of Europeans in the Aboriginal societies they studied, the Lekwammen experienced a more drawn-out and fluid process.[86] Long-standing seasonal, gender, and family-based modes of organizing labour adapted and became integrated into colonial and industrial patterns and so persisted among the Lekwammen through to the 1950s. In these circumstances gender roles inherited from the 'ethnographic moment' proved surprisingly resilient. To be sure, other facets of colonialism undermined the power of both Aboriginal women and men, as evidenced by the marginal economic position occupied by many Lekwammen in 1970 and by the decline in employment of both sexes compared to a century prior. Yet even this marginalization was relative to the original locations of individuals or their families in the pre-contact social structure. Nobles in Lekwammen society found themselves treated as anything but, as colonial society transformed into an industrial one. Yet, while colonial society also marginalized those who had been slaves in Aboriginal society, they were marginalized in common with all Aboriginal people and were no longer subject to the power of Aboriginal masters.

Microhistorical analysis reveals the gendered elements of the Canadian colonial project. Among the Lekwammen, men and women were affected by the arrival and persistence of Euro-Canadians in different and sometimes surprising ways—surprising because the complexity of the impact of colonialism over the long term has been missed in studies that have had broader spatial and shorter temporal scope. The history of the Lekwammen demonstrates the importance of long-term gendered analyses, while reminding us that gender only makes sense as an analytical category when linked to race, age, and social position.

6

'To Take an Orphan':

Gender and Family Roles Following the

1917 Halifax Explosion

Suzanne Morton

In the days following the Halifax explosion, an Alberta farm woman
who had immigrated to Canada from Holland wrote to ask, 'what
[will] they do with all the parentless children?' Frustrated with her
limited ability to communicate in English she revealed, 'I can not
explain myself the way I wanted, but I do feel sorry for all the poor
little ones. . . . I was an orphan child myself and know what it is, to be
without a home.'[1] Her letter joined hundreds of similar inquiries
addressed to Halifax bank managers, ministers, municipal officials,
and relief organizations. From across North America, offers to adopt
available orphans flooded into the city along with emergency supplies
and cash donations.

News of the December 1917 Halifax explosion generated feelings
of sadness and sympathy across North America. The accidental collision of two ships in the Halifax harbour and the ensuing destruction
brought initial reports that the number of dead would exceed 2,000
and that five times as many were homeless. Amidst the sensational
descriptions of destruction, suffering, and courage, journalists seized
upon the plight of Halifax children. Sentimental accounts in Canadian
newspapers, such as the *Montreal Star*, drew attention to the large
number of infants born immediately following the explosion and the
pitiful images of unclaimed orphans at various relief centres.[2] Reports
that the Salvation Army rescue home was 'sheltering a number of
motherless babies' aroused compassion among horrified readers.

To North Americans in 1917, overwhelmed by war and now the
tragedy at Halifax, the image of motherless children lent a human

scale to almost incomprehensible circumstances and led some individuals to action. With no local authority, the Canadian Club of New York took matters into its own hands and immediately announced it was looking for homes for over 200 explosion-orphaned children.[3] The local organizing body, the Halifax Relief Committee, received as many as a thousand requests inquiring about the availability of children.[4] Nearly 400 of these unsolicited letters survive, representing a wide variety of age, ethnic, class, and urban and rural backgrounds. These remarkable letters from both men and women described what they expected or desired in a son or a daughter, and explained why the writers felt they would be good mothers or fathers.

At the centre of it all was the family. While we acknowledge the primary role of the family in the creation of gender identity, it is easy to confuse aspects of socialization with biological destiny. The often quoted expression that you choose your friends but not your family may reflect the reality of most people's experience, but it is by no means universal. What about families that are the result of choice?

The examination of adoption permits us to untangle social and biological factors, to separate parenting from biological reproduction and thus to examine the powerful ideologies of gender around the social roles of mother, father, daughter, and son. The women and men who desired to adopt children unconsciously defined the roles of mother and father in a way that went beyond biology. Yet biology continued to play an important role. The letters reveal entrenched, distinct gender expectations for girls and boys. Preconceptions about biologically determined gender traits often complemented other concerns about heredity, such as a supposedly genetic inclination towards sexual promiscuity among certain girls.

The Halifax letters offer a unique opportunity for insight into the gendered perceptions of motherhood and fatherhood. They contain descriptions of both the traits and characteristics of the desired children and the qualifications and qualities the prospective parents believed they brought to the roles of mother and father. Certainly, it is striking that the social prescriptions surrounding these roles were shared by both men and women across a wide spectrum of society. The letters provide a clear indication of the close link between femininity and motherhood and, conversely, the more distant connection that tied fatherhood and masculinity. As a reflection of the letters, this chapter will speak in terms of ideals rather than describe practice, as the letter writers' desire for children influenced how they presented themselves and their homes.

Historical and Theoretical Background

While motherhood has been the subject of historical research, studies of it often focus on the reproductive or biological aspects, such as childbirth. Those who have approached motherhood from a more ideological perspective frequently have not been rooted in a specific historical context or emphasize prescriptive forces, especially the growing intervention of the state.[5] Fatherhood is a much more recent subject of study, with the question of the transformation from patriarchal to companionate relations between fathers and their children being central.[6] Although some American and British studies have posited the late nineteenth and early twentieth centuries as the era in which fathers were expected to make a unique and positive contribution to their children's emotional and personal development, Canadian authors have dated that shift slightly later, to the Depression or post-World War II years.[7]

A few researchers have considered non-biological family formation. The interwar period has been identified by Viviana Zelizer as a time characterized by high-profile sentimental adoptions among celebrities and an increase in legal adoptions among the general public.[8] While at the popular level there was often no great distinction between the meaning of fostering and adoption, adoptions were undergoing a process of legalization, as evident in the pioneering 1921 Ontario Adoption Law, which allowed foster parents to award foster children the same rights as natural-born children.[9]

Certainly orphans were prominent in the children's literature of the period. In her 1904 classic, *Rebecca of Sunnybrook Farm*, Kate Douglas Wiggin has 10-year-old half-orphan Rebecca Rowena Randall live with elderly spinster aunts in rural Maine. Similarly, Eleanor H. Porter's 1912 creation, *Pollyanna*, is based on the story of 11-year-old Pollyanna Whittier, who transforms the life of her spinster Aunt Polly Harrington living in a small town in Vermont. And Canada's most famous orphan, L.M. Montgomery's Anne Shirley, was popularized in 1908 in *Anne of Green Gables*, the story of a Nova Scotia orphan who goes to live with a spinster and her bachelor brother in rural Prince Edward Island. These three novels, all published in the 15 years before the explosion, involved orphan girls between the ages of 10 and 11 who brought fulfilment and love to childless women.[10]

The enrichment of these single women's lives through their involvement with a child reflected existing notions of femininity and the central role motherhood was supposed to play in the lives of all women. Historians Elaine Tyler May and Andrée Lévesque have argued that contemporary definitions of femininity were so closely linked to maternity that women who shirked motherhood were regarded as 'unnatural' or not normal.[11] Part of the reason was that children were closely associated with mothers through both their duties and responsibilities around child-rearing and the identification of women by their reproduction role, but the cultural importance of motherhood went beyond the division of labour.[12] The celebration of maternal ideology, whether expressed by women in the form of maternal feminism or by doctors and public health officials in their promotion of 'scientific motherhood', was inexorably connected to the importance of children in nation-building and family life.[13] Indeed, children were regarded as an essential component to the happy, stable home. Adoption, therefore, was a proactive solution to the implied dangers of the childless home. For example, Henry Morgenthau, an American philanthropist and former American ambassador to Turkey, made exaggerated claims in a 1923 *Literary Digest* article:

> Every adoption prevents a divorce. Divorce comes about because people have not one on whom to spend their superfluous affection. No mere husband or wife is enough for the average American, and so they have to hunt up excitement outside the home. Now this is serious because if America is to hold the moral leadership of the world, we must first get our own home in order. We must hurry to put our own domestic relations on a safe basis and to do that we must create the proper home units, each with a child or children.[14]

Morgenthau had his Canadian counterparts, such as Halifax columnist Mrs Donald Shaw, who also linked childlessness and divorce among young married couples.[15] While not all men and women in the early twentieth century accepted or conformed to the increased emphasis placed on the family as a source of satisfaction and pleasure, the majority of those who petitioned the Halifax officials for children were enthusiastic. Children were regarded as important participants in 'home units' and valued for both their labour and their company, qualities that were regarded as complementary, not mutually exclusive.[16]

Gender, Respectability, Class, Religion

Both boys and girls were needed to build families and the nation, yet they were born into a society that treated males and females very differently. This fundamental division appeared to conflict with the relatively gender-neutral child-saving movement and child-rearing advice that seldom differentiated between the treatment of girls and boys.[17] This is not to argue that the treatment of daughters and sons within a family was egalitarian but that North American attitudes towards girls were more complex than what might be suggested by scholarly generalizations about patriarchy favouring sons more than daughters.[18] Certainly, society privileged boys with opportunities in education, socialization, and employment, but broad characterizations about the patriarchal nature of North American society hide or underestimate the value placed on girls. Daughters were cherished, not only for their contribution to domestic labour but also for what were believed to be their distinct emotional attributes and qualities. The value placed on girls was especially true in the case of adoptions, where there was a consistent preference for girls over boys even among children too young to work.

By 1917, the sentimentalization of children and the intense focus on motherhood had permeated gender, class, ethnic, and regional lines across North America. This is not to claim universal values, but rather that the self-selected group who wrote these letters were indicative of how widespread these attitudes had become. A Montreal woman who was reluctant to write because 'I did not know if I should be doing right, as we are poor people', expressed similar desires to those of the former Toronto woman now married to a New York City lawyer who promised a private school education to any girl she adopted.[19] Three foremen from Canadian Vickers Limited in Montreal were willing to adopt a total of five children and 'pay all expenses', as was a man writing in Spanish from New Mexico and a Belgian woman writing in French from Connecticut.[20]

The applicants for orphans simultaneously believed in the importance of both environmental and hereditary factors on the child's well-being. Orphaned children suffered from what might be termed an environmental problem—the lack of parents—and their placements in new families was an environmental solution. Yet there was no mistaking the significance applicants placed on the child's genetic background. A suitable family environment in itself was not sufficient to ensure the proper development of a child. Without the right material, children might not develop properly, and an important aspect of this development included conforming to gender-appropriate attributes such as daughters learning to become mothers and sons apprenticing for the roles of fathers. It was therefore impossible to consider an understanding of gender that did not include the idea of good physical and moral heredity as a prerequisite for raising good girls and boys.

One of the primary potential liabilities surrounding the adoption of girls was the apprehension surrounding their sexual respectability.[21] This lay behind the specific requests of many applicants that any girl they might adopt should come from a 'decent home'. A Manitoba farm woman wrote of her earlier experience with adoption, when she had taken girls from a local children's home only to later send them back. The girls were returned to the home when she discovered that their mother had been a prostitute and 'when the girl[s] were 13 they show[ed] a tendency to follow the same path.'[22] The Manitoba woman believed that these girls lacked the moral potential to become appropriate daughters.

Therefore, we must understand that both gender and family background worked together in fostering ideal sons and daughters. This was particularly clear in the letters of well-educated applicants. A young woman from Maine who boasted of being a college graduate declared she had 'no preference as to sex but I want a healthy baby & I very much prefer that it be of light complexion. If it were possible to know anything of the baby's parentage I should wish to be convinced that its parents were not mentally deficient habitually immoral or hardened criminals.'[23] Similarly, a New York University professor's wife requested either a boy or a girl, but stipulated that the child must come from a 'from a nice family not foreign'.[24] Concern regarding a child's background was not restricted to American applicants. The importance of a child's family background was most explicit in the words of a rural Manitoban woman, who set her request in the context of her belief that 'like produces like.'[25]

Contemporary concerns about a child's origins meant that the explosion created a particularly good source of children, for they were not illegitimate, orphaned as a result of genetically unhealthy parents, or relinquished because of alcoholism, poverty, or criminality.[26] The orphans of Halifax were merely unfortunate. Popular belief that some men and women were unfit for parenthood because of their health, moral character, intelligence, or ethnic background, as expressed in the eugenics movement and campaigns for compulsory sterilization, was not relevant to the Halifax situation.[27] A Saint John man bearing the heavy responsibility of finding a little girl to educate in memory of his sister, who died in France on active nursing service, wrote that it had occurred to him 'that there would be some excellent homeless children in Halifax now.'[28] Equally explicit was the Medicine Hat, Alberta, man who explained that the explosion circumvented his usual 'fear of illegitimacy being the obstacle in the way of adopting a little one in the ordinary way'.[29] Hence, nearly every request for a child stressed the need for assurance that the orphans came from 'respectable' families.

Class also explicitly played a role. A minister writing on behalf of an influential merchant family, for example, 'would expect the child of the better class of parents', while a sponsor on behalf of the 'highly respectable' valet at the New York City Tuxedo Club noted: 'Because of the station of those good people, it is evident that the child would have to be of the more humble classes.'[30] More egalitarian but less typical was the former Nova Scotian living in Winnipeg who did not care how poor the child's family had been as long as it had been respectable.[31] Imbedded in the letters was also the assumption that wealthy parents were better able to provide a good home for the children. In a discreet inquiry made through the Methodist Church, the wife of one the partners of a prominent Toronto publishing house requested a little girl. The application, which went from her local minister to the General Secretary of the Methodist Church, was forwarded to Halifax with the request that it 'receive more than ordinary consideration' since the couple 'are devouted christian people, well to do, cultured, and would fill the position of father and mother to a child as well as any couple in Canada. . . . as being one of the most desirable homes in Canada wherein a child might be placed.'[32]

Concern about a child's background focused not only on respectability and class, but also on race. Nineteenth- and early twentieth-century immigration and settlement patterns meant that most of the population of Nova Scotia was composed of long-settled Anglo-Celtic families, with relatively few recent immigrants from southern and eastern Europe. Few Canadians or Americans appeared aware of the African-Nova Scotian population living in Halifax, since only two requests specifically referred to the desire for a 'White' child. Applicants simply assumed the orphans would be White and made requests based on ethnicity, noting the desirability of a light complexion or blue eyes.[33] Scottish, English, Canadian, and American children were the most frequently requested while English-Canadian wartime prejudices and politics were evident in a request that 'We would rather not have either German or French Canadian.'[34]

Religious tension that accompanied racism was evident in such requests as 'protestant of course' or prohibitions against Roman Catholic children.[35] In the mind of a least one Maine woman there were even specific Nova Scotian characteristics, as she desired a 'good girl from that section rather than an American as they are more obedient and stable.'[36]

The Preference for Girls

While this specific attribution of character based on residency was unusual, the preference for a girl was not. This bias is interesting, as it conflicted with a general cultural preference for male first-born children and suggests that the 'function' of male birth children and female adoptees differed. Of the 389 individual requests for Halifax orphans surviving in this collection of letters, 215 requested girls, 86 requested boys, 37 requested either boys or girls, 34 requested both, and only 17 did not state a preference. This mirrors a 1947 study of requests to the New York Children's Aid Society over the previous 50 years, which found that of the 20,994 applications, 11,665 had been for girls, 6,383 specifically for boys, 2,599 for either boys or girls, 314 for both, and 33 unstated. These applications were not related to the supply of available orphans, for the agency placed more boys than girls in families.[37] A similar study of adoptions in Minnesota in the 1920s found that 84 boys were adopted for every 100 girls.[38] Even the Halifax numbers may overstate the desire for boys, as nearly all requests for either a boy or a girl placed primary importance on the child being an infant. In fact, there appears to have been a shortage of girls available for adoption in North America—one applicant specifically pointed out that he had been trying to adopt a baby girl for some time 'but they are very hard to get hold of.'[39] Why would over half of the requests inquire after girls and less than one-quarter want a boy when society supposedly valued boys more than girls?

Qualities most desired in children change over time, and in 1917 many of the most desirable childhood characteristics were associated with the 'natural' personality of little girls. Girls supposedly possessed certain feminine traits, such as regularity, obedience, and conformity, that were highly valued by contemporary child experts.[40] In addition, Frederick Given in a 1935 article in *Canadian Magazine* suggested that a preference for adopting girls was connected to a fear of a lonely old age. Given explained that girls enriched family life since they did 'not break home ties so early as boys and outside interests do not play so large a part in their lives.'[41] Other writers assigned girls gender characteristics, such as a superior capacity for affection or a greater ability to adapt, that made them attractive new family members.[42] Finally, neither birth nor adopted daughters were important in carrying on the family surname and therefore the importance of 'blood' in the relationship had a different meaning than in the case of sons who might carry on the name.

The preference for girl adoptees and the value placed on female beauty meant considerable emphasis was placed on the appearance among those requesting little girls. Curly hair was in particular demand.[43] Requests for physical characteristics could become quite specific, such as the request for 'a little girl age between 5 and 6 years fair complexion medium brown hair with a round face blue eyes a pretty child—curly hair.'[44] Other applications simply stated prejudices against 'weak chin or turn up nose'.[45] The internal contradictions within femininity were expected even at an early age according to one woman's request for a six-year-old girl 'of an affectionate disposition and one who does not make friends easily.'[46] Some requests for physical attributes were motivated by the desire to assimilate the child into the new family. A Grimsby, Ontario, woman requested a little girl with brown eyes and hair, 'as I am very fond of dark eyes as my husband has dark eyes and hair.'[47]

Undoubtedly part of the appeal of girls was their capacity for useful labour.[48] Half of the 21 applications for girls over 13 years of age were explicitly looking for domestic help and offered wages. Other applicants felt it was necessary to address the issue of labour, such as a Manitoba farm woman who wrote: 'Dont think I want a girl just for the works sake, of course she would have to help me like my daughter'. And a New Brunswick woman promised that any girl she received 'would never have to work out of the house or anything like that but I would like her to be in the house with me when my husband was away.'[49] The frequent request that a girl would keep the woman company reminds us of the isolation of many women, especially on farms, and the real labour value of this important task. A New Brunswick widow requested a little girl for company so that she could free her two daughters to go away and teach during the winter term.[50] Similarly, a 'very lonely' Ontario woman living four miles outside of Lucknow wanted a girl for company since her daughter was at high school in town.[51] Girls were certainly open to exploitation, but since the majority of requests were for girls under six years old, it is difficult to accept they were valued only for their domestic labour.[52] Rather, girls were valued because of the combination of both their potential for labour and their attributed personal characteristics.

In her study of the British home children who came to Canada, Joy Parr also notes the centrality of labour for both boys and girls. This appears to have been true particularly in marginal or frontier farms, which could not afford the cash expense of hiring additional help.[53] While the war's interruption of a regular supply of 'labouring children' may have added to the Halifax orphans' value, the letters requesting Halifax orphans emphasized that girls' 'work' included social and emotional expectations.

The self-descriptions of families and households wanting girls or boys did not differ. Proximity to good schools and churches and fresh air were desirable qualities for both sons and daughters. One letter that offered insight into the different experiences of childhood for boys and girls was the application for a little boy by a Toronto woman, who offered 'a dog about as near perfect as it can be. Lots of room if a lad wanted other pets & the use of the back of next lot 60 ft by 60 ft for a garden.'[54] The only special attraction mentioned for a girl was the possibility of a musical education.[55]

Applications that stressed the appearance of boys were frequently motivated not by general fashion but more poignantly by the specific memory of a son who had died. Several mothers sent pictures of their deceased sons to guide in the selection of an appropriate child, while one Vancouver mother boasted that her son had resembled the baby pictured on Pears soap.[56] 'We have lost all our boys. Have you a little boy anything like the picture I am sending you . . . ?' wrote an Ottawa woman. She continued, 'This boy in the picture had brown eyes, brown curls and had fair skin and was very smart. I would like a child to take his place as our own.'[57] A Rhode Island woman married to a Canadian-born lacemaker wrote,

> It is with deep regret I must tell you that our own little boy died about five months ago, he was our only child aged two years and eight months, one of the sweetest creatures God ever created, for his sake we would gladly adopt one of these little orphans, we will give him a good home and do our best to make him happy . . . I am enclosing a small picture of myself and my little boy which was taken just twelve days before he died.[58]

Elizabeth Roberts, in her study of working-class English mothers, referred to the 'passionate sorrow' of mothers who had lost a young child.[59] This tremendous sense of loss was striking in many of the letters. A Montreal 'workingman's wife' who wrote somewhat formally that '[h]aving been deprived of my own little girl by death I am very anxious to take an orphan',[60] expressed the same emotion as an Ottawa woman who hoped that another child would 'fill in some measure the vacancy in our home caused by the death of our little son.'[61] The hope of replacing a dead child extended to both girls and boys. In the two years since the death of her 'dear daughter', a Rush, New York, woman had been unsuccessful in finding a female infant for adoption.[62] And a Montreal woman wrote: 'I was delighted to hear from you as it has given me hope. I am longing for a dear little boy to take the place of one I lost.'[63]

World War I meant that many parents whose children had survived childhood disease and accidents now met with death. Of particular sadness was the desire for daughters to replace adult sons killed during the war. A grieving Milltown, New Brunswick, woman who requested a little girl was one such case: 'I have no children having lost my only child in this terrible war and my heart yearns for something to fill the awful void in our home.'[64] A gardener living in Bowmanville, Ontario, whose 'two sons had been killed at the Front', requested a girl around six years old, while an Alberta man wrote that his 22-year-old son had been killed and that he and his wife would like to adopt a girl 'in honour of his memory'.[65] An attractive wartime characteristic of girls was that the contemporary construction of femininity meant that daughters would never have to fight in war. The two men who mentioned the deaths of their sons expressed their losses in a less emotional manner.[66] We have no idea if they felt the 'passionate sorrow' any less than their wives, but fathers did not have the same latitude in expressing emotion. Women were permitted to grieve more openly.

'Mothers' and 'Fathers'

The ability to grieve publicly was not the only place where fathers had a limited role. The aloof mourning father was consistent with the general impression of fatherhood revealed in these letters. While some men stated their own desire for children and at least in name supported the applications of their wives, we see the primary responsibility connected to fatherhood as a man's ability to support a family financially. Historian Cynthia Comacchio has described the role of father in the duties of parenting at this time as reduced 'to an accessory role'.[67] With so much emphasis placed on motherhood and the relationship between mother and child, the role of fathers was diminished. Notwithstanding their importance as breadwinners and heads of households, it was perhaps surprising to see how peripheral fathers appeared. Although the adoption of an orphan would have been an extremely important household decision, less than a third of the 389 applications came directly from a man writing on his own behalf. Women wrote nearly half of the letters, and most of the 21 letters signed on behalf of the couple were probably written by a woman. The remaining letters, written by clergy or local officials, were usually at the explicit request of a woman. Assumptions about power

within the family once again come into question as many women felt
it was within their realm to acquire children by their own initiative.
Even if this was not a reflection of power, it tells us about responsibility and how firmly children were linked with adult female caregivers.
    The men who wrote rarely defined the qualities of a good father
and these traits were more often articulated by women in their own
letters. Women described a good father by his earnings, position in
the community, abstinence, temperament, and church references.[68]
The birthplace of the father was also included and seen as relevant if
he was Canadian or English-born. In the letters written by men, some
mentioned their occupation, length of employment, and military service.[69] One man asserted what he must have considered his special
claim to respectability, being the eldest son of missionaries to China.[70]
Ideals of working-class male respectability also were present in the
declaration of a Cleveland, Ohio, man that he was 'an honest laboring
man and strictly sober at all times'.[71] However much companionate
relations between fathers and children had become popularized in
these years, those were not the terms in which men of all classes
articulated their worthiness as prospective parents.
    The limited role of fathers was apparent also in how rarely they
were mentioned in the letters of application, and when they were, the
word 'father' was nearly always accompanied by 'mother'.[72] In the
four occasions 'father' was used on its own, twice it referred to the
occupation of the woman's own father, and once it described a man
who had previously adopted children. Only once did 'father' appear
in a way that suggested an active role in a child's life. A Terrebonne,
Quebec, veteran wrote to ask for a boy to assist him on his poultry
farm and offered to 'be a father to him'.[73] This is in contrast to the frequency with which the word 'mother' appeared, both on its own and
as an adjective with love or care. As noted earlier, sentimental con-
vention led applicants to direct their pity to the 'motherless' children
of Halifax. The tragedy of loss of a mother was prominent in several
letters, such as the New Brunswick man who expressed concern for
little ones 'without home and mother'.[74]
    The quality of a mother's love was regarded as special by both
men and women. A Toronto woman promised 'the best of mother
love', while a Saskatchewan farmer's wife vowed to 'do my best to
take the place of the mother she has lost & try & make her happy &
help to forget this great tragedy in her life.'[75] Motherhood was a very
active duty that women themselves defined and promoted. Women
who promised they 'would try to be a good mother' had an ideal of
what good mothering meant and a model to which they aspired.[76]

Notwithstanding the deep love and affection of many men, children were very clearly a woman's responsibility. An Ontario man assured officials in Halifax that his wife 'would willingly be a good mother' if they decided 'to give one of these orphan girls to my wife's care'.[77]

The definition of a good mother was largely connected with the provision of basic necessities and emotional responses. Certainly an important part of this ideal was affection. The Manitoba farmer's wife who longed 'to cuddle and comfort some of the dear lonely little children' expressed this aspect.[78] Other petitioners placed greater emphasis on the skills associated with raising children. The popular ideas around scientific motherhood were present in the letters of three applicants who mentioned their training and experiences as both private and hospital nurses as relevant qualifications for motherhood.[79]

In spite of the sentimentalization of motherhood, women in the letters and in the popular press come across as more rational and practical in their selection criteria for children than men. This point was made in a 1935 article in *Canadian Magazine*, which acknowledged that the woman played the primary role in selecting children and as such possessed the determining 'preferences and prejudices'. This article is particularly interesting in its portrayal of men as more vulnerable to emotion than their wives because 'A man who is hungry for children's laughter in his home may surrender on the spot to a baby's gurgle or a Puckish grin but his wife is made of sterner stuff. She it is who is likely to raise the question of antecedents and demand a clear accounting of the child down the line.'[80] While acknowledging the father's role and his enjoyment of children, women who had primary responsibility for child-rearing had to be equipped with sterner responses—after all, a woman was the mother.

Children for Childless Homes

The power of motherhood also extended to women without children. Women who had lost their own children have been already mentioned, but another important group to apply for children were those who were not able to conceive or who had been unable to carry a child to full term. Scholars have just begun to explore the important historical experiences of infertility and miscarriage.[81] However, these women certainly were visible among the applicants, as involuntarily childless women from across North America sought children to adopt and described their marriages without children and their empty comfortable homes.[82] The inability to have children could be a devastating personal tragedy for some women since so much of women's social identity was connected to this role. These women, who approached anonymous authorities in Halifax with the most personal detail of their lives, demonstrated considerable initiative and courage in their quest for children. Their tone, while often sentimental, lacked the emotional desperation of the grieving mothers who had lost their own small children. One childless woman wrote, 'We are very anxious to have a little child in the home for there is nothing that makes a home more pleasant than a little child.'[83] Another woman in the same situation asked, 'Perhaps you know of some healthy blue eyed infant in Halifax who is in as much need of a home as our home is of a baby.'[84] Women were not alone in petitioning on behalf of childless homes. A man looking for a second child to adopt stated that their five-year-old adopted daughter 'is the delight of our home', while another concluded 'that life is a dull proposition without a youngster around the home.'[85]

Yet these men and women were not the only ones with 'childless homes'. The reduction in family size and the corresponding likelihood of no children remaining at home during middle age meant that there were now more households composed of elderly couples, widows, and widowers. The desire to replace adult daughters who had left home attested to the importance of the company and labour offered by young girls and how this loss fell hardest on women. Women of all backgrounds and living in both the city and the country experienced this change. A 45-year-old woman living in Salem, New Jersey, whose daughter had married six years ago, was one such case. A generation earlier it would have been unusual for her to be alone at 39. In her letter she explained that since her daughter had married 'I feal very lonely at times.'[86] The perception that 'a son's a son till he takes a wife but a daughter's a daughter for the rest of your life' probably had more currency in families with only boys, as mothers also felt the loss of daughters as they grew up. This did not stop families with adult sons from thinking that the situation with a girl might be different. A Montreal couple who described themselves as 50, middle class, and having 'no children except a son married', requested a girl, writing that they 'would be glad to have a young companion to brighten our home.'[87] The experience of urban Montrealers was the same as a less articulate Saskatchewan farm woman, who wrote, 'My children are grown up and all away and it would do good for [a] little one here.'[88] The impact of declining birth rates was compounded by economic dislocation. Rural depopulation meant that this was particularly felt in farm families. A southwestern Ontario farm woman believed a girl would alleviate the loneliness she and her husband had experienced since her only surviving son moved to the United States.[89]

Urbanization and migration also meant adult children were no longer available in the community to care for aging parents. Indeed, the letters contain suggestions that caring for older parents was an expectation placed on daughters. In fact, one of the most persistent inquiries for a little girl was made on behalf of an elderly couple, who were 68 and 75, by their youngest daughter. The woman explained that while she tried 'to be with them as much as possible', a girl would be 'most welcome' as all the family had married and moved away, leaving her parents on their own in a small town in the Gatineau region of Quebec.[90] But daughters did not have a monopoly on care for parents in old age according to the letter from a Toronto soldier's wife who wanted to adopt a boy. With a husband in France, the fragility of life might have been present in her request: 'What I want is a lad, whom loving kindness can change into a son if I am spared to reach old age.'[91]

The desire for the experience of motherhood also extended beyond married women and traditional perceptions of family. Explosion orphans appeared to offer an opportunity for single women to adopt children with the cloak of respectability. Applications for children made on behalf of single women were also noted in the previously mentioned 1935 article on adoption, which drew attention to the 'growing number of spinsters who take the means of rounding out their lives provided by the adoption of a child.' Nowhere was the cultural connection between satisfied women and motherhood more obvious than in Frederick Given's conclusion, 'What dreams must lie behind these records alone!'[92]

Both never-married women and widows were among the applicants for Halifax orphans and their letters betray no sense of doubt that they considered themselves to be perfectly qualified to be mothers without the assistance of a man. Certainly, the circumstances of their home life differed little from the married women whose husbands were away at war, save the important financial support a man might provide. Therefore, women without husbands took special care to provide information on their livelihood or financial resources. The applications of these single women lead us to question the extent to which rhetoric about who was an appropriate mother had been internalized and support the contention that the primary responsibility of a father was as a breadwinner and that at least the popular ideal of fatherhood did not extend to child care or assistance in child-rearing.

Like the married couples who requested children, these single women were a diverse lot. An English-born single farmer living out-side Rocky Mountain House, Alberta, wrote directly for a seven- or eight-year-old girl, as did a Buffalo, New York, schoolteacher.[93] Other single women, anxious to prove their worthiness, had a minister or employer write on their behalf attesting to their ability to support a child.[94] An Ottawa widow with two boys in their early teens and requesting a little girl challenges our usual perception of widows in her claim that in the nine years since her husband's death she had operated a small store from her home and had 'earned a living and got our home comfortable since that time.'[95] A middle-aged New Brunswick farm woman who had never married and was alone since the death of her brothers requested a boy of five or six years of age, whom she would 'bring up in the love and fear of God'. For this par-ticular woman, single parenting meant that she did not feel she could take a child younger than five as she did not keep a horse and buggy and the work of the farm meant that the child would occasionally be left alone when she had to tend to a cow.[96]

The social acceptability of single women adopting children was not universal because young single women with children risked gen-erating rumours around their own sexual respectability and chastity.[97] A Toronto middle-class family of four sisters had discussed the adop-tion of a red-haired baby boy before the explosion but had been reluc-tant to proceed 'for fear people might talk'. The tragedy in Halifax led one of the sisters, a nurse, to action: 'I have come to the conclu-sion however that one had to try and be big enough to do what they feel sure is right and not be too sensitive about what might be said.'[98]

Conclusion

Although these letters tell us a great deal about the perceptions of potential parents regarding motherhood and fatherhood and the rais-ing of sons and daughters, they did not result in any children being adopted. Very few children orphaned in the explosion were not claimed by relatives, and there was strong public opposition to send-ing Nova Scotia children out of the province.[99] Although the authors of these letters must have suffered bitter disappointments as the hope of a child or children was dashed, their letters leave us with the clear insight that this incredibly diverse group of applicants understood the roles of mothers, fathers, daughters, and sons in a way that tran-scended any strictly biological meaning of the definition of family.

The letters reveal a widespread consensus on the importance of family relations. There is no denying that biology and heredity had a place in this vision of the family, but at the same time the people who wrote to Halifax also clearly acknowledged that families could be formed in powerful relations outside of blood. The apparent paradoxical understanding of the role of the family in both 'nature' and 'nurture' is not simply an invention of latter-day historians, but rather was recognized and struggled with by a wide group of people at the time. As the letters to Halifax suggest, some parents sought to reproduce, through adoption, a family structure and familial relations they had once had. Others, like the single women who wanted to become parents, tried to create family and a maternal role for themselves that was wholly social, and that in fact contradicted notions about biological motherhood.

The requests submitted to Nova Scotia authorities offer historians a unique portrait of the gendered values and priorities held by a wide range of North Americans living in the shadow of the Great War. Although gender historians have investigated how the family has *intersected with* the state, capitalism, racism, and colonialism, ironically, it has proved challenging to garner historical insights into the gendered nature of the emotional bonds and conflicts *within* families. As the evidence presented here shows, families both reflected and shaped constituted gender roles. In this century, as in others, they have been the site where gender roles/identities began and the socially constructed gender identities of mother, father, daughter, and son were forged. There, biological beliefs about male and female— and often about race, heredity, and class—were translated into specific social identities.[100]

The sentimentalization of children, the suffering at the loss of a child, and the particular value of daughters both for their labour and for their perceived emotional qualities appear to have transcended region, class, or ethnic backgrounds. The powerful link between femininity and motherhood and the more distant connection between masculinity and fatherhood are revealed in a very specific context. The strength of these beliefs enriches our understanding of the process of gender socialization within the family, the location where gender identity was first experienced and reinforced.

7

'A Fit and Proper Person':
The Moral Regulation of Single Mothers
in Ontario, 1920–1940

Margaret Hillyard Little

For 14 years Vera Jackson[1] lived with a husband who had fits of uncontrollable rage in which he lashed out, both verbally and physically, at her and their children. In 1935 Vera made the difficult decision to leave her husband and she wrote to request Ontario Mothers' Allowance (OMA), a monthly welfare payment established in Ontario in 1920 to support single mothers and their children. Her letter clearly detailed her experience:

> My children have seen scenes since babyhood of absolute terror for them, and many times have been in real fear of my being killed by him [her husband] and his insane rages, which arose on the slightest provocation. . . . Years ago he strangled me till I lost consciousness and told me then he would kill me some day and he has kicked me all the way as I crawled across the floor on my hands and knees while carrying his babies . . . I am terrified to remain where he can come near me, the children have begged me repeatedly in the past to do something so that he can't come near us anymore. That was one reason for my change. . . . [2]

The change Vera alludes to was her decision to leave her violent husband and to find a new home for her family. Initially, the Ontario Mothers' Allowance Commission granted Vera an allowance, but it was withdrawn when it was discovered that she was socializing outside the home. Vera wrote to the OMA administration to defend her decision:

I regret that my taste of freedom after the miserable life I had for so long caused me to perhaps go out a little too much. . . . [but] my children have never wanted for food or clothing. . . . That can be proven, and as for the lies told about me in connection with a certain man, they are ridiculous. No man, neither my husband nor any other man has ever meant more to me than my children, nor ever will. Remember, there are two sides to every story. People are always ready to believe the worst about a woman.

Despite Vera's plea the allowance was never reinstated.[3]

Annie McLaren, a mother whose husband was incapacitated and 'covered with large open sores', also applied for the allowance. Her family was approved on the following grounds:

They are very worthy, reticent, Scotch people and I know Mrs. McLaren often goes without a meal in order that the children may have something. If there is any possibility of hurrying this allowance through, we would be most grateful to have it so done.[4]

How do we understand why Vera Jackson was denied OMA while Annie McLaren was strongly supported? Both were self-supporting mothers and both were clearly in economic need. Vera's and Annie's cases raise many questions about the nature of the welfare state and how it administered or refused to administer to needy single mothers in Ontario. As state administrators determined OMA eligibility they helped to construct early twentieth-century definitions of motherhood. Through an examination of the first two decades of the Ontario Mothers' Allowance policy this chapter will demonstrate how OMA helped to shape the relationship between women and the Canadian state, generally, and the lives of needy single mothers, in particular.

Historical Analysis of Gender and the Welfare State

Mothers' allowance was one of the first pillars of the Canadian welfare state. Consequently, this policy was formative in establishing a particular relationship between women and the state.[5] As one of the first welfare policies, mothers' allowance provides an important site to begin an examination of the nature of the Canadian welfare state. Did this policy help to establish a fundamentally gendered welfare state? And to what extent did this policy encourage the moral regulation of citizens? Along with a number of other Western industrialized nations, most Canadian provinces enacted legislation to provide aid to needy widows in the early 1900s. Over time this policy expanded to include a variety of impoverished single mothers.

Despite its important history, this policy has been virtually ignored by Canadian scholars, with the exception of work by Veronica Strong-Boag and James Struthers.[6] Both of these scholars have adequately established that mothers' allowance is part of a profoundly gendered welfare state; however, neither of them fully explain the intrusive features of this policy. Generally, moral concerns regarding the poor are associated with charity work prior to the twentieth century and many scholars assume that this type of moral scrutiny withered with the emergence of the welfare state.[7] But an examination of OMA reveals that not only did moral scrutiny continue in the twentieth century, but the state itself played a significant role in this process. To appreciate fully the early administration of this policy, moral regulation studies are helpful. The concept of moral regulation is used to examine how the state has scrutinized and attempted to shape its citizens' personal and intimate behaviours and subjectivities. It thus provides us with another lens under which to examine the complexities of welfare policy. This model cannot adequately *explain* why people behaved as they did, but it can help to highlight relationships and regulations that are often taken for granted. In doing so, moral regulation presents welfare state scholars with an important tool to understand better the cultural activities of the state and other social agencies.

While OMA did reinforce patriarchal and capitalist interests through the sexual division of labour, it also ensured the moral regulation of mothers and children. OMA administrators were not merely concerned with the perpetuation of the sexual division of labour within both the home and the workforce. They were also preoccupied with the *moral worthiness* of applicants. In fact, ethical questions predominated in the administration of this allowance. In economic terms it appears inefficient to expend a great deal of time and money to ensure that recipients keep a tidy house and do not use profane language or socialize frequently. Yet case files, annual reports, and other documentation clearly demonstrate the minute ways social workers and neighbours intruded into the lives of OMA recipients.

This chapter is based on provincial, municipal, and county archival research and, most particularly, on case files dating from the beginning of the policy in 1920 to 1940 from one city and two counties in southwestern Ontario (the City of London, Elgin County, and Oxford County). These case files include minute details of these mothers' lives—following them from the time they wrote out their applications, through the schooling of their children, the tabulation of their accumulating debts, and the various speculations and rumours from neighbours. To protect the anonymity of these applicants and to meet the terms under which I was permitted access to case records, I have used pseudonyms and, in recounting case histories, have either eliminated or modified biographical detail.

Everyday Administration

During these first two decades the Ontario Mothers' Allowance Act clearly stated that a mother had to be a 'fit and proper person' to receive the monthly allowance cheque.[8] This definition permitted state workers to intrude and examine almost every aspect of a low income single mother's life. In many ways OMA closely resembled the provision of nineteenth-century charity. First enacted to support poor widows, the policy quickly expanded to include deserted mothers and incapacitated fathers. The policy allowed for both intrusive scrutiny of the women's lives and enormous discretion on the part of the OMA administrators. Investigators, as the early social workers were called, were encouraged to conduct extremely thorough inquiries. In some 'particularly difficult' cases it was noted that investigators visited 'daily to advise on everything from bedding, care of children, sleeping arrangements, etc.'[9]

During the first two decades poor single mothers had to prove themselves both financially and morally deserving of the allowance. The case files reveal that seven distinct aspects of daily living were examined: finances, sexual and social activities, cleanliness, attitude, ethnicity, incapacitation, and the education of children. Each of these areas of investigation will be explored below.

The financial affairs of an applicant were the first to be examined. The husband's will would be scrutinized and the investigators would determine the financial circumstances of the mother's parents, the amount of money being earned by the children, and any other potential financial aid the mother might receive. All other avenues of financial support had to be exhausted before a mother was considered eligible for OMA. On the application form, the mother was asked to list her sources of income (profits by business; profits by sale of produce; from rent of property; from savings or insurance; from pension or annuity; from Workmen's Compensation; interest on investments; income from boarders; income from lodgers; and income from other sources) and her expenses (rent; taxes; principal; interest; house insurance; light and water; fuel; cleaning materials; food; recreation; clothing; life insurance; and sundries).[10] For the rural areas, this included a tabulation of the worth of the livestock and farm implements as well. For instance, when Ruby Maw, the wife of an

incapacitated farmer, applied in the mid-1930s the following sources
of income were carefully recorded:

> Livestock: 2 Horses $225.; 4 cows $150.; 4 pigs $24.; 24 Hens
> $12.; 2 Yearlings $30. . . .
> Implements: Hay Loader & side rake $60.; Harness $3.; 2 plows
> $16.; Harrows $2.; Disc $25.; Sleighs $5.; Essex 1929 Auto $100.[11]

Every aspect of a mother's life was examined to ensure that she was
economically destitute. If her male spouse was alive a mother had to
prove that he could not economically provide for her. In keeping with
the family wage ideology, state aid was considered a last resort, only
available in the absence of a male breadwinner.

Once the mother qualified on these financial grounds, an investigation of the home was conducted. Often these investigators would
record that the dwelling had 'no car, no radio, no liquor permit',
assuring the reader that the family did not spend money on luxury
items.[12] In some cases, the applicant's bank book would be carefully
scrutinized for every deposit and withdrawal, every bill sent to the
home would be examined. Investigators would advise mothers on
how they should spend their money. Ann Ruller's allowance was
revoked because 'it was felt that her money should have been spent
on repairs for her own home and not for a married daughter.'[13] Many
mothers, such as Frances Long, who were not considered good financial risks, had their OMA cheques payable to another person who
endorsed every cheque and in that manner had complete control over
everything her family spent.[14] This financial overseer was often a minister's wife or other leader in the community.

Investigators also advised mothers on just what type of work they
could do to earn money and still receive their allowance. Part-time
work in the home, such as piece-work and selling home-baked goods,
was encouraged. Such domestic work helped to perpetuate the sexual
division of labour within the home. In keeping with the family wage
ideology of a male breadwinner and dependent wife, full-time paid
work that might promote women's economic independence was
denied. Part-time work outside the home was also carefully scrutinized to ensure that it affirmed the sexual division of labour both
within the workforce and in the home. In some cases, the investigator
would go with the mother to the prospective employer's office to
ensure that the type and hours of work were suitable for a single
mother. As a result, OMA recipients tended to be involved in low-paid,
female-ghetto jobs that did not greatly improve their financial circumstances. It was clear that their first job was to be in the home and

that financial security would only come with remarriage. By encouraging women to focus on domestic work the OMA helped to ensure the continuance of healthy male workers and healthy future workers. At the same time, it assisted in the creation of a new source of cheap, part-time labour.

Although certain financial criteria had to be met, the OMA administrators spent the majority of their time on moral issues. Widows, whose husbands were confirmed dead, were the first group eligible and the predominant group during these two decades. These women were generally viewed favourably by the regulators—provided they did not socialize frequently, have male callers, or have only one male boarder. In short, these women were supposed to donate all their time and attention to their children and never to show any interest in a man as long as they received the OMA cheque. Just as their husbands had financially supported them in return for sexual monogamy, the state struck a similar bargain.

On the other hand, investigators and public officials were terribly concerned about living husbands. Women deserted by their husbands were the second group made eligible by the Act, but they were carefully regulated. Upon her initial application the mother had to swear that she had not seen or heard from her husband in seven years. Generally, the officials were very rigid about this length of separation, as in the case of Fanny Burlack. She had been deserted for five years by 1921 and was extremely ill in the hospital. She was very worried about how to care for her two little girls; if only she could get the OMA she could get someone else to look after them until she got well. But the OMA Commission refused because at that time a seven-year desertion period was required. Community leaders protested this decision, stating 'that the period of 7 years for deserted wives, be reduced, as this period is too long to neglect the children.'[15] While the period of desertion was reduced to three years in the late 1930s as a result of an amendment to the Act, the time restriction was one of the most common reasons deserted applicants were rejected by the commission.

The woes of deserted mothers were exacerbated during the unemployment crisis of the Depression, when more and more men left their families in a vain attempt to seek employment elsewhere. Husbands road the rails to western Canada, or went south to the United States, or even went back to their countries of origin in search of work. The Act clearly stipulated that the whereabouts of the husband must be unknown, making the status of deserted wives similar to that of widows. Nellie Todd's husband had deserted her and her family of five daughters. But another man had seen Mr Todd travelling by boat to England 'to see his Mother'. Thus, because it was believed that Mr Todd was alive and well in England, Nellie and her children were ineligible for the allowance.[16]

Mothers with incapacitated husbands were also eligible for the allowance in certain circumstances. A mother could receive OMA if her husband was 'totally and permanently incapacitated'. This case-load rapidly increased during the 1930s, perhaps due to the erosion of casual wage labour for all men, including the disabled, but also due to social pressure discouraging women from taking men's jobs in an era of economic dislocation.[17] The allowance did not cover husbands who were incapacitated prior to their marriage or who were considered only partially disabled. Often, men who had severe bouts of arthritis, or who were 'crippled', unable to stand, to walk, to exert any effort, or who were psychologically traumatized from the war were considered only partially disabled and, as such, ineligible for assistance.[18]

Incapacitation cases were carefully screened so only the most helpless were granted the allowance. And since the allowance was never enough to live on, if the husband attempted to work the allowance would be cut off. As stated by the provincial commission in Mrs Jennie Busca's case:

> From a physical standpoint the Board is of the opinion that Mr. Busca is permanently unemployable. The man however insists upon doing some type of remunerative occupation and although the earnings therefrom may be small, if the man persists in doing this type of work, he cannot be considered a total disability within the meaning of the Act.[19]

Regulators of incapacitation were not sensitive to urban and rural distinctions in work. For example, Francis Neely's husband broke his back at a barn raising, was in the hospital for six months, and was diagnosed as having a fractured lumbar vertebra, arthritis, and hernia. He could walk, unsteadily, with a cane for very brief periods. He was considered ineligible because 'outside of his disability from back and hernia he is a healthy specimen.'[20] The provincial commission believed that the husband should be able to do some type of work that would not require standing or physical motion.[21] But it remained unclear what type of work in a rural area a disabled farmer in the late 1930s would be expected to find.

The case files reveal that OMA administrators considered mothers with deserted and incapacitated husbands less deserving than widows. Any husband who was living and breathing was carefully scrutinized to ensure that he could not financially provide for his family. The OMA was only to be considered a last resort—state help was available only when a male breadwinner was no longer able to support the family due to toal incapacitation or permanent desertion. Thus, OMA administration represented a gendered welfare state—one that generally supported and reinforced the family wage ideology of the male breadwinner and economically dependent wife and children. Only in extreme circumstances was a mother permitted state help when she left this familial unit, and then she experienced menial government aid and intrusive regulations.

But the experience of the disabled male head of household also revealed a fascinating gender distinction in the moral regulation of this policy. The incapacitated father received a medical investigation but otherwise he remained free from intervention. His moral behaviour, attitude, and cleanliness were not scrutinized by OMA administrators or community leaders. Once deemed worthy due to medical reasons, he became forever worthy. His wife, on the other hand, continuously had to prove that she was a 'fit and proper person'; one month she could be declared worthy only to be found undeserving the next.

Other men, besides husbands, were also scrutinized by OMA administrators. State workers were always on the lookout for potential boyfriends. They would make surprise visits to the home, especially in the evenings, to catch the visitor. They interrogated the mother, her parents, her friends, neighbours, and public officials—asking them to comment on the number and type of visitors to the home, the number of times the mother socialized outside the home and with whom, and the type of clothing the mother bought and wore. They wrote to the suspected visitor, advising him to keep away from the home. One local investigator was much concerned about Gladys Walker and made several surprise visits to assess better the 'boyfriend'. The investigator wrote:

> I was mystified by a 'boy friend' who was in the house when I called and stayed right through the time I was there and had many suggestions as to *why* the allowance should be granted. I didn't like his manner at all—he was decidedly too much at home. I asked Mrs. Walker if he boarded there—'No, just a *close friend.*' Mrs. Walker seemed most anxious to secure the allowance at once as she needed some new clothes for a special occasion. I thought the *close friend* would likely be there for life when the *occasion* occurred.

The occasion to which the investigator referred might have been marriage. The policy and the administrators held a contradictory position on marriage. Ideally, matrimony was the prescribed goal of the policy and the administrators wrote glowingly of many cases where the mother remarried, thus taking the mother out of the hands of the state. At the same time, these administrators prevented much of the social interaction with men that would have led these women towards the chapel.

Neighbours also readily participated in this scrutiny of potential boyfriends, keeping the administrators informed about all activities surrounding the home. In one case a neighbour wrote:

> I am not in the habit of interfering with my neighbour's affairs, but as the lady stated below is drawing the Mother's Pension, I feel you ought to be informed of a few facts. . . . This woman has a single man at the house nearly every night until 1, 2, or 3 o'clock the following morning, or else goes out with him until all hours of early morning, in fact one night last week she was out all night, arriving home at 5:45 a.m.[22]

As this neighbour explained, a mother's rights to privacy from her friends and neighbours were completely lost once she was granted the mothers' allowance. Then everyone, as a taxpayer and citizen, had a right to intervene in her social life.

As well as male visitors, male boarders were also carefully scrutinized. The policy on taking in boarders was contradictory at best. Because boarding brought money into the home and did not require the mother to leave the children, this type of work was encouraged. But having one male boarder was positively disallowed. And it only took one Mrs Turmin, who ran away with a boarder, to convince the regulators that they had every reason to fear the male boarder. No one would have denied that Mrs Turmin had a difficult life, caring for her two children and an ailing husband almost 20 years her senior who was in a sanatorium. But as her neighbour explained,

> Mrs. Turmin had no possible excuse for taking in a boarder, let alone running away with him, knowing him to be a married man who had deserted his wife and two small children in the Old Country, and I consider it a direct slap in the face to those friends who provided so liberally for her and family, and to the citizens in general, by her misconduct. . . . Personally, I don't think this class of people ought to be a burden on the citizens, but should be deported.[23]

This examination of deserted and incapacitated husbands, male boarders, and boyfriends demonstrates that the administration of OMA generally reinforced the family wage ideology. All potential male breadwinners were carefully scrutinized to assess their earning ability and the nature of their relationship with the female recipient. Simultaneously, OMA caused a crack in the family wage ideal because it did permit some women to leave their familial arrangement. But freedom from this familial unit had its limitations. Accepting aid from the state subjected one to intensive scrutiny and a menial existence.

Whereas mothers with male visitors and male boarders were carefully monitored, those with illegitimate children were adamantly refused. Administrators took great pains to ensure that none were erroneously accepted, as evidenced in the case of Violet Dalton.

> The applicant was keeping company with one, John Nelson. . . . In 1931 they agreed to get married, bought the license from the City Hall in St. Thomas; Nelson then changed his mind and would not marry her; she burned the license after he refused to marry her. They lived as man and wife until 1934 when he left and she does not know where he is. . . . Applicant is not a widow but she is a mother, the [two] girls are of school age.[24]

Nothing could be done for Violet because she had not been legally married to her partner, nor for Regina Mines, a widow with two children, who had an illegitimate child with a prominent doctor who attempted to buy her silence.[25] The Mothers' Allowance Commission refused to grant her an allowance even though the mother pleaded for sympathy.

> Was it not enough that I had suffered through nine long months previous to my baby's birth, as well as constantly undergoing the humiliation for my baby's sake since her coming? What good purpose can possibly be served, by further depriving my children of the very necessary assistance to their realization of their Canadian birth right and citizenship by withholding the Mothers' Allowance . . . ?[26]

According to the records examined, illegitimacy could not be tolerated under any circumstances.

Not surprisingly, prostitution was prohibited. Given the fact that the allowance was always below the poverty line, some destitute mothers, including Lillian Jordan, turned to prostitution to make ends meet:

> This woman has always been spoken of as a doubtful character in regard to her morals. We have known her for many years and as far

back as August 1915, she was prosecuted for carrying on a house of prostitution. She has a number of children and the fathers are said to be men of different nationalities. . . . Would not think it would be right to give this woman any assistance.[27]

It was clear to all regulators that a 'deserving' applicant would not be engaging in sex or, for that matter, any social activity that might be considered to lead to sex.

Social activities and liaisons were not the only area of moral scrutiny. Cleanliness, or lack thereof, was also carefully investigated and commented upon. In *The Age of Light, Soap, and Water*, Mariana Valverde demonstrates that the Canadian social purity movement associated morality with cleanliness. Valverde and other feminist historians have illustrated that house-cleaning metaphors were used by maternal feminists to legitimize their entry into the public, so-called 'political', sphere. Both physical and moral cleanliness were important attributes for OMA recipients during the first two decades of the policy. The majority of cases made mention of the tidy or filthy condition of the home in determining whether to recommend the case. OMA investigators took pains to mention that a deserving mother tried to keep a tidy house and clean children, even though she had difficulty in making ends meet. And likewise, they almost never failed to mention the dirty condition of the house in a case they refused.

Cleanliness or lack thereof was particularly noticed in ethnic minority homes. For instance, one staff person wrote a full page on the question of one applicant's cleanliness:

I visited this home and found it in a most unsanitary condition. . . . I went into the shack, and the odor was such that the place was not healthful. . . . The place was most untidy, and looked as though the woman was a very poor manager, and certainly required some lessons on cleanliness. . . . On the table was some bread and unwashed dishes. The house consists of one living room and one bedroom. There were two beds in the room which were not made up, and the clothing was in need of attention. I consider that there was no excuse for the place being in the condition it was. I called the woman's attention to the odor, and asked her to put the place in as decent a shape as possible. She stated that she was not strong and had a young baby, and did the best she could under the circumstances.[28]

The correlation assumed between lack of cleanliness and laziness was clearly stated. Despite the fact that the woman in this case was ill, an assumption is made that she was too lazy, rather than too ill, to be tidy and clean.

It is abundantly clear that investigators and other officials of welfare organizations made a strong connection between cleanliness and godliness. The final line of a letter from the city clerk to the Relief Department inspector sums up the values of the era best of all: 'Yours for a better and cleaner city.' [29]

Moral regulation during this era also included examination and comment on the mother's attitude. Nineteenth-century charitable workers insisted that worthy recipients demonstrate a thrifty attitude. It was generally believed that the poor were financially incompetent and those who received help needed to prove otherwise. Also, humility was an important criterion to distinguish the deserving from the undeserving poor. This philosophy continued in early OMA administration. Cases where the mother did not present herself in a thankful manner were commented upon, as in Elizabeth Carpenter's situation. Her file stated:

> Mrs. C immediately greet[ed] the worker with a long list of her needs and felt the assistance from the Welfare Dept. was very inadequate and complained at length. . . . John [her son] talked a good deal about the family need and was rather demanding in his attitude. Albert [another son] is still at school but already shows evidence of the begging tendency his mother and older brother have.[30]

As a result, Mrs Carpenter was granted the allowance on a three-month trial basis to establish whether she '[had] proven herself to be a fit and proper person' during that time.

Any resistance on the part of the mother to give freely of all the details of her life was not tolerated by the investigators. If a woman refused to tell her age, the details of her husband's disappearance, the amount of debt she owed, the number of visitors she had to her home—these could be grounds for rejecting the mother as an 'unworthy' character. At the same time, administrators were sympathetic if a mother demonstrated that she had been economically self-sufficient in the past and had proudly refused any external help. In fact, the investigator would write on several application forms, 'This family has no money and has never received assistance from the public.'

If a mother did not have the thrifty, humble attitude required, the best possible option would be to repent before the investigator. Repentance could take the form of the mother attending the local church, refusing to associate with 'questionable' friends, or proclaiming that she was a 'reformed woman'. In Mrs Maud Reinhart's case, the mother 'has been in [to see the investigator] and states that she is reforming; she wants Mothers' Allowance.'[31] In this case, because the mother promised to reform, she was reconsidered. Upon repentance of a previous bad attitude, a mother might be given another chance, but with conditions. All of these mothers would undergo increased surveillance of their activities to ensure that their lives had indeed changed. And those who did repent might be granted an allowance on a one- to three-month trial basis, with the mother continuing to prove that her previous attitude had been transformed.

This moral regulation of OMA applicants was not only gendered but also race-specific. Ethnocentrism or racism was firmly entrenched in Canadian society and exhibited in the policies of this era. Throughout history the state has played a role in excluding or distinguishing between various racial and ethnic minority groups. This hierarchy of ethnic groups changes with time. At the turn of the century, there was a great concern that ethnic minority immigrants were destroying Canada's Anglo-Celtic character. The Canadian immigration policy discouraged the entry of non-British immigrants and restricted those they admitted to dangerous and low-paid jobs. All other immigrants, such as Asians and Blacks, were even less welcome and were generally restricted to short-term employment. The immigration law also allowed for the deportation of recent immigrants who were unemployed and dependent on handouts during their first three years in the country.[32]

The policy and the everyday administration of OMA reflected these racial concerns. During the first two decades only British subjects or naturalized citizens were allowed to receive the benefit. A close tabulation of all 'foreign born (naturalized)' recipients was kept throughout the first few decades of the policy. These latter recipients never consisted of more than 12 per cent of the entire case-load well into the 1940s. If one was unemployed and on relief, naturalization papers were denied. This rule explained Mrs Gladys Hertzman's ineligibility. Her husband had been on relief before he was killed by a truck and consequently had been unable to receive his naturalization papers.[33] All mothers' allowance applicants required the necessary birth, marriage, and death certificates, and obtaining these was often difficult if not impossible for those born outside of the country. For example, Lena Blosky, originally from Russia, had no marriage certificate and no possibility of obtaining one, so she and her children were refused.[34] These regulations, guaranteeing through a bureaucratic mechanism the financing of healthy Anglo-Celtic children at the expense of other racial groups, were not relaxed until 1953.

According to the case files, there appears to have been little understanding of the absolute destitution faced by many of these immigrant families, who had no relations and few charity organizations willing to support them financially. Ethnic minority women could be disqualified because they could not read or write English.[35] This was not the case for illiterate Anglo-Celtic mothers. There was also very little tolerance for the customs many of these families adhered to. Investigators complained of 'wine parties', of certain families not following Anglo-Celtic work ethics and habits, of the mobility of Aboriginal families when they worked in town during the summer and returned to the reserve in winter. The case files also clearly suggest that families from ethnic minority backgrounds underwent more intense investigation than their Anglo-Celtic counterparts. Also, neighbours were more likely to spy on and complain about minority families.

One ethnic group, however, was singled out for praise on the sole basis of an ethnic stereotype. Agnes McAllister's family was considered worthy of the allowance partly because of the characteristics ascribed to her ethnic group: 'A beautiful Scotch family, and highly recommend[ed]. The father . . . a fine upright, honest and straightforward gentleman.'[36] In the case files, no one ever mentioned how beautiful, reticent, or self-sacrificing the ethnic minority families were.

A final area of moral regulation was the public scrutiny of children. The behaviour of these offspring, the very reason for the allowance in the first place, could be cause for rejection of the monthly cheque. By the end of the 1920s, school attendance records were kept and sent in monthly in order for the mother to receive the cheque. These records would often include the student's marks, absences, number of times late, his/her attitude, and comments about the academic prospects for the future. In the 1930s, when grown men were struggling to find work, the OMA Act extended to cover families with two or more children where one child was between 16 and 18 years old and was attending school. In some ways this could be seen as the state extending its benevolent arm to mothers in need. But simultaneously it increased the regulation of children in school. These children had to demonstrate that they 'deserved' to remain in school due to their effort and academic ability. This increased the level of regulation and the amount of correspondence between the administrators of the policy and school officials. For example, Mrs Todd, whose son Earl was 16 years old, was granted OMA provided her son stayed in school. The principal of Sir Adam Beck Collegiate Institute recommended Earl's case, stating that Earl had fine attendance during his four years at the school. Citing as evidence grades that ranged from 50 in French Composition to 81 in Chemistry, the principal concluded that Earl 'has never had a failure and his standings have been uniformly high. I can recommend him on all counts as worthy of having his [allowance] continued, that he may have the chance of finishing his education.'[37] As case files reveal, the lives and behaviour of the children were closely scrutinized and affected the eligibility of their mothers for an allowance.

Conclusion

Such intrusive investigation had a profound impact on the everyday lives of OMA recipients. OMA did meet certain economic requirements. It did provide for the economically needy single mothers. Administrators encouraged these mothers to make their first priority the care of their children. But because the allowance was always below subsistence many single mothers attempted to find some paid work. OMA administrators carefully monitored any paid work in an effort to ensure that such work enhanced their domestic skills. Consequently, OMA recipients became part of the reserve army of labour participating in low-paid, part-time, domestic-skilled work when available, and OMA administration helped to perpetuate the sexual division of labour both within the home and in the labour force.

An examination of OMA administration also demonstrates that this policy generally supported and reinforced the family wage ideal. Women were ineligible for the allowance unless they could prove that the male breadwinner was totally incapacitated or permanently absent. All other men who had an acquaintance with the mother were carefully scrutinized to determine whether they should replace the state as the breadwinner. Clearly, OMA was a last resort, only available if there was no male breadwinner option. At the same time, OMA did permit some women to leave the family wage unit and live independently of men. But a menial allowance and continuous moral scrutiny ensured that this option of state aid was never too appealing.

This policy not only met certain economic and gender interests, but it was also firmly rooted in the moral preoccupations of the era and attempted to ensure they were met. As the case files demonstrate, the majority of the OMA administrators' time was spent on moral criteria. This notion of moral worthiness was closely associated with nineteenth-century notions of welfare and permitted both discretionary decision-making and intrusive and frequent investigation. The supervision of cleanliness, attitudes, and social activities was intensive and ongoing—a recipient was forced continuously to prove her deservedness, which consequently provided a greater role for the state as moral guardian of the poor, intruding into the homes of its citizens.

Through such investigation, the state and a number of societal members were intimately involved in shaping gender relations during this formative period of the welfare state. In distinguishing between deserving and undeserving single mothers, these state workers and community members were actively engaged in nourishing class, gender, and race inequality.

8

The Miner's Wife:
Working-Class Femininity in a
Masculine Context, 1920–1950

Nancy M. Forestell

From its inception in the early twentieth century, the sights and sounds of the Hollinger Consolidated Mining Company permeated the northern Ontario town of Timmins. Rising thousands of feet above the ground, its headframe dominated the local landscape. Signalling the rhythmic tenor of mining operations, its whistle blew with each shift change. Hollinger's visual and sonorous prominence enunciated the importance of this gold-mine, and other mines in the Porcupine gold-mining district, to the longterm prospects of this resource town and its inhabitants. As an additional reminder, with repeated regularity miners filled the streets on their way to or from work. In the process, the enduring and often multiple interconnections between the mining workplace and working-class households in Timmins were continuously underscored. The presence of these male workers illustrated, furthermore, the pervasive masculine environment of the community, which women and children altered but did not entirely eradicate with their arrival after the initial stages of mining development. And it would be within this particular context that working-class women negotiated, and at times contested, the gendered parameters and social meanings of being a miner's wife.

While the class-based struggles of miners in the workplace and the community have been analysed extensively by labour and working-class historians, little scholarly attention has been given to the presence and significance of women in mining towns or to the analytic importance of gender.[1] Like the field of labour and working-class history more generally, the focus has remained largely on male workers and narrowly defined workplace issues.[2] Moreover, although male workers have been the main topic of inquiry, their gender has been treated as natural and thus not subject to critical inquiry.[3] A few studies, principally by women's historians, have explored the lives of working-class women in mining communities, albeit with the quite specific focus on their involvement in mining strikes.[4] Although valuable for highlighting the pivotal community support women rendered in the midst of labour conflict during particular historical 'moments', the social dynamics of daily existence and sustenance have been obscured in these works. A notable Canadian exception remains Meg Luxton's pioneering sociological study of three generations of women in the mining town of Flin Flon, Manitoba.[5] Yet in an effort to underscore the typicality of gender roles uncovered in this community, Luxton has downplayed some of the more unique elements of a mining town and the precise impact they might have had on gender relations.

Against the distinct backdrop of an evolving multi-ethnic resource community, this chapter explores the interconnections between the mining workplace and household in shaping and reshaping the domestic priorities and marital obligations of working-class women in conjunction with those of working-class men.[6] More specifically, this study examines how the gender roles of female housewife and male breadwinner were constructed and reinforced through daily interaction and negotiation. Using a wide variety of textual sources as well as oral testimonies of long-time residents of Timmins,[7] the chapter explores and illuminates how the female gender identity of the miner's wife was continuously constituted—by the mining workplace and in the household. While this gender identity appeared to be both fixed and unitary, it was neither.[8]

The Changing Gendered Landscape

The discovery of gold in the spring of 1909 by several prospecting parties in a remote area of northern Ontario known as the Porcupine district initiated the province's first and largest gold-rush. The low-grade ore bodies being uncovered in this gold-mining camp meant that large-scale capital investment and a significant labour supply were necessary. Three mining companies with substantial capital resources assumed dominant positions: Dome, Hollinger, and McIntyre.[9] Although as many as a dozen mines were in operation in the district at any one time in the following decades, these three continued to be the largest producers.

From the outset, hiring practices introduced by district gold-mining companies would shape the contours of the mining workforce in specific ways. Following long-standing regulations stipulated in the Mining Act of Ontario, only men could or would be hired as miners. These regulations explicitly restricted women from engaging in all forms of mine employment other than the stated exception of clerical work.[10] This strict legal prohibition remained in place well past mid-century, thus ensuring the ongoing male exclusivity of mining. A pattern of hiring was also established early whereby southern and eastern European immigrants constituted the largest proportion of unskilled labourers as seasonal surface workers and, underground, as muckers, trammers, or machines helpers. By contrast, Canadians (both English and French) and British immigrants regularly filled the skilled positions of machine runners, shaftmen, timbermen, and millmen. Skill differentiation in the Porcupine gold-mines was reflected most visibly in the pay scale.

The community of Timmins was first established in 1911 to provide accommodation and services for the workforce of the nearby Hollinger mine. During the first decade of its existence this community was inhabited primarily by transient working-class men, many of whom were single but also a sizeable number of married men without resident families.[11] Most of these men resided in boarding houses or in group arrangements referred to locally as 'bachelor families' in which groups of men collectively pooled their resources and rented or bought houses together. The composition of both of these types of household were often ethnically distinct, with men who spoke the same language and who shared similar cultural values living together. No sharp distinction existed between public and private in this bachelors' community. The traditional gendered division of labour was reconfigured, at least for a time, as many working-class men did some necessary domestic work themselves. Miners here also turned frequently 'to the market', where a commercial sector offered lodging, food, and clean laundry on a cash basis. In addition to domestic labour, heterosexual relations were also largely a matter of monetary exchange in the public realm between female prostitutes and male working-class residents.

In the 1920s Timmins underwent a rapid transformation into a 'family town', in large part at the behest of Hollinger. Significant numbers of married mineworkers accompanied by wives and children began to settle permanently in the community. Hollinger actively encouraged this development by instituting preferential hiring policies for married men, building company housing rented out at low prices, and opening up a company store that offered discounts.[12] The ongoing expansion of gold-mining in Porcupine over the next several decades facilitated tremendous population growth in Timmins as it evolved into a residential community not only for Hollinger workers and their families, but also for those employed at other mines in the district.[13] Along with these changes, the significant gender imbalance evident in Timmins in the 1920s was noticeably reduced by the end of the 1940s, yet it did not disappear entirely. Overall, the ratio of males to females decreased from 163.58/100 in 1921 to 103.5/100 in 1951. Considerable disparity persisted, moreover, among non-British immigrants—European-born males continued to far outnumber European-born females. The gender imbalance within this group dropped from 260.36/100 to only 138.5/100 over the same period.[14]

As ever greater numbers of married miners settled permanently in the community with wives and children, changes occurred in the composition of working-class households as well as in the location and remuneration of domestic labour and sexual relations. Group living arrangements gradually gave way to single-family households. Domestic labour returned to the home, where unpaid housewives primarily did the necessary work. And at the same time, sexual relations largely reverted to the private realm.

The transition in household composition was both complex and uneven. One particular segment of the town's working class, tenants of a large housing tract built by Hollinger after World War I, lived in single-family dwellings with only a husband, wife, and children present from early in the 1920s. This situation did not occur by happenstance; company policy clearly stipulated that the occupants of this housing were to be restricted to the immediate family of mine employees.[15] Additional household members, such as boarders or even extended family, were clearly prohibited. Elsewhere in the community this type of household was more the exception than the rule until World War II. Instead, an array of different domestic arrangements usually involved families sharing living space with other relatives, boarders, or tenants. Furthermore, the ongoing prominence of bachelors, especially among certain immigrant ethnic groups, ensured that group households did not disappear altogether. Not until the 1940s would the nuclear family residing in a self-contained and separate dwelling become predominant among the working class.

The residential district of Timmins that evolved over these decades was divided into distinct, although not entirely exclusive, ethnic enclaves. The Hollinger townsite was inhabited primarily by Anglo-Celtics, in the mining company's view a favoured and specifically selected group of residents. Finns, Italians, Ukrainians, and other eastern Europeans, as well as French Canadians, tended to reside in different residential neighbourhoods of town.[16]

The reconfiguration of the gender division of labour, unlike the composition of household arrangements, appeared to unfold as a straightforward transition with the arrival of women to the community. Wives assumed the responsibilities of domestic labour, child care, and financial management while their husbands took on the role of primary wage-earner labouring at the mines to provide for their families. Yet this apparently 'natural' division between housekeeping and breadwinning was in fact an elaborate social construct. Formulated by the nature of paid work and the necessities of the household, by legal sanction and local custom, these gender roles (and gender identities) were shaped in the changing context of this mining town.[17] While working-class couples often held shared assumptions and expectations about marital obligations, the seeming complementarity of female housewife and male breadwinner could disguise neither the inequity nor the complexity of such relationships.

Work, Home, and Family

The rhythms of men's wage work to a great extent dictated the timing of domestic duties to be performed by wives and complicated their responsibilities for child care. Throughout the three decades of this study, the length of both the workday and workweek actually underwent few alterations. As stipulated by regulations in the Ontario Mining Act, the workday of both surface and underground workers remained at eight hours.[18] The number of shifts per week was maintained in the Porcupine district at the common standard of six. While this pattern did not diverge from other resource-sector jobs during the interwar years, miners in the district did not benefit from a contract-negotiated reduction of the workweek to 40 hours (without income rollbacks), as did those in other base-metal mining industries in the 1940s.[19] The shift schedule, both in number and timing, varied from one mine to another. Hollinger, for example, maintained a schedule of three shifts—day, afternoon, and 'graveyard'—7 a.m., 3 p.m., and 11 p.m. Other mines, such as McIntyre, instituted two shifts, one from 7 a.m. to 3 p.m., and the other from 7 p.m. to 3 a.m. And while some miners repeatedly worked the same shift, most others were obliged to follow a changing weekly rotation. The observation by various residents of the continual movement of men in the streets of Timmins at all hours of the day and night is an especially accurate one.[20] Given the erratic and exhausting work schedule, most elements of working-class women's daily labour revolved around supporting their husbands' paid labour. The timing of food preparation and the types of meal served were principally organized around a husband's shift schedule and, quite often, his personal preferences. By way of illustration, Isabel Mackinnon, the wife of a McIntyre miner, made a large meal at suppertime when John worked days and at lunchtime when he was on late evenings since he wanted his biggest meal of the day after a shift rather than before. Similar to most wives, Isabel prepared the same dinner for everyone in the family to reduce the inconvenience of this staggered schedule.[21] For women with boarders on a different shift schedule from their husbands, this domestic task became especially complicated. With two lodgers and a husband to take care of, Mary Bilenki recalled that she felt trapped at times by a seemingly endless routine of making up lunch-pails for one and dinners for another.[22]

Women also went to considerable lengths to ensure that their husbands received an extended length of sleep after working a late evening or graveyard shift. As much as possible, they restricted household tasks to ones that would not make much noise, and they remained ever vigilant with their children to keep them quiet. One informant mentioned that she even went so far as to make a sign for the front door that she would put up in such instances to warn visitors not to knock loudly.[23] Another, whose husband was an especially light sleeper, regularly took her infant child out in a carriage: 'I just walked the streets with him.'[24] Within the modest confines of most working-class homes, even muted sounds carried easily. Children, especially those who were toddlers, did not always recognize the need for hushed conversation. During the long winter months, which in northern Ontario communities spanned from late October to early April, children were especially likely to be constantly under foot. As a number of women explained, they sometimes found themselves mediating between an irritable husband and children whose boisterous behaviour had caused him to wake prematurely. Several noted that on occasion they were the focus of their husband's anger for a perceived failure to control the children properly.[25] As one miner's wife concluded, 'You never get used to [the] night shift. It cuts into your day, it cuts into what the children could do.'[26]

Domestic labour and child care filled the waking hours of most working-class women. Especially during the early decades of the community both the duration and exertion of physical labour were considerable. Since many working-class households did not have running water or electricity until the later years of the Depression, cleaning and washing clothes were especially onerous. The arrival of modern amenities and the gradual introduction of labour-saving devices such as powered washing machines and electric vacuums (which could typically be afforded only by purchase on an instalment plan) reduced women's work somewhat.[27] Numerous women mentioned that the weekly task of washing clothes became far easier, especially the dirt-filled work clothes of their husbands. Yet they also noted that these particular clothing items, because of their significant weight, caused washing machines to wear out faster than usual.[28]

While some husbands 'helped out' by performing household tasks such as cleaning up after meals, washing dishes, and watching over small children, the vast bulk of the household labour was relegated to the women. Both women and men attributed these minor efforts to the husband's physical exhaustion from mining labour and tiredness from lack of sleep due to shift work.[29] Although these circumstances played a contributing factor, one can also detect that such a rigid observance became an expected aspect of marital obligations to the benefit of most men. Responding to a newspaper survey on whether men performed any domestic labour at home, a McIntyre miner stated: 'What do you think I got married for anyway? . . . Why that's the finest thing about marriage.'[30]

The hazardous nature of mining work further complicated and at times compounded women's domestic labour.[31] Although historians have long recognized and documented the dangerous aspects of mining, few have extended their analysis beyond the narrow confines of the workplace to explore the gendered implications of disability and disease. Accident rates were extremely high during the early decades of gold-mining development and only improved marginally thereafter.[32] Furthermore, with alarming frequency, miners in this area also developed the debilitating lung disease, silicosis, which resulted from the inhalation of fine silica dust. Miners here were particularly susceptible to this occupational disease as the density of silica particles in district mines was the highest in Ontario. Of even greater consequence, silicosis predisposed men to tuberculosis, which in combination led to quite rapid physical decline and early death.[33] And still others contracted tuberculosis because labouring underground weakened lungs generally and therefore significantly reduced miners' ability to ward off such a communicable disease.

In the event of a debilitating accident or illness, most wives assumed the responsibility of taking care of the incapacitated worker. In addition to all of their other domestic duties, many women performed a variety of labour-intensive tasks in tending to their husbands, such as cooking special meals, bathing them, changing dressings, and massaging strained muscles.[34] Individual situations varied tremendously, but even a temporarily disabled husband created substantially more work at home. Although paid nursing care was provided through Ontario Workmen's Compensation several years after its implementation in 1915, and by mining company medical plans once they were introduced in the late 1930s, the bulk of this labour was still left up to wives.[35] Injuries and ill-health meant that women also had to carry out those household chores normally done by their husbands. When Steve Deveschuk sprained his back while mucking ore at the McIntyre, his wife Natalia chopped wood and shovelled snow throughout an entire winter.[36]

While some of these women must have felt overwhelmed by the physical and emotional demands of ministering to an ill spouse and resentful about running a household on their own, there is a notable silence in both the written sources and the interviews on this issue. The silence can be attributed in part to the gendered expectations of being a miner's wife, which dictated that women take on these additional obligations but precluded any emotional space for them to complain about it. Moreover, in a mining community such as Timmins these burdensome tasks were not viewed as extraordinary measures; instead, they represented necessary work that many wives performed at some point in their husband's working life. Somewhat surprisingly, feminist scholars have largely overlooked this type of unpaid female labour as an integral aspect of caring for working adults.[37] For many working-class women in Timmins at least this labour often proved to be critical in getting men back to work.

Wives were confronted by an even more daunting responsibility when husbands were permanently incapacitated by injuries or disease since they then had to look after a disabled spouse on a long-term basis. These situations were especially difficult not only because of the substantial commitment of time and effort required, but also because there was so rarely any hope of improvement. Eva Bijakowski nursed her silicotic husband for years and, as her daughter recalled, 'tried to preserve what health he had left.'[38] Similar scenarios were played out over and over again in homes throughout the community.

Beyond the disruption to domestic arrangements, mine-related accidents and disease threatened the position of the husband as the family provider just as they simultaneously posed certain challenges for the wife. And in the process, the seemingly fixed parameters of male breadwinner and female housewife were thrown open to question as well as negotiation. Among the hardrock miners in the Porcupine who took such pride in the physical strength and agility attached to their work and in their role as primary wage-earners, it is evident that debilitating accidents and disease seriously undermined their masculine identity. A series of articles in a local labour newspaper during the late 1930s on the physical and financial problems encountered by silicotics in Timmins best highlights the connection made between the incapacitated mineworker and the 'broken man'. Given the striking similarity of these stories, one could even go so far as to suggest that they constituted a quite distinctive 'silicotic narrative'. In fact, the idea for such articles was apparently spawned because of the apparent 'sameness' of these tales as told to mining union representatives in Timmins. As one article noted: 'The union office in Timmins is fast becoming a theatre, upon whose stage the souls of broken men come to tell their stories. These stories are most heartbreaking. They lay before you the spectacle of shattered dreams, shattered lives, broken-hearted wives and children.'

One January 1937 article recounted the story of a 'distressed' resident who had worked underground for 15 years but had been incapable of supporting his family for the past couple of years due to silicosis: 'I am a total physical wreck and unable to walk any more than two or three blocks without sitting down. I have a wife and two children I need to provide for.' The piece mentioned that at the end of the interview the man 'broke down and cried'.[39] Subsequent newspaper articles presented equally depressing stories of disease and despair involving once vigorous miners who were now both physically and emotionally spent. The publication of such testimonies was intended for an explicitly political purpose—to encourage union organization so as to protect better the interests of miners and their families—yet they also clearly reveal the anguish and even shame of men who could no longer fulfil their obligations as breadwinners.

While individually many incapacitated men may have felt emasculated, the widespread incidence of injuries and disease did not create a 'gender crisis' in Timmins. Various feminist scholars have posited that a gender crisis can arise when the conceptual model of the male breadwinner/female housewife has been seriously threatened, citing, in particular, periods of high male unemployment.[40] Although unsafe working conditions jeopardized the economic and social position of male wage-earners just as unemployment does, the consequences were somewhat different. Although disabled men no longer retained their position as the family provider, they remained, at least symbolically, the heads of their households. Furthermore, other members of the community recognized that these men had lost their breadwinner status involuntarily as a result of hazardous working conditions, a situation that might befall any worker. And perhaps most importantly, although wives assumed greater household responsibilities, and in some families they even became the main wage-earners, accepted gender roles were not viewed as being fundamentally challenged. Rather, they were thought to be acceptably redrawn under these particular set of circumstances. At the same time, though, such circumstances demonstrated over and over again the instability of these supposedly fixed social arrangements. Indeed, substantial physical, emotional, and financial resources were continuously mobilized to offset a gender crisis.

Whether the husband was currently working or not, one of the most essential yet stressful obligations of running a household involved converting the wages of the male breadwinner into an adequate level of subsistence. Most wives demonstrated a great deal of resourcefulness in their capacity as the 'miner's financier',[41] yet, given the particular economic constraints confronting working-class families in Timmins, many still did not manage to keep their families out of debt. Although financial management was principally the purview of wives, in many households the distribution of the 'family wage' was on occasion the subject of some negotiation between spouses or, at times, a source of intense marital conflict.[42]

The ongoing operation of working-class households in Timmins was premised largely upon the biweekly cheques issued to male workers by district gold-mines. Most family men willingly turned over their earnings directly to their wives.[43] John Mackinnon proudly noted that, 'In all the years I worked I handed every one of my paycheques over to Isabel.'[44] The findings of an informal survey conducted by the *Timmins Press* in March 1947 as to which spouse handled the finances further underscores this point. Among those surveyed, 'Miners were 100 percent for letting wifey take care of the bills.'[45] Some wives had to ensure that they actually received their husband's earnings, however, by intercepting them after shift on payday. Wives typically resorted to this type of action because their husbands had on previous occasions carelessly spent their wages, usually on alcohol and/or gambling.[46]

Such measures were clearly intended to embarrass the men publicly by revealing that they could not be depended on to live up to their duties as family providers. Grace Woodword, who often met her husband after work during the early years of their marriage, never went on pay-days at his request because 'He didn't want anyone to think I didn't trust him to bring his cheque home. He figured he'd like to come home with it rather than have to hand it to me on the street.'[47] In only a few cases did husbands actually retain control over finances, usually to the detriment of their families. Jeanne Carver discovered that emotional appeals and even nagging had minimal effect on an alcoholic husband who put his addictive needs before the financial requirements of his family. She explained: 'He was the money manager. He could spend what he wanted. I had the rest. Those were bad times in the family.'[48] For all households, the gender-specific roles such as financier had to be negotiated individually and often daily.

The pay-packet not only represented the labour performed by the mineworker, but also the fulfilment of his obligations as the breadwinner. Whether at the mine or at home, the physical exchange of the pay-cheque between husband and wife represented the symbolic transfer of responsibilities. As one retired mineworker commented, 'I earned the money, it was up to her to spend it.'[49] In effect, wives assumed the burden of family subsistence. Pat Ayers and Jan Lambertz have convincingly argued that working-class men demonstrated no small degree of self-interest by 'avoiding involvement in household affairs' in this way. As they infer, the clear separation between breadwinning and housekeeping permitted the husband to lay the blame of financial difficulties more easily on a wife's management of the household budget than on his inability to earn an adequate living or on other economic factors beyond his control.[50]

Household budgets in Timmins were seldom disrupted by bouts of unemployment, the imposition of part-time work, or seasonal patterns of employment that so adversely affected working-class families in other industrial centres, yet wives still faced a number of substantial challenges in trying to 'make ends meet'. Given the ongoing ethnic division of labour in district mines that relegated European immigrant men to lower-paying unskilled jobs, some women had less money to cover household expenses than others.[51] And almost all wives had to contend with the consequences of the bonus system widely used in Porcupine district mines. With this system workers received additional money above their base wage, or a bonus, for a measurable quantity of labour above a set minimum, such as drilling a certain length of feet or timbering a particular quantity of lumber. The bonus system was the subject of ongoing criticism not only because of the onerous physical demands placed on workers to produce above the set minimum, but also because despite constant hard work the bonuses so often fluctuated from one pay-day to the next.[52] Hence, wives on some occasions received more than expected, but just as frequently, they had less than they required. Although a husband's bonus usually did not vary substantially, even a modest amount could determine whether household bills were completely paid off or not.

The ongoing high cost of living in this northern resource town also had an especially deleterious effect on family budgets. With the exception of the homes on the Hollinger townsite that rented at a modest rate, accommodation remained expensive throughout the period. Staple grocery and fuel costs published monthly in the *Labour Gazette* repeatedly documented higher prices compared to many other urban centres in the province,[53] a reality compounded by the northern climate. Because of the long cold winter, higher expenditures for fuel and heavy clothing were compulsory.

The all-too-common occurrence of injuries and ill health had a further deleterious effect on individual household budgets. As so many families lived from pay-cheque to pay-cheque, even the brief cessation of income could hasten a financial crisis. Although in theory Workmen's Compensation was intended to provide comprehensive income protection against job-related accidents and disease, in practice it proved to be woefully deficient. This state program provided modest amounts of financial assistance to some families and some individuals, but it offered little or no protection for many others.[54]

Within these types of constraints, wives demonstrated a great deal of skill as financial managers. Many tried to budget as carefully as possible, calculating and then prioritizing the amounts required for the basic operation of the household—rent or mortgage payments, groceries, and utilities.[55] In numerous instances they also attempted to set aside a regular amount for savings to be used towards a down payment on a mortgage or the possible incapacitation of the family wage-earner. Yet in other more discretionary areas a sizeable portion was allocated for the miner out of necessity, but also out of men's sense of entitlement as the breadwinner. With specific regard to clothing expenditures, the upkeep of the 'miner's outfit' was a significant drain on finances. Although the oil pants and coat required for work had to be replaced every couple of years, purchases of overalls and woollen underwear had to be made almost monthly. By at least one estimate (based on a household of five) a gold-miner's clothing accounted for approximately half of the entire family's clothing budget annually.[56]

Typically, a small portion of the pay-packet was given back to the husband for beer and, for those who smoked, also tobacco. Often this was a negotiated settlement, although sometimes it became a source of a great deal of acrimony, and few wives questioned the acceptability of this allotment unless it reached an excessive amount.[57] For both male and female informants this spending money signified the recognition due to the husband for withstanding the physically exhausting and dangerous work involved in mine employment, and linked with that, for his position as family breadwinner. In other words, he deserved these small pleasures. For the unwaged housewife, however, no analogous amount was deemed necessary or appropriate.[58]

As a means of maximizing the wages of husbands, women gave considerable attention to their consumer habits. Shopping for the lowest possible prices for food and clothing or buying cheaper cuts of meat and day-old bread minimized expenditures, while the use of credit from local grocery stores helped women make it through from one pay day to another.[59] This latter option began to disappear, however, as various stores implemented a cash payment system in the late 1930s.

Numerous women augmented the wages of the male breadwinner by performing some form of productive labour: pickling, berry-picking, and gardening appear to have been relatively commonplace. During the early decades of the community, many working-class households also kept some type of livestock. Among the residents interviewed the wives took principal responsibility for their care. Eva Bijakowski shared a milk cow with her sister-in-law. Still others raised cows and pigs for meat.[60] Unlike most other municipalities, Timmins did not impose severe restrictions on the keeping of livestock but instead only prohibited them from roaming the streets.[61]

Some women earned money to contribute to the family income by taking in male boarders. Given the ongoing abundance of bachelors residing in the community, especially during the interwar years, such an option was easily available. At the beginning of World War II, not including a sizeable undercounting because of the informality of most arrangements, official census data reveal that 13.3 per cent of all households in Timmins had lodgers. In the following decade, however, this number would be cut by more than one half (to 5.3 per cent), precipitated at least in part by the declining number of lone men.[62] However, European immigrant families in all likelihood took in more boarders than others. The boarding system 'fit' both the economic and demographic situation of immigrants, in the same manner that James Barrett has observed in the 'jungle' of the south side of Chicago.[63] This particular convergence included the facts that married immigrant workers tended to be on the lower end of the wage scale and that bachelors from immigrant ethnic groups continued to be disproportionately represented.

While women's household duties were essential to the daily maintenance of male workers and to the economic viability of the family, many domestic tasks also served as important expressions of ethnic identity. Among both immigrant and native-born women in this community, the making of meals represented not only sustenance for their family members but also the continuation of ethnic cultural traditions or, in some contexts, the amalgamation and reformulation of various ethnic traditions. Angelina Ciaconee, who had emigrated from the Calabria region of Italy, prepared various pasta and risotto dishes for her husband and children on a regular basis. On the Hollinger townsite, Irene Hamilton followed a long-standing family tradition by serving the standard English dinner of roast beef and potatoes every Sunday. And Maria Gagnon, who cared for an Italian-born widowed father and a French-Canadian husband, often made meals that combined several ethnic cuisines.[64] Shopping was another household task signifying ethnic identification. Women often patronized stores that served them in the language of their origin and where they could purchase foodstuffs specific to their ethnic group and socialize with other women in the neighbourhood.[65] In these contexts women's household labour was doubly valued—within the class-based identity as 'miner's wife' and within the ethnically specific role as transmitter of cultural traditions.

Job-Hoarding Wives?

Few wives had the option of supplementing the earnings of the male breadwinner by going outside the home to work, even when they encountered problems in making ends meet. Both inside and outside the household, structural and ideological impediments to married women's wage labour were ongoing in this single-industry resource town. An extended discussion is warranted here as historians have so often noted this situation as being endemic to mining communities by way of assumption rather than investigation. Such an approach has failed to account for change over time and negates a needed analysis of the social construction of the division of labour in these types of communities.[66] Given the substantial physical demands of running a household on a daily basis, it is not surprising that many working-class women would have been reluctant to assume the additional burden of a full-time job. There were, of course, life-cycle variations, with domestic responsibilities being the most burdensome for women with small children.[67] One informant mentioned, 'When the children were young I had so much work to do at home from one day to the next I never even considered getting a job.'[68] A constantly changing household routine dictated by the breadwinner's shift schedule could also not be easily accommodated with women's wage employment. Among the generation of women who married in the late 1930s and 1940s many expressed the desire to seek paid employment after their children went to school, yet most did not. Some suggested that a job might have compromised their primary responsibility as housewife and mother, while still others cited exactly similar arguments stemming from their husbands.[69] Emma Wagner recalled that when she had been offered a cashier's job at a nearby grocery store her husband objected, stating that no one would be at home to cook him a 'decent meal'.[70]

Interconnected with these 'internal' constraints were even more formidable 'external' barriers. The local labour market in Timmins provided waged work primarily to men, albeit ones who were able-bodied and relatively young, while employment opportunities for all women remained quite restricted.[71] The proportion of women in the labour force increased gradually over the period, from 7.1 per cent in 1931 to 17.7 per cent in 1951, but it continued to be significantly below the rate of urban centres in southern Ontario.[72] Precise data for women wage-earners by marital status are unavailable for Timmins, but substantial evidence suggests that married women in this community accounted for a lower proportion of the female labour force than elsewhere.[73]

In a resource community such as Timmins women were not only employed in relatively small numbers, they were also relegated to a quite narrow range of occupations. Lacking any substantial secondary industries, the number of manufacturing jobs provided by the community continued to be virtually non-existent. Women were concentrated in a limited number of retail, clerical, and personal service occupations. Language qualifications for certain jobs narrowed employment opportunities even further. Many retail stores, for example, required their sales clerks to speak both English and French so that they could better serve English- and French-speaking residents in the community.[74] European immigrant women unable to speak either language fluently usually found themselves confined to positions in businesses catering to their particular ethnic group.[75] Domestic service was a notable exception to this pattern. Since domestic work did not entail 'serving the public', immigrant women could get by with only limited second-language abilities.[76] As the least-sought-after type of wage work because of the relatively low pay, yet offering flexible hours, personal service seems to have employed the largest proportion of married women in the labour force. Furthermore, such positions rarely had restrictions on the basis of marital status, as would prove to be the case with other forms of employment.

As the community developed over the interwar period, the scarcity of female employment opportunities actually became more acute as adult women accounted for an ever greater proportion of the town's population. There is little question that this situation fuelled 'cultural anger' towards married women workers in Timmins. Although in other localities married female wage-earners were subject to accusations of taking positions away from male breadwinners, especially during the Depression when jobs were generally scarce, in this mining town where the division of paid labour was so rigidly segregated along gender lines tensions arose between 'job-hoarding wives' and 'single working girls'.[77] Some allowances were made for wives whose husbands were disabled or without work, but most others were viewed with social disapproval regardless of their family's economic position. The working-class 'moral code' described by Alice Kessler-Harris as the perception that jobs were a public resource to be 'fairly' distributed among the 'deserving' simply did not apply, at least in this town, to female wage-earners who were married.[78]

Despite a booming local economy, community leaders began to notice that a female unemployment crisis was developing by the mid-1930s. They were concerned specifically about the increasing number of single female residents reaching adulthood, most of them from working-class households, who remained financially dependent on their parents because employment could not be secured. In a November 1934 letter to the provincial Minister of Labour, the president of the Timmins Board of Trade noted that 'apart from a few positions with local retailers and offices there is no outlet whatsoever for a girl graduating from high school or vocational school.'[79] Although municipal officials subsequently considered ways to attract secondary manufacturing to the community with the intention of creating more jobs for single women, no concrete plan materialized.[80] Rather than seriously addressing the underlying reason for the problem—a narrow economic base reliant on a single resource industry that only employed men—community leaders found it far simpler to try to alleviate the situation by barring married women from certain types of wage employment. Such measures were not only supported by the community's middle class but among working-class leaders as well. In November 1939 the pro-labour town council passed a resolution regarding municipal office jobs stating that 'No married woman whose husband is employed shall hold a position that can well be filled by a single woman.'[81] A number of businesses instituted formal and informal hiring policies that gave preference to single women.

The war years brought temporary relief to the local female unemployment problem as many single women filled positions vacated by male enlistments in stores and offices in town, while numerous others migrated south to secure war industry jobs.[82] Employment restrictions against married women were even lifted for a time. In the years following the war, however, a sluggish local economy combined with a maturing community meant that there were fewer positions for adult women than ever before. Jobs were in such short supply that single women were actively encouraged to move elsewhere to secure work. The local office of the National Employment Service sent scores of single working-class women to take up factory positions in a number of southern Ontario centres during the late 1940s.[83] Arguing that such measures were not sufficient, community leaders and business owners moved to reimpose restrictions on married women's employment. In January 1946 the Porcupine Rehabilitation Committee took the lead by unanimously advocating the dismissal of married women from all office work in town.[84] Even much heralded war brides discovered that they were not immune to local censure. Commenting on a lengthy January 1947 newspaper article dealing with the experiences of two Dutch war brides, one letter to the editor focused on the fact that 'these recent arrivals are working in [town] while many of our Timmins-born single girls are unemployed.'[85] Public hostility towards wage-earning wives was expressed most explicitly in a letter to the editor that appeared a month later:

> These women are animated clothes horses with an insatiable desire for nylons and fur coats and the trimmings which go with them. I was attended at a store a few days ago by one of these bejewelled Madonnas and her talons were half an inch long. Who would want a meal cooked by such hands?[86]

During this period married women throughout Canada faced employment restrictions, yet the situation in Timmins proved to be especially severe.[87]

Even women with permanently disabled husbands, who in principle were viewed as deserving of employment, had to confront local reticence to hire any married woman. Commercial enterprises like the Workers' Co-operative, a progressive working-class organization that operated a store in town, rarely suspended their preferential hiring policy of single females for married women in straitened circumstances. On one occasion, for example, a woman whose husband had been hurt in a mining accident at the McIntyre wrote to the executive board of the co-op asking that an exception be made in her case. But since her husband's injuries were not considered to be permanent, the request was denied.[88]

The inability of spouses to gain paid employment, along with the meagre earnings of mineworkers, often resulted in serious financial difficulties, with scores of families forced into substantial debt, and in all too many instances they had to default. While the commonplace configuration of female housewife and male wage-earner as sole provider offered the appearance that the family wage ideal had been achieved among the working class of Timmins, the reality proved to be quite different. At local Board of Trade meetings business people complained regularly throughout the period of the pervasive occurrence of the non-payment of bills.[89] In a critique of the inadequacy of wages in district mines, a 27 January 1937 editorial in the local newspaper argued that 'Timmins is a veritable paradise for collection agencies and credit corporations. The working people of Timmins, owe . . . at the present time $4,000,000.'[90] In 1940 twice as many divisional court actions were issued for the default of bills in Timmins and Kirkland Lake than in the far larger urban centre of Toronto.[91] Even taking into consideration that a portion of these cases would have involved families with an incapacitated breadwinner living in reduced circumstances, as well as male transients who left without paying bills, this indicates that insolvency for working-class families with a fully employed wage-earner was not at all unusual.

Conclusion

The distinct physical separation between the gold-mines of the Porcupine district and working-class households in Timmins belied the multiple interconnections that continued to exist between them. On a daily basis the demands and dangers of the mining workplace, along with the needs and privileges of male workers, fundamentally shaped the operation of households and the lives of working-class women. In large measure, the performance of domestic tasks and the allocation of financial resources were based on the exigencies of mine operations along with the well-being and earning capacity of male workers. These connections, however, did not simply flow in one direction. Mining companies *and* individual mineworkers relied on the reproductive and productive labour of women to ensure the ongoing operation of the industry.

Amidst this complex web of dependencies, the social category of the 'miner's wife' served to organize and order social relations between the sexes. Gender roles were premised on complementary responsibilities of female caregiving and male providership. Yet this complementary social arrangement was also clearly a hierarchical one, as the possessive relationship reflected within the phrase 'miner's wife' suggests. Most women exercised considerable authority within their families, but their needs were often viewed as secondary to those of the family breadwinner. Their subordinate position was further reinforced by their financial dependence. Lack of job opportunities for women in general and for married women in particular upheld a rigid boundary of female economic dependence and male providership in Timmins.

While the division between housekeeping and breadwinning was more sharply drawn here than elsewhere, it remained an inherently unstable division. Mine-related injury and ill health frequently disrupted household arrangements and the financial well-being of families. Even able-bodied mineworkers at times experienced difficulties in earning a living wage. The potential for social and economic instability that shaped this northern community constantly threw social roles into question and demanded they be continuously reconfirmed. The ongoing efforts by male community members, ranging from mine owners, local shopkeepers, town politicians, and union leadership to miners themselves, to deny married women paid work exemplifies the persisting need to restrict the freedom and opportunity of working-class women. And at the same time that the 'miner's wife' ideologically contained women in the household, it also reaffirmed the dominant social category for working-class men. Each time the 'miner's wife' was socially defined, so, too, was the 'miner'.

Within these material and ideological limits, working-class women embraced and took ownership of the identity of the 'miner's wife'. Even as the identity signified economic dependence, it did make visible some elements of their household contribution and it provided a celebrated role wherein a woman's emotional commitments to children, spouse, and at times ethnicity and class could flourish. Its persisting meaning testifies to the collective endurance of several generations of working-class women who traversed the many contradictions and complexities that confronted them as miners' wives.

9

Sex Fiends or Swish Kids?:

Gay Men in *Hush Free Press*,

1946–1956

Eric Setliff

Historians have characterized the postwar period in North America as
one of social and political conservatism. Reacting to the disruption
produced by the Depression and World War II and the new insecuri-
ties of life in the nuclear age, Americans and Canadians came to
desire security and prosperity at both the national and personal levels.
The family—consisting of a breadwinner husband and homemaker
wife along with their children—was soon viewed as the source of
social stability and individual well-being. A 'family-centred culture'
developed, which relied heavily on the 'reaffirmation of domesticity'
and on distinct gender roles.[1]

In a society increasingly dominated by an emphasis on heterosexual reproduction and narrow norms of acceptable gender and sexual
behaviour, gay men and lesbians were obvious pariahs. Indeed, historians have revealed that the postwar period was marked by an
unprecedented demonization and persecution of gay men and lesbians. John D'Emilio has shown how, in the United States, the homosexual was constructed as a national security threat at this time. From
the early fifties, gay men and lesbians were denounced by many
politicians as subversives, potential spies, and general threats to the
health of the nation. Homosexuals were soon barred from federal
employment, and millions of American workers were eventually subjected to security checks. At the same time, widespread surveillance
measures were initiated by the FBI and local police harassment of
homosexuals increased dramatically.[2]

It appears that similar events took place in Canada. In the 1950s government workers were investigated for 'character weaknesses' such as homosexuality, and after 1952 homosexuals were barred from visiting or immigrating to this country. The RCMP eventually filed reports on thousands of suspected homosexuals employed both inside and outside the civil service, and even attempted to develop a machine that would identify homosexuals.[3]

Other historians have argued that the male homosexual was labelled as a child molester in the decade following the war. George Chauncey and Estelle Freedman have both identified a sex crime panic that occurred at this time in the US and focused on violent sexual psychopaths and the dangers they posed. The mainstream press made male homosexuals central figures in the panic, associating them with violent sex crimes. As a result, the 'dominant public image of the homosexual' was 'transformed' from that of a relatively harmless individual into that of a dangerous child molester.[4] Little work on the Canadian sex crime panic has been produced, but it appears that a similar hysteria developed during this period and that the mainstream media and law enforcement officials often conflated the categories of the child molester and the male homosexual.[5]

Historians' emphasis on the labelling of gay men as security threats and/or child molesters has obscured other popular and conflicting understandings of the male homosexual during this period. This essay examines one Canadian publication, the popular 'scandal sheet' *Hush Free Press*, or *Hush*, and its depiction of gay men in the postwar decade. Even though this tabloid took full part in a Canadian sex crime panic, the male homosexual and the dangerous sex offender were not linked. Nor were any ties between homosexuality and political subversion drawn. Instead, the dominant image of the homosexual in this newspaper was that of an individual made distinct by his effeminacy. The 'swish', as he was most often termed, figured prominently in the pages of *Hush*. Numerous articles and editorials discussed the gay man's psychological condition and the various manifestations of his 'female tendencies', as well as his romantic and sexual attraction to other homosexuals. And *Hush*'s gossip columns established that gay men together constituted a vibrant and extensive community: the 'swish kids' of major Canadian cities socialized, worked, and lived together and even maintained links with similar groups across North America. As an abnormal but innocuous individual, the gay man was generally tolerated, often ridiculed, and only occasionally condemned. And in some cases, far from being demonized, the gay man was actually defended.[6]

The Tabloids

In the decade after World War II, at least four weekly tabloids were published in Toronto and distributed across Canada. The oldest and most popular of these was *Hush Free Press*, which was founded in 1920 as a 'market tip sheet' for investors and had a circulation of 48,000 by 1951.[6] *Hush* was very much a Toronto-based operation, with the editor and nine staff members working out of a suite on Queen Street and two writers based in other cities.[7] A large proportion of the tabloid's readers were located in the Toronto area as well. In 1951, half of the copies of each issue were sold in that city, while 5,000 were mailed to subscribers. The remaining issues were sold at news-stands across Canada, from Halifax to Vancouver.[8]

The tabloids were widely referred to as scandal sheets and were sometimes collectively described as the 'gutter press'.[9] Both terms were intended to reflect the content of these publications. *Hush*, like its competitors, did cater to those who—as one mainstream journalist put it—'prefer their news suggestive and spicy.'[10] Exposés on the wrongdoings of government agencies and public figures were mainstays of the paper, but even more prevalent were true tales of sex and crime, as provided by the courts of Toronto. Readers were lured with attention-grabbing headlines, the best of which combined a sexual component with criminal activity. Among the typical offerings were 'Blonde Pistol Packin' Mamma Jailed', 'Half Clad Girl Flees in Horror', and 'Rat Infested Hell Hole Houses Harlots and Babies'.[11]

While much of the subject matter and sensationalism of *Hush* set it apart from the 'serious' daily newspapers, it would be inaccurate to view the tabloid as mindless trash. *Hush* provided its readers with a humour column, reports on radio, television, and film, racing information, and a popular lonely hearts section. It campaigned vigorously for certain politicians, some of whom won despite the united opposition of the dailies, and took strong editorial stands on social and political issues. And even the mainstream press recognized that the 'scandal sheets occasionally got legitimate scoops which led to inquiries and housecleaning.'[12] Nor was the paper entirely disreputable. Toronto mayors, MLAs, and MPs took out advertisements to extend their best wishes to *Hush* readers every Christmas, and were even known to write in and thank the paper for its support. For its own part, *Hush* clearly considered itself a sort of alternative press, willing to step on the toes of the élite and explore subjects that were shunned by the hypocritical dailies despite their importance to everyday Canadians.[13]

Subversive, Sex Fiend, or Swish?

Hush did not contribute a great deal to Cold War paranoia and frowned on Senator Joseph McCarthy's activities in the US. As a result, the opportunities for links to be made between homosexuals and political subversion were limited. However, as a paper that specialized in exposés of social problems and cases of sexual misadventure, *Hush* eagerly embraced the subject of sex crimes against women and children, and it is here that one would expect references to homosexuality. True to the timing of the American sex crime panic, the subject made its debut at war's end, with a story entitled 'Society Plagued by Two Legged Rats—Sex Fiends Active Everywhere'. Such articles remained a mainstay of the publication through the mid-1950s, with *Hush* continually demanding that harsher measures be taken against sex fiends and sex beasts, particularly those who molested girls and boys.

Surprisingly, the male homosexual was never implicated or referred to in such articles, even in those cases involving the molestation of boys. In contrast to the conflation of the child molester and male homosexual described by American historians as common in the mainstream media at this time, *Hush* made no such links. Instead, gay men were subjected to a very different representation in the form of the 'swish'.

'A couple of this town's better known she-men', a *Hush* gossip columnist informed readers in 1946, 'slapped each other's wrists in public the other morning, over a good looking American blonde—male.'[14] With this, gay men made their postwar debut in the newspaper. Over the next 10 years, these 'she-men' became increasingly prominent in *Hush*'s pages, primarily in two different features of the paper: the gossip columns, as in the above instance, and the 'news' articles. The latter constituted the bulk of each edition, and were generally reports on cases being tried in the local courts. The gay men encountered in these reports had become entangled in the legal process, having been robbed by men whom they 'picked up' or arrested for gross indecency. The first of these articles was published in 1947, after which they appeared with increasing frequency.

The gossip columns dealt with gay men in more mundane circumstances. These columns consisted entirely of one- or two-sentence-long 'items' that referred to various goings-on in the local community—such as births, marriages, divorces, appearances of entertainers, minor scandals—all presented in a breezy manner. Columns for various cities were featured, written by individuals obviously well acquainted with the working-class community or, at least, certain segments of it. At different times they included 'Toronto Breeze Around', 'Montreal Street Scene', 'Winnipeg Whispers', 'Vancouver Patter', and 'Bytown Babble', titles that reflect not only the geographical scope of the columns but also their flavour and content. As was true of the articles, the frequency with which gay men appeared in the gossip columns increased over the period. In 1946, only a few 'items' appeared, but by 1955 there were over 50 such references.

On the pages of *Hush*, the dominant representation of the gay man was, to use the popular parlance of the day, the 'swish', a man whose effeminate behaviour and dress located him outside the bounds of normative masculinity. One of the most lengthy descriptions of gay men appeared in a 1951 article discussing the 'pansies' who were presently 'bloom[ing]' in a local tavern. On any Friday or Saturday night at this location, these well-dressed 'pretty boys'

> sit around like animated mannequins, flutter their eyelashes, roll their eyes and slap each other playfully as they engage in a bit of gigglish repartee. In general, they behave very much like the [private school] Branksome Hall girls at a pink tea and they make no attempt to disguise their effeminate leanings.

When one 'normal guy' punched one of the 'queers' for talking to his girlfriend, 'the high-pitched screams and shrieks that arose . . . reminded one of the time the mouse ran rampant at the ladies' sewing circle.' In all probability, the author continued, 'the pansy had not insulted the girl, but was merely enquiring as to her brand of perfume or whether she preferred the paste to the liquid deodorant. Then again he could have been objecting to the competition she afforded, for a woman has no place among "its."' [15] As revealed here, gay men were depicted as semi-women, beings who, through their gender inversion, inhabited a sort of limbo between the two sexes, neither male nor female but 'its'. And as the use of the latter term also indicates, their indeterminate gender status made them somewhat subhuman as well. In the same article, for instance, they were variously described as 'specimen[s]', 'creatures', and 'things'.

The liminality of the gay man was explicitly outlined in lengthy exposés of Liberace. This '"fairy" pianist', the paper declared, was a 'travesty of everything that constitutes true manhood!' His audiences found it difficult to determine whether or not he was 'male or female, or half and half—an average human or a homosexual. He accentuates effeminacy. He walks, talks, and looks more like a female than a male. He wears outlandish feminine-type male garments. . . . His long, wavy hair would make any woman envious.'[16] A second article outlined additional ways in which this 'giggling, simpering, school-girlish musical nonentity' failed as a 'man's man': ' "Libby" would be more at home at an afternoon tea than watching a prize fight; holding knitting needles rather than a fishing pole. . . . Men don't go around wearing white silk suits or ruffled lace shirts; they patronize barbers rather than hairdressers.' Men were also 'quite notorious for their interest in women', whereas 'outside of his mother, Liberace's inter-est in women is practically non-existent, although he has many purely platonic friendships.' As this indicates, a sexual desire for women helped to define normative masculinity; the lack of it contributed to the 'semi-female' status of Liberace and gay men in general.[17]

In *Hush*, the gay man's transgression of masculine norms was commonly signified by the adoption of elements of female dress, such as jewellery and cosmetics. In 1953 a writer described a 'weird booze party', where guests had included 'males, females and some half-and-halves': 'Ordinarily on such occasions the ladies wear lip-stick and the gentlemen get it on their cheeks and collars. This time the roles were reversed; the males or semi-males wore the paint, and they planted their carmine lips on each other's cheeks.' These 'pan-sies' had found out 'that the hot-house was not conducive to full bloom after all' when the morality squad put them all under arrest for violating the liquor laws.[18]

However, the gay man's ultimate desire, according to *Hush*, was to outfit himself entirely in feminine apparel and pose as a woman. Two articles in 1948 dealt with men arrested after dressing in drag and working as prostitutes. One such man, 'obviously . . . a queer', had walked the streets as a 'blonde of unspeakable beauty (when seen from a distance) wearing a black dress . . . a white picture hat, white shoes and white gloves'; even when deprived of his skirt and wig by the prison matron, he reportedly possessed 'a pair of legs so white and wonderfully shaped that they would rival those of Marlene Dietrich or Jane Russell any day.'[19] Apparently, the predisposition for gay men to impersonate women sometimes extended to their very physique.

The supposed desire of *all* gay men to pose as women was demon-strated in a feature on popular singer Johnny Ray, who received in the pages of *Hush* a treatment similar to that bestowed on Liberace. This singer, known for his 'effeminate mannerisms', was reported to have once been employed as a female impersonator. One particularly 'his-toric' performance was described in detail: 'donning a gown of bil-lowing black, high-heeled shoes, and make-up . . . [Ray] minced on the floor to present a show which would have made the most seasoned "lavender" lad turn green with envy.' The audience 'was heavily loaded with the type which enjoys this sort of thing'—an audience eventually left 'limp as rags in their chairs'. In *Hush*, gay men, like Johnny Ray, wished to don dresses and give their female tendencies free rein.[20]

This representation, carried to its logical conclusion, had gay men actually wanting to be physically transformed into women. In 1952, Danish doctors had revealed that such a thing was indeed possible by transforming George Jorgensen into Christine Jorgensen, an event that, not surprisingly, made its way into the pages of *Hush* several times. The following year, the paper contended that George had not been transformed into a woman at all, but was merely a castrated man. *Hush* denounced the 'grossly misleading' way in which the case had been presented, noting that it might do 'irreparable harm' to those finding themselves in George Jorgensen's 'unfortunate position', as, apparently, did 'thousands of homosexuals'. These men 'had been led wrongly, and perhaps tragically, to believe that Danish physicians are the answer to their dilemma.' Unaware of the limitations of the procedure, they were currently 'beating a path to the doors of the U.S. medical profession, seeking surgical relief from their female tendencies.'[21]

The Christine Jorgensen case provided the context for several of the attempts to explain the phenomenon of homosexuality in a pseudo-scientific fashion. 'Veritas', the pseudonymous author of the paper's worldwide news column, explained: 'Homosexuality arises by reason of emotional disturbances, usually in childhood, which cause young people to take on the social attitudes of members of the opposite sex. This is not inherited and has little to do with physical condition [i.e., it was not the same as hermaphroditism].' According to this writer, 'many such sufferers' had implored surgeons to perform operations that would 'make them look more like members of the opposite sex.'[22] The homosexuality of Johnny Ray and Liberace was also the subject of 'scholarly' analyses. *Hush* enlisted the aid of an 'eminent American psychiatrist' to explain the 'mystery of Ray's queerness'. Ray, declared the doctor, represented a person 'in whom the "war of the sexes"', that is, the battle between female and male 'tendencies', was 'waged within a single body and mind'.[23] And psychiatrists blamed Liberace's 'sexual abnormal[ity]' on Momism, his 'over-identification' with his mother and general inability 'to get away from her apron strings'.[24]

According to *Hush*'s psychiatric advisers, then, gay men suffered from a psychological condition; specifically, they were female in their mentality. Since a sex change was reportedly not a viable option, the homosexual had to look towards the psychiatrist for a cure.[25] Unfortunately, many sufferers of this condition were reported to 'refuse to take psychiatric treatment' despite the fact that it could 'restore them to a normal social life'.[26] Without such treatment, the gay man could expect no change in his mental state. He might attempt to act 'normal'. ('A well known nance is trying hard to become masculine. Even has a female girlfriend', confided one *Hush* columnist.)[27] He could even get married. ('Allen Maloney, one of this town's swish kids, has the neighborhood agog with his recent wedding to a blonde songstress', reported another.)[28] But his homosexuality would remain unchanged and such attempts at masculinity/heterosexuality were generally seen as futile. Woolworth heiress Barbara Hutton, for instance, by marrying a man who had been convicted of having a male 'lover' in Germany 17 years before, could expect nothing more than 'a platonic friendship' in the years ahead.[29]

The Gay Community

In the pages of *Hush*, male homosexuals did not suffer from their abnormality in solitude; nor did they, in most cases, hide their true nature from the world by marrying and suffering in silence. Instead, gay men were clearly shown to constitute a community. Here the gossip columns played an important part. Charged with capturing the variety of everyday urban life in Canada, columnists made local gay men and their activities a feature of their reports. Through such treatment it was established that gay men socialized together, worked together, lived together, and even vacationed together. They shared the same tastes, talents, and attitudes. In addition, they were organized on the local level and maintained links with other communities.

The terminology used to describe gay men often made reference to their status as a cohesive social grouping. 'The homo set', 'the swish set', 'the lavender set', 'the gay set', 'the wrist-slapping set', and 'the gay boys' were but a few of the popular combinations used to denote local gay communities.[30] Gay men were noted for socializing together and forming, as it was commonly put, 'queer colonies'. The Montreal columnist reported that 'The Turkish baths are the busy little joy palaces for the she-males', and, comparing them to a tavern popular with gays, described the baths as 'the poor fairies' Samovar'.[31] In Toronto, a restaurant was described as enjoying a similar popularity. Bowles' Lunch had become

a sort of meeting place for those of the male gender who like nothing better than to . . . compare notes concerning man's love for his
fellow men. So well known is this spot as a 'club-room' that police
have found it necessary to intervene at times and break up a few
meetings which have got, shall we say, out of hand.[32]

Hush's writers seemed to pride themselves on getting the scoop on
the latest gay hang-out. In Toronto in 1951, it was reported that 'the
lavender set are now making Letros Nile Room their home-away-
from-home.'[33] Two years later, Toronto's 'gay set' had 'returned to
their old haunt the Chez Paris in as large numbers as the swallows
coming back to Capistrano.'[34] And in Montreal in 1955, the 'latest
homo-haven' was the 'New Orleans Cafe'.[35]

The time gay men spent together was not limited to that passed in
nightclubs and bathhouses. In other cases, they also lived together. 'A
Jeanne Mance [street] rooming house is one of those places where the
swishy boys are welcome', ran one item in 1950.[36] And even on vacation they congregated, visiting the same spots, knowledge of which
quickly spread throughout the community. A 'small Miami hotel', for
instance, was identified as 'the favorite inn of Montreal's homosexual
set'. The establishment had 'first made local contacts' two years
before, and its Montreal 'biz' had since 'boomed'.[37]

Gay men were also shown to have common places of employment,
often flocking to certain fields because they possessed a common
vocation for the work required. *Hush* had a particular obsession with
the number of gay men working in the display department of Simpson's department store in Toronto. A 1951 article claimed that gay men
were 'as common as cockroaches in a cafeteria' there, outnumbering
straight men nine to one.[38] Such a concentration was not surprising, the
columnist facetiously explained, because 'the darlings are so artistic,
don't you know.'[39] The CBC received the same treatment. In Toronto, it
was felt to be 'a pity' that the CBC cameras couldn't give viewers

> intimate shots of the 'arty boys' who work behind the scenes at the
> Jarvis Street studios. Berets, ascot scarves, and goatees are the
> order of the day, even for electricians' assistants and, for that mat-
> ter, the cleaning staff. Obviously there is a school of thought at the
> CBC that limp-wrists are a sign of genius.[40]

And in Montreal, one had no hope of becoming involved in television
production unless one was 'that way'.[41]

As the references to the artistic nature of gay men indicate, homosexuals were felt to share the same interests and tastes. The Toronto

columnist reported that, while Johnny Ray's popularity was faltering among the 'normal', this 'fad-style vocalist (please Mr. Printer, don't make that fag-style)' was still drawing 'considerable support from the lavender set' who considered him 'a doll'.[42] And other musical acts were described as having, 'for some reason or other . . . a great appeal for the lavender set'.[43]

Often these 'wrist-slappers' appeared to constitute a private club or society. Its members developed ways of distinguishing themselves from men who might victimize them, as in one Winnipeg report: 'The homo set have taken to painting one fingernail as a means of identifying each other. Too many have been hooked and then robbed by psuedo-queers [sic].'[44] They looked after each other and sought to provide jobs for other members of the community. 'Those Washington State Department "wrist slappers" who got fired, can always find jobs here through a certain nitery manager',[45] wrote a columnist on the advent of the McCarthy era. They even possessed their own magazine, which, like nail polish in Winnipeg, was used in Montreal as a means of identification: 'Copies of the homosexual publication "One" are starting to show up around town. The queeries are leaving them in various taverns, etc., and using them to attract strangers who may also be "one".'[46]

As many of these items indicate, the network of gay men was far-reaching. Through 'contacts' and word of mouth, pertinent knowledge was widely disseminated both within the confines of the local community and beyond. In Montreal in 1955, 'queers' were said to be 'holding regular huddles to plan where to hang out if there is a police crackdown.'[47] Later that year, the 'news that homosexuals are thronging' the same city due to a decline in police interference was said to have reached New York. The latter city, in turn, had dutifully sent up a 'delegation of queers from Greenwich Village', presently 'mincing around the theatre district'.[48]

Love, Sex, and the 'Swish'

As the 'swish', the gay man was defined in large part by his effeminacy, and this quality most visibly linked him with others to form a community. However, gays in *Hush* were also connected by their romantic and sexual interest in members of their own sex. Although the gay man's sex life rarely received as much attention as his make-up and 'wrist-slapping', under some circumstances it became the focus of *Hush*'s reports. It was discussed often enough to make it an important theme, and to make it clear that the 'swish', that is, the effeminate man, was interchangeable with the man sexually active with members of his own sex.

One of the prime concerns of the gossip columns was local romance, and this applied to both heterosexuals and homosexuals. Gay men competed for the attentions of men, as in the case of 'two of the better known Peel Street swish boys' who had 'fallen out over an entertainer'.[49] In Winnipeg in 1955, 'local homos' were reported to be 'vieing [*sic*] for the affections of an Ellice Avenue newcomer from Calgary'. His popularity was no surprise, according to the columnist, for the Calgarian was 'quite cute, especially after taking his quarterly Toni Silverkurl'.[50] Swish romances sometimes turned sour, as it did for a man identified only by the initials O.L., when the object of his affection, a 'Main Street swish', developed 'a yen for a new boyfriend'. The paper suggested that the scorned party 'change his perfume' for better luck in the future.[51]

Above all, what such items made clear was that gay men were romantically involved with and attracted to their 'own kind'—other gay men. This was explicitly stated in an article that referred to a man who advertised as a drama coach in the classified sections of the daily papers. *Hush* suspected that it was through this medium that this 'member of Toronto's "gay-boy set"' was 'issu[ing] his mating call to others of his ilk'.[52] And another gay man, recognizable by his 'peculiar mannerisms', spent thousands of dollars on parties at which he 'surrounded himself with men . . . of his own kind'.[53] Of course, the desire for other gay men did not preclude an interest in 'normal' men as well. A 'local chorus boy', for instance, who 'never hides the fact that he's a swisher', was described as 'trying to convince a couple of the regulars that he can be sooo much fun'.[54] But it was more typical for gay men to stick to each other as far as their love lives were concerned.

The gay interest in men was often portrayed as more romantic— and 'feminine'—than sexual, as befitted men who could make no claim on the virility traditionally associated with masculinity. To express his interest in someone, the gay man was liable to 'flutter' his eyelids and 'pucker' his lips 'into a coy smile'.[55] They enticed men with 'coy' suggestions,[56] and their 'warm little hand[s] . . . pressed . . . calling card[s]' into the palms of potential dates.[57] However, gay men were also presented in a sexualized context. At a gay party, for example, the lipstick-covered guests 'leered at one another' for much of the evening. With their 'bodies swaying . . . [and] lips pursed lewdly to the sounds of sensual music', the get-together was 'reminiscent of Sodom and Gomorrah'.[58] Thus, the 'swish' could be associated with sex and not lose his feminine qualities.

The coverage of trials of men charged with gross indecency meant that *Hush* writers also had to deal with gay men in a context that was primarily and explicitly sexual. While the tone of most of these articles was generally more subdued, *Hush*'s writers grouped these men together with the effeminate swishes as well. One man charged with gross indecency apparently made this a relatively easy task for the reporter:

> the defendant proved to be the best-dressed 'it' in court when he appeared wearing a station-wagon coat with a fur collar. Knotted around his lily-white throat was a silk-chiffon scarf decorated with gayly colored flowers and giving him all the resemblance of a pansy proudly growing in a bed of petunias.[59]

Another man involved in a trial with clear homosexual overtones arrived in court with 'his black hair shining like patent leather and his svelte figure encased in an immaculate blue suit'. His membership in the 'lavender set' was confirmed for readers when 'he tiptoed to the witness box with mincing step.'[60] In another case of a man with 'homosexual leanings', the accused was pictured 'twisting his hands rather effeminately and staring straight ahead as if bewildered by all the fuss'.[61] And a man arrested for making advances towards a plain-clothesman in a theatre, while 'rather good-looking', was said to possess 'the voice and actions of a female'.[62]

In some cases, the connections between effeminacy and men arrested for homosexual offences were much less explicit. Descriptions of the accused as 'a bespectacled wisp of a fellow'[63] or as 'a slightly built man . . . with a rather high-pitched voice'[64] probably represented attempts to hint at a lack of masculinity. At other times, the link with 'the swish' was achieved solely through the usage of slang terms commonly associated with this representation. An article on two men arrested for gross indecency refers to them as 'men', 'petunias', and 'members of the lavender set', although nothing is said of their actual behaviour or appearance.[65] In most such cases the headline, at least, ensured that these men were associated with the dominant image of the gay man. 'Union Station Washroom "Swish Boys" Love Nest' was emblazoned on the top of a page in 1949, and '"Pansies" Bloom in Bowles' Lunch' appeared two years later.[66]

The extent of the common association of gay men, effeminate behaviour, and homosexual sex was most vividly demonstrated in a comment from a 1955 article. A fork-truck operator had laid charges against his employer, a supervisor at a paint company, for performing 'an indecent act in his presence' and 'invit[ing] him to participate'.

The supervisor had denied the charges, and the *Hush* reporter found the case extremely perplexing: both men seemed 'reliable' and, more importantly, 'the accused's mannerisms gave no outward sign of possible guilt.'[67] The man who partook in homosexual sexual activity was expected to betray himself through his effeminate behaviour.

Attitudes towards Gay Men in *Hush*

The writers of *Hush* expressed a complex variety of attitudes towards gay men. In general, gay men were tolerated, if only because of the potential for humorous ridicule their continued presence represented. From time to time they were bullied and harassed, while on other occasions they were defended. In all cases, the tone of any particular article depended very much on the circumstances surrounding the gay men in question.

As some of the material quoted above demonstrates, gay men were afforded a basic toleration in *Hush*. The paper never called for the mass arrest of gay men, as it did for vagrants and other 'undesirables', and seemed to accept them as a permanent fixture on the social landscape. Homosexuality was not approved of, but could be endured. This attitude was well encapsulated in the stock phrase the paper used in reference to gays: 'To each his own.' In 1951, for instance, this was the reply offered by the editor to a reader who wrote complaining about the portrayal of gay men in a recent article. 'Here in the Maritimes we believe in the live and let live', proclaimed the reader, and, judging by the paper's response, it appeared that *Hush* recognized the wisdom of such an approach.[68] In 1953, the phrase received a reworking when a reader wrote the editor to defend homosexuals as 'natural' and condemn bisexuals as 'perverted heterosexuals'. 'To each his own and ours is neither, thank God', ran the editor's response, reflecting the journal's toleration, along with its unwavering belief that homosexuality was an abnormal and unenviable condition.[69]

That homosexuality was seen in these terms—as a condition—had much to do with the toleration afforded those who 'suffered' from it, and also explained the occasions when this toleration was combined with pity. As sufferers of insanity or alcoholism could not be faulted for their disease or the nature of its expression, the homosexual could not be blamed for his 'strange sexual make-up' or his actions.[70] Instead, as 'pitiable creatures' suffering from 'an unfortunate condition' and deserving of 'sympathy',[71] homosexuals were 'merely victims of a disease which they regret as much as anyone.'[72]

Expressions of pity had limited entertainment value, so, not surprisingly, gay men were more often ridiculed. Indeed, it often appeared impossible for the writers to resist mocking them, and the opportunity to make derisive quips probably served as the initial inspiration for many articles and items. The only circumstances under which gay men were 'appreciated' (in a perverse sense of the term) was when they served as entertainment for heterosexuals. 'If you want to get a few laffs', wrote a columnist, 'hit the Chez Paree [club] some nite when it is really rolling. The Bloor Street spot is a favorite hangout for the "sa-wish" kids. When Jimmy Roulston plays the piano, the whole audience swoons. Honest dearie, they do.'[73] In Montreal, gay men at wrestling matches were presented as a good source of amusement, their supposed fawning over wrestler Gorgeous George 'even a better show than the gorgeous one' himself.[74] And in the same city a 'middle-aged romeo' known as 'Georgette', who resembled 'something out of a comic opera', was noted for his appearances at a local restaurant, where he ogled the waiters and 'swishes around to everyone's amusement'.[75]

Tim O'Rourke, the man responsible for the Toronto gossip column, often turned to ridiculing gay men. A favourite topic was their preponderance at Simpson's: 'didja know that every time we mention the "swish" colony employed in the display department, ten per cent of the department get so annoyed they could punch our head in, and the other ninety per cent get so furious that they could slap our wrist. Whoops dearie.'[76] At times the ridicule in such columns and in articles was remarkable for its sheer pettiness, unrelieved by any attempt at cleverness. One gay man appearing in court for a minor infraction was described as showing 'signs of having used peroxide to enliven his natural brunette'. He 'would have been surprised', the reporter wrote cattily, 'to know how much dark hair was showing at the roots.'[77]

Even in the most mean-spirited cases of ridicule, toleration of homosexuals was still implicit; there is a distance between mocking a group and calling for its wholesale persecution. But this toleration was always extremely conditional, and gay men had to tread a fine line not to lose it. A shift in attitude generally occurred when gays were felt to be too prominent by virtue of their audacious behaviour, their large numbers, or, in the case of individuals, their fame. In such circumstances, gay men were bullied and attacked.

Hush offered tacit approval, for example, when two 'female impersonators' were thrown out of a café for their brazen behaviour in 1949. The men were 'applying rouge and powder and acting in so effeminate a manner that they disgusted the young toughs around

them', who 'ordered the perverts out'. One of the gay men was then
beaten up. *Hush* identified the actual assault on the man as a 'mistake', but whether this was so because it netted one 'tough' a 30-day
jail sentence or because the gay man did not deserve an actual beating
is not clear. At any rate, that the gay men had been behaving in such a
provocative manner was seen as justifying the 'leniency' of the sentences imposed.[78]

When gay men became too prominent through sheer numbers or
concentration they were also attacked. In 1950, the Ottawa gossip
columnist predicted threateningly:

> One of these fine days . . . someone is going to smash the hell out
> of that club of 'Nancys' who take up all the room in the Chateau
> Laurier's cocktail lounge. If there is anything we cannot stand
> under any circumstances, it's the mincing, prancing walk of these
> creatures and their high-pitched, lisping voices. But, then, we are a
> nasty fellow, aren't we?[79]

Here the familiar ridicule was joined by a violent edge, brought on by
the fact that gay men were taking up 'all the room' in this lounge.[80] In
Montreal, the limits of toleration were reached in 1955. Early in the
year, the morality squad had apparently rid the 'hotel-theatre district'
of prostitutes, and since that time 'homosexuals' had been appearing
in the area in increasing numbers. These developments were closely
followed by the columnist for some months, until he eventually spread
the alarm that 'homosexuals' had 'taken over': 'This has been itemed
here before, but now the situation is serious. The young queers, some
in full make-up, have just about taken over the Peel and St. Kay intersection and given it a nauseous look. Wonder what tourists think of
this French town these days?'[81] Gays had once more reached the point
where their numbers were threatening; the sense that they had 'taken
over' was enhanced by the fact that they were declaring their homosexuality, through the wearing of make-up, so boldly.[82]

The process by which gay men went from being tolerable, and
entertaining, to constituting a 'serious' problem was outlined in 1951.
An article on the gay presence in Toronto's Letros Tavern stated that
while 'we have no objections to such creatures being served', gay
men should not be 'allowed to overcrowd a room, [and] abuse regulations by standing in groups while drinking and blocking the aisles.'
The author speculated that, as '"queer" colonies always attract a certain number of amused spectators', the bar was exploiting its gay
patrons as an alternative to hiring professional entertainment. *Hush*
wished to inform the management, however, that

the entertainers are far outnumbering their normal patrons which is not a very good policy. There are quite enough of these dimpled darlings running around and getting into people's hair without encouraging them. It is up to the police and the Liquor authorities to investigate, but if they fail to act then fumigation appears to be the only solution.[83]

It was clearly felt that Toronto had reached its saturation point as far as gay men were concerned.

The tabloid's 'policy' on gays was further clarified several months later, in the editor's reply to a letter. 'An American' had informed the editor that, according to Dr Kinsey, homosexuality was the result of 'natural impulses' and therefore could not be 'termed a crime', as he felt it had been in the article noted above. The editor replied that the paper had never 'determine[d] homosexuality as a crime'. Rather, the point of the article had been that 'encouragement of them [gays] to congregate in a public place because [the] monetary desire [of the management leads them to allow gay men] to carry on in their fashion, and yet invite the other public to also frequent the same establishment where the latter may be subject to embarrassment and insults, is far from proper.'[84] Here *Hush* appeared to feel that gay men did have a right to congregate and 'carry on', but not in the presence of innocent, unsuspecting heterosexuals who might be upset.

Gay men also incurred the wrath of *Hush*'s writers when, as individuals, they became too prominent on an international level, usually as entertainers. Johnny Ray and Liberace, for instance, were subjected to caustic attacks. Ray was presented as a 'weeping, wailing, wild-eyed freak', an alcoholic, possibly a former inmate of a mental hospital, and, worst of all and at the root of all these problems, a 'queer'.[85] To the 'intelligent minority', and especially to 'he-men', Liberace was 'obnoxious and nauseating'. 'Most men', *Hush* declared, 'would like nothing better than to take him out and knock some of the nonsense out of him.'[86] Liberace found himself in the same position as those 'female impersonators' in the cafe above— deserving of a beating that would 'put him in his place'.

In both cases, the popularity of these stars with women was particularly resented. 'One would think', ran an article on Liberace,

> that such effeminacy and fol-de-rol . . . would disgust all intelligent womanhood. . . . But young girls dote on this dolled-up darling, thinking him cute and clever and handsome; they dream of him. And older women, particularly those who have lived frustrated lives or are at loose ends, almost go crazy in his presence.

Ray's appeal to young women was also galling. That he had achieved such vast popularity with only a '10 cent brain and a 50 cent voice' was seen as indicative not only of the 'millions of morons' in the population, but of the overall decline of civilization: 'It is a weird commentary on this age and generation that a freak like this, half male, half female, in his mental make-up, can cause hordes of bobby-soxers to follow him frantically, just as the rats followed the Pied Piper of Hamlin [sic].' The author, apparently disgusted with the entire free world, concluded: 'Johnny Ray epitomizes democracy in this Twentieth Century.'[87]

In all of these cases, the limited toleration of gays and the ease with which even this could be lost are reminiscent of the toleration extended to any type of oppressed group. At the base of *Hush*'s attitude was the belief that gays were inferior beings who could be denied the rights enjoyed by full citizens. As people who occupied a lower position in the social hierarchy, they were required to behave in a deferential and humble manner. When they did not conduct themselves appropriately, they were viewed as infringing on the privileges of 'normal' citizens and constituting an affront to society. If disciplinary action was not taken under such circumstances, the principles by which society was governed would crumble, along with civilization.

There was also a genre of story in *Hush* in which gay men were defended and supported. Again, certain circumstances were required for gays to merit this treatment—specifically, it was necessary that they be victimized by criminals. The most common scenario involved straight men who specialized in robbing homosexuals. By 1953, this was identified as 'a big-scale criminal racket'.[88] The criminals in question searched for 'those of suggested lavendar [sic] leanings',[89] often by frequenting Toronto's 'pansy plots'.[90] They then 'lure them into unfavorable places and positions; set upon them and leave them stripped and perhaps half dead.'[91] The 'human petunia' involved, 'shunning publicity because of his strange leanings', could be relied on to take no legal action, having been warned by his assailant that any complaint would 'result in the "lah-dedah's" activities being made public.'[92] And when such a criminal was arrested, he inevitably proclaimed that his actions had been part of an effort to defend himself against the advances of a homosexual.

In these articles, the gay men, who were always referred to as 'victims', were contrasted favourably with straight 'criminals', the latter labelled 'leaches [sic]', 'punks', and 'human vermin' who 'make a living on duping innocent and helpless suckers'.[93] *Hush*'s depiction of these incidents is surprising in an era wherein the Criminal Code defined sexually active gay men as criminals. The publication did not suggest that gay men were receiving just punishment for their nefarious search for sex, nor did it propose that the victims' sexual motivations diminished their innocence. Instead, *Hush* presented the gay man's sexual interest in an almost comic tone. One victim, for instance, was depicted as earnestly attempting to convince the criminal 'that it would be the ideal climax to a jolly evening to spend the night together.' Plying him 'with all sorts of inducements', the gay man finally offered him dinner out and an opportunity to borrow his clothes for the occasion. The criminal donned the apparel, but 'duck[ed] out on the passionate host', avoiding the 'amorous climax'.[94]

The most significant factor contributing to the support gay men received in these situations was the immorality of the criminals. The criminals were robbing and assaulting people, something *Hush* disapproved of at the best of times. But what made these men truly despicable was their willingness to involve themselves in gay sex in their quest for money and goods. These heterosexuals would 'submit to disgusting and sickening abominations' and thought 'little or nothing of participating in . . . male love orgies' for financial gain.[95] The involvement of gay men in such activity, on the other hand, was taken for granted and seen as the inevitable expression of their strange mentality.

For this reason, the typical defence of this type of criminal, that he was 'defend[ing] his virtue and morality' against 'a pervert'[96] or that he had 'struck a blow for manhood',[97] was scoffed at. For one thing, these men had no virtue to defend. As one article sarcastically began: 'They are becoming very moral fellows, these Toronto thugs and gangsters—moral, that is, except for a few little lapses such as assaulting females, beating and robbing males, practising devilment, and using vile language at all times.' It was clear, the article continued, that 'their morality amounts to nothing more than words.'[98]

Inevitably, the defence of gay men in the pages of *Hush* was extremely conditional. Those who attacked or robbed gay men were only condemned if they were immoral criminals. A 1950 case demonstrated that this was so. A man who received a six-year prison sentence for stabbing a professor he had met in a bar popular with gays was defended in the paper. The convicted man claimed that he had been subjected to 'a homosexual attack' and had stabbed his 'heated' pursuer in order to 'defend his honor'. *Hush* supported his claim and decried the punishment imposed. '[A]pparently it is a crime for a man to defend his honor and he may be sentenced at any time merely because he is a normal sex-minded individual.' What made this case so different was the fact that the straight man appeared to be 'clean'.

He had no criminal record, and he had not stolen anything from the professor he stabbed. In addition, the professor was reported to have pursued boxing as a hobby, which may have made him more of a plausible threat than the average 'swish'.[99]

But if the conditions were met, gay men could be treated extremely positively for the time. In some cases, for instance, they were absolved of wrongdoing even in circumstances that would at first appear to be particularly damning. In 1953, *Hush* published a report on two men the police had found engaging in acts 'for which "pansies" are noted' with seven 'youths'. While the latter were referred to as 'boys' and 'youngsters', and go unnamed because of their age (although they were at least old enough to drive), the gay men were not attacked for their actions. Instead, they were described as the 'victims' of these young 'punks'. The youths had 'willingly submitted themselves' to the sexual acts and had no doubt demanded money, as the gay men claimed in court. The writer expressed hope that these 'punks will attempt to . . . start a decent way of life', although he doubted this would occur. And he scolded the gay men for having 'ignored the risk of dealing with strange youths'.[100]

At other times, the paper's toleration of gay men showed signs of expanding to a wider acceptance. This liberalization of attitude was demonstrated in an article about a gay man who had been robbed. '[W]e are in agreement that those of a homosexual nature do have a place in society', wrote the author.[101] And in another instance, a man who killed a homosexual, using as his defence the fact that the latter was a 'pervert' who had made sexual advances, was condemned, as was the shortness of the sentence he received for manslaughter. 'Undoubtedly there was a good deal of sympathy for [the killer] in the minds of the jury because of the character of his victim; the prejudice against a pervert overwhelmed the horror of homicide. However, many thinking people . . . feel that the trial jury were too lenient.' *Hush* felt that the killer deserved a longer sentence or even the death penalty; 'the fact that he was dealing with a sex pervert was no condemnation considering the circumstances.' Predictably, these included the fact that the killer was 'no angel' himself; rather, he was 'a wanderer and a wastrel who had undoubtedly been with [the victim] on previous occasions' and so 'knew what to expect'. Certainly, murdering a gay man to protect one's virtue was seen as an overreaction. 'Even if he had been an innocent stranger he was quite able to ward off any sexual advances without using extreme violence.' The murderer had 'killed a man deliberately and in cold blood, and added to his crime by concealing the body as if it were a dead dog. He

committed MURDER, nothing but murder, and he should have been
found guilty of murder.'

The author went on to editorialize on gay men in general. 'Gay
guys', he wrote, are 'as a rule good citizens and hard workers', and
'few of them are criminals at heart.' He quoted the opinion of a 'correspondent', who, because he or she worked in a department store with
' "quite a few gay people" ', seems to have been considered an expert
on the subject. According to this person, ' "gay boys . . . are about the
most reliable in the store. They are always neat and clean; they work
hard and mind their own business, making good citizens."' And yet
' "bums" ' who ' "never work a day a week" ' and find gay men ' "an
easy prey" ' are permitted to rob them and ' "even go the limit of
murder . . . and get very little punishment"?' The author, perhaps having employed the 'correspondent' as a device to express controversial
views for which he did not want to bear direct responsibility, did pro-
claim that 'there is wisdom in these words, disagreeable though it may
be to the public.' Allowing these 'bums to batter the lives out of "gay
guys" on pretence of self-defence, and rewarding them in the courts, is
something which this nation should not tolerate.'[102]

The tolerance afforded gay men in these examples should not, of
course, be overemphasized. For gay men to merit such treatment it
was necessary for very specific conditions to be fulfilled, as has been
illustrated. And it is telling that the most sympathetic discussion of
gays ever published in this paper required that a gay man be brutally
murdered in order to be written. Elsewhere in the tabloid, gay men
were generally being mocked and bullied; *Hush*'s writers were variously calling for police action, fumigation, and vigilantism to keep
gays in their place. But at the same time, the fact that any articles as
positive as those described above were published when, elsewhere,
homosexuals were being demonized remains remarkable.

Conclusion

As this discussion of the 'homosexual content' of *Hush* in the postwar
decade reveals, the discourse on male homosexuality during this
period was more varied and contradictory than historians have
argued. In this tabloid, the homosexual was depicted as effeminate
and usually innocuous and as a member of visible urban communities, rather than as a hidden, predatory threat to society.

In the mainstream publications examined by American historians
in their studies of homosexuality at this time, on the other hand, it
seems doubtful that the 'swish' was much of a presence, if he existed

at all. The more respectable newspapers and journals were simply not interested in the subject matter that *Hush* found so alluring, and, as a result, odds were against their coming into contact with, or writing about, identifiably gay men with any frequency. They did not publish articles about transvestite prostitutes, 'queer' parties, and 'human petunias' who had their pants stolen by men they brought home from bars. Their gossip columnists, when they even had them, did not take delight in caricaturing local gays as limp-wristed, giggling 'she-men'. The mainstream press was not even able to spread rumours about the flamboyant Liberace—when one daily paper went so far as to call him 'fruit-flavoured' in 1956, Liberace sued for libel and was awarded $24,000 in damages.[103] Thus, when the homosexual did appear in these publications, in discussions of sex crimes or subversion, he had not been provided with the context that, in *Hush*, helped to make the gay man seem unrelated to these topics, as indeed he was.

While it seems probable that the 'swish' did not appear with much frequency in dignified, respectable publications, it remains to be seen to what extent this stereotype remained popular in society. It is likely that some of *Hush*'s views of and attitudes towards gay men were also held by a significant portion of the population. Further studies are required to see whether this was indeed the case and to identify the importance of the 'swish'—and the functions served by this figure—in postwar Canada and the United States. Finally, further study is also required to determine the impact that *Hush* and tabloids like it had on the gay community. While *Hush*'s coverage undoubtedly fuelled homophobic attitudes and stereotypes, it also validated the existence of homosexuals and their right to that existence. In *Hush*'s pages, life as a gay man was presented as a real—if undesirable— possibility and gay communities were revealed to be local realities. In all probability, *Hush* came to be used as a resource by homosexuals themselves, informing isolated individuals of the existence of homosexuality and of a gay subculture, and providing directions on how to find and involve oneself in this world.[104] In this way, *Hush* helped in the creation of the community it was so fascinated with exploiting, unwittingly adding to the growing ranks of 'swish kids' in cities across Canada.

10

'The Case of the Kissing Nurse':

Femininity, Sexuality, and Canadian

Nursing, 1900–1970

Kathryn McPherson

On a lazy Sunday afternoon in January of 1959 Mrs Bew and Mrs Sulman discovered they had a problem. Right in front of their office window sat a parked car in which a young couple were engaged in passionate kissing. As matrons of the Vancouver General Hospital nurses' residence, Bew and Sulman were responsible for ensuring that more than 500 student nurses adhered to the residence rules and thereby maintained a sterling reputation for the school and hospital. Here lay the dilemma. Owing to the nature of the activity in the car, the matrons could not see the woman's face. If she was a Vancouver General Hospital student, the school representatives could interrupt the couple and insist that the woman return to her residence. After all, not only was her behaviour unseemly, but it was past 2:30 p.m. and all student nurses were expected to be back in the hospital a half-hour before their 3 p.m. shift began. If she was *not* a Vancouver General Hospital student, could the matrons rightfully request the couple to move to another location? Just as the diligent overseers had decided to take action, the car door slammed and the young woman—a senior nursing student—sauntered towards the residence. The matrons intercepted the student, reported her to the school authorities, and the student was suspended for two weeks.

To be sent home for a fortnight was a stern penalty, though not unusually so. Yet the prospect of the student having to return home to explain to her parents why she had been reprimanded was severe enough to prompt immediate sympathy from her colleagues in the nursing school. Protesting what they considered harsh and inconsistent punishment, the student nurses threatened to strike if the errant nurse was not reinstated. News of the conflict leaked to the press and by the end of the week was receiving not only local but national coverage. Faced with public humiliation and the potential loss of 500 bedside attendants, the hospital administration met, first with the vigilant matrons to sort out the details of the case and then with the student council to negotiate the rules governing residence life and nurses' leisure time.[1] Meanwhile, newspapers, radio stations, and television networks debated the 'Case of the Kissing Nurse' to understand why, as the *Toronto Daily Star* put it, 'are certain women's professions discriminated against in romance?'[2]

The high public profile this conflict garnered was unprecedented, but in other ways events at Vancouver General Hospital in 1959 revealed long-standing social and occupational tensions over how nurses' sexuality, femininity, and respectability would be defined. This chapter unravels those tensions as they played out in three historical contexts, beginning in the late nineteenth and early twentieth centuries, when the 'modern' trained nurse first appeared, through the interwar years, and then into the post-World War II decades. In spite of the many changes in the structure and content of nursing work, throughout the era under study most nurses received their training in hospital apprenticeship programs. For two or three years, apprentices were schooled in the many rules and regulations they were to carry into paid work, and thus the educational process was a dominant factor in shaping nurses' social role. Drawing on historical documentation from institutional records, oral interviews, and popular culture, this essay explores how ordinary or 'rank-and-file' nurses, during their apprenticeship and as graduates, negotiated their occupational identity. Sexuality was a central component of that identity. Although same-sex relations constituted an important, and woefully understudied, dimension of nursing's past, this discussion focuses on the dominant regulatory regime of heterosexual symbol and practice.[3]

To do so, this essay employs Judith Butler's theoretical framework of gender as performance. Butler likens the gendered roles of men and women to those of theatrical performance. She argues that there is no core gender or sexual identity expressed through social roles. Rather, men and women develop or put on masculine and feminine identities through the 'stylized repetition of acts' performed daily. But not just any set of acts will do. Gendered acts are developed within specific social and historical contexts: women and men learn and develop their roles within the confines of social taboos and expectations. Because, as Butler states, 'the gendered body acts its part in a culturally restricted corporeal space and enacts interpretations within the confines of already existing directives',[4] individuals may make gendered roles 'their own' but performing one's role wrong incurs the wrath of social censure| In Butler's conceptualization the human body is critical not only as the vehicle for gendered performances but also as the site where sexuality or 'desire' is socially constructed. Bodies 'do' gender in part to 'do' desire.[5]

This framework is useful for understanding nursing's relationship to social definitions of appropriate femininity in several ways. First, Butler's assertion that there is no core or 'essential' femaleness (or maleness) being expressed through gender stands as a reminder that there is no core or essential 'nurse' being expressed in the workplace. The category of 'nurse' is wholly a social creation, a role being played, not an essentialized nurturing identity being expressed. Like actors, nurses had to learn their part, not only in terms of the occupationally specific skills and responsibilities they took on, but also in terms of the behaviour and attitudes they had to exhibit. Playing the part wrong invoked powerful social sanctions. And like actors, nurses had to dress the part. The modern nurse donned an occupationally specific uniform, a costume that distinguished her from other women or other caregivers. As well, Butler's focus on sexuality is particularly germane for nursing, an occupation bedevilled by its members' intimate knowledge of the human body.

Finally, Butler's emphasis on the historical specificity of gender roles underscores the importance of identifying how nurses' occupational identity was created, contested, and constrained according to the specific social rules operating at a given point in time. For rank-and-file nurses, the workplace identities they developed, over time and through repetition, were scripted by several potent social forces: social definitions of respectable femininity, the political economy of health care, and the legal and social norms developed by nursing leaders, administrators, and educators—what I call the nursing élite. These three scripts were not always autonomous; when any one of these factors changed with time, so, too, were the other sets of influences reconfigured.[6] And while the focus of analysis here is the relationship between gender and sexuality, class and race were equally powerful influences on nursing's occupational identities.[7]

The 'Modern' Nurse

The 'modern' nurse stepped onto Canada's historical stage in the late nineteenth and early twentieth centuries, when hospitals implemented a radical restructuring of institutional staffing. As part of the wider campaign to make institutions respectable and reliable providers of modern scientific medical treatment for all classes of patient, hospi-_ tals established nursing schools. There, apprenticing students laboured on the wards for three years in exchange for training and certification as 'graduate' nurses. Under the supervision of small staffs of graduate nurse supervisors, students offered hospitals cheap, subordinate, and flexible patient care staff. Unlike the working-class widowed or married women who preceded them, the young, single, White women from a range of class and ethnic backgrounds who filled the ranks of apprenticeship programs were expected to embody the social standards of bourgeois femininity.

The first stage of this grooming process was the introduction of standardized uniforms. While each institution added its own distinctive features, most adopted the basic design of a long blue dress, covered by a white apron and crowned with a cap. The uniform was inspired by that worn by domestic servants in élite households and, like domestic servants, nurses endured uniform styles that were slightly out of style. Trained nurses were expected to dress differently from other working women, but not the same as their patients.[8]

Uniforms promised to fulfil several symbolic functions. Standardized dress eradicated differences of class or ethnicity or even personality that distinguished young recruits from one another. Whatever features differentiated the uniforms adopted by individual schools, the commonalities were sufficient to create an occupationally specific code that indicated nurses' status as 'on duty'. And while the uniform represented the work that nurses performed, it simultaneously identified nurses as different from any other female wage-earners. Especially important was the clear demarcation between nurses and the only other group of working women who had intimate contact with the bodies of strangers—prostitutes. Like religious habits, nurses' uniforms signified the desexualized status of the women wearing them, simultaneously containing female sexuality even as the bodies wearing the uniforms learned about the human body.

The uniform, then, located nurses symbolically as workers, as women, as serving society, and as sexually contained. In doing so, the uniform drew on gender-specific images—after all, only women were nurses—but at the same time distinguished nurses from other women. Given the complexity of this symbolic order, it was not surprising that women who donned the nurses' costume found their role difficult to learn. Efforts to entice trained nurses to comply with the Victorian ideology of middle-class femininity and sexual respectability under-scored the fundamental contradiction that tending the bodies of strangers created for working women, as events at Halifax's Victoria General Hospital in 1896 revealed. That year, the Lady Superintendent of the Hospital and of the Nursing School, Miss Elliot, introduced a 'new rule' mandating that apprenticing students assume the tasks involved in cleaning and treating male patients' private parts. The possibility of direct contact with male genitalia provoked substantial discontent among the nurses, as well as among the patients, who found themselves waiting for long periods to receive attendance. The situation peaked when one well-to-do male patient complained so vociferously that a commission was struck to investigate the matter.

The commissioners' report highlighted the difficulty nursing faced drawing clear lines between appropriate occupational behaviour and the broader social standards of feminine behaviour upon which nursing rested. The commissioners reiterated the hospital's general principle that 'Nursing is a woman's work, for which she is peculiarly fitted', but conceded that 'there are obviously limitations to her usefulness, imposed both by modesty and her want of physical strength.' But the commissioners were unequivocal that the students' insubordination contravened both the occupational and social standards to which the young women were expected to comply.[9]

> A young woman entering the profession of nursing ought to make up her mind to the discharge of a great many unpleasant and even repulsive duties for patients, irrespective of sex. If she cannot, then she has no business in the profession, either in a hospital or in private practice. What is wanted is the proper spirit of the profession. . . .

To inculcate the 'proper spirit of the profession' nursing élites endeavoured to distinguish professional from carnal knowledge. They did so by establishing two sets of complex rituals, one that shaped therapeutic treatment performed at the bedside, the other that shaped social behaviour on duty and off. The former defined nurses as skilled in modern scientific therapeutics. The latter played on an exaggerated vision of Victorian femininity to claim an asexual status for working nurses. Mary Poovey has described this occupational image as the 'sexless, moralizing angel',[10] but nursing's reliance on both femaleness and sexuality were never completely denied. After all, the modern nurse was born out of the gender division of medical labour, and her position within the health-care system was premised on heterosexual complementariness, as the 'wife' to the male doctor or administrator. Even hospital residences did not serve to cloister students: the weekly 'theatre leave', provisions for 'receiving' male guests in the residence lobby, and school-sponsored dances all accommodated heterosexual activity within strict limits.[11]

Rather than try to deny nurses' sexuality or the gendered nature of the occupation, nursing leaders sought to reformulate what Mariana Valverde terms the 'ethical subjectivity' of student and staff nurses by not merely repressing desire but redefining it.[12] Building on the symbolism of nursing uniforms, the professional élite developed a vision of femininity that overstated contemporary standards of social deference, sexual passivity, and ladylike gentility. The key element of ladylike behaviour was restraint: from being noisy, from smoking, from drinking alcohol, from gossiping, or from challenging hospital authorities. Sexual behaviour was central to this regulatory regime. Student nurses were warned not to flirt, 'pose', or show 'familiarity' towards male patients, orderlies, or medical staff.[13] In a crucial inversion of the chivalric code, nurses were instructed to 'stand at attention' or give up their seat or place in an elevator when in the presence of any doctor or senior nursing staff.[14] These various elements of social and sexual restraint were considered as a single goal. As late as 1935 a superintendent of nursing disciplined her charges for smoking, on the basis that 'smoking leads to alcohol and progresses to promiscuity.'[15]

For three years, six and a half days per week, twelve hours per day, apprenticing nurses were encouraged, corrected, and chastened in the details of this regulatory regime. The performative ritual began each morning when students had to assemble in the foyer of the nursing residence to participate in morning prayers and have their uniforms inspected. After a brief breakfast they went on the wards, wherein their therapeutic and social behaviour was monitored by staff nurses or even senior students. Successful adherence to the prescribed rituals was rewarded with promotion to the next rank of student. Punishment for transgressing school rules usually involved some public display of discipline, such as having late leave revoked or being denied the right to wear the nursing cap when on duty.[16] Serious or frequent flaunting of rules would result in the errant apprentices being summoned to the nursing superintendent's office.

At the end of each workday, a shift change also signalled an identity change. Student nurses took off their uniforms (and, indeed, were forbidden from wearing their uniform off duty), donned civilian clothes, and then, no longer asexual nurses, were obliged to adhere to the rules of respectable femininity that residence life demanded.[17] For several short hours, between the end of their shift and residence curfew, students could participate in the social pursuits enjoyed by other young women. In this way, the entire system of regulation developed by hospitals was designed to constrain female sexuality off duty and to neutralize it completely on the wards. After three years, students had learned the clear demarcation between them and other women, in terms of skills they had acquired but also in terms of the sexual scripts they performed.

Understandably, some students interpreted the nuances of this occupational script with ease, others with anxiety. Hospital records indicate that nursing administrators regularly admonished their students for failure to conform to the behaviour norm. Students who chose not to participate in their occupation's performative rituals resigned, sometimes because of marriage and in other cases due to conflicts with school administrators.[18] Despite these actions, relatively few apprenticing nurses abandoned their training, in part because in the years before World War I the Victorian image of respectable femininity did not appear old-fashioned or outmoded compared to that being prescribed for other women. If anything, the model devised within nursing reinforced Victorian notions of bourgeois femininity, so that nurses simply performed a more extreme version of the model of femininity and sexuality being advocated for all women, especially those of the middle class.

Challenges to Victorian Femininity, 1920–1942

By the 1920s, however, nursing's vision of respectable sexuality began to stand in contrast with the liberated sexual mores being advocated for the new woman. Christina Simmons, a historian of sexuality, has examined how in the 1920s the 'Myth of Victorian Repression' was constructed to signal what was wrong with American gender relations and why a sexual revolution was needed to revise them. The new woman of the 1920s was sexually liberated and actively pursuing heterosexual relations. By condemning the repression of pre-World War I gender relations, social commentators indicated that healthy sexual lives demanded expression, not repression. Within this context, nursing appeared anomalous. The feminine persona reinforced by nursing leaders and educators in the 1920s and 1930s was emblematic of the Victorian sexual restraint that by the 1920s was considered outmoded and dangerous.[19]

The most obvious symbol of this disparity was nurses' dress. Throughout the 1920s and 1930s, nursing schools across the country maintained the traditional uniform style and continued to rely on it to signify their occupational identity. Blue dresses with tight bodices, full skirts, high collars, and long sleeves constituted the standard apparel. White aprons and bibs were worn over the blue dress, with starched white collars, cuffs, and ties added according to student status and school style. Each day students donned their costume, and each day that dress was inspected. As students progressed through their years as probationer, junior, intermediate, and then senior nurse, additions to their uniform signified the maturation process. Upon graduation, practitioners were permitted to wear an entirely white costume—dress, cap, stockings, and shoes. The symbolic inversion of traditional female imagery, wherein the colour white signified nurses' workplace experience rather than a bride's sexual inexperience, was reinforced by the elaborate graduation ceremonies (modelled after wedding ceremonies and, to a lesser degree, religious initiation rites) sponsored by training schools and alumnae across the Dominion. Such rites of passage also reaffirmed the asexual status of trained nurses: they graduated out of the cloistered world of hospital apprenticeship sexually and socially pure, driven by vocation and profession, not by marriage or sexuality.

Given the power of the symbolism, it is not surprising that nursing educators and administrators vigorously defended the dress code they had established. Only on the question of hair did supervisors fail to impose their standards. As bobbed hair became all the rage with North American women, superintendents of nursing resisted the fashion, punishing students who bobbed their locks and insisting that students wear their hair long, in a bun on the back of the head, with the cap perched on top. One student nurse at Halifax's Victoria General decided to use her day off to acquire a bob. When she returned to the ward the nursing superintendent demanded that the student retrieve her shorn hair and pin it back onto her head so that she might continue to conform to the conventional look.[20] In this battle, the older generation lost and bobbed hair became the standard coiffure, but on other issues the old guard held fast. In the fashion world of the flapper, hemlines were rising and waistlines dropping, but within nursing the uniform remained pinched at the waist, and seven inches off the floor.[21]

Nursing leaders were not unaware of the differential that had developed between their staffs and the dress and ethos of other women, but maintained that the 'problem' of modern femininity had not penetrated their ranks. As one superintendent of nursing put it: 'In spite of the criticism given the so-called "flapper" of today . . . there is a large proportion amongst our pupils who measure up to the best in the past not only of our own school but of the nursing world in general.'[22] Emboldened by the limited job opportunities available to potential recruits, nursing leaders clung tenaciously to the asexual feminine persona fashioned by their predecessors.

Working nurses were less decided that the scripts defining their occupational identity needed to differ so dramatically from that of modern femininity. Clearly, some rank-and-file nurses sought to integrate elements of a more modern, sexualized feminine persona into their workplace identity. Graduates modernized their dress as soon as they were liberated from training programs,[23] while students openly defied institutional rules by breaking curfew, flirting with patients, and dating male hospital personnel.[24] Tensions between modern femininity and occupational standards emerged as a central theme in nurses' popular culture of the interwar years, as students used their publications to mock regulatory regimes. Vancouver General's 1939 *Nurses' Annual* included a cartoon depicting morning roll call. Although students in the front row were conforming to the military discipline of this morning ritual, those in the back row were finishing their morning toilet, which included getting dressed and applying make-up.[25] The 'stylized repetition of acts' that constituted morning roll call was undermined by an equally 'stylized' set of acts derived from modern femininity, such as putting on lingerie and lipstick.

SOURCE: Vancouver General Hospital, *Nurses' Annual*, 1939.

Nurses' popular culture also subverted the sexual sanctity of the uniform by linking nurses' heterosexual conquests to their occupation and dress. The cheeky 1928 poem, 'The Nurse's Chance', began:

> It seems to me a nurse has got
> A most delightful life
> Since she has many chances
> To become a rich man's wife

Their 'slick' uniform offered nurses a 'mean advantage' over 'mushy' male patients on the mend. Advising nurses to 'strike while the iron is hot', the poem concluded:

> For men assume the wife will be
> Just like the nurse who cooled
> Their fevered brow so patiently
> But oh! how men are fooled [26]

Bedside labour permitted nurses to improve their class position by becoming 'a rich man's wife' but also to undermine conventional gender relations within marriage.

Such articulation of the sexual tension inherent in bedside care served to challenge the conventional occupational identity endorsed by nursing educators in schools across the country. At the same time, the contradictions inherent in the political economy of interwar health care prompted many working nurses to foster the traditional nursing image. Most graduate trained nurses made their living in the private health-care market, caring for individuals in the patients' homes or private hospital rooms. A small minority of practitioners were employed as public health nurses, travelling from house to house or working in local, sometimes mobile, health clinics. As women not contained in home, factory, or office, nurses had to negotiate daily with male doctors, administrators, patients, and members of the community. To mediate their position as women traversing the 'public' world of private or community health services, many nurses accommodated themselves to the traditional asexual image of nursing.

For instance, to secure work, nurses often relied on recommendations from male doctors and often travelled unchaperoned with male doctors to attend patients. Adhering to carefully delineated rules of personal and sexual propriety helped nurses defend against unwanted sexual advances, rumours of sexual impropriety, or allegations of professional advancement through sexual relations. [27] Relations with patients could prove equally challenging to negotiate. In her 1920 *The Girl of the New Day*, feminist author Ellen Knox acknowledged the perils to purity that private health care posed: 'what are you to do', she asked rhetorically, if a patient 'flatters you or says low, common things, better left unsaid.'[28]

That such transgressions might well result in allegations of improper behaviour and dismissal were alluded to in a poem reproduced several times in nursing publications:

> Some people think that nurses
> Fall in love the very day
> They come to count a sick man's pulse
> Or bring his dinner tray.

Insisting that invalid males were far from attractive and that 'fair romance' was not inspired by a 'man without a collar who's as cranky as a bear', the poem concluded:

> So cheer up, wives and sweethearts,
> Because it is not true
> That artful vampires in white caps
> Would wish to steal from you
> To tell the truth, before a week
> The poor nurse is a wreck:
> The love for your man is only this—
> The love to wring his neck.[29]

Critiquing the sexual appeal of male patients, the poem denied that nurses were 'artful vampires in white caps' and assured 'wives and sweethearts' that nurses posed no sexual threat. The poem's humorous conclusion, which made light of the dangerous image of nurse as sexual predator, recognized the reality that in private practice any threat to domestic and marital relations might cost nurses their jobs.

The poem's denial of the potential sexuality symbolized by the uniform was echoed in working nurses' interpretation of their place in the public sphere. Nurses working in public health and private duty often found themselves alone in rough neighbourhoods in the middle of the night, travelling on the outskirts of a city or in an isolated rural district, or accepting rides from strangers. In such contexts, nurses were proud to report, as did a nurse working for Winnipeg's Margaret Scott Nursing Mission (MSNM): 'I am not afraid to go anywhere at any time in my uniform as all our friends and patients know us.'[30] Men from all classes could be counted on to treat MSNM staff with respect. Riding home on the streetcar, 'tired, wornout workmen . . . offer us their seats if we are in uniform', while 'truck drivers . . . private cars, the doctors and anyone going in our direction' would offer nurses rides to patients in outlying districts. For these women, conforming to the behavioural and dress restrictions of the nursing establishment held tangible rewards. The asexual persona served to neutralize even the most sexually dangerous men, turning working-class and bourgeois males alike into gentlemen. Clearly, there were limits to the symbolic work a uniform could do, as one nurse learned when, walking home from a patient's house in the middle of the night, she was harassed by a local man. But her response to the man revealed the depth of nurses' confidence in their occupational identity: she chastised her harasser, 'If you don't respect me you might have respected the uniform.'[31]

Maintaining boundaries between the more sexualized persona of modern femininity and the traditional asexual occupational image proved a potent means for working nurses to negotiate their daily lives. The occupational identity acquired, however painfully, as apprentices was certainly open to critique. Graduating students used their school publications to mount that critique, albeit often in humorous terms. But nurses' place within the interwar political economy of health also necessitated that ordinary practitioners deploy the asexual feminine persona if they were to serve the public health and private homes safely and respectably. The performative rituals that shaped nurses' occupational identity were re-enacted daily as working nurses sought to legitimate their presence in the world of work.

Compulsory Heterosexuality: Nursing in the 1940s and 1950s

Just as the political economy of private health care shaped the stage on which interwar nurses played their parts, so, too, did changes to the health-care system during and after World War II influence the dominant definition of nursing that developed. Wartime and postwar economies provided, for the first time, a stable funding base for Canadian hospitals and with it both a dramatic growth in institutional health services and the decline of the private health-care market. Nursing administrators, recognizing the new occupational options young women enjoyed, tried to increase dramatically the numbers of staff and student nurses by making nursing an attractive occupational option. To do so, they modernized nursing's sexual and social feminine image, thereby ensuring that the occupation would remain, in this era, women's work.[32]

Changes in nurses' uniforms served as the most telling evidence of the new feminine ideal being promoted. During World War II nursing schools moved to bring nurses' official dress into line with other uniformed women. This time it was not domestic servants who inspired nurses' costume but women in the military.[33] While it is unclear whether this was a self-conscious manoeuvre to capitalize on the positive image of service women or simply part of the larger fashion trend of the day, nursing schools raised the hemlines, tailored their skirts, shortened the sleeves, relaxed the collar, and, eventually, removed the apron.[34] Leaders were anxious to publicize the makeover their occupation was undergoing. When, for example, the Toronto General Hospital decided to redesign its institutional costume, it consulted an 'internationally known designer who has definite ideas concerning the uniforms'. The designer's advice, that 'a charming appearance in every field of activity is a helpful tonic and especially so in nursing', obviously struck a chord in the health-care world. When the all-white uniform was introduced the *Canadian Hospital Magazine* reported its debut in the language of a model's runway and fashion show.

> This Class wore smart white uniforms with short sleeves and deep inset side pockets, thus doing away with starched cuffs, collars, bibs and aprons. The all-white uniform is a departure which will establish a precedent at the Hospital. Not only is it attractive in appearance but it is practical and should prove very popular.[35]

Whatever concessions to modern fashion nursing leaders were willing to make, they still hoped to signify heterosexual possibility, not experience. This became clear in the 1950s, when many hospitals introduced uniforms with full, soft skirts, a design that conformed to what historian of fashion Maureen Turim has termed the 'sweetheart line' of female dress design. With respect to Hollywood's uses of the sweetheart line, Turim argues that this shape was able to 'annex the connotations of princess, debutante, or bride that became attached to this exaggerated feminine' appearance and that it contrasted with the 'slinkier tight skirt . . . [that represented] women as sexual warriors and golddiggers'.[36] Like debutantes, not golddiggers, nurses were represented as conforming to feminine norms, available for heterosexual relations if not yet experienced in them.

The image of the 'exaggerated feminine' was central to nursing leaders' recruiting efforts in the postwar decades. High school girls learned that nursing offered more than a job: parties, travel, and socializing all accompanied an occupation 'studded with opportunities and adventure'.[37] Part of the adventure was romance. No longer portrayed as an occupation women pursued until marriage or in place of marriage, nursing was promoted as an occupation that prepared women for, and could be pursued after, matrimony. Leaders campaigned to resolve the dichotomies between heterosexual pursuits and paid work by emphasizing that nursing training enhanced not only women's marital prospects but also their skills at making a marriage successful. As one promotional article declared: 'it's not surprising that the matrimonial rate among nurses is higher than in any other profession.'[38] Thus, the renovation of the occupational dress did not only serve to expose more leg and accentuate more curves, it also served as a powerful symbol of the fundamentally heterosexual status of nurses.[39]

Once again, the nursing uniform served a symbolic function. Through it nursing leaders articulated the highly stylized public persona nurses were expected to embody, a persona that signified the sexual possibility that nurses, like all young women, possessed. The contradiction, of course, was that nurses' actual heterosexuality was to be developed or practised only when they were out of uniform. At no point did occupational leaders expect that the rituals of deference that governed patient care would be replaced by rituals of flirtation or romance on the wards. It was the hours after work, in residence, wherein apprentices were encouraged to fuse contemporary sexual and social norms with their occupational identity.

Nursing schools facilitated heterosexual contact through dating, class formals, and seasonal dances, sometimes organized in conjunction with engineering students at the local university. A 1958 Vancouver General yearbook photograph of a young woman, decked out in a full-length, sleeveless 'sweetheart' gown, walking down the steps of the nurses' residence holding the hand of a dapper young man wearing a tuxedo, reminded nursing and non-nursing readers that apprenticeship training did not insulate nurses from the wider heterosexual culture of post-World War II Canada.[40]

At the same time, residence rules were relaxed to facilitate young nurses' participation in modern cultural forms. Institutions like the Winnipeg General Hospital established a 'smoker' wherein nurses could enjoy cigarettes without having to sneak onto the roof or into a nearby café as they had done in the previous generation. One Winnipeg alumna recalled that until she enrolled, 'I don't think I'd ever seen a woman smoke.' But because 'the smoking room was where all the fun was . . . all the student nurses went in that room, usually after every shift, that's where the people got rid of their tensions, and told all the jokes', the student realized that if she wanted to be part of the after-hours socializing she had to 'smoke in self-defence'.[41] Activities that in a previous generation were defined as deviant were now part of the normative socio-sexual self. Just as the rituals of nursing education had done in the past, the daily rituals of convening in the smoker allowed nurses to socialize and be socialized, to participate in the domain of contemporary femininity even as they met as working women.

The popular culture created by nursing students clearly articulated the heterosexual femininity of their occupation. The 1949 Calgary General Hospital yearbook included the following cartoon. The student's mind wandered from her gynecology text to her romantic fantasies, while the cobwebs growing in her desk suggested that she spent more time dreaming than at her studies. That the student wore pajamas, the uniform of leisure and bed, rather than a nursing garb located her firmly within a gendered rather than vocational role. Within the new political economy of health care, the closer alignment between nursing and heterosexuality was possible precisely because all nurses, staff and students, were now contained within institutional walls. As hospitals emerged as the primary location of employment,

SOURCE: Calgary General Hospital, *In Uniform and Cap*, 1949.

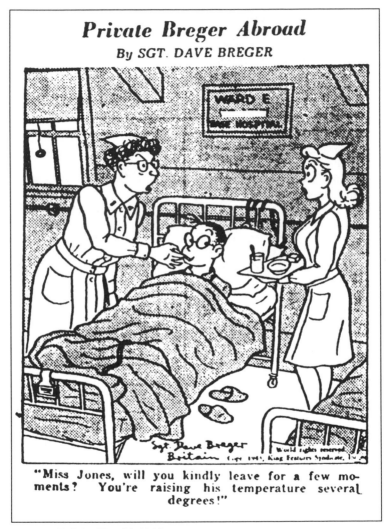

Private Breger Abroad
By SGT. DAVE BREGER

"Miss Jones, will you kindly leave for a few moments? You're raising his temperature several degrees!"

SOURCE: *Halifax Herald*, 1945.

nurses were less frequently called to individual homes where private doctors, family members, or men on the street might harass them or misinterpret their behaviour. In hospitals, institutional structures overrode the specific dynamics of private households and familial employment, and the 'low common things' said to nurses were less likely to compromise their employment status.

Of course, as nurses' heterosexuality became part of public discourse, the pendulum threatened to swing too far. Non-nurse publications and commentators picked up the question of nurses' sexuality and the image of the sexually knowledgeable nurse began to appear. For example, a 1945 cartoon from the *Halifax Herald* depicted two nurses at the bedside of a young male patient. As the patient, not terrifically attractive himself, sucked on a thermometer his eyes bugged out at the big-chested 'Betty Boop'-like nurse. The second, older, grey-haired, bespectacled nurse requested her colleague to leave the bedside because she was causing the patient's temperature to rise unnaturally high. Scientific medicine was being interrupted by female sexuality.

At the same time, the fact that the patient was a young man who was clearly more responsive to the ministrations of the curvacious young nurse suggested that sexuality and science could be combined in powerful ways. When, for instance, a 1950 issue of the University of Manitoba Students' Union newspaper, *The Manitoban*, announced that the Red Cross would be on campus that week the article began: 'Roll up your sleeve and smile for the cute little blonde nurse, boys— she wants some of your blood for her collection.'[42] The nurse's professional mandate to administer a blood bank was recast *à la Dracula*, as if it was *her* collection and her sexual appeal lured potential victims. In this context, it was the public, not nurses, who capitalized on the image of nurses as 'artful vampires in white caps'.

By the late 1960s and early 1970s, the sexualized image of the nurse would be carried one step further. Within American popular culture characters like *M.A.S.H.*'s 'Hot Lips' Hoolihan and Ken Kesey's 'Big Nurse', Nurse Ratched in *One Flew Over the Cuckoo's Nest*, were depicted by left-liberal writers as symbolic of women's heterosexual and socially damaging power. At a more grassroots level, popular culture positioned nurses as more sexually knowledgeable than other women, as nurse-characters' frequent appearances in pornographic films and novels suggested.[43]

Given these circumstances, nurses sought to locate themselves as feminine, sexual, *and* respectable. Many accomplished this by marrying—in fact, this new sexual-social occupational paradigm legitimated the decision made by many women in the postwar era to combine nursing careers with marriage. But the unmarried women, who still comprised the majority of graduates, confronted a definition of femininity in which sexual space was in some ways even more difficult to negotiate than it had been before. Nurses were encouraged to participate in the youth culture of heterosexual and heterosocial activities, but at the same time they had to avoid crossing the line into promiscuity.

The 1959 'Case of the Kissing Nurse' exemplified this tension. When the Vancouver General administrators met to resolve the conflict, their discussion centred not on whether the kissing had occurred but whether it had continued past the point of the respectable. One matron proclaimed, 'I'm not a prude but 25 minutes is too long.' Another administrator asked, 'Who initiated the contact?' and another queried, 'Were his hands in evidence at all times?'[44] Yet while hospital administrators worried that the 'kissing nurse' had gone too far, news reporters queried whether nurses were not allowed to go far enough: Was nursing 'discriminated against in romance?'[45]

Nurses' claims to respectable femininity hinged on their ability to negotiate the mixed messages and ambiguous limits they encountered. Not surprisingly, then, the essence of student complaints at Vancouver General was not about rules regarding deportment *per se* but about the inconsistency with which those rules were applied. Facing powerful social sanctions if they performed their gender wrong, the students demanded what Butler would call a clearly delineated script. This point was not lost on all observers. Mr McNaughton, second vice-chairman of the Hospital Board, commented that at 10:30 at night he had often seen seven cars lined up outside the residence as students said good-bye to their boyfriends, and asked, 'was it a crime to kiss your boyfriend at 2:30 in the afternoon but not one at 10:30 at night?'[46] Here McNaughton captured the crux of the problem. Heterosexual desire was to be applauded and encouraged in daylight, but practised only after dark, preferably with a man who would become your husband.

Within the new political economy of health services that developed after World War II, nursing leaders scripted a subtle change in their occupational identity. As in previous eras, nurses were encouraged to use their leisure time to pursue 'normal' heterosexual options, but unlike during the pre-war decades, nursing work itself was heralded as enhancing women's sexual appeal. In doing so, leaders were able to capitalize on the powerful youth culture of the postwar era wherein 'innocent' sexual encounters between the sexes were considered healthy and women's sexual possibility was highly visible. As Canadian nursing élites emphasized the heterosexual complementariness of their occupation, they had to come to terms with the possibility of open displays of heterosexual activity—whether in front of the nursing residence or in popular representations of nurses. Meanwhile, working nurses had to navigate the narrow path between being 'kissing nurses' and 'artful vampires'.

Conclusion

In recent years, historians of nursing have reckoned with the gendered contours of the occupation's past. Emphasizing the asymmetrical division of labour and authority that has ordered relations of power between nurses and the male medical profession, historians have confronted the ways gendered notions have infused the structure and content of nursing work. Such historiographical shifts in interpretation speak to the success of women's history, especially in making gender visible within an occupation that has been so shaped by notions of femininity that it has at times been taken as natural. Much less scholarly attention has been paid to the ways that sexuality shaped nursing's gendered reputation. As the research presented here demonstrates, nurses' close working relationship with the bodies of strangers signalled their potential as 'artful vampires'. To contain or capitalize on that potential, occupational leaders and working nurses scripted specific workplace identities, learned through the highly 'stylized' repetition of acts.

If nursing history has much to learn from gender history, so, too, can studies of femininity and masculinity benefit from the lessons offered from nursing's past. Researchers frequently assert that gender is 'socially constructed', but articulating the precise mechanisms whereby such constructions occurred in the past is often complicated by unavailability of sources. As a thoroughly gendered occupation with a rich primary resource base, nursing offers a site wherein 'normative' sexuality can be interrogated. Historians of Canadian women have tended to address the question of sexuality by examining regulatory regimes or prescriptive codes and then considering the 'deviants' who transgressed those rules. The implication of such studies is that fear of being 'deviant' inspired 'normal' women to adhere to the prescriptive code: heterosexual monogamy emerges as the default position women adopted if they wanted to resist being labelled sex radical, prostitute, or lesbian.[47]

The example of nurses reveals, however, that normal sexuality was not simply a function of expression/repression, but rather a complex process whereby particular combinations of acceptable behaviour were scripted and then learned through occupationally specific rituals of performance in the workplace and during leisure hours. And, as

Butler warns, the process of learning normative sexual and gendered identities was often painful: 'Gender is what is put on, invariably, under constraint, daily and incessantly, with anxiety and pleasure'.[48] The nursing identities developed by apprentices took three years and often involved a great deal of negative reinforcement, but once formed they proved powerful. The power of those identities lay in the authority nursing educators and leaders held over apprentices and in the political economy of health that shaped working nurses' conditions of employment. Rejecting the dominant occupational definition held very real consequences for student and graduate nurse alike. At the same time, the occupation could not exist too far outside contemporary heterosocial and sexual norms for fear of public censure or trouble attracting new recruits.

Feminist theorists have also challenged us to think about gender not only as the experiences of women and men, but also as a system of signifying power—that gender can be at work even if real women, or men, are not.[49] And, theorists assert, gender identities are relational—they are formed against or with their socially constructed opposite. There is no doubt that for nurses in this century different and sometimes competing versions of masculinity were constantly lurking about: the sexual partner, the sexual predator, and the supportive gentlemen were powerful images invoked to signify the legitimacy or logic of nurses' various occupational scripts. Hypothetical male behaviour was indeed a potent system of signifying power. But it is equally important that however much nurses used masculine imagery to construct their social roles, the actual cast of characters was entirely female. Women with substantial occupational power scripted a social identity that less powerful women embraced, resisted, or modified. In the effort to chart the relations between the genders, historians must not lose sight of the substantial power women wielded over each other or the potential for self-definition they sometimes realized.

11

Defending Honour, Demanding Respect:
Manly Discourse and Gendered Practice
in Two Construction Strikes, Toronto,
1960–1961

Franca Iacovetta

Neither historians of masculinity nor their subjects—men—are monolithic groups. The emerging field of gender history, though sometimes considered a site reserved for reified post-modern exercises in literary deconstruction, already has produced a literature marked by various approaches and topics.[1] Earlier polarized debates over the role of 'representation' versus 'structure' in shaping history—debates that saw discourse analysts and historical materialists locked in battle—have given way to sophisticated efforts by scholars, including both class-oriented feminists and Marxists, to consider ways of integrating key insights from both approaches.[2] The willingness of some 'social determinists' to entertain post-structuralist insights regarding, for instance, the power of linguistic symbols and discourse is not so surprising given that, as Neville Kirk has astutely observed, these historians have been far more attuned to such complicating issues than their detractors have admitted.[3]

More specifically, historians of masculinity have begun demonstrating that masculinity, like femininity, is neither a biological state of being nor a fixed and unitary set of practices and identities. As a relational construct, masculinity, like femininity, is forged in particular contexts and by the critical forces, including class, race-ethnicity, state power, patriarchy, and ideology, that shape such contexts. Sympathetic accounts of male cultures, whether the gentlemanly ambience of the men's club or the class-conscious camaraderie of the union hall, are not sufficient. Nor are studies intended solely to map the diversity of masculine identities. Just as women's history has shown that femininity cannot be grasped without a consideration of women's oppression, studies of masculinity must seriously dissect men's privilege and power, especially in relation to 'the other', whether women, gay men, or racial-ethnic minorities.[4]

But if the critical aim of the history of masculinity is the excavation of male power and privilege, how, then, do we write about men who belonged to a marginal male group? What happens when we shift the lens to male subjects who were themselves 'othered'—in this case, as exploited immigrants who escaped a hostile homeland only to occupy, in their adopted home, the unenviable position of pick-and-shovel man, racially inferior newcomer, and dangerous foreigner? This paper revisits two strikes that rocked the Toronto construction trades in the early 1960s. My 1992 study, *Such Hardworking People*, analysed the class and ethnic dimensions of those conflicts; this study uses recent scholarship in gender history to focus more closely on the male images and immigrant (and racial) discourses that helped give shape to the campaigns.[5] The strikes were triggered by Italian immigrants, mostly former peasants and rural artisans from southern Italy, and they featured mass rallies, brutal class exploitation, charismatic labour leaders, and violence. The essay argues that the workers' grievances became forcefully articulated within an immigrant discourse that coalesced around the image of the honourable family man whose proven capacity for hard work, 'nation-building', and self-sacrifice entitled him to respect and better treatment. Such discontents and demands were encapsulated in a striker's rallying cry: 'End immigrant slavery—Think of your families.'

In highlighting the masculine discourses of the strikes, this chapter in no way suggests that symbols, rhetoric, and ritual alone propelled Italian workers to strike. The discourse of the honourable immigrant took shape in the real and overlapping contexts of workplace, household, neighbourhood, and community, and drew on a combination of Old World and New World patterns and beliefs, both mixing and colliding. But while language and ritual may not have created the harsh class conditions of Toronto's postwar construction trades, they were the means by which Italian immigrant workers gave meaning to events and experiences. Such men were negotiating their gender identities, like their class, racial-ethnic, and newcomer status, amid the challenges occasioned by their transition from peasants in a marginal and inhospitable rural economy to urban, industrial waged workers in a booming but hostile New World metropolis. Workplace experiences interacted with and were filtered through the men's perceptions of themselves as honourable workers. That image was based on their capacity to endure tough and dangerous work, and in their (shifting) capacity to act as the family's chief provider and protector, especially amid the new uncertainties engendered by immigration. It was also rooted in their privileges as the acknowledged head of the household, even while they negotiated with wives who might challenge that status. Indeed, though the strikes were male dramas, women and the gender dynamics of immigrant households played decisive roles. Once articulated and transformed into a strike platform, manly discourse helped to crystallize a defining moment for the strikers: their transition from foreign greenhorns tolerating slaughterhouse conditions to skilled tradesmen and experienced labourers demanding humane treatment. Militancy was fuelled by masculinist ideology that, as men, strikers had the prerogative and obligation to fight injustice, but manly militance also threatened to represent strikers as hooligans and bullies when picket-line violence erupted. Contrasting racial images of 'slave' versus 'free' labour and a desire to improve their racial status as Toronto's 'almost black' newcomers also infused this discourse, suggesting that the strikes illuminate as well how Italian immigrant workers came to define themselves as White Canadians. In short, a discourse of 'defending honour' and 'demanding respect' became an effective tool for mobilizing Italian workers precisely because it resonated so deeply with the men's real lives and aspirations.

Greenhorns Enter 'the Jungle'

The construction industry is a deeply gendered, intensely male work world, one associated with risky jobs, dangerous worksites, and rough men. Historically, images of construction workers have ranged widely: accomplished craftsmen carrying on established traditions, exploited immigrants performing brute labour on the resource frontier, tough-talking, cigar-chomping union bosses, and uncouth louts who harass women walking past building sites. In recent years, the industry's tough, machismo image derives from a notoriety fuelled by countless court inquiries, royal commissions, and media exposés investigating charges of fraudulent business practices, employer abuses, and union corruption.[6]

The association of Italian immigrant men with construction jobs has been a strong and enduring one. The predominant image is of wage-hungry, dark-skinned, and ever-mobile peasants transformed into 'human steam shovels' who, by brute force and sheer doggedness, built the infrastructure of the world capitalist economy—railroads, tunnels, sewers, houses, subways, factories, highways, and skyscrapers.[7] To that, we could add the racist metaphors that offered cruel caricature of their marginal class position and 'in-between' racial status as undesirable southern Europeans: 'sweatback', 'the Chinese of Europe', 'Australia's olive peril', 'pick-and-shovel men', and, from the men's own mouths, *'lavoratori de diavuli'* (the devil's workers). All are subhuman metaphors that help capture the brutal exploitation and racial derision to which millions of Italian migrant and immigrant men, particularly southerners, have been subjected.[8] This image dominates despite the presence of skilled craftsmen and the diverse work patterns actually exhibited by Italian immigrants throughout the nineteenth and twentieth centuries.[9]

In Toronto, the association of Italian men with construction work, though evident earlier, was solidified in the two decades after World War II. So strong did their identification with construction become that some observers virtually ascribed to Italian men an innate, racial affinity for mortar, bricks, and wheelbarrow. Such equations overlapped with racist depictions of culturally backward and, in the words of one Torontonian, 'ignorant, almost black'[10] men. In an era before significant migration of immigrants of colour from Asia, the Caribbean, and elsewhere, southern Italians in early postwar Toronto occupied a vulnerable racial status. Italian men were acutely aware of this fact; for some, the 1960 and 1961 union drives would mark their refusal to continue to accept anything less than the rights enjoyed by White, unionized Canadian workers.

The Italian influx of Toronto's construction trades was part of the so-called Italian 'invasion' of postwar Toronto, which saw well over 100,000 Italians arrive in the city by 1965. Post-1945 boom conditions and a rapidly expanding metropolis created a huge demand for construction workers. By 1961, more than 15,000 Italians, or fully one-third of Toronto's working Italian men, were employed in construction, and they represented one-third of the city's total construction workforce.

As developers and builders eagerly exploited the seemingly insatiable demand for postwar housing and services, new roads, sewers, and houses and apartments were extended into the city's sprawling suburbs. Whether single, recently married, or fathers of young children, men in their twenties and thirties from the agro-villages of the impoverished Italian south dominated the ranks of greenhorns who took on risky and dangerous outdoor jobs. They infiltrated the entire industry, working on building sites erecting residential, industrial, and commercial structures and on engineering projects building roads, bridges, and sewage systems. Their daily work life was daunting. 'Sandhogs' (tunnellers) on sewage and hydro sites worked deep underground. Others quickly earned the scars, sore backs, and gnarled hands of ditchdigger, digging trenches for the installation of gas mains or sewers. Braced against early winter winds or the soaring heat of summer, workers faced daily the risk of injury, including death by cave-ins. Men on road-building and paving sites were exposed to gas leaks and explosions that could maim or kill. The oral testimonies of Italian construction workers unleash painful memories of injuries experienced or witnessed: men's limbs impaled on pipes; backs broken from falls from poorly assembled scaffolds, skyscraper beams, or elevator shafts; hands and feet cracked and frozen from exposure; and faces cut from shattered glass.[11]

By far the largest Italian concentration developed in the house and apartment sector: approximately 65 per cent for the field, and 85 per cent for certain trades, such as bricklaying and carpentry. Unlike large sections of the non-residential field, where craft unions affiliated with the American Federation of Labor (AFL) maintained closed shops and safeguarded apprenticeship programs, the housing field was unorganized, permitting informal methods of recruitment and training to flourish. Many Italians who became tradesmen, for example, actually performed semi-skilled work learned 'on the job', mostly in the non-certified trades such as carpentry, bricklaying, and cement finishing— a situation that reinforced demeaning stereotypes of Italians as inferior pick-and-shovel men masquerading as craftsmen.[12] Italians also became employers, but at the lowest levels, running small trade-specific subcontracting firms and assembling work crews from among former co-workers, kin, and *paesani*. The profusion of firms best served the interests of the developers and builders who engaged in bid-peddling that left many subcontractors to run their businesses on a shoestring.[13] The latter had little legal recourse if builders declared their work substandard and withheld payment.

Most victimized of all, however, were the workers. The AFL unions (also called 'commercial' or 'old-line' unions) had failed to organize the residential field, where the features that generally hampered union drives in construction—volatile markets, numerous small employers, scattered work crews, large supplies of newcomers, and intense job competition—found extreme expression by the recession years of the late 1950s. Hard times made Canadian unionists even less inclined to organize immigrants, especially those whom they considered to be 'inferior craftsmen', whose presence might undercut union wages. Italian residential workers were thus especially vulnerable to employer cost-cutting techniques. In an effort to cover their losses on tenders for which they had underbid, and under pressure from their own 'bosses'—builders and developers—to complete projects on time, subcontractors subjected their workers to speed-ups and long workdays, ignored costly and time-consuming safety regulations, and withheld wages. With growing regularity, Italian workers complained of hours inexplicably 'docked' from their pay-cheques. Fly-by-night contractors (both Italian and non-Italian) also arrived, ruthlessly exploiting their work crews in order to finish projects for which they had grossly underbid—and then disappeared before pay-cheques bounced at the bank. To compete amid this cutthroat competition, legitimate small contractors resorted to similar tactics, including kickback schemes wherein a worker returned a portion of his wages to the employer as a condition of his employment. As employers ignored safety codes, accidents and injuries continued. Already trailing behind the commercial trades, residential wages plummeted.[14] Employer violations of the Vacations with Pay Act, Workmen's Compensation Act, Unemployment Insurance, and other protective legislation increased.

Fighting Back: Men without Women?

In recalling these events, immigrant bricklayer Marco Abate observed that such crippling conditions threatened to dehumanize the men who worked daily in a context that exploited and demeaned them. 'The residential field', he said, 'was a jungle, a no man's land. . . . It was like our life was so cheap, not worth anything. Like we could hear a builder saying, "Some Italians die today, got injured. Oh well, send us another load." ' In describing a brutal regime, Abate used a popular, racial image of the jungle as a remote place where lawlessness and subhuman or primitive conditions prevailed. As Mediterraneans acutely aware of their 'undesirable' racial status among White Canadians, Italian workers probably would have agreed with Abate's efforts to distinguish themselves as White ethnics far removed from the jungles of faraway worlds. They likely would have agreed with the rest of Abate's comments—that reforming Toronto's residential sector would also serve to rehabilitate themselves from popular images of southern Italians as a culturally backward people accustomed to substandard treatment and subhuman conditions. Unless Italian workers 'fought back', Abate declared in the tough words of a blue-collar worker, 'we were doomed' to a brutal life.[15]

The event that prompted men to fight back occurred on 17 March 1960, when five Italian workers installing an underground water main beneath the Don River at Hogg's Hollow, on Toronto's northern limits, were killed. A fire had swept through the tunnel's main shaft, leaving the men to suffocate under an avalanche of mud. A subsequent inquiry revealed that the project had violated numerous safety standards and inspection had been inadequate. The rescue mission had been sabotaged by faulty equipment.[16]

The Hogg's Hollow disaster highlighted features central to Italian immigrant men's lives, including their vulnerability in the face of dangerous work. It also vividly captured their status as gendered subjects: whether husbands, fathers, or sons, these men occupied a critical link in their family's transition from peasants or artisans in a marginal rural economy to urban wage-earners in an industrial city. At the time of the disaster, one of the victims, John Fusile, 27, had been boarding with his four brothers while sending money overseas to his elderly parents and his wife and awaiting the arrival of wife and baby. Alexandro and Guido Mantella, both in their early 20s, and another brother also working in construction, had been supporting a family still residing in Italy. So had 27-year-old Pasquale Allegrezza. John Corrigle, 46, was the eldest victim and the only one who had been reunited with his family. He had also met another goal for which thousands of immigrant couples would endure years of indebtedness, thrift, and financial sacrifice to attain—home-ownership.[17]

Of course, not all men, once abroad, fulfilled their obligations to family and kin. Some squandered their pay-cheques, whether out of wilful abandon, resentment, or despair. Others 'opted out' of family networks, deserting elderly parents or abandoning wives and children back home. (The 'bigamist' and his 'American' wife are recurring images in migrant folktales and songs.) Even men who fulfilled most family-designated expectations were not necessarily beyond reproach in their personal treatment—or mistreatment—of women and children. Still, most of Toronto's Italian men closely resembled the Hogg's Hollow victims in their apparent willingness to carry out family-defined goals. That so many did so was not solely a reflection of men's emotional commitment to wife, parents, and children, though the ties of sentiment that bond immigrant families could be very intense indeed. It also attests to the crucial importance that allegiance to the family and a family-defined code of honour played in Italian men's self-identity and self-respect as honourable men. The activities that shaped their lives in Toronto—earning wages, sending home remittances, living as 'bachelors' on an impossible budget until the others arrived, filling out sponsorship papers to secure the entry of kin, and making preparations to purchase a modest house—were simultaneously strategies of economic survival long familiar to immigrants and critical markers of Italian men's trustworthiness as family providers and protectors.

The published biographies of the Hogg's Hollow victims helped rescue them as hard-working members of struggling Italian families. Moreover, many Italian workers saw in Hogg's Hollow their own stories of pain and the varied sources of their masculine self-identity: fathers, sons, and brothers with familial obligations, working-class foreigners relegated to unsafe jobs, and immigrants determined to improve their lives and demand respect. The tragedy, of course, also exposed their vulnerability and graphically displayed how unsafe and risky jobs could sabotage dreams and destroy families. If Italian men derived considerable *onore* (honour) from their capacity to act as family protectors and providers, the reverse engendered *vergogna* (shame) and an acute sense of failure. As one man put it, 'you came here to make a better life, when you can't you feel ashamed, you want to do for your family.' Such transplanted notions of manly honour informed and reinforced the strong class discontent that Italian workers had developed over the brutal conditions of their work.[18]

Although the fatalities had occurred outside the housing field, Hogg's Hollow triggered a massive union campaign among Italian residential workers. For some observers, Hogg's Hollow was yet one more indication of the industry's brutal regime. As one journalist quipped: 'For years, they've been dying in ones and twos in Don Mills and Scarborough. Falling off rickety scaffolds with no safety hats, no work boots, not even gloves. . . . The only thing different about . . . Hogg's Hollow is that five guys died in a hellhole underground.'[19] But for the workers inside 'the jungle', most of them immigrants whose experience with unions in Italy had been confined to fascist-imposed organizations, the event marked a political awakening and a profound shift in vantage point—from that of unskilled foreign greenhorn prepared to endure a brutal regime to established tradesman and experienced labourer declaring entitlement to decent working wages and safe jobs.

At the time of the disaster, the two men who would dominate the leadership of the immigrant organizing campaigns, Bruno Zanini and

Charles Irvine, had already scored some union gains among several
trades. Now, Italian workers flooded the new residential unions that
collectively became known as the Brandon Union Group.[20] The Brandon Group was composed of five trades (each with its own AFL char-
ter)—the bricklayers, cement masons, plasterers, carpenters, and
labourers—and an executive consisting of immigrant organizers and
seasoned unionists.[21] But real power resided with Irvine, an old-line
unionist and an international vice-president with the AFL's Plasterers
and Cement Masons, and Zanini, a union novice but a quick study.
Brashness characterized their style. A member of Toronto's small pre-
war Italian community and the city's interwar youth gang culture, the
stocky Zanini was a bricklayer and frustrated opera singer now bent
on securing fame as champion of underdogs. Equally tough and
authoritarian was the tall and rangy Scottish-born Charles Irvine.
While Irvine knew that his own membership would be more secure if
the Italians were organized, he was an opportunist as well as a maver-
ick who had initiated the early immigrant drives without notifying his
superiors in Washington.

Irvine and Zanini called an (illegal) organizational walkout for
1 August 1960; it turned into a fierce, three-week struggle that
involved an estimated 6,000 Italian workers.[22] Despite numerous
obstacles,[23] the Brandon Group workers, supported by Teamsters and
some commercial locals,[24] won a union contract. They had sabotaged
the residential field, forcing numerous contractors to form associa-
tions, strike negotiating committees, and hammer out contracts,[25]
while inaugurating a working relationship with old-line unionists and
the labour movement.[26] Still, the campaign had unionized less than
half of the residential firms, and before long it was clear that many
employers were resorting to familiar cost-cutting tactics. By spring
1961, more than 1,000 union grievances had been filed with the
Ontario Labour Relations Board.

Determined to organize a greater portion of the field, Brandon
leaders called a second strike. Though reeling from winter lay-offs,
Italian men responded enthusiastically. The 1961 strike, from 29 May
to 15 July, involved far greater numbers and the support of the old-
line unions, whose sympathy strikes shut down subway, road-paving,
and other projects. In the fourth week, more than 15,000 men were
out and some 12,000 public utilities employees looked perched to follow. A solidarity rally held at the Canadian National Exhibition
grandstand drew some 17,000 supporters.[27] The state took the strike
seriously, as evidenced by Premier Leslie Frost's 'peace plan' proposal providing for more safety inspectors, a royal commission to

investigate labour relations, and a special arbitration board to adjudi-cate alleged contract violations. These measures brought the 1961 dispute to an end, although subsequent inquiries and strikes made clear that basic conflicts were never fully resolved. That local leaders had sought help from the controversial US Teamster leader, Jimmy Hoffa, ensured that the 1961 strike even contributed to the industry's notoriety.

The issue of notoriety begs the question: were Italians tricked by the charismatic personalities who led the strikes? Did the image of adoring crowds of Italian men huddled around Irvine and Zanini con-jure up fascist-era stereotypes of Italians as 'sheep' (rather than 'men') easily misled by orators? These issues worried some men yet did not deter thousands from walking off the job. Workers recognized the leaders' talents and hoped to benefit from them. Both men were effective grassroots organizers, especially Zanini, who spent hours talking with men at job sites and in the street corners, billiard halls, and other male gathering places of Toronto's Little Italies. In the ongoing exchanges of stories about unpaid wages, on-site injuries, and family tragedies, Zanini tapped into the men's deep-seated sense of workplace injustice. He also drew effectively on the vocabulary that resonated deeply with the men's self-identity as hard-working, self-respecting, and honourable family men. Irvine especially met the men's evident desire for dynamic leadership. 'Charlie had such a way', recalled one worker. 'Nobody knew English, but the way he talked, it made sense to everyone. He inspired so much confidence, a born leader.'[28]

The Italian men who joined the campaign did so in defiance of powerful building interests and Italian community élites, most of them Italo-Canadian professionals and businessmen fearful that the strike would generate negative publicity and that the union bosses might displace their own dominance. Also opposed was the Catholic Church, whose Italian-speaking parish priests defended the integrity of the hard-pressed Italian subcontractors, whom they depicted as equally hard-working family men making ends meet. Defence of manly honour, then, was not confined to strikers. Critics invoked sim-ilar images when trying to discredit the workers' actions. Gianni Gro-hovaz, editor of the mainstream Italo-Canadian newspaper, the *Corriere Canadese*, claimed sympathy for the workers yet denounced Zanini's 'selfish desire to be *il capo* (the head) of all the Italian work-ers'. Grohovaz also partly blamed the workers for the crisis, writing that 'the immigrants, by accepting work that was unsafe or paid less than the legal rate, were letting themselves be treated as if they were second-class citizens.' His accusation that at union meetings 'gossip, profane language and political speeches had taken the place of a proper program' inferred that strikers were behaving as less than honourable men. In 1960, Italian residential workers received no support from the old-line unions, save for Teamsters truck drivers who refused to deliver supplies to housing sites. Indeed, a rivalry developed in this strike between the Brandon campaign and an AFL-Building Trades Council certification campaign.[29]

Just as family and community intersected with daily workplace life, a worker's decision to strike was not made exclusively on the building site but, rather, within the overlapping arenas of work, union hall, family, household, and community. It was influenced by transplanted familial strategies and traditions and by the networks of reciprocity that characterized relations among kin and co-villagers in the households and neighbourhoods of the immigrant wards. Here it is worth considering the basis of decision-making within Italian households. Many of Toronto's Italians brought with them a family-centred culture of work characteristic of peasant family economies, one in which household members sacrificed individual pursuits to contribute (through labour and/or earning power) to the financial well-being of the family unit. Artisanal families, though organized around a different type of work, had a similar family-oriented work ethos. It combined an assumption of patriarchal authority with a commitment to economic co-operation. As heads of the households, married men in particular enjoyed power and prestige over wives, children, and even elderly parents. Of course, some men abused their power, although, unfortunately, my evidence is silent on this issue. The immigrants described here, however, clearly felt the pressures attached to their status and derived pride from their capacity to meet their duties. As one construction worker put it: 'You make sacrifices, get up at 5 o'clock in the morning and wait for the truck to take you to sometimes you don't know where. And for what? To clean out the mud and mix cement for hours so the family can make a better life.'[30]

On both sides of the ocean, Italian men enjoyed greater freedoms, especially sexual liberties, than women, and southern European cultures are replete with double standards or codes of honour denying women the opportunities and choices permitted men. Moreover, women's sexual infractions, including adultery, were treated as dangerous transgressions that undermined the moral authority of cuckolded husbands and brought shame to the entire family. Still, Italian families, like most families, though patriarchal in organization, were social arenas of negotiation, even if among members with unequal status, power, and resources. Within pre-migration and immigrant households, women were essential to family survival—a reality that men recognized—and many did lay claim to certain rights and privileges. An Italian woman's public acknowledgement of her husband's 'superior' status did not deter her from placing herself at the centre of wide networks of family, kin, and *paesani*. Nor did it prevent her from negotiating aggressively with her husband, working around and behind him, hiding information from him, or seeking help from allies if he placed unreasonable barriers in her way. By the same token, men who might publicly boast about their authority could act differently once beyond the purview of fellow men and willingly share decision-making with their wives.[31]

In immigrant families across the diaspora, Italian peasant women appear to have maintained their customary 'power of the purse', making front-line decisions about the family budget.[32] This pattern prevailed in postwar Toronto. But Toronto's postwar Italian women differed from their counterparts in earlier and other immigrant contexts in their propensity for waged work. In Toronto, many assumed timely roles as critical wage-earners. By 1961, more than 40 per cent of adult Italian women in Toronto, mostly immigrants, were registered in the city's female labour force, mainly in low- and semi-skilled factory jobs. Thousands more worked in the informal economy, making money 'under the table' as babysitters and cleaning ladies. This pattern reflected, of course, the gap between the male breadwinner ideology and the reality of insufficient and inconsistent male wages. On average, Italian women earned half the wages of Italian men,[33] yet their income was so indispensable that it calls into question the definition of women as secondary wage-earners. Wives earned year-round wages while husbands faced seasonal or regular unemployment, and women's wages were a main source of income when men were sidelined by injury, illness, or strikes.

It is therefore not surprising that while Italian workers envisioned the strike as a battle of honour among men, they had made the decision to join, or not, in consultation with wives (and, in some cases, parents) and by weighing several factors. The reluctance of some couples to participate reflected a deep desire to secure work, at virtually any cost, out of sheer economic need. This was especially true of recent arrivals, but could also prompt those who had overextended themselves by buying a house or starting up a subcontracting firm. Uncertain of their legal rights as immigrants, some genuinely feared that the government might deport strikers. Most fearful were those immigrants who had quietly greased the palms of semi-legitimate middlemen to secure exit visas, the families of contract workers who had prematurely jumped jobs or been unceremoniously released before their one-year labour contract had officially expired, and others who for various reasons had 'fudged the facts' on their immigration papers. Some employers exploited such fears, threatening job dismissal and deportation. But in other cases workers felt loyal to the employer, frequently a relative, who had sponsored and hired them, especially when work bonds reinforced the ties of kin, village, and community. Given these conflicting demands, men's use of breadwinner rhetoric—that as male heads of household they were striking to ensure their families' survival—may have served to soften any sense of disloyalty to family or friends and resolve any sense of guilt that they were imperilling their family's status in Canada.

Indeed, consultation with wives is a recurring theme in the recollections of married strikers. According to a Brandon agent, Frank Colantonio, a peasant-turned-carpenter and immigrant organizer, negotiations with wives involved endless talk about whether the couple or family could weather the storm financially. Were their modest savings sufficient? Could a wife's earnings cover necessary costs for the duration? Could they borrow money? For some families, this meant cultivating a credit rating with local Italian store owners; for others, it meant turning to a relative who might be modestly better off. Given the youthfulness of Toronto's Italian families, many couples could not turn to older children as additional or substitute wage-earners. Those with children over 16 had to decide whether to take the child out of school to earn money. Where a son or daughter was already working, detailed calculations were made about how far such incomes could be stretched. And it was the women, of course, who found ways to feed and clothe the family and pay bills on a much reduced income. The wife of a Brandon organizer, who at the time had two toddlers, recalled that 'it was a hard time, thinking for the children, worrying about the money. But I supported my husband, was doing good things to help Italian workers, to help ourselves.'[34] For people accustomed to making sacrifices with long-term goals in mind, the decision to endure short-term pain for the prospect of greater security and safety was a difficult but not unfamiliar one.

Still, Italian women played no public role in the 1960 or 1961 strikes and their conspicuous absence from the streets and community halls deserves more explanation. As labour historians have documented, women's strike support activities, including crowd protests, picketing, and morale-building events, have featured prominently in strikes involving considerable community mobilization. Mining and textile towns 'on strike', for example, revealed women's strong ties to their community and their capacity for being 'radicals of the worst sort'—troublemakers, street fighters, and boycotters, rather than orthodox unionists.[35] While Toronto was hardly a single-industry town, the construction drives did require effective mobilization within the Italian community and beyond. Women's absence from the public events can best be explained by several related factors. First, it was partially linked to the logistics involved in waging a construction strike, where pickets were scattered across a large region—in this case, a vast territory encompassing the city's neighbouring and distant suburban and ex-urban areas of development. For many Italian women, whose daily lives were rooted in the neighbourhoods and workshops of the city, especially in the west-end wards, the work sites were largely out of their frame of reference. As one woman put it, the suburbs 'for us then, was still farm country'.[36] Also, few women would have obtained a driver's licence, making them dependent on public transportation (which could be infrequent in barely developed ex-urban areas) or men with available cars and pick-up trucks. Also important was the high ratio of women with small children, which limited women's capacity for public action. But answers related to logistics alone will not suffice. After all, car and truck pools could have been organized, had organizers considered it important. It also cannot entirely explain why women did not attend the morning rallies and solidarity events, which took place in local venues. Furthermore, Italian mothers with young children could usually find the resources for child care within their own neighbourhood and community.

Second, cultural and ideological factors were also at play. Doubtless, women's public absence reflected in part the prevailing cultural and patriarchal norms among Italian men regarding female honour and women's proper place—which, at least ideally, did not include the aggressively male sphere of a muddy, unsafe, and even violent building site. That Italian men did not envision a public role for women in these union drives is born out in the campaign rallies, slogans, and even recollections of strikers, all of which invoked the exclusively male image of men acting on the family's behalf. Nor did Italian women (like other women) find welcoming the masculine culture of union hall or construction site. Too much, however, should not be made of cultural explanations of immigrant women's behaviour, as they invariably draw on and confirm misleading racial-ethnic stereotypes. Historians have largely exploded the myth of the 'cowering' Italian woman by documenting instances of their militancy, both as strike supporters and strikers.[37] Like other women from rural or working-class backgrounds, Italian women were not necessarily constrained by a North American code of femininity that associated respectability with demure, ladylike behaviour. When they did strike, they became enthusiastic participants in shouting matches, aggressive picket-line duty, and other defiant actions.[38]

Probably the most important factor accounting for women's public absence from the construction campaigns resulted from their critical position as family wage-earners. We must return to their remarkably high rate of labour force participation in Toronto's postwar economy. The importance of their wage-earning capacity during these strikes cannot be exaggerated. In a mixed industrial economy that did offer women jobs, Italian women with construction worker husbands on strike were not confined to supporting roles. Those who had been employed continued to work, often taking on longer workdays for modest but critical pay increases. Others landed their first Canadian jobs during these campaigns, though their inexperience meant their relegation to low-skilled and low-paid work. Women's full-time and part-time jobs took on enormous importance among striking families at the same time as they imposed huge pressures on women, who faced the strains of the double day and the added pressures of stretching even more from even less.

Women's contribution to household budgets did receive public recognition during the 1961 strike when the press began probing the price being paid by strikers and their families. As in the past, strikers did not enjoy regular strike pay, and as the campaign moved into its fourth, fifth, and sixth weeks, families suffered. Some couples lost homes by defaulting on mortgages, while others could not pay the rent. In requesting financial aid from the internationals in Washington, immigrant organizer Marino Toppan noted: 'We are going to win but meantime we have hundreds of people begging for their children.'[39] But neither the occasional donations from unions nor the aid of kin and neighbours could replace the efforts of wives, who again stretched dwindling resources and toiled in shops and factories. The press highlighted Italian women's shift into the role of family breadwinner. In her profiles of striking wives, reporter Rosemary Boxer noted a depressingly familiar irony: the situation had forced many women, including the steam press operators and garment workers she interviewed, to tolerate substandard conditions, poor wages, and kickback schemes. Even at that, these women were earning the family's sole wages. Women's absence from public rallies and pickets was more than matched by their wage-earning efforts.[40]

'End Immigrant Slavery—Think of Your Families!'

The morning rally that kicked off the 1960 campaign became a recurring public spectacle in both strikes. Taking place in the smoke-filled and overcrowded rooms of an Italian movie theatre in the west end, the morning rallies began on a ceremonial note, as Irvine and Zanini led the men in silent prayer. They then quickly transformed into highly boisterous events, complete with fiery speeches and spontaneous outbursts from the floor. The costumes and artefacts of the construction worker, objects characterized by manliness, were everywhere in evidence: young men in workpants and heavy construction boots (but dressed up with inexpensive suit jackets); hundreds of small pick-up trucks parked outside the theatre; and the carpenter's two-by-four 'plank', which was waved about at meetings. The strike leaders cultivated such manly symbols as a sign of the workers' aggressive determination to win. Irvine brandished his own two-by-four, this one with a spike driven through it, calling it a workingman's 'plank of action'.

Strike leaders and organizers appealed to various themes close to workers' hearts. In speeches Irvine and Zanini stressed the integrity of the immigrants' struggle and denounced the developers and builders who opposed them. They appealed to the seriousness that men attached to their self-definition as the family's breadwinner and the fears or shame unleashed by their inability to perform it. During one meeting, Zanini dramatically took the stage with his pockets stuffed with cheques stamped NSF. Waving them furiously about, he shouted: 'This is the sort of exploitation that should be stopped. Canada is a free country and immigrants should be treated the same as Canadians!' As the crowd roared its approval, more men jumped onto the platform to produce their NSF pay-cheques. Organizer Marino Toppan shouted: 'An end to immigrant slavery—think of your families!' In response, men chanted, 'Canadian wages, Canadian hours!'[41]

Aggressive rhetoric and symbols were obvious appeals to the strikers' masculinity. Refusing to be treated like second-class citizens, Italian workers loudly defended the honour of their work and boldly asserted their right to be accorded the same respect as Canadian workers. The campaigns, recalled Abate, were 'an Italian uprising. . . . We were saying "Enough to this kind of exploitation." '[42] In articulating a masculine discourse of immigrant honour, Italian workers also drew on contrasting images of manly versus unmanly behaviour and human versus subhuman treatment. This included compelling racial metaphors, especially that of 'free' worker versus unfree 'slave'. Such distinctions, as recent scholarship reveals, have long informed the public discourse of White workers in North American labour movements. It has also shaped the discourse of marginal 'White ethnic' workers keen to dissociate themselves from the most despised racial minorities, namely Blacks and Asians, and link themselves more closely with the dominant majority.[43] Toronto's Italian workers drew a link between eliminating the 'jungle' status of the industry and gaining greater respectability within the wider society. Similar conclusions might be drawn about the recurring metaphor of the construction industry as a 'slaughterhouse'. By fighting back, it was argued, men could humanize the industry and themselves. These themes converge in Colantonio's recent memoir, in which he recalls what he said when delivering his first speech at a morning rally:

> I talked about the years of broken laws and low wages, the cut-throat competition that forced so many contractors to take advantage of Italians desperate for work, the crooked contractors who didn't hesitate to treat us like slaves and then cheat us on our wages. 'Low wages and phoney cheques are bad enough,' I said. . . . 'Even worse is the complete disregard for safety. Just take a trip out to the WCB [Workmen's Compensation Board] Rehab Centre. . . . My dear countrymen, this is not an industry. This is a slaughterhouse. . . .' I tried to appeal to the pride that I knew so many of us felt as men who worked so hard for such long hours to provide for our families, only to be treated like farm animals on the job and dangerous foreigners on the street. 'Show the world you are human beings and not the bunch of jackasses some people think you are. Show them you want a union. Show them you want a contract!'[44]

Strikers defined their actions as the angry but reasonable responses of hard-working men who had been shabbily treated, which became abundantly clear in an incident during the 1960 drive involving Johnny Lombardi, an Italian-Canadian entertainment promoter and self-proclaimed 'mayor' of 'Little Italy'. Insisting that most immigrants are 'very very happy', Lombardi blamed 'the recent noise' on a few 'young rabblerousers' and 'poolroom, coffee-counter hangers-on' who 'have no right to speak for the Italian community'. 'The statements they are making about exploitation', he added, 'is hurting the well-meaning immigrants—the one who needs a job and will work at anything to provide for his family.' Once again, a critic had invoked the image of the honourable immigrant family man to denounce the strikers. The strikers responded with a rash of angry pickets around Lombardi's grocery store. An organizer for the Laborers, Nick Gileno, told reporters: 'We are hard-working people. Lombardi lives with us and should tell the truth.' Toppan added, 'I am a good bricklayer and have worked myself up. I want Lombardi to know that I haven't time for poolrooms—I have worked every day since coming to Canada.' The strikers won this battle: Lombardi apologized and subsequently supported the 1961 strike.[45]

Convincing the wider community was a more difficult task. Italian strikers had to defend themselves against a competing, anti-immigrant discourse in which contradictory but consistently negative images of them as selfish and calculating schemers, easily manipulated dupes, and violence-prone minorities dominated. Dozens of Torontonians wrote to the city's English-language newspapers expressing disapproval, even contempt, for the strikers. The violence that marked each campaign fuelled the ire of bigots who dubbed Italians as 'hot-blooded' and incapable of respecting the law or dismissed them as a mob-like 'gang of union men'.[46]

The issue of male violence deserves scrutiny. Although strikers saw builders and developers as the villains, much of the actual conflict occurred at the job sites, where Italian picketers confronted hostile Italian and other workers whom they hoped to recruit into their union movement. Emotions ran high at the sites and assaults inevitably occurred. During the 1961 strike, for example, a housing site in Markham saw 150 strikers and workers engaged in a brick-throwing exchange, which resulted in several serious injuries and put some of the duelling men in hospital. The Toronto Builders Exchange took advantage of the situation, portraying picketers as 'goon squads' and 'ruffians' savagely destroying property and machinery.[47]

When violence did erupt, union leaders blamed employers and police. Police arrests of contractors for intimidating strikers and, in one case, waving a gun at pickets gave some credence to union charges.[48] When, for instance, strikers in North York were arrested in 1961 after allegedly trying to prevent a police officer on a motorcycle from driving through the crowd of picketers in an effort to disperse them, the Brandon executive charged police with arbitrarily confiscating picket signs from workers, rough-handling them, and calling them wops, DPs, and other derogatory names.[49] Strike organizers downplayed the violence. While admitting that men sometimes got 'carried away' during the face-to-face heckling at the sites, they insisted that order, not chaos, characterized these encounters. Their presence, insisted union organizers, gave many of the working men the encouragement they needed to join the campaign. According to Colantonio, organizers stayed calm, reminding strikers: 'We're here to communicate, to behave like gentlemen.'[50]

The question of responding with violence was a delicate one for leaders to navigate. To maintain the public claims that strikers were honourable men, defending their families and trying to win justice, union leaders had to insist that strikers were not hooligans or gangsters, but responsible and legitimate members of Canadian society. But to maintain solidarity among the striking men, leaders needed to reinforce men's claims to masculinity, among which was a sense that as men they were obliged to take action when threatened, to respond with force when necessary. Irvine's 'plank of action' was not just words—it was a board with a nail, a symbol of the workers' trades but also a potential weapon. The potential for physical force and for violence, which in part defined men's social role, had to be symbolically deployed, even as real acts of violence had to be contained.

Defending their manly honour against charges of picket-line harassment and vigilante violence became crucial, particularly during the 1961 strike when police and the courts intensified their efforts to demonize the strikers. 'Arrests will be made', promised Toronto's deputy police chief in 1961, 'as long as groups of men roam the city and terrorize other workers, contractors, and citizens.' The police tried to intimidate strikers into submission by increasing surveillance, ordering 'special details' to watch over larger sites, and arresting hundreds of strikers. Etobicoke's chief of police put it bluntly: 'We're going to take them up by the truckload and dump strikers in the Don [jail].'[51] Since few strikers could afford bail, arrested men inevitably spent some time in jail. In an incident that caused police authorities some embarrassment, police patrols rounded up strikers in Etobicoke and then, during questioning, hinted at the possibility of deportation. According to strikers' recollections, police also used other intimidation techniques, 'manhandling' the men during arrest and sometimes beating them.[52]

The courts seemed equally bent on achieving submission, but by making an example of some men. In 1961, they chose 20-year-old Giancarlo (John) Stefanini, an organizer with the Common Laborers arrested on obstruction charges. Police testified that Stefanini had incited strikers to harass working men and then refused to disperse the group when ordered to do so. Since Stefanini had spoken in Italian, the police probably had not understood him. But he was convicted and the judge endorsed Crown counsel's proposal for a stiff jail sentence: six months.[53]

But the most heavy-handed tactics of all were those of the builders and critics who raised the bogeyman of deportation. In so doing, they transformed a whispering campaign of rumour and innuendo into a public debate over the rights of Italian men to defend their honour and demand respect in a context in which they were 'othered', as foreign workers and non-citizens. The deportation question revealed the competing discourses of critics determined to undermine the strikers' legitimacy by conjuring up lurid images of hooligans disrespectful of the law and demagogue-led ruffians bent on destruction. The strikes were indeed contested terrain. Contrasting images of the honourable immigrant versus dangerous foreigner, like the contrasting explanations of the recurring violence, were more than merely linguistic symbols and rhetorical flourishes unleashed by the strike. Once articulated and effectively manipulated, they helped shape the contours of the conflict, including its escalation into a deportation affair.

H.P. Hyatt, president of the Metropolitan Toronto House and Building Association, triggered the deportation debate in June of 1961 when he requested the Minister of Immigration, Ellen Fairclough, to deport immigrants convicted of strike-related violence.[54] Fairclough refused, but the request provoked critics and supporters to respond. The discourse deployed by both groups drew on contrasting images of honourable and dishonourable men. Critics included unionists and staunch conservatives. The former revealed their distrust of Italians as unionists, usually by dubbing them the authors of their own misfortune. As one Canadian worker put it, Italians were 'willing to accept lower wages than the standard' but 'now faced with the problem of a strike, they want people to feel sorry for them.' Other unionists blamed immigrant selfishness, claiming that Italian workers had placed their desires for houses, cars, and other luxuries before the greater cause of working men. In short, Italians had failed to measure up to the honourable traditions of the labour movement.[55] Ironically, conservative anti-labour critics, keen on deportation and quick to attribute the strikes to demagogues and 'hot-blooded' Italians, also invoked images of the Italian strikers as dishonourable, untrustworthy, and even dangerous men. In a letter to the *Globe and Mail*, one writer said the strike had 'shattered' her 'confidence in Canadian democracy' because it had permitted 'a gang of union men to converge upon a construction development and intimidate the workers until naked fear makes them rush to protect their families.' Others argued that as strikers kept others from exercising their right to work, all of them should be deported. Perhaps the most unequivocal of all was the critic who described the strikers as 'nothing but a howling, screaming pack of unruly hooligans'.[56]

The strikers countered with familiar claims about peaceful information pickets and controlled crowds. Yet the debate clearly exposed their vulnerability as non-citizens and unleashed deep-seated fears. For men who brought with them well-aged suspicions of the state, as well as recent experiences with fascism and a war fought in their own backyards, the idea that governments might run roughshod over people's rights was not an entirely foreign one—the assurances of the Immigration Minister notwithstanding.

What Italian strikers could not have predicted, however, was that the deportation affair would mobilize enormous support for their campaign from within the immigrant and wider communities. Initially, Toronto's daily newspapers welcomed the strikes as a chance to eliminate immigrant exploitation in construction, though *Globe and Mail* editorials expressed concern over union rivalries and the illegality issue. The support was linked at first to the Hogg's Hollow revelations, which had graphically revealed exploitative conditions and abusive employers. A *Telegram* editorial that captured media outrage over Hogg's Hollow also mirrored the Italian workers' own claims as nation-builders: 'Men who labor beneath the surface of a city provide physical comforts and civic security to hundreds of thousands. What a lavish expenditure of energy and sacrifice to give city dwellers the most commonplace conveniences of modern life.'[57] Indeed, the conservative *Telegram* remained surprisingly sympathetic during both strikes, in part because of its labour columnist, Frank Drea, a young muckraking, crusading reporter. His columns offered 'human portraits' of beleaguered strikers and chronicled the demanding daily routines of men that, as in the case of labourer Dominic Moscone, involved 'rising at 4 am to walk fifteen miles to his pick-up depot and not returning home until after dark—all for the princely sum of $1.00 an hour.' Drea reported on injuries and woefully inadequate compensation awards, and his columns also reinforced the workers' projected image, calling them upstanding immigrants—not radicals or Communists—entitled to better protections.[58]

The greater public support was engendered in 1961. Convinced that nativists were running a smear campaign against all Italians, previously unsympathetic élites in the immigrant community came on side, including Grohovaz, who declared: 'The battle of the Italian workers has now become our battle. . . . [it] is not only about a labour dispute but involves us all in the inalienable rights of the Italian immigrants.'[59] In the face of growing violence, the English-language dailies (as in 1960) had begun to waver in their support of the strikers, but they now switched gears, condemning the builders and deportation advocates. In defending Italian men's honour, Rosemary Boxer drew on romantic stereotypes of 'sunny Italy', declaring that 'violence is not their normal way. Italians are gay and fun loving, sentimental and emotional.' But she also blamed matters on Canadian failure to 'understand' or 'help' immigrants, saying 'this whole situation is an open sore on our community and society.' A *Star* editorial expressed astonishment at such 'unwarranted intimidation' of immigrants addressing legitimate grievances. 'Canadian law', another warned, 'should not be used as a club to scare men into docile acceptance of bad working conditions.' The *Globe and Mail* agreed: 'the deportation request', it declared, 'is so contrary to the principles of democracy that one is left wondering if the builders are aware that they live in a democracy.'⁶⁰

Sympathetic Torontonians also condemned the deportation request and defended the strikers as hard-working immigrants and family men. A Canadian woman living in an Italian neighbourhood wrote: 'I have watched the men go out with their lunch boxes in the morning [and] come home at dark, bone tired and weary but always with a smile and a laugh to quiet their children. I have talked to shopkeepers who marvel they don't starve.' Another writer, H. Dust, defended the Italians against charges of staging an illegal strike with claims that it was '[e]qually abhorant [*sic*] for some contractors to take unfair advantage of immigrants'. And if unionists were among the strike's opponents, they also numbered among its strong supporters, applauding the Italians for their courage and welcoming the opportunity to create a more unified labour movement. As one Canadian worker put it: 'the immigrants are fighting our fight, along with their own.' Finally, the city's labour leaders endorsed a resolution condemning the Home Builders Association. Significantly, its wording echoed the strikers' discourse of the manly, honourable immigrant. 'What should be deported', it read, 'is long hours, low pay, deplorable and dangerous working conditions and the exploitation and cheating of immigrants who wish only to build for themselves and their families a better life in Canada.'⁶¹

The debate over deportation suggests the ways that claims to honourable masculinity could support broader claims to citizenship. Just as their claims to familial leadership justified their participation in union action, Italian working men's claims to honourable masculinity underscored their rights as members of a democratic society. Others claimed status as nation-builders. 'Italians', P. Palozzi declared in a letter to the press, 'did not come to Canada to steal jobs or to work at low rates, but to build a better, stronger Canada. We don't know where the race track is, or where Florida and California are in winter—but we know where our job is.'[62] If designed and maintained properly, the gendered norms of masculinity, forged out of particular class and ethnic context, held the power to signify citizenship and nation-building, even for the least powerful groups of immigrant working people.

Masculinity—Some Theoretical and Political Issues

For labour scholars, unionists, and Italian workers, the impact of the immigrant union drives on industrial relations in the construction industry remains open for debate.[63] But the strikes offer an opportunity to explore the dynamic processes involved in the formation of the gender identities of immigrant male workers, to probe the shifting boundaries, transitions, and transformative moments, the configurations of work, household, and community, and the interplay of transplanted and emergent strategies, customs, and gender relations as they unfolded in an immigrant context.

A central question has framed this particular rendering of the strikes: how did men who otherwise felt disadvantaged, marginal, and exploited derive a sense of manly honour? In seeking to address that question, this chapter draws some larger conclusions. It argues against a static, snapshot view of masculinity (and, indeed, femininity) or idealist constructions of manhood. It speaks in favour of studies of masculinity that both acknowledge the active role that language, symbols, and discourse can play in the construction of class, gender, and racial-ethnic identities *and* seek to integrate a sensitivity to discursive practices into, as Kirk suggests, a 'wider framework of analysis which embraces agency and structure, saying and doing, the conscious and unconscious, and the willed and intended consequences of individual and social action and thought.'[64] Gender, like class or ethnicity, is neither a static structure nor a neatly packaged set of prescribed practices and identities. It is an evolving, relational process. The gender identity of Italian immigrant construction workers did not arrive fully formed upon their arrival in postwar Toronto but was negotiated and remade in changing and challenging contexts. Men articulated and projected their masculine image and manly discourse amid the transitional contexts occasioned by their migration experience and the class exploitation, gendered practices, immigrant households, racial derision, and material sacrifice that helped define that experience. The dominant masculine discourse of the honourable immigrant that emerged within the overlapping contexts of rickety scaffolds, crowded flats, multi-family households, neighbourhood parks, and union halls both articulated and reinforced Italian men's determination to earn public respect for labours performed and rehabilitate their customary status and privilege as family breadwinner and protector.

Second, an explicit assumption underlying this paper, namely, that historians seriously take up the challenge of scrutinizing men as gendered subjects, is intended as more than an élitist exercise in deconstructing the multiple meanings embedded in the metaphors, 'Italian human steam shovel', 'wetback', or 'almost black' pick-and-shovel man. As an exercise in politically engaged scholarship, this study reminds us of the crucial role that women and the politics of gender play in the political mobilization of male workers and working-class communities. On the surface, the construction strikes appeared to be exclusively male dramas orchestrated by Italian men (and their male allies). Yet, the men's decision to 'fight back' and their capacity to endure two long and bitter struggles without benefit of strike pay were contingent in large part on women's wage-earning and other forms of support and, to a lesser degree, on the support mobilized within the immigrant and wider communities. The union drives were limited in scope, aiming at concrete bread-and-butter issues, yet they hint at the wisdom of labour strategies aimed at cultivating cross-gender, community, and broad-based alliances.

Finally, this chapter suggests that we think carefully about a hierarchy of masculinities.[65] Even a study aimed at retrieving the dignity of men treated abysmally by more powerful men and vested capitalist interests cannot ignore the patriarchal privileges and advantages that even marginal immigrant men enjoyed compared to their wives and other women in their community. Nor can we continue to celebrate naïvely the violent actions of men on strike.[66] Yet we need also to acknowledge that masculinities, like real men, do not enjoy equal status, power, and influence. In the same spirit in which feminist labour historians have argued against monolithic, essentialist models of patriarchy,[67] this essay suggests the need to discern between the masculinities of powerful men and those of homosexuals, racial-ethnic minorities, workers, and the poor.

Notes

McPherson, Morgan, Forestell, Introduction

1. This phrase is customarily attributed to Joan Scott (see 'Gender: A Useful Category of Historical Analysis', in her *Gender and the Politics of History* [New York, 1988], 28–50), but it was also used by Elizabeth Fox-Genovese, who wrote in 1982 that 'we must adopt gender systems as a fundamental category of historical analysis, understanding that such systems are historically, not biologically, determined.' Fox-Genovese, 'Placing Women's History in History', *New Left Review* 133 (May-June 1982): 6.

   Recent international publications in gender history include the journal *Gender and History*, as well as collections such as Laura Frader and Sonya Rose, eds, *Gender and Class in Modern Europe* (Ithaca, NY, 1996); Lynn Abrams and Elizabeth Harvey, eds, *Gender Relations in German History: Power, Agency and Experience from the Sixteenth to the Twentieth Century* (Durham, NC, 1997); and Robert Shoemaker and Mary Vincent, eds, *Gender and History in Western Europe* (London, 1998).

2. Gisela Bock, 'Women's History and Gender History: Aspects of An International Debate', *Gender and History* 1, 1 (1989): 18.

3. Joy Parr provides a most useful summary of these debates among feminist historians in 'Gender History and Historical Practice', *Canadian Historical Review* 76, 3 (Sept. 1995): 354–76. See also Judith Bennett, 'Feminism and History', *Gender and History* 1, 3 (Autumn 1989): 252–72; Joan Hoff, 'The Pernicious Effects of Poststructuralism on Women's History', *The Chronicle of Higher Education* (Oct. 1993):

B3–5. The Canadian debate on this was initiated in Franca Iacovetta and Mariana Valverde, eds, *Gender Conflicts: New Essays in Women's History* (Toronto, 1992). The debate was sharpened through an exchange in *Left History*. See Joan Sangster, 'Beyond Dichotomies: Reassessing Gender History and Women's History in Canada', *Left History* 3, 1 (Spring/Summer 1995): 109–21; Karen Dubinsky and Lynne Marks, 'Beyond Purity: A Response to Sangster', and Franca Iacovetta and Linda Kealey, 'Women's History, Gender History and Debating Dichotomies', *Left History* 3, 2 and 4, 1 (Fall 1995/Spring 1996): 205–37.

4. These debates have been pronounced in North America in part because fledgling programs in women's history (and women's studies) sometimes appear jeopardized by proposals for gender history (or gender studies) alternatives. Robert Shoemaker and Mary Vincent, 'Introduction', in Shoemaker and Vincent, eds, *Gender and History in Western Europe*, 7, provide a non-North American perspective on this question.

5. Neville Kirk, 'History, language, ideas and post-modernism: a materialist view', in Keith Jenkins, ed., *The Postmodern History Reader* (London, 1997).

6. Mariana Valverde, 'Gender History/Women's History', *Journal of Women's History* 5, 1 (1993): 121–8.

7. Scott, 'Gender: A Useful Category of Historical Analysis', 42–5. Ruth Pierson's *'They're Still Women After All': The Second World War and Canadian Womanhood* (Toronto, 1986) provides an excellent example of the military's concern with gender relations as a way of maintaining hierarchy. See also Cynthia Enloe, *Bananas, Beaches and Bases: Making Feminist Sense of International Politics* (London, 1989).

8. Michele Barrett, 'Words and Things: Materialism and Method in Contemporary Feminist Analysis', in Barrett and Anne Phillips, eds, *Destabilizing Theory: Contemporary Feminist Debates* (Stanford, Calif., 1992), 201–19.

9. For a ground-breaking exploration of the concept of women's vs men's experiences, see Joan Kelly, 'Did Women Have a Renaissance?', in *The Selected Essays of Joan Kelly* (Chicago, 1984).

10. See E.P. Thompson, *The Making of the English Working Class* (New York, 1963). Christine Stansell's *City of Women: Sex and Class in New York, 1789–1860* (Chicago, 1987) and Barbara Taylor's *Eve and the New Jerusalem: Socialism and Feminism in the Nineteenth Century* (London, 1984) are excellent examples of socialist-feminist work that probes the ideological dimensions of working-class womanhood, women's experiences, and their resistance to class and gender inequities.

11. Christine Stansell, 'Response to Joan Scott', *International Labor and Working Class History* 31 (Spring 1987).

12. See Mariana Valverde, 'Poststructuralist Gender Historians: Are We Those Names?', *Labout/Le Travail* 25 (Spring 1990): 227–36.

13. For an earlier example of such work in Canadian women's history, see Linda Kealey, ed., *A Not Unreasonable Claim: Women and Reform, 1880s to 1920s* (Toronto, 1979).

14. See, for example, Jacqueline Jones, *Labor of Love, Labor of Sorrow: Black Women, Work and the Family from Slavery to the Present* (New York, 1985); Ellen Carol Dubois and Vicki L. Ruiz, eds, *Unequal Sisters: A Multicultural Reader in U.S. Women's History* (New York and London, 1990). For a theoretical discussion, see Elizabeth Spelman, *Inessential Woman: Problems of Exclusion in Feminist Thought* (Boston, 1988).

15. See, for example, *Gender and History*, Special Issue on Gender, Nationalisms and National Identities 5, 2 (Summer 1993); also *History Workshop Journal*, Special Issue on Colonial and Post-Colonial History 36 (Autumn 1993).

16. For example, see Anna Davin, 'Imperialism and Motherhood', *History Workshop Journal* 5 (Spring 1978): 9–65; Vron Ware, *Beyond the Pale: White Women, Racism and History* (London, 1992); Carroll Smith-Rosenberg, 'Captured Subjects/Savage Others: Violently Engendering the New American', *Gender and History* 5, 2 (Summer 1993): 177–95.

17. See Parr, 'Gender History and Historical Practice', 372–3, for a discussion of the need for specificity.

18. These issues are taken up by John Tosh, 'What Should Historians Do With Masculinity? Reflections on Nineteenth-Century Britain', *History Workshop Journal* 38 (Autumn 1994): 179–202. See also Joy Parr, *The Gender of Breadwinners: Women, Men and Change in Two Industrial Towns, 1880–1950* (Toronto, 1990).

19. See, for example, J.A. Mangan and James Walvin, eds, *Manliness and Morality: Middle-Class Masculinity in Britain and America, 1800–1940* (Manchester, UK, 1987).

20. See Ava Baron, 'On Looking at Men: Masculinity and the Making of a Gendered Working-Class History', in Anne-Louise Shapiro, ed., *Feminists Revision History* (New Brunswick, NJ, 1994).

21. For examples of such scholarship, see George Chauncey, *Gay New York: Gender, Urban Culture and the Making of the Gay Male* (New York, 1994); Alan Bérubé, *Coming Out Under Fire: The History of Gay Men and Women in World War II* (New York, 1990).

22. For a discussion of the problematics surrounding the category 'lesbian' in history, see Martha Vicinus, ' "They Wonder To Which Sex I Belong": The Historical Roots of the Modern Lesbian Identity', *Feminist Studies* 18, 3 (Fall 1992): 467–97.

23. Gail Bederman, *Manliness and Civilization: A Cultural History of Gender and Race in the United States, 1880–1917* (Chicago, 1995), 5.

24. Bettina Bradbury, Peter Gossage, Evelyn Kolish, and Alan Stewart, 'Property and Marriage: The Law and the Practice in Early Nineteenth Century Montreal', *Histoire sociale/Social History* 26, 51 (May 1993): 9–39.

25. See Janice Potter-MacKinnon, *While the Women Only Wept: Loyalist Refugee Women in Eastern Ontario* (Montreal and Kingston, 1993).

26. See Elizabeth Jane Errington, *Wives and Mothers, Schoolmistresses and Scullery Maids: Working Women in Upper Canada, 1790–1840* (Montreal and Kingston, 1995); Katherine M.J. McKenna, 'The Role of Women in the Establishment of Social Status in Early Upper Canada', *Ontario History* 83, 3 (Sept. 1990): 179–206.

27. See Katherine M.J. McKenna, *A Life of Propriety: Anne Murray Powell and Her Family, 1753–1849* (Montreal and Kingston, 1994); Constance Backhouse, *Petticoats and Prejudice: Women and Law in Nineteenth-Century Canada* (Toronto, 1991).

28. See, for example, Kealey, ed., *A Not Unreasonable Claim*.

29. See Ruth Frager, *Sweatshop Strife: Class, Ethnicity, and Gender in the Jewish Labour Movement of Toronto 1900–1939* (Toronto, 1993); Graham Lowe, *Women and the Administrative Revolution* (Toronto, 1987).

30. Carolyn Strange, *Toronto's Girl Problem: The Perils and Pleasures of the City, 1880–1920* (Toronto, 1995).

31. Cynthia Commachio, *'Nations Are Built of Babies': Saving Ontario's Mothers and Children, 1900–1940* (Montreal and Kingston, 1993); Agnes Calliste, 'Race, Gender, and Canadian Immigration Policy: Blacks from the Caribbean, 1900–1932', in Joy Parr and Mark Rosenfeld, eds, *Gender and History in Canada* (Toronto, 1996).

32. Meg Luxton, *More Than a Labour of Love: Three Generations of Women's Work in the Home* (Toronto, 1980); Joan Sangster, *Earning Respect: The Lives of Working Women in Small-Town Ontario, 1920–1960* (Toronto, 1995); Pamela Sugiman, *Labour's Dilemma: The Gender Politics of Auto Workers in Canada, 1939–79* (Toronto, 1994).

33. Mary Louise Adams, *The Trouble With Normal* (Toronto, 1997); Line Chamberland, 'Remembering Lesbian Bars: Montréal, 1955–1975', *Journal of Homosexuality* 25, 3 (1993): 231–69; Becki Ross, *The House That Jill Built: A Lesbian Nation in Formation* (Toronto, 1995).

34. Jack Granatstein, 'Foreword', in Parr and Rosenfeld, eds, *Gender and History in Canada*, v.

35. Natalie Davis, a practitioner of gender history well before the term was coined, recently observed how her teaching and scholarship were shaped by the interrelatedness of women's history and 'men's history—what we

used to call the "relations between the sexes"', paper presented at Celebrating Twenty-Five Years: Women's Studies at the University of Toronto, 2 Oct. 1996. For her earlier observations on the field of women's history, see 'Women's History in Transition: The European Case', *Feminist Studies* 3, 3/4 (Spring/Summer 1976).

Chapter 1
Morgan, 'When Bad Men Conspire, Good Men Must Unite'

I would like to thank the University of Toronto Press for permission to use material from my book, *Public Men and Virtuous Women: The Gendered Languages of Religion and Politics in Upper Canada, 1791–1850* (1996).

1. For the meanings of loyalty to Britain and her political institutions in Upper Canada, see David Mills, *The Idea of Loyalty in Upper Canada, 1784–1850* (Montreal and Kingston, 1988).

2. See, for example, J.A. Mangan and James Walvin, eds, *Manliness and Morality: Middle-Class Masculinity in Britain and America* (Manchester, UK, 1987); Mark C. Carnes and Clyde Griffen, eds, *Meanings for Masculinity: Constructions of Masculinity in Victorian America* (Chicago, 1990).

3. The literature in this field is enormous, but see, for example, Linda Kerber, *Women of the Republic: Intellect and Ideology in Revolutionary America* (Chapel Hill, NC, 1980); Ruth H. Bloch, 'The Gendered Meanings of Virtue in Revolutionary America', *Signs* 13, 1 (Autumn 1987): 37–57. For France, Joan Landes, *Women and the Public Sphere in the Age of the French Revolution* (Ithaca, NY, 1988). For Britain, Dorothy Thompson, 'Women and Nineteenth-Century Radical Politics: A Lost Dimension', in Juliet Mitchell and Ann Oakley, eds, *The Rights and Wrongs of Women* (Harmondsworth, 1976); Anna Clarke, 'The Rhetoric of Chartist Domesticity: Gender, Language and Class in the 1830s and 1840s', *Journal of British Studies* 31 (Jan. 1992): 62–88.

4. Joan Scott, *Gender and the Politics of History* (New York, 1988), 39.

5. Carroll Smith-Rosenberg, 'Discovering the Subject of the "Great Constitutional Discussion," 1786–1789,' *Journal of American History* 79, 3 (Dec. 1992): 845.

6. The literature on Upper Canadian politics is extensive. For an overview of political developments, see Gerald M. Craig, *Upper Canada: The Formative Years, 1784–1841* (Toronto, 1963); J.M.S. Careless, *The Union of the Canadas: The Growth of Canadian Institutions, 1841–1857* (Toronto, 1967); Colin Read, 'Conflict to Consensus: The Political Culture of Upper Canada', *Acadiensis* 19, 2 (Spring 1990): 169–85.

7. See issues of the *Upper Canada Gazette*, 1804–10; also Craig, *Upper Canada*, 57–65.
8. Many historians of Upper Canada, particularly of political issues, have made use of the colonial press. Two recent works make extensive use of newspapers; see Jane Errington, *The Lion, the Eagle, and Upper Canada: A Developing Colonial Ideology* (Montreal and Kingston, 1987); Mills, *The Idea of Loyalty*. To date there is no comprehensive study of the Upper Canadian press, but see W.H. Kesterton, *A History of Journalism in Canada* (Toronto, 1967), 11–24; also Carl Benn, 'The Upper Canadian Press, 1793–1814', *Ontario History* 70, 2 (June 1978): 91–114; J.J. Talman, 'The Newspapers of Upper Canada a Century Ago', *Canadian Historical Review* 19 (1938): 9–23. It is difficult, if not impossible, to determine circulation figures for this period and to state with any certainty the percentage of the population that participated in shaping political discourses. Kesterton (p. 11) suggests that, in 1833, the 30 papers in the province had a combined circulation of 20,000; the province's Euro-Canadian population at that time was approximately 234,000. Historians have noted, however, that Upper Canadians continued the eighteenth-century practice of passing newspapers around and reading them aloud in homes, churches, taverns, and workplaces, so that it is possible that literacy was not always required to participate in political debates. See Graeme Patterson, *History and Communications: Harold Innis, Marshall McLuhan, the Interpretation of History* (Toronto, 1990), 194; Paul Rutherford, *The Making of the Canadian Media* (Toronto, 1978), 7.
9. Francis Collins, who had arrived in the colony in 1818 from Ireland, was the publisher and editor of the reform paper the *Canadian Freeman*, which published from 1825 to just before Collins's death from cholera, in 1834. H.P. Gundy, *Dictionary of Canadian Biography* (*DCB*), VI (1987), 164–6. William Lyon Mackenzie (1795–1861) came to Canada in 1820 and began his career as a journalist and merchant, publishing the *Colonial Advocate* in 1824 from his home in Queenston and then in York, where he launched into full-blown attacks on the political élite of that town. He was elected in 1827 as the member of the assembly for York; in 1834, with York's incorporation as Toronto, he became an alderman and then mayor. Mackenzie continued in his opposition of what he perceived to be official corruption, an opposition that culminated in his leadership of the armed Rebellion in Upper Canada in December 1837. Along with many others who had taken up arms, Mackenzie fled to New York state and spent the 1840s there until granted a pardon by the Upper Canadian government in 1849. He re-entered politics in 1851 as the representative for Haldimand County, a seat he held until his resignation in 1858. See

Frederick H. Armstrong and Ronald J. Stagg, *DCB*, IX, 496–510. Jesse Ketchum, the American-born tanner, reformer, and philanthropist, was active in York and provincial politics from 1820 to 1834, during which time he opposed state funding for the Church of England, sat for York as a member of the assembly with Mackenzie, and worked for the latter's reinstatement on the many occasions when he was expelled from the assembly. See Lilian F. Gates, 'Jesse Ketchum', *DCB*, IX, 422–34. Other, similar papers were the *St Thomas Liberal*, 1832–7 (surviving issues, 1832–3) and the *Niagara Spectator*, published at Niagara by Bartemus Ferguson, 1817–19.

10. Rutherford, *The Making of the Canadian Media*, 7.
11. An analysis of Canadian political culture that acknowledges such links is Gordon T. Stewart, *The Origins of Canadian Politics: A Comparative Approach* (Vancouver, 1986).
12. See Olivia Smith, *The Politics of Language: 1791–1819* (Oxford, 1984), 20, for a discussion of the hegemonic effects of Johnson's *Dictionary*.
13. 'Front Page Exchange', *Upper Canada Gazette*, 25 Jan. 1823.
14. See also 'Always Something New', *Niagara Gleaner*, 31 Aug. 1833. In her *Enlightened Absences: Neo-Classical Configurations of the Feminine* (Urbana, Ill., 1988), Ruth Salvaggio examines the ways in which 'woman' personified hysteria and excess for writers such as Swift.
15. See the work on the French Revolution, most notably that of Lynn Hunt, *Politics, Culture, and Class in the French Revolution* (Berkeley, 1984), 39.
16. *Upper Canada Gazette*, 24 Feb. 1825; ibid., 7 July 1827.
17. *Niagara Spectator*, 6 Nov. 1824.
18. *Patriot and Farmers' Monitor*, 31 May 1833. The paper was also fond of identifying reformers as the faction of the 'knife, firebrand, and bludgeon'.
19. *Ibid.*, 29 Aug. 1833.
20. Mackenzie's son James was born in 1814 in Alyth, Scotland (*DCB*, IX, 497). He was cared for by his grandmother, Elizabeth Mackenzie, and in 1822 emigrated to Upper Canada with her to join his father, where he worked as an apprentice in his printing shop. While the circumstances of James's birth were not seized upon by his father's enemies, Mackenzie was accused of beating and abusing James in order to upset Elizabeth (*Canadian Freeman*, 7 Oct. 1830).
21. For a discussion of such fears, see Morgan, *Public Men and Virtuous Women*, 81–3, 106–7. See also Lynne Marks's essay in this volume.
22. *Upper Canada Gazette*, 26 May 1827.
23. *Kingston Chronicle*, 1 Feb. 1822.
24. *Patriot*, 14 June 1833.

25. Samuel P. Jarvis, *Statement of Facts, Relating to the Trespass, on the Printing Press, in the Possession of Mr. William Lyon Mackenzie, in June 1826* (York, 1828), 9.

26. *Ibid.*, 14, 15–16.

27. For a discussion of such defences of female honour, see Cecilia Morgan, '"In Search of the Phantom Misnamed Honour": Duelling in Upper Canada', *Canadian Historical Review* 76, 4 (1995): 529–62.

28. This description of 'country' rhetoric is necessarily reductionist. For a more complex and nuanced analysis, see J. Pocock, 'The Varieties of Whiggism', in his *Virtue, Commerce, and History: Essays on Political Thought and History* (Cambridge, 1985). See also Paul Romney, 'From the Rule of Law to Responsible Government: Ontario Political Culture and the Origins of Canadian Statism', *Historical Papers* (1988): 91–7, for a discussion of some of the problems with the use of a 'court-country' model in the Upper Canadian context.

29. 'When Bad Men Conspire and Good Men Must Unite', *Colonial Advocate*, 7 May 1829.

30. 'The Editor's Address to the Public', ibid., 18 May 1824.

31. Francis Collins's attacks on Mackenzie, Egerton Ryerson, and Jesse Ketchum in the pages of the *Canadian Freeman* were an exception.

32. See Paul Romney, 'A Conservative Reformer in Upper Canada: Charles Fothergill, Responsible Government and the "British Party," 1824–1840', *Historical Papers* (1984): 42–62.

33. *Colonial Advocate*, 29 Dec. 1825.

34. 'To the Electors of Members of Assembly', ibid., 18 May 1824; see also 'To the Independent Electors of the County of York', ibid., 8 Nov. 1832.

35. Letter from 'A Friend to Liberty', ibid., 3 Jan. 1833; 'To the Electors of Upper Canada', ibid., 8 July 1824; 'Appeals to the People of Upper Canada', ibid., 9 Sept. 1830; 'To the Mechanics and Labourers of Toronto', ibid., 20 Mar. 1834; report of York Constitutional Meeting, *Canadian Freeman*, 21 Aug. 1828; 'Another Triumph for the People', ibid., 25 Sept. 1828.

36. 'A Friend to Liberty', *Colonial Advocate*, 3 Jan. 1833; see also 'Address of the Markham Township meeting to William Lyon Mackenzie', ibid., 6 Feb. 1834.

37. For this material in Upper Canada, see Morgan, *Public Men and Virtuous Women*, ch. 1. Loyalist women's ambivalent relationship to patriotic language is examined in Janice Potter Mackinnon, *While the Women Only Wept: Loyalist Refugee Women in Eastern Ontario* (Montreal and Kingston, 1993).

38. 'To the Electors of Members of Assembly', *Colonial Advocate*, 18 May 1824. French republicans also equate the *ancien régime*'s absolutism

with effeminacy and women's power in government. See Landes, *Women and the Public Sphere*, 147.

39. Mackenzie, letter to John Beverley Robinson, *Colonial Advocate*, 3 June 1824; 'On the State of the Colony', ibid ., 10 Jan. 1828; resolutions of Yarmouth public meetings, ibid., 3 Apr. 1834; editorial, ibid., 9 Aug. 1834; editorial, ibid., 24 Sept. 1835; Appendix F, 'Independence!', in Colin Lindsey, *The Life and Times of William Lyon Mackenzie* (Toronto, 1862), 358–62.

40. 'Address to Independent Electors of County of York', *Colonial Advocate*, 8 Nov. 1832.

41. Editorial, ibid., 18 July 1833.

42. 'Address of the Markham Township Meeting', ibid., 6 Feb. 1834.

43. *Colonial Advocate*, 3 Nov. 1831.

44. Ibid., 6 Sept. 1834; see editorial, ibid., 3 Nov. 1831.

45. Ibid.; also 25 May 1826.

46. Ibid., 4 July 1836.

47. For discussions of women and the family in the French and American Revolutions, see Landes, *Women and the Public Sphere*, 147–8; Kerber, *Women of the Republic*, 269–88; Bloch, 'The Gendered Meanings of Virtue', 46–7.

48. 'To the Electors of Members of Assembly', *Colonial Advocate*, 18 May 1824. Although reformer Charles Cuncombe discussed both the family and the importance of women's education in his *Report on Education*, his was a rare consideration of the private realm.

49. Carol Pateman, *The Sexual Contract* (Stanford, Calif., 1988), 70.

50. 'The Declaration of the Reformers of the City of Toronto to their Fellow Reformers of Upper Canada', 2 Aug. 1837, reprinted in Lindsey, *Life and Times*, 344.

51. See Paula Baker, 'The Domestication of Politics: Women and American Political Society, 1780–1920', *American Historical Review* 89, 3 (1984): 624–5; Kerber, *Women of the Republic*, 27–41; Bloch, 'The Gendered Meanings of Virtue', 45–6.

52. Dorothy Thompson, 'The Women', in her *The Chartists* (London, 1984).

53. While we lack a truly comprehensive analysis of reformers' political philosophies, see Romney, 'From the Rule of Law to Responsible Government'. My comparison here is with the French Revolution. 'Through their language, images, and daily political activities, revolutionaries worked to reconstitute society and social relations. They consciously sought to break with the French past and to establish the basis for a new national community.' Hunt, *Politics, Culture, and Class*, 12.

54. See Mills, 'The Controversy over Legitimate Opposition: Reform Loyalty before the Rebellion', in his *The Idea of Loyalty*.

55. See, for example, 'The Declaration of the Reformers of the City of Toronto', 2 Aug. 1837, reprinted in Lindsey, *Life and Times*, 334–44; *The Constitution*, 11 Oct. 1837; *Mackenzie's Gazette*, 17 Apr. 1838.

56. Lower Canada had been occasionally defined as feminine, a province that had been outraged and must be delivered by independent manhood. See *Colonial Advocate*, 22 Feb. 1834. Mackenzie had also depicted the Bank of Upper Canada as a 'jealous old lady', ugly and malicious. *Colonial Advocate*, 19 Feb. 1835; *The Constitution*, 21 May 1837.

57. See Allan Greer, 'La république des hommes, les Patriotes de 1837 face aux femmes', *Revue d'histoire de l'Amérique française* 44, 4 (printemps 1991): 507–28.

58. *St Thomas Liberal* as quoted in *The Constitution*, 30 Aug. 1837.

59. *The Constitution*, 22 Nov. 1837.

60. *Mackenzie's Gazette*, 17 Apr. 1838; 'Wholesale Robbery', ibid., 12 May 1838; 'A Letter to the Friends of Freedom in Upper Canada', ibid., 4 Aug. 1838.

61. Ibid.

62. Ibid.

63. Colin Coates examines the use of insult and rumour, particularly around illegitimate sexuality, in attacking authority in 'Authority and Illegitimacy in New France: The Burial of Bishop Vallier and Madeleine de Vérchéres vs. the Priest of Batiscan', *Histoire sociale/Social History* 22, 43 (May 1989): 65–90.

64. *Mackenzie's Gazette*, 12 May 1838.

65. Ibid., 19 Sept. 1838.

66. Ibid., 23 June 1838.

67. Ibid., 26 May 1838; 1 Sept. 1838; 10 Nov. 1838.

68. Conservatives appealed to men as heads of households in attempts to rouse opposition to the Rebellion (see 'To the Men of the Home District', *Patriot*, 3 Nov. 1837; ibid., 8 Dec. 1837). See also Samuel Thompson, *Reminiscences of a Canadian Pioneer for the Last Fifty Years* (Toronto, 1884), 118, who attributed his and his peers' loyalty to the government to Bond Head's rhetoric, which called to fathers and sons to protect hearth and home. Joseph Hilts, *Experiences of a Backwoods Preacher* (Toronto, 1892), 22, recalled a similar experience, although it was his father and older family members who talked him out of his support for the Rebellion.

69. See Jon P. Klancher, *The Making of the English Reading Audience, 1790–1832* (Madison, Wis., 1987), 77, for a discussion of the multiple meanings of signs in the popular press, especially the notion of 'the crowd'.

70. For a discussion of some literate Euro-Canadian women's reactions to and participation in Upper Canadian politics, see Morgan, *Public Men and Virtuous Women*, 94–6.

Chapter 2
Poutanen, The Homeless, the Whore, the Drunkard, and the Disorderly

1. Quarter Sessions Documents (QSD), 2–9–1836.
2. QSD, 8–9–1841.
3. QSD, 19–2–1841.
4. These ideas were originally presented in Tamara Myers and Mary Anne Poutanen, 'Tales of Women's Lives on the Streets: A Comparative Study of the Policing of Female Vagrants in Montreal, 1810–1842 and 1890–1930', paper presented at the 1994 CHA meeting at the University of Calgary. This current study is part of a much larger investigation that examines male and female vagrancy in Montreal, 1780–1843. See Tamara Myers, 'Criminal Women and Bad Girls: Regulation and Punishment in Montreal, 1890–1930', Ph.D. thesis (McGill University, 1996), ch. 2.
5. See, for instance, the work of Paul T. Ringenbach, *Tramps and Reformers 1873–1916: The Discovery of Unemployment in New York* (Westport, Conn., 1973); Sidney Harring, *Policing a Class Society: The Experience of American Cities, 1865–1915* (New Brunswick, NJ, 1983); James Pitsula, 'The Treatment of Tramps in Late Nineteenth Century Toronto', *Historical Papers* (1980); Eric H. Monkkonen, 'A Disorderly People? Urban Order in the Nineteenth and Twentieth Centuries', *Journal of American History* 68 (Dec. 1981); Jeffrey S. Adler, 'Vagging the Demons and Scoundrels: Vagrancy and the Growth of St. Louis, 1830–1861', *Journal of Urban History* 13, 1 (Nov. 1986).
6. The most important work in this area is Christine Stansell, *City of Women: Sex and Class in New York, 1789–1860* (Chicago, 1986). Other studies include Penelope J. Corfield, 'Walking the City Streets: The Urban Odyssey in Eighteenth-Century England', *Journal of Urban History* 16, 2 (Feb. 1990); Mary P. Ryan, *Women in Public: Between Banners and Ballots, 1825–1880* (Baltimore, 1990); Marilynn Wood Hill, *Their Sisters' Keepers: Prostitution in New York City, 1830–1870* (New York, 1993).
7. Cases involving vagrancy were heard outside of the formal courts, in Petty Sessions, and before one or more justices of the peace. This tribunal, which met at a time and place determined by the justices, dealt with minor misdemeanours punishable by fine or imprisonment. Donald Fyson, *The Court Structure of Quebec and Lower Canada, 1764 to 1860* (Montreal, 1994), 59.
8. Less than one-tenth of the incidents involved women where occupation of the father or husband is known. Consequently, I have not included a discussion of social class, which awaits more rigorous family reconstitution.

9. The remaining 0.7 per cent comprised a minuscule group who could not be categorized as Francophone or non-Francophone.

10. Jean-Claude Robert, *Atlas Historique de Montréal* (Montreal, 1994), 79.

11. National Archives (NA), RG4 B14, Police Register, vol. 38, 9–12–1836.

12. Those arrested six or more times represented 11 per cent of the total.

13. QSD, 5–1–1831.

14. QSD, 26–10–1831.

15. Traveller R.H. Bonnycastle, *The Canadas in 1841* (Wakefield, Que., 1968): 76–7, described the hustle and bustle of Montreal street activity:

> In this city, one is amused by seeing the never changing lineaments, the long queue, the bonnet-rouge, and the incessant garrulity, of Jean Baptiste, mingling with the sober demeanour, the equally unchanging feature, and the national plaid, of the Highlander; whilst the untutored sons of labour, from the green isle of the ocean, are here as thoughtless, as ragged, and as numerous, as at Quebec. Amongst all these, the shrewd and calculating citizen from the neighbouring republic drives his hard bargains with all his wonted zeal and industry, amid the fumes of Jamaica and gin-sling. These remarks apply, of course, to the streets only.

16. In contrast to the denseness of the old city, the Montreal suburbs were described as containing a number of residences often surrounded by pleasure-grounds of great beauty. See, for example, Thomas Hamilton, *Men and Manners* (London, [1833] 1843), 421–2). The streets were depicted as airy, wide, and running the entire length of the city. See Joseph Bouchette, *A Topographical Description of the Province of Lower Canada, with Remarks upon Upper Canada and on the Relative connexion of Both Provinces with the USA* (London, 1815), 142.

17. George Henry (Hume), *The emigrant's guide; or, Canada as it is. Comprising details related to the domestic policy, commerce and agriculture, of the Upper and Lower Provinces, comprising matter of general information and interest, especially intended for the use of settlers and emigrants* (New York, 1832), 10.

18. Thomas Fowler, *The journal of a tour through British America to the falls of Niagara* (Aberdeen, 1832), 126.

19. Buckingham, *Canada, Nova Scotia, New Brunswick and the Other British Provinces in North America* (London, 1843), 150; Adam Hodgson, *Letters from North America, written during a tour in the United States and Canada* (London, 1824), 374; John McDonald, *Narrative of a voyage to Quebec and journey from thence to New Lanark in Upper Canada. Detailing the hardships and difficulties which an emigrant has to encounter, before and after his settlement; with an account of the*

country, as it regards its climate, soil, and the actual condition of its inhabitants (Edinburgh, 1823), 31.

20. William Henry Atherton, *Montreal 1535–1914, vol. 2, Under British Rule 1760–1914* (Montreal, 1914), 131.

21. Jacob Marston, the High Constable for the District of Montreal, requested the presiding justice of the peace on 10 July 1817 to 'summon two or more constables to attend the beach at least on Sunday to see that the said regulation be strictly observed.' QSD, Presentment of the Grand Jury, 19–7–1817.

22. Corfield, 'Walking the City Streets', 159.

23. Stansell, *City of Women*, 41–2.

24. Ibid., 75.

25. Elizabeth Blackmar, *Manhattan for Rent, 1785–1850* (Ithaca, NY, 1989), 151.

26. Jean-Marie Fecteau, 'La pauvrete, le crime, l'État: Essai sur l'économie politique du contrôle social au Québec, 1791–1840', Thèse du doctorat (U. de Paris, VII, 1983), 302–5.

27. See Jan Noel, *Canada Dry: Temperance Crusades before Confederation* (Toronto, 1995), 58–66.

28. For example, the Montreal Ladies Benevolent Society separated applicants for their charity into the deserving and undeserving poor. See *Gazette*, 5–10–1833.

29. Prominent public male figures who made up the grand juries were concerned about the influence of female criminals on their younger counterparts in the prisons. QSD, Presentment of the Grand Jury, 19–1–1842.

30. My examination of the registers of the police court show that public order offences made up almost three-quarters of the total charges brought before the Police Stipendiary between 1838 and 1842. (Archives Nationales du Québec à Montréal [ANQM], Registers of the Police Court, vols. 1–6, June 1838–Jan. 1842.) Although I do not have similar figures from an earlier period for comparison, Donald Fyson's research shows that interpersonal violence made up the greatest proportion of Quarter Sessions complaints between 1785 and 1830. See Fyson, 'Criminal Justice, Civil Society and the Local State: The Justices of the Peace in the District of Montreal, 1764–1830', Ph.D. thesis (Université de Montréal, 1995), 286–93. Unfortunately, sources such as police registers and duty books do not exist prior to 1836. Such documents would provide a glimpse into police activity that did not always lead to formal complaints and official police intervention. For instance, court records show that Montrealers were seldom arrested for drunkenness before 1838. Because drunkards do not appear in judicial dossiers or prison registers, it does not indicate that Montreal was a teetotalling society or that Montrealers

were clever at avoiding arrest. Rather, they may simply not have been arrested or they may have been incarcerated overnight and then released without being charged.

31. By 1802, with the establishment of a House of Correction in Montreal, constables were expected to apprehend all vagrants or idle and disorderly persons except those permitted to solicit alms, distinguished by the letters P and M, cut in red or blue cloth, worn on the upper right-hand sleeve of their clothing. (Quarter Sessions Registers [QSR], 10–7–1803.) Begging was eventually outlawed in 1819 in anticipation that a House of Industry, which was about to open, could accommodate this population. By 1822 application for permission to seek alms was once again reinstated. Even in 1833, when beggars and vagrants were to serve three months in the Common Gaol, begging being outlawed, a provision for some beggars to apply for permission to beg remained. The original licensing system of beggars was once again reinstituted in 1821, while ordinances prohibiting begging remained. According to Fyson, the coexistence of this edict with a licensing system directed at so-called proper objects of charity permitted authorities to arrest those deemed improper. (Fyson, 'Criminal Justice, Civil Society', 61.) Despite the evolution of this law, which empowered the police to arrest these indigents, the public continued to voice concern, in local newspapers, about the growing number of beggars and vagrants in the streets of the city and the suburbs. These vagrancy-related regulations remained the law until the Rebellions.

32. At the beginning of the century, vagrants, according to English law, were defined as 'such as wake on the night, and sleep on the day, and haunt customable taverns, and ale-houses, and routs about; and no man wot from whence they come, nor whither they go.' (Joseph Chitty, *Commentaries on the Laws of England: By the Late Sir W. Blackstone*, IV [London, 1826], 169.) Vagrants were divided into three classes: idle and disorderly, rogues and vagabonds, and incorrigible rogues. While all offended the public order, each class had a specific punishment. Idle and disorderly persons were to be confined in the House of Correction for one month. Rogues and vagabonds were to be whipped and imprisoned up to six months. Incorrigible rogues were to be whipped and imprisoned up to two years. Being idle and disorderly, or a vagrant without having any visible means of support, was grounds for immediate arrest. (Richard Burn, *The Justice of the Peace and Parish Officer* [London, 1788], 103–4.)

33. In 1838 the ordinance establishing a new system of policing in the cities of Montreal and Quebec also provided guidelines for magistrates and the police to deal with loose, idle, and disorderly persons. This law enabled a policeman on duty 'to apprehend all loose, idle and disorderly persons whom he shall find disturbing the public peace, or whom he shall have

just cause to suspect of any evil designs, and all persons whom he shall find lying in any field, highway, yard or other place, or loitering therein, and not giving a satisfactory account of themselves'. Drunkenness was also included in the definition of a disorderly person. In addition, if any person described as loose, idle, and disorderly was suspected of being 'harboured or concealed in any house or houses of ill fame, tavern or taverns, boarding house or boarding houses', then a warrant could be issued so that a constable could enter any of these establishments to arrest all persons found within to appear before a justice of the peace. These individuals could be treated in the same manner as loose, idle, and disorderly persons and thus imprisoned in the Common Gaol or House of Correction. *Governor and Special Council of Lower Canada Ordinances*, vol. 1–3, 2 Vic c 2, 28–6–1838.

34. Nicholas Rogers, 'Policing the Poor in Eighteenth-Century London: The Vagrancy Laws and Their Administration', *Histoire sociale/Social History* 24, 47 (May 1991): 131.
35. Judith Walkowitz, 'The Making of an Outcast Group: Prostitutes and Working Women in Nineteenth-Century Plymouth and Southampton', in M. Vicinus, ed., *A Widening Sphere: Changing Roles of Victorian Women* (Bloomington, Ind., 1977), 147, 72.
36. NA, RG4 B14, Police Register, vol. 38, 19–11–1836.
37. NA, RG4 B14, Police Register, vol. 34, 4–6–1841.
38. QSD, 20–5–1815.
39. We know from a list of Watch Rules and Regulations that police patrolled twice nightly between June and August, and three times a night between September and May. These rules and regulations were cancelled in December of 1827.
40. While petitioners in 1818 were granted their request that a watch be established in the St Antoine suburb, we do not know if it was ever put into practice.
41. QSD, 12–7–1824.
42. QSD, 1–7–1839.
43. See, for example, QSR, Presentment of the Grand Jury, 19–7–1823.
44. Some historians of police, such as Greg Marquis, have argued that the new police institutions of the nineteenth century emphasized public order, resulting in the preoccupation of the lower courts with public-order offences. Vagrancy, public drunkenness, and disturbing the peace became the major public-order offences for both sexes. Marquis suggests that public-order offences were the 'bread and butter' of municipal police. See Marquis, *Policing Canada's Century: A History of the Canadian Association of Chiefs of Police* (Toronto, 1993), 37–8. Some authors have described the state of Montreal's policing agencies in the early nineteenth

century as non-existent or inefficient. Allan Greer argues that until the establishment of a new police force in the late 1830s, city and colonial governments were unable to exercise control over civil society directly and consistently. While constables and watchmen might arrest the occasional thief, and badger vagrants and unlicensed tavernkeepers, they could not control the city streets. Greer, 'The Birth of the Police', in Allan Greer and Ian Radforth, eds, *Colonial Leviathan: State Formation in Mid-Nineteenth-Century Canada* (Toronto, 1992), 18–19.

Others have shown there was more continuity between the old and new forms of policing than previously acknowledged. See Ruth Paley, ' "An Imperfect, Inadequate & Wretched System"? Policing London before Peel', *Criminal Justice History* 10 (1989): 95; Elaine A. Reynolds, 'St. Marylebone: Local Police Reform in London, 1755–1829', *The Historian* 51, 3 (1989): 446–63. While the present study demonstrates that the arrest levels of female vagrants rose significantly after 1838 when the police force was reorganized, the fact that there were more policemen patrolling a greater area of the city influenced these numbers. Police court registers show that after 1843 these numbers declined, when the complement of constables was once again reduced.

45. Philippa Levine, 'Women and Prostitution: Metaphor, Reality, History', *Canadian Journal of History/Annales canadiennes d'histoire* 28 (Dec. 1993): 484–7.
46. NA, RG4 B14, Police Register, vol. 31, 3–9–1840.
47. NA, RG4 B14, Police Register, vol. 31, 24–9–1840.
48. QSD, 13–7–1819.
49. *Montreal Transcript*, 18 Feb. 1841.
50. Corfield, 'Walking the City Streets', 148, noted that over the century the streets became more differentiated in function, developing red-light districts for the first time. Timothy Gilfoyle demonstrates that the urban landscape of New York underwent similar changes. Initially, prostitutes competed with other residents for use and control of the public space, but by mid-century New York's first red-light district was established in Soho. Gilfoyle, 'The Urban Geography of Commercial Sex: Prostitution in New York City, 1790–1860', *Journal of Urban History* 13, 4 (Aug. 1987): 376–82.
51. Even as early as 1798 a description in a deposition shows that this was a popular area for Montreal prostitutes. Nine streetwalkers were named in a grand jury presentment as being in 'the daily habit of frequenting the rampart near the powder magazine'. QSD, 30–4–1798.
52. NA, RG4 B14, Police Register, vol. 34, 29–5–1841.
53. NA, RG4 B14, Police Register, vol. 50, 15–6–1842.

54. NA, RG4 B15, Police Register, vol. 58, 19–9–1839.
55. QSD, 5–1–1831.
56. QSD, 24–7–1835.
57. QSD, 16–2–1833.
58. QSD, 9–9–1841.
59. QSD, 16–6–1831.
60. QSD, 13–6–1835.
61. QSD, 20–8–1841.
62. Constance Backhouse, *Petticoats and Prejudice: Women and Law in Nineteenth-Century Canada* (Toronto, 1991), 230.
63. Jeffrey S. Adler, 'Streetwalkers, Degraded Outcasts, and Good-for-Nothing Huzzies: Women and the Dangerous Class in Antebellum St. Louis', *Journal of Social History* 25, 4 (1992). 744–5.
64. QSD, 9–3–1835.
65. NA, RG4 B14, Police Register, 26–4–1840.
66. QSD, 7–5–1841.
67. NA, RG4 B14, Police Register, vol. 38, 2–3–1837.
68. Phillips relates seasonal cycles in the economy to incarceration rates for vagrancy. Poor relief was generally more available in the winter, and the population was more sympathetic at this time of year. See Jim Phillips, 'Poverty, Unemployment, and the Administration of the Criminal Law: Vagrancy Laws in Halifax, 1864–1890', in Philip Girard and Jim Phillips, eds, *Essays in the History of Canadian Law*, vol. 3, *Nova Scotia.* (Toronto, 1990), 134–42.
69. Nicholas Rogers, 'Policing the Poor in Eighteenth-Century London: The Vagrancy Laws and Their Administration', *Histoire sociale/Social History* 24, 47 (May 1991): 136–7.
70. QSD, *Calendar of the House of Correction*, 16–4–1822.
71. ANQM, Coroner's Report, 24–11–1842.
72. QSD, 26–2–1820.
73. QSD, 18–4–1835.
74. For some historians of police, the debates have been quite polarized. For instance, Allan Greer, 'The Birth of the Police', 24, argues that police activity tended to have a moral-reform thrust with pronounced class and gender bias. Michael McCulloch, 'Most Assuredly Perpetual Motion: Police and Policing in Quebec City, 1838–58', *Urban History Review/Revue historique urbaine* 19, 2 (Oct. 1990): 109, maintains that the police acted as agents of social welfare, providing shelter to the homeless, and were preoccupied with petty crimes such as drunkenness, vagrancy, and regulating the activities of known brothels. Other historians recognize the dual purpose of maintaining public order—curbing immorality and integrating moral reform into police duties. See, for

example, Nicholas Rogers, 'Serving Toronto the Good: The Development of the City Police Force', in Victor Russell, ed., *Forging a Consensus: Historical Essays on Toronto* (Toronto, 1984), 132–5.

75. See, for example, Fyson, *Criminal Justice, Civil Society*, and my own work on prostitution, ' "To Indulge Their Carnal Appetites": Early Nineteenth-Century Prostitution in Montreal, 1810–1842', Thèse de doctorat (Université de Montréal, 1996).

76. NA, RG4 B14, Police Register, vol. 54, 20–2–1842.

77. QSD, 20–1–1836.

78. Conditions were harsh in the Common Gaol. The grand jury, which habitually examined the Common Gaol, described chronic problems of overcrowding, vermin, poor ventilation, and inadequate heating. It frequently complained about broken window-panes during the winter, complicated further by the inadequate clothing of prisoners, who often sold their apparel in order to purchase food. Diet consisted of bread and water through the week; meat was added on Sundays and holidays. Conditions were not much better in the House of Corrections.

79. QSD, 10–1–1836.

80. QSR, 30–4–1839.

81. QSD, 30–4–1812.

82. QSR, 19–7–1813.

83. QSR, 19–7–1819.

84. QSD, 13–4–1841.

85. QSD, 19–2–1841.

86. QSD, 12–2–1841.

87. QSD, 16–8–1839.

Chapter 3
Marks, No Double Standard?

I would like to acknowledge the financial support provided by a University of Victoria internal SSHRC grant and work-study positions in funding much of the research for this paper. I would also like to acknowledge the excellent research work of Chris Dorigo, Lisa Codd, Karen Duder, Carol Chamberlain, and Natania East, as well as the helpful comments of John Blakely, Karen Dubinsky, Nancy Forestell, Annalee Golz, Cecilia Morgan, Suzanne Morton, Mariana Valverde, and Elizabeth Vibert on earlier drafts of this paper. I am also grateful to Duff Crerar for his generosity in sharing his research findings on eastern Ontario Presbyterian Church discipline cases with me.

1. Canadian Presbyterian Archives (CPA), Session minutes, Bond Head Presbyterian Church, 18 Sept. 1836.

2. See Lynne Marks, 'Christian Harmony: Family, Neighbours and Community in Upper Canadian Church Discipline Records', in Franca Iacovetta and Wendy Mitchinson, eds, *On the Case* (Toronto, 1998); Annalee Golz, 'Abusive and Murdering Husbands: The Historical Relationship between Wife Abuse and Wife Murder in Nineteenth and Early Twentieth Century Ontario', paper presented at the Family History Conference, Ottawa, May 1994.

3. For American literature on this subject, see, for example, Curtis D. Johnson, *Islands of Holiness: Rural Religion in Upstate New York, 1790–1860* (Ithaca, NY, 1989); Jean E. Friedman, *The Enclosed Garden: Women and Community in the Evangelical South, 1830–1900* (Chapel Hill, NC, 1985); Christopher Waldrep, ' "So Much Sin": The Decline of Religious Discipline and the "Tidal Wave of Crime" ', *Journal of Social History* (Spring 1990); Randolph A. Roth, *The Democratic Dilemma: Religion, Reform and the Social Order in the Connecticut River Valley of Vermont, 1791–1850* (Cambridge, Mass., 1987). In the British context, see Rosalind Mitchinson and Leah Heneman, *Sexuality and Social Control* (Oxford, 1989). For a brief discussion of church discipline in the context of Upper Canadian social history, see Peter Ward, *Courtship, Love and Marriage in Nineteenth Century English Canada* (Montreal and Kingston, 1990), ch.1.

4. See, for example, Duff Willis Crerar, 'Church and Community: The Presbyterian Kirk-Session in the District of Bathurst, Upper Canada', MA thesis (University of Western Ontario, 1979). Cecilia Morgan, 'Gender, Religion, and Rural Society: Quaker Women in Norwich, Ontario, 1820–1880', *Ontario History* (Dec. 1990), deals with the gendered nature of church discipline, but only among Quakers.

5. Cecilia Morgan, *Public Men and Virtuous Women: The Gendered Languages of Religion and Politics in Upper Canada, 1791–1850* (Toronto, 1996). For recent work on Upper Canadian women's history, see Jane Errington, *Wives and Mothers, Schoolmistresses and Scullery Maids: Working Women in Upper Canada, 1790–1840* (Montreal, 1995); Katherine McKenna, *A Life of Propriety: Anne Murray Powell and Her Family, 1755–1849* (Montreal, 1994); Janice Potter-MacKinnon, *While Women Only Wept: Loyalist Refugee Women in Eastern Ontario* (Montreal, 1993).

6. See Susan Lewthwaite, 'Violence, Law and Community in Rural Upper Canada', in Jim Phillips, Tina Loo, and Susan Lewthwaite, eds, *Essays in the History of Canadian Law, vol. 5: Crime and Criminal Justice* (Toronto, 1994); J.M.S. Careless, *The Union of the Canadas* (Toronto, 1967); Allan Greer and Ian Radforth, eds, *Colonial Leviathan: State Formation in Mid-Nineteenth Century Canada* (Toronto, 1989); Bryan

Palmer, 'Discordant Music: Charivaris and Whitecapping in Nineteenth-Century North America', *Labour/Le Travailleur* 3 (1978); John Webster Grant, *A Profusion of Spires: Religion in Nineteenth Century Ontario* (Toronto, 1988); Margaret Banks, 'The Evolution of the Ontario Courts, 1788–1981', in David Flaherty, ed., *Essays in the History of Canadian Law*, vol. 2 (Toronto, 1983).

7. The Presbyterians were far more numerous, at about 20 per cent of the population, while the Baptists always made up less than 5 per cent of the total population. Each denomination was divided into various subdenominations, which further divided and reunited over the period. A major difference between the Baptists and the Presbyterians was that Upper Canadian Presbyterians were closely linked to their Scottish or Irish origins and were thus a more ethnically homogeneous group than were the Baptists. Baptists tended to be of American origin, but this ethnic commonality did not create the tight-knit communities based on shared Irish or Scottish origins that were common among Presbyterians.

8. Friedman, *The Enclosed Garden*, 11.

9. Johnson, *Islands of Holiness*. Also see Roth, *The Democratic Dilemma*; Susan Juster, *Disorderly Women: Sexual Politics and Evangelicalism in Revolutionary New England* (Ithaca, NY, 1994); and in the Upper Canadian context, William Westfall, *Two Worlds: The Protestant Culture of Nineteenth Century Ontario* (Montreal and Kingston, 1989).

10. See Judith Colwell, 'The Role of Women in the Nineteenth Century Church of Ontario', unpublished paper, 1985, Canadian Baptist Archives (CBA), 8–9.

11. See Marks, 'Christian Harmony'.

12. CBA, Boston Baptist Church minutes, 17 Aug. 1839.

13. CBA, Vittoria Baptist Church minutes, Murray Meldrum notes, Feb. 1843.

14. CBA, Oxford Baptist Church minutes, 12 Mar. 1825, Apr. 1827. For the censure of a member for attending 'profane concerts', see CBA, Woodstock Baptist Church minutes, 29 Mar. 1856.

15. CBA, Boston Baptist Church minutes, Murrary Meldrum notes, 24 Mar. 1809.

16. The Baptist Church records show that eight men and 12 women were censured for dancing. CBA, Wicklow Baptist Church minutes, July 1823.

17. Nine women and 62 men.

18. CPA, Session minutes, Boston Presbyterian Church, 10 Aug. 1856, 1 Apr. 1837.

19. CPA, Session minutes, Dundas Presbyterian Church, 20 Jan., 5 Feb. 1846.

20. CBA, Dundas Baptist Church minutes, 10 Jan. 1847.

21. CBA, Wicklow Baptist Church minutes, Oct. 1819.

22. Cheryl Krasnick Warsh, '"Oh, Lord, pour a cordial in her wounded heart": The Drinking Woman in Victorian and Edwardian Canada', in Warsh, ed., *Drink in Canada* (Montreal and Kingston, 1993), 89.
23. See Constance Backhouse, *Petticoats and Prejudice: Women and Law in Nineteenth Century Canada* (Toronto, 1991).
24. See ibid.; Karen Dubinsky, *Improper Advances* (Chicago, 1993).
25. See, for example, United Church Archives (UCA), Session minutes, Franktown Presbyterian Church, 18 Jan. 1840.
26. CPA, Session minutes, Niagara-on-the-Lake Presbyterian Church, 29 Oct. 1851, 23 Jan., 27 Sept., 18 Oct. 1852.
27. CBA, St Catharines Baptist Church minutes, 30 Nov. 1844.
28. CBA, Yarmouth Baptist Church minutes, 13 May 1838.
29. CBA, Oxford Baptist Church minutes, Oct 1843.
30. CPA, Session minutes, Brockville Presbyterian Church, 29 Nov. 1849.
31. CPA, Session minutes, Franktown Presbyterian Church, 14 July 1839. The Elora Presbyterian Church also refused to restore a John L. to church privileges because he was more than once charged with sexual misconduct. See Family History Archives (Church of the Latter Day Saints), Knox Presbyterian Church, Elora, 13 Feb. 1861.
32. Thirteen women and seven men.
33. All cases of sexual misconduct n=166; cases involving only women being charged n=62; cases involving only men n=40; cases involving both partners n=62.
34. The Session or the Baptist committees overseeing such issues often seem to have been made aware of such issues through such networks. For a discussion of the role of gossip in church discipline cases, see Lynne Marks, 'Railing, Tattling, General Rumour and Common Fame: Speech, Gossip, Gender and Church Regulation in Upper Canada', paper presented at the Canadian Historical Association, St Catharines, Ont., May 1996.
35. See, for example, Ann Douglas, *The Feminization of American Culture* (New York, 1977); Lynne Marks, *Revivals and Roller Rinks: Religion, Leisure and Identity in Late Nineteenth Century Small Town Ontario* (Toronto, 1996).
36. National Archives, Session minutes, Peterborough Presbyterian Church, 15 July 1835. For another example of a man who simply left town, UCA Session minutes, Franktown Presbyterian Church, 8 Aug. 1847.
37. See Backhouse, *Petticoats and Prejudice*.
38. This case is complicated by the fact that after Peter M. confessed to fornication, it was also discovered that he and his wife were guilty of antenuptial fornication and had to be admonished for that as well. CPA, Session minutes, Fergus Presbyterian Church, Mar.–June 1840.

39. CPA, Session minutes, Fergus Presbyterian Church, May, June, Aug. 1840.
40. For other cases of men refusing to appear to face charges of sexual misconduct, see CPA, Session minutes, Fergus Presbyterian Church, 31 Jan. 1850, Feb. 1848; UCA, Session minutes, Renfrew Presbyterian Church, 28 Oct. 1844; UCA, Session minutes, St Ann's Presbyterian Church, 25 Feb. 1835.
41. For Presbyterians n=15 and for Baptists n=42. For a discussion of the fact that Baptists were more likely to challenge church authority, see Marks, 'Christian Harmony'.
42. CBA, Vittoria Baptist Church minutes, Murray Meldrum notes, Aug. 1850.
43. CBA, Beamsville Baptist Church minutes, Murray Meldrum notes, 23 Feb. 1822.
44. CBA, Woodstock Baptist Church minutes, 30 Apr. 1831.
45. CBA, Boston Baptist Church minutes, 19 Dec. 1807; Family History Archives, Iona Station Baptist Church minutes, 28 Nov. 1829.
46. Crerar, 'Church and Community', 113. For poor relief to widows among Baptists, see Colwell, 'The Role of Women', 4. Also see CBA, Oxford Baptist Church minutes, 1808; CBA, Brantford Baptist Church, 1 Apr. 1855. For a discussion of the limitations of secular social welfare in this period, see David R. Murray, 'The Cold Hand of Charity: The Court of Quarter Sessions and Poor Relief in the Niagara District, 1828–1841', in W. Wesley Pue and Barry Wright, eds, *Canadian Perspectives on Law and Society: Issues in Legal History* (Ottawa, 1988).
47. For a discussion of these newer ideals of masculinity, see Leonore Davidoff and Catherine Hall, *Family Fortunes: Men and Women of the English Middle Class 1780–1850* (London, 1987); Morgan, *Public Men and Virtuous Women*.
48. Crerar, 'Church and Community', argues that the Free Church Presbyterians retained church discipline practices into the 1860s, after they had been largely abandoned among other Presbyterians. Neil Semple argues that Methodists also largely abandoned church discipline practices after mid-century. See Semple, 'The Impact of Urbanization on the Methodist Church of Canada, 1854–1884', *Papers*, Canadian Society of Church History (1976).
49. Church attendance remains the primary form of behaviour to be regulated by the churches in this period.
50. See, for example, Semple, 'The Impact of Urbanization'.
51. Johnson, *Islands of Holiness*, 169.
52. See Marks, 'Christian Harmony'.
53. Mariana Valverde, *The Age of Light, Soap, and Water: Moral Reform in English Canada, 1885–1925* (Toronto, 1991).

Chapter 4
Dubinsky and Givertz, 'It Was Only a Matter of Passion'

We would like to thank Kate McPherson and Cecilia Morgan, as well as Annalee Golz, Atina Grossmann, Angus McLaren, and Bay Ryley, for their comments.

1. Michael Roper and John Tosh, 'Historians and the Politics of Masculinity', in Roper and Tosh, eds, *Manful Assertions: Masculinities in Britain since 1800* (London and New York, 1991), 2.

2. Recent works on the history of masculinity, which address masculine heterosexuality, include Angus McLaren, *The Trials of Masculinity: Policing Sexual Boundaries, 1870–1930* (Chicago, 1997); Lesley A. Hall, *Hidden Anxieties: Male Sexuality, 1900–1950* (Cambridge, 1991); Kevin White, *The First Sexual Revolution: The Emergence of Male Heterosexuality in Modern America* (New York, 1993); E. Anthony Rotundo, *American Manhood: Transformations in Masculinity from the Revolution to the Modern Era* (New York, 1993); Jonathan Katz, *The Invention of Heterosexuality* (New York, 1995).

3. See, for example, Christine Stansell, *City of Women: Sex and Class in New York, 1789–1860* (New York, 1986); Françoise Barret-Ducrocq, *Love in the Time of Victoria* (London, 1991); John D'Emilio and Estelle Freedman, *Intimate Matters: A History of Sexuality in America* (New York, 1988); Beth Bailey, *From Front Porch to Back Seat: Courtship in Twentieth-Century America* (Baltimore, 1988); Joanne Meyerowitz, *Women Adrift: Independent Wage Earners in Chicago, 1880–1930* (Chicago, 1988); Kathy Peiss, *Cheap Amusements: Working Women and Leisure in Turn-of-the-Century New York* (Philadelphia, 1986); Carolyn Strange, *Toronto's Girl Problem* (Toronto, 1995); Steven Seidman, *Romantic Longings: Love in America, 1830–1980* (New York, 1991).

4. For further details about our methodology and the history of sexual crime in the Ontario court system in this era, see Karen Dubinsky, *Improper Advances: Rape and Heterosexual Conflict in Ontario, 1880–1929* (Chicago, 1993); Adam Givertz, 'Sex and Order: The Regulation of Sexuality and the Prosecution of Sexual Assault in Hamilton, Ontario, 1880–1929', MA thesis (Queen's University, 1992).

5. Ibid. Further historical analyses of rape prosecutions in the courts include Marybeth Hamilton Arnold, 'The Life of a Citizen in the Hands of a Woman: Sexual Assault in New York City, 1790–1820', in Kathy Peiss and Christina Simmons, eds, *Passion and Power: Sexuality in History* (Philadelphia, 1989), 35–57; Constance Backhouse, *Petticoats and Prejudice: Women and Law in Nineteenth-Century Canada* (Toronto, 1991), 81–111; Anna Clark, *Women's Silence, Men's Violence: Sexual*

Assault in England, 1770–1845 (London, 1987); Barbara Linemann, 'To Ravish and Carnally Know: Rape in Eighteenth-Century Massachusetts', *Signs* 10, 1 (Autumn 1984): 63–82; Guido Ruggiero, *The Boundaries of Eros: Sex Crime and Sexuality in Renaissance Venice* (New York, 1985).

6. See Dubinsky, *Improper Advances*.
7. Criminal Assize Indictment (CAI), case M., Peterborough County, 1922.
8. Barret-Ducrocq, *Love in the Time of Victoria*, 110.
9. Rotundo, *American Manhood*, 232.
10. CAI, case M., Lincoln County, 1922.
11. Provincial Archives of Ontario (PAO), RG 22, County Court Judges Criminal Court (CCJCC), L., Ontario County, 1903; emphasis added.
12. *Oshawa Daily Reformer*, 27 Nov. 1926.
13. On sexual scandals in this era in Ontario, see Dubinsky, *Improper Advances*, 86–112.
14. *Hamilton Spectator*, 14 Apr. 1883; CAI, case R., Wentworth County, 1925; *Hamilton Spectator*, 1 Oct. 1925.
15. Jack the Ripper, of course, remains the most enduring example of this phenomenon. Judith Walkowitz, *City of Dreadful Delight* (Chicago, 1992).
16. Wendy Holloway, 'I Just Wanted to Kill a Woman: Why? The Ripper and Male Sexuality', in Feminist Review, ed., *Sexuality: A Reader* (London, 1987). See also Walkowitz, *City of Dreadful Delight*; Angus McLaren, *A Prescription for Murder: The Serial Killings of Dr. Thomas Neill Cream* (Chicago, 1993).
17. Assaults by strangers account for approximately one-third of our sample.
18. Emily Murphy, *The Black Candle* (Toronto, 1922; reprint, 1973), 134.
19. *Stratford Evening Beacon*, 29 Oct. 1894. For a discussion of the murder trials of transient men convicted of sexual assault and murder, see Dubinsky, *Improper Advances*, 99–103.
20. On the sexual politics of the Knights of Labor, see Karen Dubinsky, 'The Modern Chivalry: Women and the Knights of Labor in Ontario, 1880–1891', MA thesis (Carleton University, 1985); Givertz, 'Sex and Order'; Robert B. Kristofferson, ' "True Knights are We": Unity, Conflict and Masculine Discourse: The Knights of Labor in Hamilton', Major Research Paper, York University, Sept. 1992. This labour program of self-regulation is an interesting counterpart to the way the American bourgeoisie defined itself at the same time by advising women to look to middle-class male protectors in case of trouble from working-class men. See John P. Kasson, *Rudeness and Civility: Manners in Nineteenth-Century America* (New York, 1990).
21. For an extended discussion of Jack the Hugger, see Dubinsky, *Improper Advances*, 39–43.

22. *Palladium of Labor*, 10 Oct. 1885.

23. Ibid., 11 Oct. 1884.

24. The extreme exploitation of Italian navvies was alluded to ibid., 6 Sept. 1884. In addition, the racism of the Knights of Labor was not consistently directed at all non-Whites. For example, according to Deborah King the Knights encouraged the organization of Black men and women workers. 'Multiple Jeopardy, Multiple Consciousness: The Context of a Black Feminist Ideology', in Micheline R. Malson et al., eds, *Feminist Theory in Practice and Process* (Chicago, 1989), 99. Similarly, David Montgomery notes that the Knights were affiliated with unions of domestics in Black communities in the southern US: *The Fall of the House of Labor: The Workplace, the State and American Labor Activism, 1865–1925* (Cambridge, 1987), 147. Thus, labour's racism was contingent. Still, Blacks were not immune from working-class racism. One article, picked up from the *Bobcaygeon Independent*, told the story of a 'colored' woman 'enticing white girls to evil ways' and warned that 'All Christian lands are reeking with immorality, are rotten with vice.' *Palladium of Labor*, 1 Aug. 1885.

25. See, for example, Patricia Roy, *A White Man's Province: British Columbia Politicians and Chinese and Japanese Immigrants, 1858–1914* (Vancouver, 1989); Edgar Wickberg, ed., *From China to Canada: A History of the Chinese Communities in Canada* (Toronto, 1982).

26. Valverde found that the intersection of sexual purity, national purity, and the advocation of stricter control over immigration in middle-class reformers' discourse only became prominent during the second and more forceful wave of the White slavery panic, 1909–14. Mariana Valverde, *The Age of Light, Soap, and Water: Moral Reform in English Canada, 1885–1925* (Toronto, 1991), 53, 92, 186–7 n. 70. See also Madge Pon, 'Like a Chinese Puzzle: The Construction of Chinese Masculinity in *Jack Canuck*', in Joy Parr and Mark Rosenfeld, eds, *Gender and History in Canada* (Toronto, 1996), 88–100.

27. Gail Bederman, *Manliness and Civilization* (Chicago, 1993).

28. *Vancouver Sun*, 4 Apr. 1914.

29. Kay J. Anderson, *Vancouver's Chinatown: Racial Discourse in Canada, 1875–1980* (Montreal and Kingston, 1991), 56; Constance Backhouse, 'The White Women's Labor Laws: Anti-Chinese Racism in Early Twentieth-Century Canada', *Law and History Review* (Fall, 1996): 315–68.

30. Marjorie Garber, *Vested Interests: Cross-Dressing and Cultural Anxiety* (New York, 1993), 234–66. In Hwang's play, the Judge presiding over Rene Gallimard's espionage trial asks Song Liling, Gallimard's cross-dressed lover, how he had been able to trick Gallimard into believing that

he was really a woman. Song Liling answers: 'One, because when he finally met his fantasy woman he wanted more than anything to believe that she was, in fact, a woman. And second, I am an Oriental. And being an Oriental, I could never be completely a man.' David Hwang, *M. Butterfly* (New York, 1989), cited in Garber, *Vested Interests*, 240.

31. This account of Kong's story is drawn mainly from newspaper reports. See *Vancouver Sun, Vancouver Daily Province, Victoria Daily Times*, 3, 4 Apr. 1914, and during Kong's preliminary hearing and trial, 16, 17 Apr., 18, 19, 20, 21, 22 May 1914. See also Roy, *A White Man's Province*, 14–15; Anderson, *Vancouver's Chinatown*, 90–1. Kong had the historical misfortune to come to trial just as the *Komagata Maru* was making its way to the Vancouver harbour—a boat carrying immigrants from India that was prevented from landing in Vancouver by an angry mob and, eventually, turned around. This simply exacerbated what was destined to be an enormous anti-Asian panic throughout the province. For days, headlines such as 'Boatload of Hindus on its Way' fought for space alongside 'China Boy's tale of Killing is Denied by Medical Expert'. On the *Komagata Maru*, see Hugh Johnson, *The Voyage of the Komagata Maru: The Sikh Challenge to Canada's Colour Bar* (Vancouver, 1988).

32. On the moral panics surrounding Black and French-Canadian men charged with murder in this era in Canada, see Dubinsky, *Improper Advances*, 98–104.

33. Anderson, *Vancouver's Chinatown*, 92–5.

34. *New Westminister News*, 6 Apr. 1914. See also the discussion of Kong in the *Vancouver Sunday Sunset*, 11 Apr. 1914, which asserts that 'the Chinese are as different from Canada and Canadians as nature and traditions can make them. Their minds do not run in the same channels.'

35. *Vancouver Sun*, 6 Apr. 1914.

36. Ibid.; *New Westminister News*, 6 Apr. 1914.

37. *Vancouver Province*, 9 Apr. 1914.

38. *BC Federationist*, 10 Apr. 1914. The paper also pointed out that, 'owing to the large number of unemployed women now seeking jobs in Vancouver, they can be hired cheaper than a Chinaman.'

39. Jean Barman, *The West Beyond the West: A History of British Columbia* (Toronto, 1991), 134; *Report of the Royal Commission on Chinese Immigration* (1885), cited in Backhouse, 'White Women's Labor Laws', 337.

40. Anne McClintock, *Imperial Leather: Race, Gender and Sexuality in the Colonial Context* (New York, 1995), 86.

41. Ibid., 103.

42. Ibid., 164.

43. *Vancouver Sun*, 6 Apr. 1914.

44. Another intriguing example of a lust-driven 'monster man' is the case of Vachar the Ripper, a serial killer who stalked the countryside in nineteenth-century France. See McLaren, *Trials of Masculinity*, 158–81.

45 *Toronto Evening Telegram*, 8 Apr. 1914.

46. In fact, the bill never received royal assent but remained amidst the statutes of that year as an unproclaimed bill. But when Ontario's statute law was collected and rationalized in 1927 in a single bill, the *Revised Statutes of Ontario*, the unproclaimed bill, because of a technical error, became law. Perhaps more interesting is the fact that several communities, shortly after proclamation, called on the Attorney-General to enforce the law. In a letter from Dr J.W. MacMillian of the Minimum Wage Board to Attorney-General W.H. Price (30 Aug. 1928), MacMillian reported that though the Board had corrected wages in a number of Chinese restaurants', it had 'received no evidence of misconduct on the part of the Chinese proprietors toward this class of help' (White female waitresses). Nevertheless, MacMillian reported it was his 'feeling that the law in question was a good one'. In addition to the desire for enforcement, Attorney-General Price also received a letter from the Chinese Consul-General (1 Sept. 1928) protesting the Act and asking that the government act 'in a manner most creditable to Christian civilization as well as Western democracy, and conducive to the best interests of Canada and China.' In the midst of all this the City of Toronto commenced prosecution of a restaurant owner named Ing, apparently at the insistence of Mayor McBride who was generating momentum for his fall campaign for re-election. At the same time, a group of 69 waitresses petitioned the Lieutenant-Governor of Ontario requesting that he rescind the legislation, stating that they were well satisfied with their present employment. Ultimately, the Act was amended under the *Statute Law Amendment Act* (1929) to return it to its unproclaimed state. PAO, RG 4–32, 1928–916.

47. *Toronto Evening Telegram*, 8 Apr. 1914.

48. Ibid., 14 Apr. 1914.

49. In 1924 and 1931, for example, two other high-profile British Columbia cases, in which a White woman was murdered and a Chinese male the suspect, triggered a panic about sexually dangerous Chinese, including attempts to bar White women from working in Chinese-owned establishments. There are interesting parallels and convergences in the case of Wong Foon Sing, another Chinese domestic servant charged with the murder of a White woman in Vancouver in 1924. The death of Scottish nursemaid Janet Smith, Sing's fellow employee in the household of F.L. Baker, raised many complications: party rivalries, rumours of drug trafficking on the part of the prominent Baker family, and an incredible kidnapping and six-week torture—by police—of Sing. While there were certainly several

possible explanations for Smith's death (including suicide), many—particularly the Scottish community and Smith's domestic servant friends—were instantly suspicious of Sing. In this case, the 'sexually threatening Asian man' became a plausible and readily understood character. See Edward Starkins, *Who Killed Janet Smith* (Toronto, 1984). According to Kay Anderson, the 1931 murder of Mary Shaw, a White waitress in Chinatown, allegedly by her Chinese admirer Lee Dick, renewed civic campaigns through the 1930s to bar White women from working in Chinese establishments. Anderson, *Vancouver's Chinatown*, 158–64.

50. Linda Gordon, *Heroes of Their Own Lives: The Politics and History of Family Violence* (New York, 1988), 3–6.

51. On this point, see Adele Perry, 'Oh, I'm just sick of the faces of men: Gender Imbalance, Race, Sexuality and Sociability in Nineteenth-Century British Columbia', *BC Studies* (1995). On how the construction of White femininity has played an important historical role in maintaining racial hierarchies, see Antoinette Burton, *Burdens of History: British Feminists, Indian Women and Imperial Culture, 1865–1915* (Chapel Hill, NC, 1994); Vron Ware, *Beyond the Pale: White Women, Racism and History* (London, 1992); Nancy MacLean, *The Making of the Second Ku Klux Klan* (New York, 1994).

52. McLaren, *Trials of Masculinity*, 111.

53. *Vancouver Province*, 30 June 1914.

54. Backhouse, 'The White Women's Labor Laws'.

Chapter 5
Lutz, Gender and Work in Lekwammen Families

This article has been much improved thanks to the comments of Cheryl Coull, Chad Gaffield, Kathryn McPherson, and Cecilia Morgan. The research was conducted with the help of funding from the Social Sciences and Humanities Research Council of Canada.

1. See especially Margaret Jolly and M. Macintyre, *Family and Gender in the Pacific: Domestic Contradictions and Colonial Impact* (Sydney, 1988).

2. Until recently the Lekwammen were known to Euro-Canadians as 'Songhees' and this remains the legal name of the band and their reserve on the Department of Indian Affairs files. They have changed their name back to a term that identifies them by the dialect they speak.

3. Karen Anderson, *Chain Her By One Foot: The Subjugation of Native Women in Seventeenth Century New France* (New York, 1993); Jo-Anne Fiske, 'Colonization and The Decline of Women's Status: The Tsimshian

Case', *Feminist Studies* 17, 3 (Fall 1991): 509–35; Eleanor Leacock, 'Montagnais Women and the Jesuit Program for Colonization', in M. Etienne and E. Leacock, eds, *Women and Colonization: Anthropological Perspectives* (New York, 1980); Ron Bourgeault, 'The Indian, the Métis and the Fur Trade: Class, Sexism and Racism in the Transition from "Communism" to Capitalism', *Studies in Political Economy* 12 (Fall 1983): 45–80.

4. Nancy Bonvillain, 'Gender Relations in Native North America', *American Indian Culture and Research Journal* 13, 2 (1989): 1–28.

5. Compare the different conclusions of Carol Cooper, 'Native Women of the Northern Pacific Coast: An Historical Perspective, 1830–1900', *Journal of Canadian Studies* 27, 4 (Winter 1992–3): 44–73, who looks at upper- and mid-ranking Tsimshian women, with Fiske, 'Colonization and the Decline', who focused only on the upper-ranked. Though there has been very little attention paid to slaves, I draw this conclusion from recent research by Susan Marsden, presented in 'The Life of Tahlama', paper given to the BC Gender History Conference, Victoria, June 1995.

6. Microhistory is a method of historical analysis involving the detailed examination of individuals within a specific setting, such as a community, workplace, or household. See Giovanni Levi, 'On Microhistory', in Peter Burke, ed., *New Perspectives on Historical Writing* (University Park, Pa., 1991), 93–113. Although she does not use the term 'microhistory', Dorothy Smith argues for this approach in *Texts, Facts and Femininity: Exploring the Relations of Ruling* (London, 1990).

7. Wilson Duff, 'Fort Victoria Treaties', *BC Studies* 3 (Fall 1969): 3–57; Robert T. Boyd, 'Demographic History, 1774–1874', in Wayne Suttles, ed., *Handbook of North American Indians*, vol. 7 (Washington, 1990), 135–48.

8. The main ethnographers who have studied the Lekwammen, including such luminaries in the field as Franz Boas, Diamond Jenness, Charles Hill-Tout, Homer Barnett, and Wayne Suttles, have all been men using primarily male informants.

9. For a discussion of this problem as systemic in ethnographic literature, see Marjorie Mitchell and Anna Franklin, 'When You Don't Know the Language, Listen to the Silence: An Historical Overview of Native Indian Women in B.C.', in B.K. Latham and R.J. Pazdro, eds, *Not Just Pin Money* (Victoria, BC, 1984), 17–36; Bonvillain, 'Gender Relations in Native North America'.

10. Laura Klein, ' "She's One of Us, You Know": The Public Life of Tlingit Women, Traditional, Historical and Contemporary Perspectives', *Western Canadian Journal of Anthropology* 6, 3 (1976): 164–83; Homer Barnett, *Coast Salish of British Columbia* (Eugene, Ore., 1955), 246–9.

11. Barnett, *Coast Salish*, 250–1.

12. Hill-Tout believed the *siem* constituted a separate class and that there was an intermediary class who were not of the nobility but who had acquired considerable wealth. Wayne Suttles, 'Private Knowledge, Morality and Social Classes among the Coast Salish', in Suttles, ed., *Coast Salish Essays* (Seattle, 1987), 3–14; Charles Hill-Tout, *The Salish People* (Vancouver, 1977), 130.

13. J.M. Yale's 1839 census included one of the Lekwammen extended families. He records for them 12 families, which included 57 'people', plus 70 male and female 'followers' or slaves. The large number of slaves may have been a recent adaptation. British Columbia Archives and Record Services (BCARS), B/20/1853, James Douglas, Private Papers, 2nd ser., 5–31.

14. Paul Kane, *Wanderings of an Artist . . .* (1859; reprinted Edmonton, 1968), 152; Gary J. Morris, *Straits Salish Prehistory* (Lopez Island, BC, 1993), 11.

15. Chee-al-thuk was generally known to the Whites as King Freezie. He was 'chief' of the Lekwammen until his death in 1864.

16. Barnett, *Coast Salish*, 241–4.

17. There are accounts from various sources, unfortunately none particularly reliable, that Chee-al-thuk had 15 wives at one time. I believe this to be exaggerated. In the 1839 Yale census, cited above, there were 12 heads of families enumerated and only 14 mature women.

18. Thomas Buckley and Alma Gottlieb, *Blood Magic: The Anthropology of Menstruation* (Berkeley, 1982), 3–50. The most direct Salish male testimony comes from John Fornsby, 'John Fornsby: The Personal Document of a Coast Salish Indian', compiled by June Collins, in Marian Smith, ed., *Indians of the Urban Northwest* (New York, 1949), 287–341; Mourning Dove, *Mourning Dove: A Salishan Autobiography*, ed. Jay Miller (Lincoln, Neb., 1986), 38, 42.

19. Wayne Suttles, *Economic Life of the Coast Salish of Haro and Rosario Straits* (New York, 1974), 57, 69, 235–40. Captain George Vancouver, visiting a Salish village in 1790, described 'nearly the while of the inhabitants . . . about 80 or 100 men, women and children, were busily engaged . . . rooting up this beautiful verdant meadow in quest of a species of wild onion.' George Vancouver, *A Voyage of Discovery to the North Pacific Ocean and Round the World* (London, 1798; reprint, ed. W. Kaye Lamb, 1984), 545.

20. Franz Boas, 'The Lku'ñgen' Report of the British Association for the Advancement of Science (1890), 571. Among some of the Lekwammen neighbours we know of specific examples where women dressed as men and engaged in male occupations, including hunting. How this was

reconciled with menstrual taboos is not known. See Wilson Duff, *The Upper Stalo Indians of the Fraser River of B.C.* (Victoria, BC, 1952), 79; Walter L. Williams, *The Spirit and the Flesh: Sexual Diversity in American Indian Culture* (Boston, 1986), 194–216.

21. Food was exchanged for other food and could only be converted into wealth indirectly; surplus food could be given as 'gifts' to one's in-laws for which they were bound to return wealth goods. Otherwise, surpluses of food were only convertible through the freeing up of labour to be dedicated to the production of wealth goods. See Suttles, *Coast Salish Essays*, 15–25.

22. Ibid., 8, 17. There is an enormous ethnographic literature on the potlatch. A good bibliography can be found in D. Cole and I. Chaikin, *An Iron Hand upon the People* (Vancouver, 1990), 213–23.

23. Cecil Jane, *A Spanish Voyage to Vancouver and the North-West Coast of America* (London, 1930), 34–5; Vancouver, *Voyage of Discovery*, 524.

24. Myron Eells, *The Indians of Puget Sound: The Notebooks of Myron Eells* (Seattle, 1985), 122; F.W. Howay, 'The Dog's Hair Blankets of the Coast Salish', *Washington Historical Quarterly* 9, 2 (Apr. 1918): 83–91. One of Paul Kane's paintings at the Royal Ontario Museum shows a Lekwammen women weaving such a blanket and another spinning dog wool with a sheared dog in the foreground.

25. Judith Brown, 'Economic Organization and the Position of Women among the Iroquois', *Ethnohistory* 17 (1990): 151–67.

26. Bolduc, in Father P.J. De Smet, *Oregon Missions and Travels over the Rocky Mountains in 1845 and 1846* (New York, 1847), 57–8; BCARS, James Douglas, Private Papers, 2nd ser., B 20 1853; Captain Wilson, 'Report on the Indian Tribes inhabiting the country in the vicinity of the 49th Parallel of North Latitude', *Transactions of the Ethnological Society of London* n.s., 14 (1866): 275–332; National Archives (NA), RG 88, vol. 499, 1876–7; Canada Census, Manuscript, 1891; Department of Indian Affairs, *Annual Report*, 1911; Esquimalt band is counted with the Songhees.

27. For an elaboration of this point, see John Lutz, 'Work, Wages and Welfare in Aboriginal-Non-Aboriginal Relations, British Columbia 1843–1970', Ph.D. thesis (University of Ottawa, 1994), ch. 2.

28. Robert H. Ruby and John A. Brown, *A Guide to Indian Tribes of the Pacific Northwest* (Norman, Okla., 1992), 225; Boas, 'Lku'ñgen', 566; W.F. Tolmie, 'Utilization of the Indians', *The Resources of British Columbia* 1/12 (1 Feb. 1884): 7.

29. Douglas to Governor and Committee, 27 Oct. 1849, in Hartwell Bowsfield, *Fort Victoria Letters 1846–1851* (Winnipeg, 1979), 63; Sophia Cracroft, *Lady Franklin Visits the Pacific Northwest* (Victoria, BC, 1974), 79.

30. BCARS, E/B/B34.2, Charles A. Bayley, 'Early Life on Vancouver Island'; Sylvia Van Kirk, *'Many Tender Ties': Women in Fur-Trade Society in Western Canada, 1670–1870* (Winnipeg, 1980), discusses the widespread phenomenon of fur traders marrying Aboriginal women and the benefits such liaisons brought to both parties.

31. Fornsby, 'John Fornsby', discusses the prevalence in Puget Sound; see also Jean Barman, 'Imagining the "Halfbreed": British Columbia in the Late Nineteenth Century', paper presented to the American Historical Association, 1992.

32. BCARS, James Douglas, Private Papers, 2nd ser., B 20 1853; for more discussion of Lekwammen population changes, see Lutz, 'Work, Wages and Welfare', ch. 6.

33. Fornsby is quite explicit about the relative wealth of the Lekwammen in his account of one such marriage between a Lekwammen *siem* and a Swinomish woman, in 'John Fornsby'. William W. Elmendorf, *Twana Narratives: Native Historical Accounts of a Coast Salish Culture* (Seattle, 1993), 41; BCARS, ms. Diamond Jenness, 'The Saanich Indians of Vancouver Island', 83–4; Charles Hill-Tout, 'Report on the Ethnology of the South-Eastern Tribes of Vancouver Island, B.C.', 1907, reprinted in Ralph Maud, ed., *The Salish People*, vol. 4 (Vancouver, 1978), 132–4.

34. Caroline Ralston, 'Ordinary Women in Early Post-Contact Hawaii', in Margaret Jolly and Martha Macintyre, *Family and Gender in the Pacific: Domestic Contradictions and the Colonial Impact* (Cambridge, 1989), 57.

35. Fiske makes this point in 'Colonization and Tsimshian Women', 523; Cooper, 'Native Women of the Northern Pacific Coast', 59; NA, Church Missionary Society (CMS), C.2./0 Appendix C, Reel A–105, William Duncan, First Report Fort Simpson, Feb. 1858; Franz Boas, *Contributions to the Ethnography of the Kwakiutl* (New York, 1925), 93–4.

36. Ellice B. Gonzalez, *Changing Economic Roles for Micmac Men and Women: An Ethnohistorical Analysis* (Ottawa, 1981), 111.

37. When widowed, Lekwammen Sarah Albany worked in canneries and her children, including future Lekwammen chief John Albany, earned 10¢ an hour washing cans. Esquimalt Municipal Archives, 'Interview with Joyce Albany'; BCARS, Add. Mss. B1/C21, Alfred Carmichael, 'Account of a season's work at a Salmon Cannery'.

38. Canada, *Sessional Papers*, 1887, 5, 92; 1888, 13, 105. Studies of other coastal groups suggest that the separation of the earnings of husbands and wives was common elsewhere as well: Cooper, 'Native Women of the Northern Pacific Coast', 56; Klein, 'She's One of Us', 167; Cairn Crockford, 'Changing Economic Activities of the Nuu-chah-nulth of Vancouver Island, 1840–1920', Honours thesis (University of Victoria, 1991), 43.

39. Canada, *Sessional Papers*, 1883, 61, reports 1,300 Aboriginal men employed at the fisheries and paid an average of $1.75/day for a season of 90 days, while the canneries employed 400 Aboriginal women in the same season, who earned $1/day; Vowell in Canada, *Sessional Papers*, 1902, no. 27, 284–9; NA, RG 10, vol. 3988, file 154,635, Lomas to Vowell, 30 Mar. 1897; Canada, *Sessional Papers*, 1892, vol. 10, no. 14, 115–18; Canada, *Sessional Papers*, 1904, vol. 11, no. 27, 254–61.

40. NA, RG 10, vol. 1349, reel C–13917, item 412, Great West Packing Co. Ltd to W.R. Robertson, Cowichan Indian Agent, 20 Feb. 1913; British Columbia, *Sessional Papers*, 1893, 'B.C. Fishery Commission Report', testimony of F.L. Lord, 117; RG 10, vol. 3908, Black Series, file 107297–2, reel C–10160, 'Minutes of a Royal Commission at Victoria involving the fishing privileges of Indians of British Columbia', 1915.

41. Canada, *Sessional Papers*, 1887, 5, 92; 1888, 13, 105.

42. Ibid., 1885, 105.

43. Ibid.; NA, RG 10, vol. 3772, file 35139, Loren P. Lewis to A.W. Vowell, 29 Jan. 1887.

44. Canada, Census Mss. 1891, 1901; NA, RG 10, vol. 11,050, file 33/3, part 7, 'Census of the Songhees Band of Indians', 1910; Anglican Church of Canada, Ecclesiastical Province of British Columbia and the Yukon Archives (ACC), Bishop Hills's Diary, 17 Jan. 1860.

45. Lomas in Canada, *Sessional Papers*, 1888, 13, 105.

46. Mss. Census, 1901; NA, RG 10, vol. 11,050, 33/3, part 7. Among the Lekwammen there were seven widows in 1901 with an average age of 54 and three widowers with an average age of 67; in 1910 there were six widows with average age of 67 and two widowers, whose average age was 74. The special disadvantage that widows faced is discussed by Alice Bee Kasakoff, 'Who Cared For Those Who Couldn't Care For Themselves in Traditional Northwest Coast Societies?', *Canadian Journal of Native Studies* 12, 2 (1992): 299–302; Marjorie Mitchell, 'Social and Cultural Consequences for Native Indian Women on a British Columbia Reserve', *Atlantis* 4, 2 (Spring 1979).

47. Of the eight single Lekwammen women under 25 in the 1901 census for which there was information on marriage, all married non-Indians. Only two of the nine single Lekwammen men under 25 listed in the 1910 census, and for whom marriage information is available, married non-Indians. Since Aboriginal men less frequently married non-Aboriginal women, the pool of partners available to them declined. Four of the single Lekwammen men under 25 in 1901, who lived past 40, never married. This information is drawn from the Canada 1901 Mss. Census and compared to genealogy tables derived from estate files from 1903 to 1965, in NA, RG 10, Series B 3 g, reel 2739–40, file 37–3–23, and supplemented by the Cowichan agency correspondence files.

48. A.W. Vowell in Annual Report of the British Columbia Indian Superintendent's Office, 19 July 1906, in Canada, *Sessional Papers*, 1907, No. 27, 268; this passage is repeated nearly verbatim in all the reports through this decade.

49. As early as 1862 Bishop Hills found women sewing dresses on the Songhees reserve; in the 1880s, when relief was issued to men, it included a shirt and trousers, but when issued to women, it included needles and nine yards of both flannel and cotton. NA, RG 10, vol. 3803, reel C–10,141; Indian Affairs, Black Series, 53,283, H. Moffat to Superintendent General of Indian Affairs, 21 Dec. 1888; ACC, Hills Diary, 1 Feb., 13 Mar. 1862.

50. Barbara Lane, 'The Cowichan Knitting Industry', *Anthropology in British Columbia* 2 (1951): 18–19.

51. NA, RG 10, vol. 11,050, 33/3, part 7; BCARS, GR 1995, reel B–1454; transcripts, McKenna-McBride Commission, 10 June 1913, 198–9.

52. United Church Archives, Toronto, 78.092c, file 97, E.K. Nichols to A.B. Sutherland, 19 June 1909; *Colonist*, 13 June 1906, 9; 12 July 1907, 5; *Vancouver Province* 18 Sept. 1909, 1; Peter Baskerville, *Beyond the Island: An Illustrated History of Victoria* (Burlington, Ont., 1986), 68.

53. The following information for 1910 is taken from NA, RG 10, vol. 11,050, file 33.3, part 7, 'Census of the Songhees Band of Indians', 21–5 Nov. 1910.

54. This has since changed with recent revisions to the Indian Act. See Bruce Miller, 'Women and Politics: Comparative Evidence from the Northwest Coast', *Ethnology* 31, 4 (Oct. 1992): 367–83.

55. Mitchell, 'Social and Cultural Consequences', 183.

56. Thomas Crosby, *Among the Ankomenums or Flathead Tribes of Indians of the Pacific Coast* (Toronto, 1907), 107.

57. The improvements were collectively valued at $20,172. *Colonist*, 22 Mar. 1916, 3; British Columbia, *Sessional Papers*, 1912, C270; Canada, *Statutes of Canada*, 1911, vols 1–2, ch. 24, 225–7.

58. NA, RG 10, vol. 11,050, file 33/3, part 7.

59. Department of Indian Affairs, Annual Report (hereafter DIA), 'Report of the Deputy Superintendent', 1935, 10; J.L. Taylor, *Canadian Indian Policy During the Inter-War Years, 1918–1939* (Ottawa, 1984) 93.

60. NA, RG 10, vol. 9,170, file B–45, Mrs Percy Ross to H. Graham, 8 Jan. 1935; H. Graham to George Davidson, BC Superintendent of Welfare, 17 Jan. 1935.

61. NA, RG 10, vol. 9,170, file B–44, George Pragnell, Inspector of Indian Agencies, to Secretary, DIA, 14 Dec. 1934; file B–48, Mrs Susan Cooper to H. Graham, Indian agent, 15 Mar. 1933; Mrs Elsie Kamia to H. Graham, 6 Dec. 1933; Ron Baird, 'World Famous Cowichan Sweaters', *BC*

Motorist (Sept.-Oct. 1965): 10–11; and the 1935 price from a March 1994 interview with 'Priscilla' quoted in Sylvia Olsen, 'Cowichan Indian Sweaters', unpublished paper, University of Victoria, 1994, 13. In his October 1930 report the Inspector of Indian Agencies wrote that in the Cowichan agency the sale of Indian sweaters was constantly increasing. NA, RG 10, vol. 9,170, file B–44, George S. Pragnell, Inspector of Indian Agencies, to the Secretary of DIA, 26 Oct. 1935.

62. 'Cecilia', in Olsen, 'Cowichan Sweaters'.

63. NA, RG 10, vol. 9,170, file B–45, Mrs Percy Ross to H. Graham, 8 Jan. 1935; Robbie Davis to H. Graham, 8 Dec. 1934.

64. NA, RG 10, vol. 9,170, file B–44, George Pragnell to Secretary, DIA, 15 June 1933; Pragnell to Secretary, DIA, 30 July 1932; file B–45, Frank George to H. Graham, 4 Apr. 1933. 'Please continue my relief as the strawberries are getting on soon and then we won't be bothering you any more.'

65. NA, RG 10, vol. 9,172, file B–57, Percy Ross to R.H. Moore, 21 May 1943, also file B–58. For women's occupations, see British Columbia, Department of Labour, *Annual Reports*, in British Columbia, *Sessional Papers*, 1940–5.

66. Information on employment at Empire Cannery comes from University of British Columbia Special Collections (UBC-SC), J.H. Todd and Sons Business Records, boxes 2–6; DIA, *Annual Report*, 1944, 46.

67. NA, RG 10, vol. 9,172, file B–58, Minutes of Songhees Band Council meeting 25 June 1944; Percy Ross to R.H. Moore, 20 July 1944; Moore to W.A. Green, 19 Feb. 1945; file B–49, A.H. Brown, DND Dependents Allowance Board, to R.H. Moore, Indian agent, 14 Apr. 1941.

68. DIA, Annual Report, 1946, 197.

69. In 1946 and 1947 the *Annual Report* of the Department of Indian Affairs noted that Cowichan sweaters were turned out 'in considerable quantity' at 'higher than prewar prices'. DIA, *Annual Report*, 1947, 206–7.

70. Ibid., 1954.

71. In 1948 the Department of Indian Affairs started paying Indians over 70, $8 per month in lieu of Old Age Security. In 1950 this was raised to $25 per month. NA, RG 10, vol. 2375, file 275-3–4[1], 'Indians Transferred from Aged Assistance to Old Age Security', 31 Dec. 1951; NA, RG 29, Department of National Health and Welfare, vol. 1,889, file R170/110, J.I. Clark to Joy Peacock, 2 Nov. 1968.

72. NA, Vancouver Regional Repository (hereafter NA-VRR), RG 10, V1984–85/316, Box 21, file 988/29–5, part 1, Indian Affairs Branch to All Indian Agents, 26 Apr. 1948, 1 June 1950; NA, RG 29, vol. 1889, file R170/110, J.I. Clark, Principal Research Officer, Department of Health and Welfare, to Joy Peacock, 2 Nov. 1968; *Thunderbird,* 1 June 1949, 8 Nov. supplement, 1950, 4.

73. DIA, 974/21–1, vol. 1, J.V. Boys, 1 Feb. 1956.

74. DIA, Central Registry, Ottawa, file 9748/21–1, vol. 1, J.V. Boys, Superintendent, Cowichan agency, 'Report for the Quarter Ending December 31, 1955'; E. Blanche Norcross, 'Cowichan Indian Sweaters', *The Beaver* (Dec. 1945): 18–19; Norman Lougheed, quoted in Olsen, 'Cowichan Sweaters', 16.

75. Olsen, 'Cowichan Sweaters'; Lane, 'Cowichan Knitting Industry', 14–17; NA, RG 10, vol. 9,170, various letters; George S. Pragnell, Inspector of Indian Agencies, to Secretary, DIA, 'Cowichan Indian Agency Report No. 6', 26 Oct. 1935.

76. Olsen, 'Cowichan Sweaters'.

77. Mitchell, 'Social and Cultural Consequences', 183.

78. Kathleen A. Mooney, 'Urban and Reserve Indian Economies and Domestic Organization', Ph.D. dissertation (University of Michigan, 1976), 89; the reserve she mentions is the Tsawout Reserve, 30 km north of the Lekwammen's.

79. NA, RG 10, vol. 6,933, file 901/29–1, part 1, K.R. Brown to W.S. Arneil, 26 Mar. 1954.

80. Joyce Albany's account of schooling provided by the Department of Indian Affairs shows that it was not up to the standard provided by the province in public schools. Moreover, high school was free for 'provincial tax-payers' but Indians had to pay fees. Albany was hired as a secretary for a law firm and eventually the school board but said that her sisters looked for work in Vancouver because they were known as 'Indians' in Victoria. See Esquimalt Municipal Archives, 'Joyce Albany Interview'.

81. Mooney, 'Urban and Reserve Coast Salish Employment', 399; Mitchell, 'Social and Cultural Consequences', 183, 184.

82. In addition, 145 families received Family Allowance in the Cowichan agency and 106 individuals received old-age or disability pensions. NAVRR, RG 10, V84–5, vol. 500351, file 41–12; DIA, Central Registry, Ottawa, file 208/29–1.

83. Canada, *Sessional Papers*, 1891; Capital Region Planning Board of BC, Indian Communities, appendix 1.

84. No Lekwammen women were listed as having an occupation in the 1967 survey.

85. In this respect they fit into a national pattern evident in Linda Gerber, 'Multiple Jeopardy: A Socio-Economic Comparison of Women Among the Indian, Metis and Inuit Peoples of Canada', *Canadian Ethnic Studies* 22, 3 (1990): 69–84.

86. A drawn-out process is also suggested by Cooper, 'Native Women of the Northern Pacific Coast', and by Gonzalez, *Changing Economic Roles for Micmac Men and Women.*

Chapter 6
Morton, 'To Take an Orphan'

I am grateful for the comments of the editors and Tamara Myers and for the last-minute research of Sarah Schmidt.

1. Public Archives of Nova Scotia [PANS], MG 27, Children's Aid Society, vol. 11, Halifax Explosion Adoption Letters, 175. All spelling appears as in the original letters.

2. *Montreal Star*, 10 Dec. 1917.

3. *Montreal Gazette*, 11, 13 Dec. 1917.

4. United Church Archives, Methodist Church (Canada) Department of Temperance, Prohibition and Moral Reform, Social Service and Evangelism, 1902 26; Box 6, file 102, Rev. A.S. Rogers, Halifax, to Rev. T. A. Moore, Toronto, 17 Jan. 1918.

5. See Nancy Pottishman Weiss, 'The Mother-Child Dyad Revisited: Perceptions of Mothers and Children in Twentieth-Century Child Rearing Manuals', *Journal of Social Issues* 34, 2 (1978): 29–43; Jay Mechling, 'Advice to Historians on Advice to Mothers', *Journal of Social History* 2 (1975–6): 46–63. For examples of literature that concentrated on medical and childbirth themes, see Katherine Arnup, Andrée Lévesque, and Ruth Roach Pierson, with Margaret Brennan, eds, *Delivering Motherhood: Maternal Ideologies and Practices in the 19th and 20th Centuries* (London, 1990); see also Adrienne Rich, *Of Woman Born: Motherhood as Experience and Institution* (New York, 1986 [1976]); Ann G. Dally, *Inventing Motherhood: The Consequences of the Ideal* (London, 1982). Important studies of how maternal ideologies were formed are Katherine Arnup, *Education for Motherhood: Advice for Mothers in Twentieth Century Canada* (Toronto, 1994); Cynthia R. Comacchio, *'Nations Are Built of Babies': Saving Ontario's Mothers and Children, 1900–1940* (Montreal and Kingston, 1993); Ellen Ross, *Love and Toil: Motherhood in Outcast London, 1870–1918* (Oxford, 1993). See Elaine Tyler May, *Barren in the Promised Land: Childless Americans and the Pursuit of Happiness* (New York, 1995), for a discussion of childlessness.

6. Robert L Griswold, *Fatherhood in America: A History* (New York, 1993); Kerry Daly, 'Reshaping Fatherhood: Finding the Models', *Journal of Family Issues* 14 (1993): 510–30; John Demos, 'The Changing Face of Fatherhood', in Demos, *Past, Present and Personal: The Family and Life Course in American History* (Oxford, 1986); Joseph Fleck, 'American Fathering in Historical Perspective', in Michael Kimmel, ed., *Changing Men: New Directions in Research on Men and Masculinity* (Newbury Park, Calif., 1987), 83–97; E. Anthony Rotundo, *American Manhood: Transformations in Masculinity from the Revolution to the Modern Era*

(New York, 1993); E. Anthony Rotundo, 'Patriarchs and Participants: A Historical Perspective on Fatherhood in the United States', in Michael Kaufman, ed., *Beyond Patriarchy: Essays by Men on Pleasure, Power and Change* (Toronto, 1987); Margaret Marsh, 'Suburban Men and Masculine Domesticity, 1870–1917', *American Quarterly* 40 (1988): 165–86.

7. See Cynthia Commachio, ' "A Postscript for Father": Defining a New Fatherhood in Interwar Canada', *Canadian Historical Review* 78, 3 (Sept. 1997): 385–408; Robert Rutherdale, 'Fatherhood and the Social Construction of Memory: Breadwinning and Male Parenting on the Job Frontier, 1945–1966', in Joy Parr and Mark Rosenfeld, eds, *Gender and History in Canada* (Toronto, 1996).

8. Viviana A. Zelizer, *Pricing the Priceless Child: The Changing Social Value of Children* (New York, 1985), 189; Paula Pfeffer, 'Homeless Children, Childless Homes', *Chicago History* 16, 1 (Spring 1987): 57.

9. Andrew Jones and Leonard Rutman, *In the Children's Aid: J.J. Kelso and Child Welfare in Ontario* (Toronto, 1981), 161; Pfeffer, 'Homeless Children, Childless Homes'. Despite these changes it should be noted that in 1922 the federal Department of Justice ruled that the Civil Service Insurance Act excluded adopted children as beneficiaries. National Archives of Canada, RG 13, Department of Justice, vol. 2183, 1829/1924.

10. Kate Douglas Wiggin, *Rebecca of Sunnybrook Farm* (1904); Eleanor H. Porter, *Pollyanna* (1912); L.M. Montgomery, *Anne of Green Gables* (1908). The comic strip 'Little Orphan Annie' began publication in 1924. Arthur Asa Berger, *The Comic-Stripped American* (New York, 1973), 80.

11. Elaine Tyler May, *Great Expectations: Marriage and Divorce in Post-Victorian America* (Chicago, 1980), 88; Andrée Lévesque, *Making and Breaking the Rules: Women in Quebec, 1919–1939* (Toronto, 1994).

12. Veronica Strong-Boag, 'Intruders in the Nursery: Childcare Professionals Reshape the Years One to Five, 1920–1940', in Joy Parr, ed., *Childhood and Family in Canadian History* (Toronto, 1982), 160–78.

13. For medical aspects, see Comacchio, *'Nations Are Built of Babies'*; Linda Kealey, *A Not Unreasonable Claim: Women and Reform in Canada* (Toronto, 1979); Veronica Strong-Boag, *The New Day Recalled: Lives of Girls and Women in English Canada, 1919–1939* (Toronto, 1988).

14. Henry Morgenthau, 'Cradles Instead of Divorces', *Literary Digest*, 14 Apr. 1923, 35–6.

15. Mrs Donald Shaw, 'The Right and Wrong of Birth Control', in Ian McKay, ed., *The Challenge of Modernity: A Reader in Post-Confederation Canada* (Toronto, 1992), 341.

16. John Bullen, 'Orphans, Idiots, Lunatics, and Historians: Recent Approaches to the History of Child Welfare in Canada', *Histoire sociale/Social History* 18 (May 1985): 133–45; Bullen, 'Hidden Workers: Child Labour and the Family Economy in Late Nineteenth-Century

Urban Ontario', *Labour/Le Travail* 18 (Fall 1986): 163–87; Joy Parr, *Labouring Children: British Immigrant Apprentices to Canada, 1869–1924* (Montreal, 1980); Neil Sutherland, *Children in English-Canadian Society: Framing the Twentieth Century Consensus* (Toronto, 1976); Sutherland, '"We always had things to do": The Paid and Unpaid Work of Anglophone Children Between the 1920s and the 1960s', *Labour/Le Travail* 25 (Spring 1990): 105–41; Sutherland, '"I Can't Recall When I Didn't Help": The Lives of Pioneering Children in Twentieth-Century British Columbia', *Histoire sociale/Social History* 24, 48 (Nov. 1991): 263–88.

17. Comacchio, *'Nations Are Built of Babies'*, 142.
18. Strong-Boag, *The New Day Recalled*, 8. In understanding why choice in adoption appeared to conflict with societal prejudices, some of the value placed on males may have been connected to the practice by which they carried the patrimonial surname. This significance may have been diminished when the name was not reinforced or connected by blood.
19. PANS, MG 27, vol. 11, 80, 218.
20. Ibid., 85, 411, 112.
21. Parr, *Labouring Children*, 114; May, *Barren in the Promised Land*, 103. May notes that American eugenicist Charles Benedict Davenport was 'obsessed with sexual transgressions'.
22. PANS, MG 27, vol. 11, 292.
23. Ibid., 93. See Angus McLaren, *Our Own Master Race: Eugenics in Canada, 1885–1945* (Toronto, 1990).
24. PANS, MG 27, vol. 11, 287, 322.
25. Ibid., 292.
26. See E. Ann Kaplan, *Motherhood and Representation: The Mother in Popular Culture and Melodrama* (London, 1992), 174. For discussion of illegitimacy in nineteenth-century Canada, see W. Peter Ward, 'Unwed Motherhood in Nineteenth-Century English Canada', Canadian Historical Association *Historical Papers* (Halifax, 1981), 34–56; Peter Gossage, 'Abandoned Children in Nineteenth-Century Montreal', MA thesis (McGill University, 1983); Rickie Solinger, *Wake-Up Little Susie: Single Pregnancy and Race Before Roe v Wade* (New York, 1992), 148; Mary E. Odem, *Delinquent Daughters: Protecting and Policing Adolescent Female Sexuality in the United States, 1855–1920* (Chapel Hill, NC, 1995).
27. McLaren, *Our Own Master Race*.
28. PANS, MG 27, vol. 11, 377.
29. Ibid., 8. An Alabama woman wanted 'some listing of their parentage. . . . Would want to be sure the child had no disease and no tubercular and other inherited trouble and would have none but a legitimate child.' Ibid., 219.
30. Ibid., 173, 320.

31. Ibid., 105.
32. United Church Archives, Methodist Church (Canada), Department of Temperance, Prohibition and Moral Reform, Social Service and Evangelism, 1902–26, Box 6, file 102, Rev. T.A. Moore to Rev. A.S. Rogers, 2 Jan. 1918.
33. See PANS, MG 27, vol. 11, 387, 394. A letter from Chattanooga, Tennessee asked specifically about 'negro girls. I presumed there are negro children in Halifax, but, I have no idea how many and I wanted to help them, as they'd apt to be the last ones to be permanently provided for.' Ibid., 362. Another example about prejudice and background comes from L.M. Montgomery's *Anne of Green Gables* (Toronto, 1969), 7. The lack of local farm help available except for 'those stupid, half-grown little French boys' caused Matthew to suggest requesting a Home child from Britain. Marilla rejected this proposal, saying, 'They may be all right—I'm not saying they're not—but no London Street Arabs for me. . . . Give me a native born at least. There'll be a risk, no matter who we get. But I'll feel easier in my mind and sleep sounder at nights if we get a born Canadian.'
34. PANS, MG 27, vol. 11, 135, 88, 199. It should be noted that the explosion occurred in the midst of a bitter federal election campaign that saw the election of a pro-conscription Union government on 17 December 1917.
35. Ibid., 212, 220.
36. Ibid., 376.
37. Lockridge (1947), noted in Nancy Williamson, *Sons or Daughters* (Beverly Hills, Calif., 1976), 112–13.
38. Alice M. Leahy, 'Some Characteristics of Adoptive Parents', *American Journal of Sociology* 38 (Jan. 1933): 561–2.
39. PANS, MG 27, vol. 11, 413.
40. Duane Alwin, 'Changes in Qualities Valued in Children in the United States, 1964–1984', *Social Science Research* 18 (1989): 195–236; Steven Mintz and Susan Kellogg, *Domestic Revolutions: A Social History of American Family Life* (New York, 1988), 122.
41. Frederick A. Given, 'Bargains in Babies', *Canadian Magazine* 83 (Apr. 1935): 29.
42. The emotional work performed by daughters within the family has not been investigated by historians. The emotional responsibilities of homemakers has been acknowledged by Meg Luxton in *More Than a Labour of Love: Three Generations of Women's Work in the Home* (Toronto, 1980) and by Strong-Boag in *The New Day Recalled*, but perhaps this work was shared by other female household members.
43. For example, PANS, MG 27, vol. 11, 394, 395.
44. Ibid., 179.
45. Ibid., 158, 321, 364. Qualities such as red hair brought both positive and negative responses, as it was both specifically requested and declined.

46. Ibid., 366.
47. Ibid., 188.
48. Williamson, *Sons or Daughters*, 23; Zelizer, *Pricing*, 194.
49. PANS, MG 27, vol. 11, 66, 267.
50. Ibid., 277.
51. Ibid., 285.
52. Parr, *Labouring Children*, 102.
53. Ibid., 87.
54. PANS, MG 27, vol. 11, 124.
55. Ibid., 366.
56. Ibid., 187.
57. Ibid., 315.
58. Ibid., 91.
59. Elizabeth Roberts, *A Woman's Place: An Oral History of Working Class Women 1890–1940* (Oxford, 1985), 103.
60. PANS, MG 27, vol. 11, 40.
61. Ibid., 86.
62. Ibid., 366.
63. Ibid., 254. This desperate demand for children led to the illegal sale of infants during the 1930s and 1940s at the Ideal Maternity Home near Chester, Nova Scotia. Bette Cahill, *Butterbox Babies* (Toronto, 1992).
64. PANS, MG 27, vol. 11, 146.
65. Ibid., 406, 330. Other women simultaneously faced the deaths of an infant and a grown son. A Canadian living in Trenton, New Jersey, who described her family as 'working people', explained, 'My oldest boy joined the Canadian army and my baby boy died last August. I lost two in one year. I gave one for my country and I would take one for my country.' The baby had been two years and three months when he died. Ibid., 181.
66. Ibid., 183, 207. A Toronto man wrote: 'We lost our eldest child, who would now have been 18 years of age.' A man from Moncton said, 'We had three boys of our own and lost the two older one. The one left is eight years old.'
67. Comacchio, *'Nations Are Built of Babies'*, 138.
68. PANS, MG 27, vol. 11, 392, 371, 416, 135.
69. Ibid., 375, 389.
70. Ibid., 183.
71. Ibid., 144.
72. 'Father' appeared only 13 times in the 389 individual requests, and nine times it was used in conjunction with 'mother'. Moreover, in six of these nine examples 'mother' and 'father' were used to describe the condition of the Halifax orphans, not the households requesting the children. Ibid., 188, 245, 150, 116, 33, 79.
73. Ibid., 389.

74. Ibid., 200, 29, 92, 146.
75. Ibid., 16, 65.
76. Ibid., 277. For other examples, see the wife of a British Columbian rancher, postmaster, and stagecoach driver who concluded her application formally with the sincere 'hope that I shall be allowed to give a good home and the love of a mother to one of them.' A Toronto woman simply wrote, 'I've no one to mother.' Ibid., 62, 124.
77. Ibid., 406.
78. Ibid., 292.
79. Ibid., 170, 194, 62.
80. Given, 'Bargains in Babies', 29.
81. May, *Barren in the Promised Land*; Barbara Katz Rothman and Wendy Simonds, *Centuries of Solace: Expressions of Maternal Grief in Popular Literature* (Philadelphia, 1992).
82. PANS, MG 27, vol. 11, 417, 206, 219.
83. Ibid., 158.
84. Ibid., 93.
85. Ibid., 367, 413. This sentimentalization of children and the focus they had in family life were also evident in the connections made between possible adoptions and the coming of Christmas. In three of the four households that asked that the child arrive before Christmas, the adoption was explicitly to replace a child who had died. Ibid., 86, 194, 366.
86. Ibid., 416.
87. Ibid., 152.
88. Ibid., 385.
89. Ibid., 150.
90. Ibid., 308.
91. Ibid., 124.
92. Given, 'Bargains in Babies', 31.
93. PANS, MG 27, vol. 11, 101, 17, 358.
94. Ibid., 19, 27, 319.
95. Ibid., 95.
96. Ibid., 410.
97. An example of this is portrayed in Nellie McClung, *Purple Springs* (Toronto, 1992 [1921]).
98. PANS, MG 27, vol. 11, 321.
99. Ibid., Arthur Barnstead, 193, Whitman, 78, 10 Jan. 1918. See Patricia Rooke and R.L. Schnell, 'Charlotte Whitton and the "Babies for Export" Controversy, 1947–48', *Alberta History* 30, 1 (1982): 11–16.
100. The analytical significance of probing gender formation within families has been forcefully demonstrated in Leonore Davidoff and Catherine Hall, *Family Fortunes: Men and Women of the English Middle Class, 1780–1850* (Chicago, 1987).

Chapter 7
Little, 'A Fit and Proper Person'

1. All names of OMA applicants have been changed to meet the requirements of my research agreements with the archives I have used. I have chosen pseudonyms that attempt to maintain the ethno-racial integrity of the applicants' names.
2. Letter from mother to Local Mothers' Allowance Board, Sept. 1935, Mothers' Allowance Case Files, London, Ont., D.B. Weldon Western Ontario Regional Collection (DBW).
3. Letter from Mrs McGee to Local Mothers' Allowance Board, 25 Mar. 1936, Mothers' Allowance Case Files, DBW.
4. Letter from the Local Board to the Provincial Commission, Mothers' Allowance Case Files, DBW.
5. There is a large body of literature on the gendered nature of the welfare state and on moral regulation. For useful overviews, see Jane Ursel, *Private Lives, Public Policy: 100 Years of State Intervention in the Family* (Toronto, 1992); Mariana Valverde and Lorna Weir, 'The Struggles of the Immoral: Preliminary Remarks on Moral Regulation', *Resources for Feminist Research* 17, 3 (Sept. 1988): 31–4; Valverde, *The Age of Light, Soap, and Water: Moral Reform in English Canada, 1885–1925* (Toronto, 1991).
6. Veronica Strong-Boag, 'Wages for Housework: Mothers' Allowances and the Beginning of Social Security in Canada', *Journal of Canadian Studies* 14, 1 (1979): 24–34; Strong-Boag, 'Canada's Early Experience with Income Supplements: The Introduction of Mothers' Allowances', *Atlantis: A Women's Studies Journal* 4, 2 (Spring 1979): 35–43; Strong-Boag, 'Working Women and the State: The Case of Canada, 1889–1945', *Atlantis* 6, 2 (Spring 1981): 1–9; Megan Davies, 'Services Rendered, Rearing Children for the State: Mothers' Pensions in British Columbia, 1919–1931', in Barbara Latham and Roberta Pazdro, eds, *Not Just Pin Money: Selected Essays on the History of Women's Work in British Columbia* (Victoria, BC, 1984), 249–64; James Struthers, *The Limits of Affluence: Welfare in Ontario, 1920–1970* (Toronto, 1994), esp. ch. 1.
7. Questions of morality and welfare have not been adequately addressed in the Canadian welfare state literature generally, which tends to focus on issues such as federalism, production, or the relationship between production and reproduction. See, for example, Keith G. Banting, *The Welfare State and Canadian Federalism* (Montreal and Kingston, 1982); Alvin Finkel, 'Origins of the welfare state in Canada', in Leo Panitch, ed., *The Canadian State* (Toronto, 1977), 344–72; Donald Swartz, 'The politics of reform: conflict and accommodation in Canadian health policy', ibid., 311–43.

8. 'Ontario Mothers' Allowance Act', *Statutes of Ontario*, First Session of the 15th Legislature, ch. 89, 1920.
9. 'Second Annual Report of the Ontario Mothers' Allowance Commission', *Ontario Sessional Papers*, vol. 55, part 8, 1921–2.
10. A typical application form, 1936, Mothers' Allowance Case Files, DBW.
11. Application form, Mar. 1937, Mothers' Allowance Case Files, Elgin County Library (ECL), St Thomas, Ont.
12. Application Form, Apr. 1931, Mothers' Allowance Case Files, DBW.
13. Local Board Meeting, 7 June 1923, Mothers' Allowance Local Board Minutes, Simcoe County Archives (SCA), Simcoe County.
14. Letter from Senior Investigator to woman responsible for the cheques to the mother, Jan. 1931, Mothers' Allowance Case Files, DBW.
15. Simcoe County Local Mothers' Allowance Board Minutes, 25 Nov. 1920, SCA.
16. Mothers' Allowance Case Files, Elgin County, ECL.
17. Veronica Strong-Boag, *The New Day Recalled: Lives of Girls and Women in English Canada, 1919–1939* (Toronto, 1988).
18. Of the case files studied, those who were considered ineligible included applicants with symptoms as serious as chronic asthmatic bronchitis with chronic myocardial degeneration, silicosis, cataracts in good eye and no vision in other eye, chronic lead poisoning, chronic Bright's disease, broken back, multiple lung abscesses, manic depressive psychosis, hernia, and lost limbs. Those considered eligible included applicants with schizophrenia, recurrent brain tumour, epileptic fits, indulant fever, open sores over entire body, multiple sclerosis, and arterio sclerotic heart disease.
19. Letter from Provincial Commission to City Clerk, 19 Feb. 1937, Mothers' Allowance Case Files, DBW.
20. Medical Certificate by Provincial Medical Examiner, Aug. 1939, Mothers' Allowance Case Files, Elgin County, ECL.
21. Provincial Commission declares the case ineligible in its written correspondence, 5 June 1939, 3 Oct. 1939, 19 Feb. 1940, 27 Jan. 1941, 25 Aug. 1941, 6 Jan. 1944, Mothers' Allowance Case Files, Elgin County, ECL.
22. Letter to London City Clerk's Office, 31 Jan. 1930, Mothers' Allowance Case Files, DBW.
23. Letter to the London City Clerk, 26 Apr. 1926, Mothers' Allowance Case Files, DBW.
24. Letter from Division Registrar to Elgin County Clerk, 26 Nov. 1940, Mothers' Allowance Case Files, Elgin County, Box 42, file 3, ECL.
25. Letter from Secretary of Local Board to the Local Board members, 19 Oct. 1933, Mothers' Allowance Case Files, DBW.
26. Letter from mother to Local Board, 26 Apr. 1934, Mothers' Allowance Case Files, DBW.

27. Letter from official to Local Board, Mar. 1930, Mothers' Allowance Case Files, DBW.
28. Letter from Inspector from Relief Department to City Clerk, 19 Aug. 1926, Mothers' Allowance Case Files, DBW.
29. Letter from City Clerk to Relief Department Inspector, 24 May 1926, Mothers' Allowance Case Files, DBW.
30. Report from Local Children's Aid Society to Local Board, 1928, Mothers' Allowance Case Files, DBW.
31. Letter from City Clerk to investigator, 31 Jan. 1930, Mothers' Allowance Case Files, DBW.
32. For discussions of racism and ethnocentrism in early twentieth-century Canada, see Don Avery, *'Dangerous Foreigners': European Immigrant Workers and Labour Radicalism in Canada, 1896–1932* (Toronto, 1979); Mariana Valverde, ' "When the Mother of the Race is Free": Race, Reproduction, and Sexuality in First-Wave Feminism', in Mariana Valverde and Franca Iocavetta, eds, *Gendered Conflicts: New Essays in Women's History* (Toronto, 1992).
33. Mothers' Allowance Local Board Minutes, 3 June 1941, Simcoe County, SCA.
34. Mothers' Allowance Local Board Minutes, Aug. 1940, Prince Edward County, County of Prince Edward Archives, Picton, Ont.
35. Mothers' Allowance Local Board Minutes, 18 May 1921, London, Ont., London City Hall Archives.
36. Letter from the Board of Education to the investigator, 1 Nov. 1934, Mothers' Allowance Case Files, DBW.
37. Generally, marks of the pupil were not included in the determination of school attendance. Letter from principal of Sir Adam Beck Collegiate Institute to the Provincial Commission, 18 Feb. 1935, Mothers' Allowance Case Files, DBW.

Chapter 8
Forestell, The Miner's Wife

1. In the Canadian context, see Allen Seager, 'A Proletariat in Wild Rose Country: The Alberta Miners, 1915–1945', Ph.D. thesis (York University, 1982); Allen Seager, 'Class, Ethnicity and Politics in the Alberta Coalfields, 1905–1945', in Dirk Hoerder, ed., *'Struggle a Hard Battle': Essays on Working-Class Immigrants* (De Kalb, Ill., 1986), 304–25; David Frank, 'The Cape Breton Coal Miners, 1917–1926', Ph.D. thesis (Dalhousie University, 1979); Ian McKay, 'Industry, Work and Community in the Cumberland Coalfields, 1848–1927', Ph.D. thesis (Dalhousie University, 1983). For one of the only studies on Ontario miners, see

Doug Baldwin, 'A Study in Social Control: The Life of the Silver Miner in Northern Ontario', *Labour/Le Travailleur* 2 (1977): 79–109.

2. Bettina Bradbury, 'Women's History and Working Class History', *Labour/Le Travail* 19 (Spring 1987): 39; Ava Baron, 'Gender and Labor History: Learning from the Past, Looking to the Future', in Baron, ed., *Work Engendered: Toward a New History of American Labor* (Ithaca, NY, 1991): 3–39; Alice Kessler-Harris, 'Treating the Male as "Other": Redefining the Parameters of Labor History', *Labor History* (Fall 1994): 190–204.

3. Ava Baron, 'On Looking at Men: Masculinity and the Making of a Gendered Working-Class History', in Ann-Louise Shapiro, ed., *Feminists Revision History* (New Brunswick, NJ, 1994), 146–7; Elizabeth Faue, 'Gender and the Reconstruction of Labor History: An Introduction', *Labor History* (Fall 1994): 169–73.

4. For Canada, see Meg Luxton, 'From Ladies' Auxiliaries to the Wives' Committee', in Linda Briskin and Lynda Yanz, eds, *Union Sisters: Women in the Labour Movement* (Toronto, 1983), 33–47; Steven Penfold, 'Have You No Manhood In You?: Gender and Class in the Cape Breton Coal Towns, 1920–1926', *Acadiensis* 23, 2 (Spring 1994): 21–44. For the United States, see Ann Schofield, 'An Army of Amazons: The Language of Protest in a Kansas Mining Community, 1921–1922', *American Quarterly* 37, 5 (1985): 686–701; Priscilla Long, 'The Women of the Colorado Iron and Fuel Strike, 1913–1914', in Ruth Milkman, ed., *Women, Work and Protest* (New York, 1985), 62–85; Elizabeth Jameson, 'Imperfect Unions: Class and Gender in Cripple Creek, 1894–1904', in M. Cantor and B. Laurie, eds, *Class, Sex and the Woman Worker* (Westport, Conn., 1977), 166–206; Judy Aulette and Trudy Mills, 'Something Old, Something New: Auxiliary Work in the 1983–1986 Copper Strike', *Feminist Studies* 14, 2 (Summer 1988): 251–67; Barbara Kingsolver, *Holding the Line: Women in the Great Arizona Mine Strike of 1983* (New York, 1988).

5. See Meg Luxton, *More Than a Labour of Love: Three Generations of Women's Work in the Home* (Toronto, 1980).

6. In many respects class designation in a mining community is fairly straightforward because of the distinct and acknowledged occupational hierarchy in the mining industry. Yet while this may have been the case for men, for women, especially since so few worked either before or after marriage, class designation is less straightforward. There has been some debate in the feminist literature on the question of ascertaining the class of women. Pat and Hugh Armstrong have pointed out the weaknesses of various theoretical positions: 'Theories that lump all women together as a class ignore class differences amongst women. Theories that attach women to their husbands or families ignore women's subordination, their domestic labour or their labour force work. Theories which locate

women in terms of their own paid employment forget both the segregation of the labour force work, and the domestic labour that most women
perform. Theories that are blind to sex differences obscure not only divisions fundamental to all classes, but also the structure of capitalism.' See
Pat and Hugh Armstrong, 'Beyond Sexless Class and Classless Sex', in
Roberta Hamilton and Michele Barrett, eds, *Politics of Diversity* (London, 1987), 208–40.

7. Supplemented by a wide array of textual material, oral testimonies of
long-time residents of Timmins, both women and men, compose an
important source for this study. Forty interviews in all were conducted
with community residents, 23 women and 17 men. To ensure their
anonymity, pseudonyms have been used.

Oral history does not so much provide an 'unfiltered' version of the
past, as various scholars have recently pointed out, as offer valuable
insights about the historically contingent and contextually specific
memories of those interviewed. Furthermore, it is possible to discern
gendered differences in terms of individuals' recollections of the past.
For a recent excellent discussion on the use of oral history, see Joan
Sangster, 'Telling Our Stories: Feminist Debates and the Use of Oral
History', *Women's History Review* 3, 1 (1994): 5–28. See also Personal
Narratives Group, *Interpreting Women's Lives: Feminist Theory and
Personal Narratives* (Bloomington, Ind., 1989); Sherna Gluck and
Daphne Patai, eds, *Women's Words: The Feminist Practice of Oral His-
tory* (New York, 1991).

8. For a recent and innovative consideration of identity and difference by a
feminist historian, see Nancy Hewitt, 'Compounding Differences', *Feminist Studies* 18, 2 (Summer 1992): 313–26. For Canadian studies that
take a similar approach, see Joy Parr, *The Gender of Breadwinner:
Women, Men and Change in Two Industrial Towns, 1880–1950* (Toronto,
1990); Suzanne Morton, *Ideal Surroundings: Domestic Life in a Working-Class Suburb in the 1920s* (Toronto, 1994); Mark Rosenfeld, ' "She
Was a Hard Life": Work, Family, Politics, and Ideology in the Railway
Ward of a Central Ontario Town, 1900–1960', Ph.D. thesis (York University, 1990); Lynne Marks, *Revivals and Roller Rinks: Religion, Leisure
and Identity in Late Nineteenth-Century Small-Town Ontario* (Toronto,
1996). For recent studies that give due attention to ethnicity as well, see
Franca Iacovetta, *Such Hardworking People: Italian Immigrants in Post-
war Toronto* (Montreal and Kingston, 1992); Ruth Frager, *Sweatshop
Strife: Class, Ethnicity and Gender in the Jewish Labour Movement of
Toronto, 1900–1939* (Toronto, 1992).

9. Harold Innis, 'Settlement of the Mining Frontier', in A.R.M. Lower, *Settlement and the Forest in Eastern Canada: Settlement and the Mining
Frontier* (Toronto, 1936), 350.

10. In Ontario, legislation was first introduced to prohibit women's employment in the mines in 1893. In various localities in Britain during the nineteenth century, women were hired to work both below and above ground in coalmining. Legislative restrictions were placed on their employment by the British Parliament from the 1880s onwards. As far as can be determined, women were never employed in any mining operations in Canada. On British women in coalmining, see Angela John, *By the Sweat of Their Brow: Women Workers in Victorian Coal Mines* (London, 1984).

11. For a more detailed discussion of social relations in Timmins during this initial stage of development, see Nancy Forestell, 'Bachelors, Boarding-houses and Blind Pigs: Gender Construction in a Multi-Ethnic Mining Camp, 1909–1920', in Franca Iacovetta, ed., with Paula Draper and Robert Ventresca, *A Nation of Immigrants: Readings in Canadian History, 1840s–1960s* (Toronto, 1998).

12. Hollinger erected 150 houses in the spring of 1921 and an additional 100 in the spring of 1922. See *Porcupine Advance*, 20 Apr. 1921, 10 May 1922. During this same period, the company also opened a store.

13. The population of Timmins grew from 14,200 in 1921 to 28,799 in 1941. Over the next decade the population would decrease slightly, to 27,393 in 1951.

14. Canada, *Ninth Census of Canada*, 1951, vol. 1, Table 148.

15. *Annual Report of Hollinger Gold Mines Limited*, 1922.

16. For a more detailed description of these ethnic enclaves, see Peter Vasiliadis, *Dangerous Truth: Interethnic Competition in a Northeastern Ontario Goldmining Center*, 113–19. For a discussion of ethnic neighbourhoods in other urban centres, see, for example, Robert Harney, 'Ethnicity and Neighbourhoods', in Harney, ed., *Gathering Place: People and Neighbourhoods in Toronto, 1900–1945* (Toronto, 1985), 1–24.

17. The precise connection between domestic labour and wage labour in an industrial capitalist economy has been the subject of much debate. See, for example, Bonnie Fox, ed., *Hidden in the Household: Women's Domestic Labour Under Capitalism* (Toronto, 1980). For more recent reassessments, Angela Miles, 'Economism and Feminism: A Comment on the Domestic Labour Debate', in Roberta Hamilton and Michele Barrett, eds, *The Politics of Diversity* (London, 1986), 168–79; Bonnie Fox, 'Never Done: The Struggle to Understand Domestic Labour and Women's Oppression', in Hamilton and Barrett, eds, *The Politics of Diversity*, 180–9; Wally Seccombe, 'Reflections on the Domestic Labour Debate and Prospects for Marxist-Feminist Synthesis', in Hamilton and Barrett, eds, *The Politics of Diversity*, 190–207.

18. Ontario, 'An Act to amend the Mining Act of Ontario in respect to the Hours of Underground Employment', *Statutes of Ontario*, 1913, ch. 23, 2

George V. This amendment stipulated that 'No workman shall remain or be allowed to remain underground in any mine for more than eight hours.'

19. United Steelworkers of America, 'A Submission to the Special Committee to Inquire into the Socio-Economic Problems of the Goldmining Industry in Ontario, 1954', 4. This report documented that while miners in the Porcupine still worked a 48-hour week, those in the nickel mines of Sudbury laboured only 40.
20. Lion's Club, Timmins, Ont., *The Book of Timmins and the Porcupine*, 39.
21. Interview with Isabel Mackinnon, born 1923.
22. Interview with Mary Bilenki, born 1921.
23. Interview with Jeanne Carver, born 1914.
24. Interview with Grace Woodward, born 1912.
25. Interviews with Kathleen Beauchamp, born 1923; Edna Pulmitaka, born 1927; Isabel Mackinnon, born 1923.
26. Interview with Yvette Blanchard, born 1919.
27. On the increasing usage of domestic appliances during the interwar period, see Veronica Strong-Boag, *The New Day Recalled: Lives of Girls and Women in English Canada* (Toronto, 1988), 115–18.
28. Interviews with Anna Colavincenzo, born 1924; Marguerite Tremblay, born 1923; Anne Ritchie, born 1915.
29. Interviews with John Forget, born 1913; Andrew Robinson, born 1908; Edna Pulmitaka; Nelly King, born 1915.
30. *Timmins Press*, 10 Feb. 1947.
31. This section only addresses instances of non-fatal accidents. On the incidence of fatalities and their implications for miners' families, see Nancy Forestell, '"You Never Give Up Worrying": The Consequences of a Hazardous Mine Environment for Working-Class Families in Timmins, 1915–1950', in Margaret Kechnie and Marge Reitsma-Street, eds, *Changing Lives: Women in Northern Ontario* (Toronto, 1996), 199–212.
32. Prior to 1930 approximately one-third of the mining labour force sustained some form of workplace injury on an annual basis. In over half of these cases the injuries were serious enough to warrant more than a week off work. After that point, the accident rate declined somewhat but still did not drop below 25 per cent until the late 1940s.
33. Gerald Markowitz and David Rosner, '"The Street of Walking Death": Silicosis, Health and Labor in the Tri-State Region, 1900–1950', *Journal of American History* (Sept. 1990): 252. See also David Rosner and Gerald Markowitz, *Deadly Dusty: Silicosis and the Politics of Occupational Disease in Twentieth-Century America* (Princeton, NJ, 1992). On the incidence of tuberculosis in silicosis for Ontario miners, see Ontario, Department of Mines, *Silicosis in Hardrock Miners in Ontario* (1958), 53. During the period 1926 to 1930, 82.7 per cent of silicotic miners also had tuberculosis; in 1946 to 1950, 43.6 per cent also had TB.

34. Interviews with Jeanne Carver, Kathleen Beauchamp, Anne Ritchie.
35. Workmen's Compensation was enacted by the Ontario government in 1915. As of 1917, injured workers were remitted for medical expenses, including nursing care when it was warranted. See Ontario, *Annual Report of the Workmen's Compensation Board, 1917*, 18. The Hollinger medical plan, for example, permitted nursing care for all family members although individuals had to pay for each visit. See Provincial Archives of Ontario (PAO), F 1350, Box 43, Medical Plans, Hollinger Employees' Medical Services Association Rules and Regulations, 1944.
36. Interview with Steve Deveschuk, born 1905. The wife of an ill fluorspar miner in Newfoundland aptly described this type of situation: 'I'm the man and the woman since he got sick. I got to be man and woman because if anything at all turns up, he's just right useless.' Elliott Leyton, *Dying Hard: The Ravages of Industrial Carnage* (Toronto, 1975), 101.
37. In an otherwise comprehensive discussion of domestic labour, Meg Luxton fails to mention these tasks. See Luxton, *More Than a Labour Of Love*, 117–59. See also Veronica Strong-Boag, 'Keeping House in God's Country: Canadian Women at Work in the Home', in Craig Heron and Robert Storey, eds, *On the Job* (Montreal and Kingston, 1986), 124–51. Even Susan Kleinberg, who details the effects of dangerous conditions in Pittsburgh steel mills on working-class families, does not address this issue. See Kleinberg, *The Shadow of the Mills: Working-Class Families in Pittsburgh, 1870–1907* (Pittsburgh, 1989).
38. Interview with Mary Bilenki.
39. *Union News*, 27 Jan. 1937. This disabled mineworker received a partial pension from Workmen's Compensation, but it was inadequate to support his family. For similar articles, see ibid., 10 July 1937, 22 July 1938.
40. See, for example, Ruth Roach Pierson, 'Gender and the Unemployment Debates, 1934–1940', *Labour/Le Travail* 25 (Spring 1990): 77–104; Margaret Hobbs, 'Rethinking Antifeminism in the 1930s: Gender Crisis or Workplace Justice? A Response to Alice Kessler-Harris', *Gender and History* 5, 1 (Spring 1993): 4–15.
41. The well-known Nova Scotia labour leader, J.B. McLaughlan, characterized the miner's wife as 'the greatest financier in the world'. See David Frank, 'The Miner's Financier: Women in the Cape Breton Coal Towns, 1917', *Atlantis* 8, 2 (Spring 1983): 137. Although McLaughlan clearly viewed this statement as an affirmation of the thriftiness and hard work employed by women in budget management, ironically, it had the unintended effect of negating that these financiers, at least in a community such as Timmins, continually found themselves close to insolvency.
42. The feminist theoretical debate over the gendered implications of the 'family wage' for working-class men and women has been long and intense. See Jane Humphries, 'Class Struggle and the Persistence of the

Working Class Family', *Cambridge Journal of Economics* 1, 3 (1977): 241–58; Jane Humphries, 'The Working Class Family, Women's Liberation and Class Struggle: The Case of Nineteenth Century British History', *Review of Radical Political Economics* 9, 3 (Fall 1977): 25–41; Michelle Barrett and Mary McIntosh, 'The Family Wage: Some Problems for Socialists and Feminists', *Capital and Class* 2 (Summer 1980): 51–72; Hilary Land, 'The Family Wage', *Feminist Review* 6 (1980): 55–72; Johanna Brenner and Maria Ramas, 'Rethinking Women's Oppression', *New Left Review* 144 (Mar.–Apr. 1984): 33–71.

43. Interviews with Steve Deveschuk; William Bertolo, born 1912; John Forget; Tony Colavincenzo, born 1921.

44. Interview with John Mackinnon, born 1913.

45. *Timmins Press*, 19 Apr. 1947.

46. Mark Rosenfeld has observed that even among the respectable working class in the railway ward of Allandale, Ontario, some wives went to the station on pay-days to 'provide protection against the spending habits of husbands'. See Mark Rosenfeld, ' "It was a Hard Life": Class and Gender in the Work and Family Rhythms of a Railway Town, 1920–1950', in Bettina Bradbury, ed., *Canadian Family History: Selected Readings* (Toronto, 1992), 253.

47. Interview with Grace Woodward.

48. Interview with Jeanne Carver.

49. Interview with Thomas Desjardins, born 1923.

50. Pat Ayers and Jan Lambertz, 'Marriage Relations, Money and Domestic Violence in Working-Class Liverpool, 1919–1939', in Jane Lewis, ed., *Labour and Love: Women's Experiences of Home and Family, 1850–1940* (London, 1986), 201.

51. On the construction and reconstruction of the ethnic division of labour in the Porcupine gold-mines, see Nancy Forestell, 'All That Glitters is Not Gold: The Gendered Dimensions of Work, Family and Community Life in the Northern Ontario Goldmining Town of Timmins, 1909–1950', Ph.D. thesis (University of Toronto, 1993), ch. 1.

52. Interviews with Arvi Riihinen, born 1907; Tony Colavincenzo; Daniel Blanchard, born 1919. Bonus sheets were posted at the end of each pay period, as a supposedly public affirmation of 'good workers'. It would appear that while many miners were critical of the bonus system, its logic caught them in such a way that the only perceived way of increasing their income was by speeding up their labour. Local labour leaders repeatedly called for the abolition of bonuses, in part because it encouraged workers to take added risks in already dangerous jobs and because of the unfair financial benefits gained by the mining companies. See *Union News*, July 1936, 10 Apr. 1937, 8 June 1937. A modified version of bonuses continues to this day.

53. See, for example, *Labour Gazette*, Feb. 1939, 340–4. While the average provincial price per pound of a 90-pound bag of potatoes was 1.416¢, the price in Timmins was 2.099¢. Similarly, the difference per pound for granulated sugar was 6.2¢ versus 6.4¢. In a 1941 study conducted by labour activists in the gold-mining town of Kirkland Lake, the basic cost of living was estimated to be 11 per cent higher than in Toronto. PAO, F 1350, Dome Mines, Box 14, 'Brief Submitted by International Union of Mine, Mill and Smelter Workers, Local 240', Oct. 1941, 15.

54. For an extended discussion of the limited coverage offered by Workmen's Compensation as well as the formulation and administration of this program as an upper 'male' tier of a gendered two-tiered welfare state, see Forestell, 'All That Glitters', ch. 4.

55. Interviews with Molly Buzowski, born 1918; Alice Pichete, born 1921; Irene Hamilton, born 1901.

56. One newspaper report in 1937 stated that it cost a minimum of $20 for men starting out in mining work, and thereafter an additional expenditure of $5 per month would be required. *Union News*, 10 Apr. 1937. For annual clothing budget estimate, see PAO, F 1350, Box 14, 'Brief Submitted by the International Union of Mine, Mill and Smelter Workers, Local 240', Oct. 1941, 15.

57. At one point in the mid-1930s Hollinger maintained that 11.4 per cent of its payroll went to alcohol and tobacco. This figure should be viewed with some scepticism because of the lack of its precise source as well as the fact that it was offered amidst the first large-scale union drive in more than two decades. *Porcupine Advance*, 21 Feb. 1936.

58. Interviews with Andrew Robinson, born 1908; Daniel Blanchard, born 1919; Yvette Blanchard; Elsie Latimer, born 1899.

59. Interviews with Kathleen Beauchaump; Edna Andruchuk, born 1910; Helen Kukala, born 1936.

60. Interview with Mary Bilenki.

61. According to the current by-law officer livestock can still be lawfully kept within the boundaries of Timmins. As Bettina Bradbury has shown, in large industrializing cities such as Montreal during the nineteenth century the municipality systematically restricted the keeping of livestock. See Bettina Bradbury, 'Pigs, Cows and Boarders: Non-Wage Forms of Survival Among Montreal Families, 1861–1891', *Labour/Le Travailleur* 14 (Fall 1984): 9–46.

62. Canada, *Eighth Census of Canada, 1941*, vol. 5, Table 5. Canada, *Ninth Census of Canada, 1951*, vol. 3, Table 50. As a snapshot of a given time, census data obscure the fact that many other households may have had boarders at particular points in the family life cycle. Meg Luxton found that of the 100 women she interviewed, 69 had taken in boarders. Luxton, *More Than a Labour of Love*, 173.

63. James Barrett, *Work and Community in the Jungle: Chicago's Packinghouse Workers, 1894–1922* (Bloomington, Ind., 1985), 73.

64. Interviews with Angelina Ciaconne, born 1912; Irene Hamilton; Maria Gagnon, born 1922.

65. With the founding of two working-class co-ops, one in 1926 and the other in 1932, consumption also became tied to political identification as much for those who bought goods there as for those who did not. The first, the Workers' Co-op, had a clientele of both Ukrainian and Finnish immigrants with formal and informal affiliations with the Communist Party. The second, the Consumers' Co-op, representing a breakaway group from Workers', tended to attract social democratic Finnish immigrants.

66. The increasing participation of married working-class women in the Canadian wage labour force during the first half of the twentieth century, albeit incrementally, has been documented as a necessary corrective to the previously accepted stereotype of the female worker as single and living at home. In addition, studies on particular industrial sectors such as knit goods have noted the particular prominence of married women. Yet their relative absence in resource communities has usually been noted only in passing. For a broad overview of female labour force participation, see Paul Phillips and Erin Phillips, *Women at Work: Inequality in the Labour Market*, 2nd edn (Toronto, 1987). On the knit goods industry, see Parr, *Gender of Breadwinners*, 86–90.

67. For a description of how life-cycle patterns have influenced women's participation in the wage labour force, see Gail Cuthbert Brandt, ' "Weaving it together": Life Cycle and the Industrial Experience of Female Cotton Workers in Quebec', *Labour/Le Travailleur* 7 (Spring 1981): 113–26; Nancy Forestell, ' "Times Were Hard": The Pattern of Women's Paid Labour in St. John's Between the Two World Wars', *Labour/Le Travail* 24 (Fall 1989): 149–68. See also Tamara Haraven, *Family Time and Industrial Time: The Relationship Between Family and Work in a New England Industrial Community* (New York, 1982); Louise Lamphere, *From Working Daughters to Working Mothers: Immigrant Women in a New England Community* (Ithaca, NY, 1987).

68. Interview with Irene Hamilton.

69. Interviews with Lempi Riihinen, born 1918; Maud Newbury, born 1917; Maria Gagnon; Marguerite Tremblay.

70. Interview with Emma Wagner, born 1924.

71. By means of contrast, 85.3 per cent of males over the age of 14 in this community were employed in 1951 (the first year the published census tabulated such figures for Timmins), compared to only 18 per cent of females above that age. Canada, *Ninth Census of Canada, 1951*, vol. 3, Table 24.

72. Unfortunately, the 1921 census does not provide labour force data for Timmins. Over this same period the proportion of female wage-earners

in Toronto, for example, rose from 25.3 to 30.2 per cent. Canada, *Seventh Census of Canada, 1931*, vol. 6, Table 7. *Eighth Census of Canada, 1941*, vol. 2, Table 9; *Ninth Census of Canada*, 1951, vol. 3, Table 6.

73. The Canadian census does not include labour force data by gender and marital status for Timmins during the entire period of the study.

74. Advertisements such as the following appeared regularly: 'Wanted for store work. Must speak English and French.' *Porcupine Advance*, 8 Oct. 1924; see also ibid., 19 July 1922, 17 Jan. 1923, 2 Nov. 1931.

75. Interviews with Edna Andruchuk; Peggy Boychuck, born 1913. Aili Schneider, who was employed for a time in her father's bakery, noted in her autobiography that it took her a long time to learn English because 'We had very few customers who did speak English.' See Aili Gronlund Schneider, *The Finnish Baker's Daughter* (Toronto, 1986), 28.

76. Finnish women in particular pursued domestic work. Advertisements appeared continually in the local newspaper placed by Finnish women seeking work as domestics. See *Porcupine Advance*, 31 Aug. 1921, 18 Mar. 1926, 19 Aug. 1935. For a discussion of the general trend of Finnish immigrant women as domestics, see Varpu Lindstrom-Best, *Defiant Sisters: A Social History of Finnish Immigrant Women in Canada* (Toronto, 1988), 84–114.

77. For a discussion of 'cultural anger' towards married working women in Canada during the Depression, see Margaret Hobbs, 'Equality and Difference: Feminism and the Defence of Women Workers During the Depression', *Labour/Le Travail* 32 (Fall 1993): 201–23.

78. See Alice Kessler-Harris, 'Gender Ideology in Historical Reconstruction: A Case Study from the 1930s', *Gender and History* 1, 1 (Spring 1989): 31–49. Kessler-Harris's assertion that 'jobs belonged to the providers' regardless of their gender has been subsequently challenged by other feminist scholars such as Ruth Pierson, who argue that men still tended to be privileged over women. See Ruth Roach Pierson, 'Gender and the Unemployment Insurance Debates in Canada, 1934–1940', *Labour/Le Travail* 25 (Spring 1990): 80.

79. *Porcupine Advance*, 1 Nov. 1934.

80. *Timmins Press*, 19 Aug., 7 Oct. 1935.

81. *Porcupine Advance*, 23 Nov. 1939.

82. Job opportunities for women did not expand to the degree that they did elsewhere because of the significant out-migration during those years and the consequent retraction of the local economy. For the definitive work on World War II and women's employment in Canada, see Ruth Roach Pierson, *'They're Still Women After All': The Second World War and Canadian Womanhood* (Toronto, 1986).

83. On one such occasion over 50 young women from Timmins were hired by General Electric in Peterborough as a result of arrangements made

by this government office. See *Timmins Press*, 15 Feb., 6 Mar., 31 July 1947.

84. Ibid., 15 Jan. 1946.
85. Ibid., 14 Jan. 1947.
86. Ibid., 19 Feb. 1947.
87. Pierson, *'They're Still Women After All'*, 215–16; Joan Sangster, 'Doing Two Jobs: The Wage Earning Mother, 1945–1970', in Joy Parr, ed., *Diversity of Women: Ontario, 1945–1980* (Toronto, 1995), 98–134; Veronica Strong-Boag, 'Canada's Wage-Earning Wives and the Construction of the Middle Class, 1945–1960', *Journal of Canadian Studies* 29, 3 (Fall 1994): 5–25.
88. Ukrainian Museum, Workers' Co-operative, Minutes, 1 Apr. 1930.
89. See, for example, *Porcupine Advance*, 3 Oct. 1925, 29 May 1929, 23 Aug. 1933, 15 Apr. 1948.
90. *Union News*, 27 Jan. 1937.
91. As cited in Laurel Sefton MacDowell, *'Remember Kirkland Lake': The History and Effects of the Kirkland Lake Gold Miners' Strike, 1941–42* (Toronto, 1982), 45.

Chapter 9
Setliff, Sex Fiends or Swish Kids?

This paper was written over the summer of 1994 in fulfilment of the requirements of the Master's degree program of the History Department at the University of Toronto. The author would like to thank his adviser, Prof. Ian Radforth, and Prof. Kathryn McPherson, as well as his parents and sister.

1. Elaine Tyler May, *Homeward Bound: American Families in the Cold War Era* (New York, 1988), 11, 9. See also Veronica Strong-Boag, 'Home Dreams: Women and the Suburban Experiment in Canada, 1945–1960', *Canadian Historical Review* 72, 4 (1991): 471–504.
2. John D'Emilio, 'The Homosexual Menace: The Politics of Sexuality in Cold War America', in Kathy Peiss and Christina Simmons, with Robert A. Padgug, eds, *Passion and Power: Sexuality in History* (Philadelphia, 1989), 226–40.
3. Daniel J. Robinson and David Kimmel, 'The Queer Career of Homosexual Security Vetting in Cold War Canada', *Canadian Historical Review* 75, 3 (1994): 319–45.
4. George Chauncey, Jr, 'The Postwar Sex Crime Panic', in William Graebner, ed., *True Stories from the American Past* (New York, 1993), 171; Estelle Freedman, ' "Uncontrolled Desires": The Response to the Sexual Psychopath, 1920–1960', in Peiss and Simmons, with Padgug, eds, *Passion and Power*.

5. See, for example, Sidney Katz, 'The Truth About Sex Criminals', *Maclean's*, 1 July 1947, 12, 46–8; J.D. Ketchum, 'The Prude is Father to the Pervert', *Maclean's*, 15 Jan. 1948, 9, 42–4; W.C.J. Meredith, 'Law and the Sex Criminal', *Saturday Night*, 18 Oct. 1952, 1, 26–7; June Callwood, 'The Parents Strike Back Against Sex Criminals', *Maclean's*, 23 July 1955, 7–9, 48–51.

6. H.R. How, 'Half a Million for Sex and Scandal', *Canadian Business* (July 1951): 35, 34.

7. Ibid., 66.

8. Ibid., 35.

9. Ibid., 34.

10. Ibid.

11. 'Blonde Pistol Packin' Mamma Jailed', *Hush Free Press*, 30 Nov. 1946, 1. (Hereafter, unless otherwise indicated, all references are to *Hush*. 'Rat Infested Hell Hole Houses Harlots and Babies', 5 Jan. 1946, 1; 'Half Clad Girl Flees in Horror', 7 Apr. 1951, 10.

12. How, 'Half a Million for Sex and Scandal', 35.

13. 'The Editor Looks Back: A Review of 1945 Achievements', 19 Jan. 1946, 9.

14. 'Montreal Street Scene', 5 Oct. 1946, 12.

15. ' "Pansies" Bloom in Cocktail Bar', 17 Mar. 1951, 6.

16. 'Liberace Queer Antics Exposed—Press Agents Fake Normal Sex-Life', 12 Feb. 1955, 4.

17. ' "Queer" Stories Backfire on Liberace—Doll Face on Skids', 21 July 1956, 4.

18. 'Morality Cops Raid Weird Booze Party', 19 Aug. 1953, 10; 'Montreal Street Scene', 5 Mar. 1955, 13.

19. 'Cops Spoil "Fairy" Tale—Joy Girl Really Joy Boy,' 4 Sept. 1948, 6.

20. 'Johnnie Ray's Strange Sex Life', 4 Apr. 1953, 4.

21. 'Exclusive—"She" Is a "He"—Doctors Expose Fake', 9 May 1953, 8.

22. 'Reading Between the Lines', 3 Jan. 1953, 5.

23. 'Johnnie Ray's Strange Sex Life', 4.

24. 'Liberace Queer Antics Exposed', 4.

25. The man 'with strong female tendencies', *Hush* explained, 'can only obtain relief from psychiatry or psychoanalysis.' 'Exclusive—"She" Is a "He"—Doctors Expose Fake', 8.

26. 'Reading Between the Lines', 5.

27. 'Montreal Street Scene', 3 Sept. 1955, 13.

28. 'Toronto Breeze Around', 2 Oct. 1948, 7.

29. 'Woolworth Heiress Babs Hutton To Marry Sex Criminal', 5 Nov. 1955, 4.

30. 'The swishes are very annoyed at Hal Courney for snubbing them at a Peel Street restaurant', read a typical item. 'Montreal Street Scene', 14 Aug. 1948, 13.

31. 'Montreal Street Scene', 17 Jan. 1948, 10.
32. '"Gay-Boys" Nabbed in Bowles Lunch', 11 Aug. 1951, 6.
33. 'Toronto Breeze Around', 3 Feb. 1951, 9.
34. 'Toronto Breeze Around', 18 July 1953, 13.
35. 'Montreal Street Scene', 27 Oct. 1955, 13.
36. 'Montreal Street Scene', 25 Mar. 1950, 13.
37. 'Montreal Street Scene,' 5 Mar. 1955, 13.
38. Gay men were, in the words of the columnist, 'as common as cockroaches in a cafeteria. In fact the normal male members of that department have formed what they call the "Ten Per Cent Club" because they feel that these "sweet things" outnumber them 9 to 1.' '"Pansies" Bloom in Cocktail Bar', 6.
39. In 1955 there were still 'so many "gay" characters floating around Simpson's' that it was 'tough to tell the males from the "shemales" without a program.' 'Toronto Breeze Around', 26 Nov. 1955, 9.
40. 'Toronto Breeze Around', 7 Apr. 1956, 9.
41. 'Montreal Street Scene', 21 Jan. 1956, 13.
42. 'Toronto Breeze Around', 11 July 1953, 9
43. 'Toronto Breeze Around', 6 Oct. 1951, 9.
44. 'Winnipeg Whispers', 9 Apr. 1955, 13.
45. 'Montreal Street Scene', 22 Apr. 1950, 13.
46. 'Montreal Street Scene', 12 Feb. 1955, 13. One, a magazine dedicated to presenting 'the homosexual viewpoint', was, in fact, one of the few gay publications being produced in North America at this time.
47. 'Montreal Street Scene', 2 Apr. 1955, 13.
48. 'Montreal Street Scene', 30 July 1955, 13.
49. 'Montreal Street Scene', 28 Dec. 1946, 12.
50. 'Winnipeg Whispers', 29 Jan. 1955, 13.
51. 'Montreal Street Scene', 19 Feb. 1949, 13.
52. 'Newspaper Advertisements Contacts for Degenerates', 15 Sept. 1951, 6.
53. 'Grandma's Life Savings Blown in $20,000 Partying Swindle', 5 Mar. 1949, 12.
54. 'Montreal Street Scene', 18 July 1953, 13.
55. '"Pansies" Bloom in Cocktail Bar', 6. Other stories proclaimed that gays 'swoon[ed]' when local entertainers played the piano, and liked to 'make with the eyes' at professional wrestlers. 'Toronto Breeze Around', 9 Oct. 1948, 7; 'Montreal Street Scene', 20 Nov. 1948, 13.
56. 'Newspaper Advertisements Contacts for Degenerates', 6.
57. '"Pansies" Bloom in Cocktail Bar', 6.
58. 'Morality Cops Raid Weird Booze Party', 10.
59. '"Pansies" Bloom in Cocktail Bar', 6.
60. 'Bedroom "Fairy Story" Farce? Male Nurse Alleges Robbery', 8 Feb. 1947, 10.

61. 'C.B.C. Ballet Dancer Guilty of Sex Perversion', 8 Oct. 1955, 6.
62. ' "Matinee" Pervert Prowls Theatre', 28 Apr. 1951, 6.
63. 'Parasite Convicted of Robbery at King Eddie', 11 July 1953, 6.
64. ' "Gay-Boys" Nabbed in Bowles Lunch', 6.
65. 'All Night Restaurant "Lavender Set" Hang-Out', 1 Aug. 1953, 11.
66. 'Union Station Washroom "Swish Boys" Love Nest', 20 Aug. 1949, 11;
    ' "Pansies" Bloom in Bowles' Lunch', 5 Sept. 1953, 9.
67. 'Imperial Varnish Employee Charges Boss with Indecent Assault',
    14 May 1955, 8.
68. 'Voice Your Views: No Objection to "Blooming Pansies" ', 14 Apr. 1951,
    10.
69. 'Voice Your Views: RE Bi and Homosexual', 10 Jan. 1953, 13.
70. ' "Hubby Likes Boys"—Wife Seeks Annulment', 26 May 1951, 11.
71. 'Elevator Operator Robs "King Eddie" Hotel Guest', 14 Mar. 1953, 4;
    ' "Matinee" Pervert Prowls Theatre', 6; 'C.B.C. Ballet Dancer Guilty of Sex
    Perversion', 6; 'Sex Perverts Infest Large City Locales', 17 May 1952, 11.
72. 'Killed Gets 10 Year Sentence—Sentenced 10 Years for Sex Fiend',
    3 Dec. 1949, 2.
73. 'Toronto Breeze Around', 9 Oct. 1948, 7.
74. 'Montreal Street Scene', 20 Nov. 1948, 13.
75. 'Montreal Street Scene', 5 Aug. 1950, 13.
76. 'Toronto Breeze Around', 17 June 1950, 9. A year later he included this
    report in his column: 'Whoops dearies, but we wouldn't have believed it
    unless we had seen it with our own eyes. A coin operated perfume spray
    machine in the "men's" washroom at Letros Tavern. "Tabu" and
    "Evening in Paris" were two choices offered. We were so angry when we
    found "My Sin" missing that we tore a Kleenex tissue in half. Brute that
    we are.' 'Toronto Breeze Around', 20 Oct. 1951, 9.
77. 'Morality Cops Raid Weird Booze Party', 10.
78. ' "Pretty Boy" Bounced by Teen Age Tough', 7 May 1949, 6.
79. 'Bytown Babble', 11 Feb. 1950, 13.
80. A year before, the same columnist had complained that the ' "half-sex"
    class of people' were disturbing those who wished 'to sip their drinks in
    quietude' in the same bar. 'Bytown Babble', 13 Aug. 1949, 13.
81. 'Montreal Street Scene', 4 June 1955, 13.
82. In Toronto, Tim O'Rourke seemed to be making a similar call for action
    against gays when he wrote on the many complaints being made about a
    local bathhouse. The main annoyance here was 'the army of "purple
    boys" who have made this joint a hangout.' O'Rourke admitted that it
    would be difficult for the management to keep out 'all the swish kids in
    Toronto', but he urged them 'to act on complaints instead of merely
    pooh-pawhing them'. 'Toronto Breeze Around', 11 Nov. 1950, 9.

83. ' "Pansies" Bloom in Cocktail Bar', 7.
84. 'Voice Your Views: Opinion on Homosexuality', 4 Aug. 1951, 10.
85. 'Johnnie Ray's Strange Sex Life', 4.
86. 'Liberace Queer Antics Exposed—Press Agents Fake Normal Sex-Life', 4.
87. 'Johnnie Ray's Strange Sex Life', 4.
88. 'Parasite Convicted of Robbery at King Eddie', 6.
89. 'Elevator Operator Robs "King Eddie" Hotel Guest', 4.
90. 'All Night Restaurant "Lavender Set" Hang-Out', 11.
91. 'Parasite Convicted of Robbery at King Eddie', 6.
92. 'Elevator Operator Robs "King Eddie" Hotel Guest', 4.
93. 'All Night Restaurant "Lavender Set" Hang-Out', 11; 'Elevator Operator Robs "King Eddie" Hotel Guest', 4.
94. Ibid.
95. 'All Night Restaurant "Lavender Set" Hang-Out', 11.
96. 'Parasite Convicted of Robbery at King Eddie', 6.
97. 'Elevator Operator Robs "King Eddie" Hotel Guest', 4.
98. 'Parasite Convicted of Robbery at King Eddie', 6.
99. 'Attacker Jailed—Nude Victim Denies Charges', 18 Nov. 1950, 6.
100. 'All Night Restaurant "Lavender Set" Hang-Out', 11.
101. For their own safety, however, gay men were warned that they would be 'far wiser to keep to their own company rather than flirt with outsiders'. 'Elevator Operator Robs "King Eddie" Hotel Guest', 4.
102. 'Killed Gets 10 Year Sentence—Sentenced 10 Years for Sex Fiend', 2.
103. Bob Thomas, *Liberace: The True Story* (New York, 1987), 121, 146.
104. Ross Higgins and Line Chamberland have come to a similar conclusion in their look at the Montreal yellow press of the 1950s, suggesting that these newspapers, by supplying information on the gay world, functioned as 'predecessors of the later gay press'. See their 'Mixed Messages: Gays and Lesbians in Montreal Yellow Papers in the 1950s', in Ian McKay, ed., *The Challenge of Modernity: A Reader on Post-Confederation Canada* (Toronto, 1992), 421–31.

Chapter 10
McPherson, 'The Case of the Kissing Nurse'

This article was original prepared for this volume of essays. Much of the research presented here was subsequently reworked for inclusion in my 1996 book, *Bedside Matters: The Transformation of Canadian Nursing, 1900–1990* (Toronto, 1996), especially material presented in ch. 5, 'The Case of the Kissing Nurse'. I would like to thank Oxford University Press (Canada) for permission to use material presented in *Bedside Matters* for this article.

Thanks are also extended to John Lutz, Adele Perry, and Cecilia Morgan for comments on earlier drafts. York University Faculty of Arts Fellowship support made possible the time to draft the original version of this article.

1. Vancouver City Archives (VCA), Vancouver General Hospital (VanGH), Minutes, Meeting, 15, 16 Jan. 1959.
2. Jeannine Locke, 'Nurses Denied Romance by Prudish Profession', *Toronto Daily Star*. See also 'Hospital to "Kiss, Make Up" With its Student Nurses', *Vancouver Sun*, 16 Jan. 1959 (VCA, VanGH collection.)
3. I consider the homosocial space created by nursing's occupationally specific gender and sexual identities in McPherson, *Bedside Matters*, ch. 5.
4. Judith Butler, 'Performative Acts and Gender Constitution: An Essay in Phenomenology and Feminist Theory', in Sue Ellen Case, ed., *Performing Feminisms: Feminist Critical Theory and Theatre* (Baltimore, 1990), 277.
5. Judith Butler, *Gender Trouble: Feminism and the Subversion of Identity* (New York, 1989).
6. For an overview of the changing structure and content of nursing work over the twentieth century, see McPherson, *Bedside Matters*.
7. See McPherson, *Bedside Matters*; McPherson, 'Carving Out a Past: Canadian Nurses Association War Memorial', *Histoire sociale/Social History* 29, 58 (Nov. 1996): 417–39; McPherson, 'Working With Whiteness', paper presented to the Canadian Association for Medical History, Ottawa, June 1998.
8. Elizabeth Wilson, a historian of fashion, argues that 'By the 1890s it had become customary for maid-servants to wear black, and, like nurses at the same period, to have women's caps from an earlier period.' Wilson, *Adorned in Dreams: Fashion and Modernity* (London, 1985), 36. Irene Poplin demonstrates that within German nursing the 'brilliant strategy to make the attire worn by Kaiserswerth nurses central to the strategy for reforming nursing and women's public role the nurse uniform acquired singular importance. It became an instrument for change.' Poplin, 'Nursing Uniforms: Romantic Idea, Functional Attire, or Instruments of Social Change?', *Nursing History Review* 2 (1994): 164.
9. Provincial Archives of Nova Scotia (PANS), Victoria General Hospital (VicGH), 'Report of Commissioners Appointed to Enquire into Management', *Nova Scotia Journal of the Legislative Assembly*, App. 15, 1896.
10. Mary Poovey, *Uneven Developments: The Ideological Work of Gender in Mid-Victorian England* (Chicago, 1988), 14.
11. At the Winnipeg General Hospital (WGH), students were granted late leave until 11:30 once per week, and once a month that could be extended to midnight for 'Theatre Leave'.

12. Mariana Valverde, *The Age of Light, Soap, and Water: Moral Reform in English Canada, 1885–1925* (Toronto, 1991).

13. Winnipeg General Hospital Nurses Alumnae Association Archives (WGHNAAA), WGH, *Student Register*, 1903–6, uncatalogued. See also PANS, MG 20, vol. 1000, no. 1, VicGH, *Chronological Record of Ward Service*, Mar. 1912–Mar. 1920.

14. See, for example, Brandon General Hospital Archives (BGHA), Brandon General Hospital (BGH), *Rules and Regulations for Nurses*, 1906, Box 55.

15. St Boniface General Hospital School of Nursing Alumnae Room Archives, unpublished history of the St Boniface School of Nursing, n.d. (*circa* 1976), 14–15.

16. When one Vancouver General student was caught smoking in her room she lost her cap for six months. Nora Kelly, *Quest for a Profession: The History of the Vancouver General Hospital School of Nursing* (Vancouver, 1973), 36. At the Royal Jubilee in Victoria one student lost the right to wear her cap for a week when she failed to report a patient's death right away. Anne Pearson, *The Royal Jubilee Hospital* (Victoria, n.d.), 24.

17. In the nurses' home, students had to entertain visitors in the reception room and could not have visitors, other than perhaps mothers and sisters, in their own rooms. Permission had to be sought if nurses wanted to receive a male patient or ex-patient at the residence. Provincial Archives of Manitoba (PAM), WGH collection, 'House Rules for Nurses approved by the board August 1920', WGH, House Committee, Minutes, 25 Aug. 1920.

18. WGHNAAA, WGH, Register, 1903–6. See also PANS, VicGH, *Ward Register*, 1900–20.

19. Christina Simmons, 'Modern Sexuality and the Myth of Victorian Repression', in Kathy Peiss and Christina Simmons, eds, *Passion and Power: Sexuality in History* (Philadelphia, 1989), 157–77. See also John d'Emilio and Estelle Freedman, *Intimate Matters: A History of Sexuality in America* (New York, 1988). In the Canadian context, Veronica Strong-Boag's *The New Day Recalled: The Lives of Girls and Women in English Canada, 1919–1939* (Toronto, 1988) and Andrée Lévesque's *Making and Breaking the Rules: Women in Quebec, 1919–1939* (Toronto, 1994) focus on the continuing prescriptive emphasis on motherhood. Simmons acknowledges that 'Women's celebrated "new freedom" was most salient for single women since most white wives did not remain long in the labor force', but since most nurses were single, the prescriptions for sexual 'liberation' continued to have resonance for them.

20. Martha Stewart, interview by author, Halifax, 1981. The many references to bobbed hair in students' yearbooks suggest the degree of controversy over the new fashion in hair.

21. For a discussion of the influence of 'American' fashion on images of female sexuality in Quebec, see Lévesque, *Making and Breaking the Rules*, 55–7.

22. WGHNAAA, 'Miss Grant Addresses the Alumnae Association', *WGH Nurses' Alumnae Journal* 18, 23 (1927): 13–14.

23. 'Are Uniforms all Alike?', MGH *Blue and Gold*, 1928, 57. See also *Blue and Gold*, 1933, 'New 1933 Styles in Crisp White Uniforms'. Some agencies, hoping to attract graduate nurses onto their staffs, provided uniforms that, like the images in the Eaton's advertisements and yearbook cartoons, were distinctly modern. The Victorian Order of Nurses uniform, for example, included a drop-waisted dress, a tie, and a cloche hat.

24. PANS, RG 25, Box 10, VicGH, *Ward Nursing Register*, 1920–4.

25. VanGH, *Nurses' Annual*, 1939, 45.

26. 'The Nurse's Chance', WGH *Blue and White*, 1928, 45.

27. For an example of one nurse whose appointment was questioned because of allegations of sexual relations with her employer, see Provincial Archives of British Columbia, GR 496, A.D. Lapp, Superintendent of Tranquille Sanatorium, to Mr P. Walker, Deputy Provincial Secretary, Victoria, 9 Jan. 1936.

28. Ellen Knox, *The Girl of the New Day* (Toronto, 1920), 51.

29. 'Love', WGH *Blue and White*, 1931, 61; VanGH, *Nurses' Annual*, 1928, 84.

30. PAM, MSNM file, *Report*, Dec. 1935, 1503–4.

31. Mary Shepherd, tape-recorded interview by author, Winnipeg, 18 June 1987. Members of the American Frontier Nursing Service also celebrated the shield their uniform provided. FNS nurse Betty Lester recalled, 'It is one of our few rules that no nurse rides alone at night but . . . we nurses are safe. Our uniform allows us to go anywhere in the mountains, and it is only fear of accident which prevents our riding alone at night.' Cited in Donna Parker, 'Made to Fit a Woman: Riding Uniforms of the Frontier Nursing Service', *Dress* 20 (1993): 53.

32. Concerns about shortages of graduate nurses abounded throughout the postwar era. See, for example, VicGH, *Annual Report*, 1948, 23–5, and 1953, 30. See also John R. Smiley, Isabel Black, Andrew Kapos, and Boyde G. Gill, *The Untapped Pool: A Survey of Ontario Nurses* (1968); Registered Nurses Association of British Columbia, *Submission to the Royal Commission on Health Services* (1962), 11–24.

33. In her *'They're Still Women After All'*, Ruth Pierson has demonstrated that the wartime propaganda campaign to recruit women into military and civilian production hinged on the depiction of women in uniform—whether a CWAC dress or a welder's suit—as uncompromisingly heterosexual and feminine. Ruth Roach Pierson, *'They're Still Women After All': The Second World War and Canadian Womanhood* (Toronto, 1986).

34. *Hamilton General Hospital School of Nursing* (Hamilton, 1956) describes that school's efforts to modernize their uniform. See also 'Trends in Nursing', *Canadian Nurse (CN)* 49, 3 (Mar. 1953): 209, for a discussion of the Demonstration School at Windsor that eliminated the capping ceremony and allowed students to wear the full uniform from the first day of training. This strategy was taken to '[protect] our new students from that feeling of being different, without a cap and not yet a nurse, [in order to apply] some of that mental hygiene we discuss so much about.' The article also applauded other changes to the regulation dress. 'Can you remember when short sleeves were rather looked down upon as being unprofessional? Better to dabble our cuffs in bath water than to show our elbows!' For other discussions of changes to nurses' costume, see Ethel Johns, '. . . Off . . . Duty . . .', *CN* 38, 5 (May 1942): 350; 'Is the Cap a Symbol?', *CN* 37, 4 (Apr. 1941): 262–3; L. Grace Giles, 'A Cap is Part of a Uniform', *CN* 37, 3 (Mar. 1941): 173–4.

35. 'Toronto General Hospital Student Nurses' Uniform', *The Quarterly* 7, 6 (Winter 1949): 1. See also 'New Uniforms', *In Cap and Uniform*, 1952, 44, Calgary General Hospital Nurses' Alumnae Association Archives, uncatalogued.

36. Maureen Turim, 'Designing Women: The Emergence of the New Sweetheart Line', in Jane Gaines and Charlotte Herzog, eds, *Fabrications: Costume and the Female Body* (New York, 1990), 225–6. In her exploration of why this particular design connoted the feminine image it did, Turim (p. 227) concludes: 'Just as these decorative dresses were often very uncomfortable and impractical to wear, so the decorative and passive function assigned to women by their metaphorical inscription in such clothing was the ugly underside of the charming appearance. In fact, the sweetheart line can also be seen as a form of gilded bondage. . . . This style, by enforcing symbolic femininity, allowed for a great restriction of the female role to be attached to the very notion of the feminine.'

37. Canadian Nurses' Association, 'What Nursing Holds For You', (n.d.). In addition to celebrating the many job options nursing offered, the pamphlet underscored the important social role played by nurses. 'Her place in the community is an important one. She takes part in the drama of life and is often called upon to play many roles.'

38. 'Woman in Service', *Vancouver Daily Province*, 8 July 1944, 8.

39. See Jane Gaines, 'Costume and Narrative: How Dress Tells the Woman's Story', in Gaines and Herzog, eds, *Fabrications*.

40. VanGH, *Nurses' Annual*, 1958.

41. Marjorie McLeod, tape-recorded interview by author, 6 Sept. 1992.

42. 'Red Cross Seeking Students' Red Blood', *The Manitoban* 37, 14 (10 Nov. 1950): 1.

43. For analyses of the sexualized image of nurses in American popular culture, see Philip A. Kalisch and Beatrice J. Kalisch, *The Changing Image of the Nurse* (Menlo Park, Calif., 1987); Barbara Melosh, 'Doctors, Patients, and "Big Nurse": Work and Gender in the Postwar Hospital', in E.C. Lagemman, ed., *Nursing History: New Perspectives, New Possibilities* (Philadelphia, 1984).

44. VanGH, Minutes, Meeting, 15, 16 Jan., 1959.

45. Locke, 'Nurses Denied Romance by Prudish Profession'. See also 'At Hospital: "Kissing Nurse" Case Put on Ice', *Vancouver Sun*, 17 Jan. 1959, 9; 'New Rule for Nurses', *Vancouver Sun*, 27 Jan. 1959. A letter to the editor entitled 'Good Night, Nurse', apparently written by an ex-patient of VanGH, defended the students' rights to a social life on the grounds that they received so little financial remuneration for their hard work that the least they deserved was some romance to maintain their femininity: 'More power and happiness to her and student nurses like her . . . these student nurses . . . don't get enough pin money to keep them in lipstick or a few other female necessities.' *Vancouver Sun*, 1959, VCA, Add. mss. 320.

46. VanGH, Minutes, Meeting, 15, 16 Jan. 1959.

47. For example, see Lévesque, *Making and Breaking the Rules*.

48. Butler, 'Performative Acts', 282. Butler emphasizes the coercive or non-volitional dimension of identity formation and acquisition in 'The Body You Want: Liz Kotz Interviews Judith Butler', *Artforum International* (Nov. 1992): 82–9.

49. Joan Scott, 'Gender: a useful category of historical analysis', *American Historical Review* 91, 5 (1986).

Chapter 11
Iacovetta, Defending Honour, Demanding Respect

1. Consider, for example, this small sample: Leonore Davidoff and Catherine Hall, *Family Fortunes: Men and Women of the English Middle Class, 1780–1850* (Chicago, 1987); Joy Parr, *The Gender of Breadwinners: Women, Men and Change in Two Industrial Towns* (Toronto, 1990); Michael Roper and John Tosh, eds, *Manful Assertions: Masculinities in Britain Since 1800* (London and New York, 1991); Ava Baron, ed., *Work Engendered: Toward a New History of American Labor History* (Ithaca, NY, 1991); George Chauncey, *Gay New York: Gender, Urban Culture and the Gay Male World, 1890–1940* (New York, 1994); Keith Jenkins, ed., *The Postmodern History Reader* (New York, 1997).

2. For example, the essays in *Signs* 19, 2 (Summer 1994); Regina Kunzel, 'Pulp Fiction and Problem Girls: Reading and Rewriting Single Pregnancy in the Postwar United States', *American Historical Review*

100 (Dec. 1995); Franca Iacovetta and Wendy Mitchinson, eds, *On the Case: Explorations in Social History* (Toronto, 1998).

3. Neville Kirk, 'History, language, ideas and post-modernism: a materialist view', in Jenkins, ed., *The Postmodern History Reader*. See also Christine Stansell, 'Response to Joan Scott', *International and Labor Working Class History* 31 (Spring 1987).

4. See Michael Roper and John Tosh, 'Introduction', in Roper and Tosh, eds, *Manful Assertions*; and the introduction to this volume.

5. Franca Iacovetta, *Such Hardworking People: Italian Immigrants in Postwar Toronto* (Montreal and Kingston, 1992). While I remain committed to the materialist focus of my original portrayal (ch. 5), this version highlights the varied gender dynamics involved, incorporates some poststructuralist insights regarding the role of language in giving shape to experience, discontents, and demands, and adds some new material.

6. See, for example, *The Goldenberg Report* (Ottawa, 1962); Catherine Wismer, *Sweethearts: The Builders, the Mob, and the Men* (Toronto, 1968); H.C. Goldenberg and J.H. Crispo, eds, *Construction Labour Relations* (Toronto, 1968).

7. A fuller discussion is in Donna Gabaccia and Franca Iacovetta, 'Women, Work, and Protest in the Italian Diaspora: An International Research Agenda', *Labour/Le Travail* 42 (Fall 1998).

8. See, for example, Michael La Sorte, *La Merica: Images of Italian Greenhorn Experience* (Philadelphia, 1985); Donna Gabaccia and Fraser Ottanelli, 'Diaspora or International Proletariate?', *Diasporas* 6 (Spring 1997); James R. Barrett and David Roediger, 'The In Between Peoples: Race, Nationality, and the "New Immigrant" Working Class', *Journal of American Ethnic History* 16 (Spring 1997).

9. On the image and reality of the 'pick-and-shovel' metaphor in its many national and continental contexts, see George E. Pozzetta and Bruno Ramirez, eds, *The Italian Diaspora Across the Globe* (Toronto, 1992).

10. Archives of Ontario, Department of Planning and Development, Immigration Branch Files, F.J. Love to Premier Leslie Frost, 1 Sept. 1954. See also Iacovetta, *Such Hardworking People*, ch. 5.

11. Interviews with author.

12. *Toronto Telegram*, letter to editor, A.E Chapman et al., 5 Apr. 1960; interviews with author.

13. Bid-peddling refers to the practice whereby builders pressured a contractor into lowering his price below his competitor's by revealing the latter's bid. Such practices violated the principle of competitive tendering of contracts.

14. In bricklaying and carpentry, hourly rates dropped by half, from $2.50 to between $1.00–$1.50. Labourers earned as low as 80 cents an hour.

15. Interview with author (pseudonym).
16. Iacovetta, *Such Hardworking People*, ch. 2.
17. By 1971, approximately 77 per cent of Canada's Italians owned their homes, compared with 55 per cent of the general population. For Toronto, Italians recorded the highest proportion, with over 83 per cent of Italians owning their own homes. Anthony Richmond and Warren Kalback, *Factors in the Adjustment of Immigrants and Their Descendants* (Ottawa, 1980), 404–7.
18. Interview with author.
19. Reporter Frank Drea, cited in Frank Colantonio, *From the Ground Up: An Italian Immigrant's Story* (Toronto, 1997). I gratefully acknowledge the generosity of Frank Colantonio, who sadly passed away before his memoir was published, for sharing his manuscript with me.
20. The union met in a hall in an Italian neighbourhood of west-end Toronto, on Brandon Ave.
21. The Brandon locals were: Bricklayers, Masons, and Plasterers' International Union of America, Local 40; International Hod Carriers, Building and Common Laborers' Union of America, Local 811; United Brotherhood of Carpenters and Joiners of America, Local 1190; Operative Plasterers and Cement Masons' International Association of the United States and Canada, Local 117 (Plasterers) and Local 117–C (Cement Masons).
22. The 1960 strike was illegal because it was a recognition strike. Under the Ontario Labour Relations Act, strikes are prohibited until a union has been certified or voluntarily recognized by the employer and until conciliation procedures have been completed. The 1961 strike was a recognition strike for some and hence illegal; for those under contract, the strike was illegal because the Labour Relations Act prohibited strikes during the life of a collective agreement.
23. This included the rival AFL union campaign, which was launched with the official support of mainstream labour organizations such as the Canadian Labour Congress.
24. Local 211 (Teamsters) voted in favour of a sympathy strike, interrupting truck deliveries of ready-mix cement and other materials to non-union projects. So did the Commercial Bricklayers' Union, Local 183, which had a large Italian membership, and the Plasterers.
25. The final contracts, covering over 200 firms and some 7,000 workers, set a 40-hour week (for labourers, 45 hours), general increases of 40–50 cents, 4 per cent vacation pay, and some safety provisions. This raised the official hourly rate of the highest paid trade, bricklayers, from $2.60 to $3.05, and the lowest paid, labourers, from $1.55 to $2.00.
26. *Toronto Star*, 8 Aug. 1960; *Labour Gazette*, Aug. 1960.
27. *Toronto Telegram*, 26 June 1961.

28. Interview with author. An unflattering portrait of Zanini is in Colantonio, *From the Ground Up.*

29. Irvine and Zanini had jumped the gun on the AFL's plan to lead a union drive among immigrants on the grounds, they claimed, that the old-line unions could not be trusted.

30. Cited in Frank Drea, *Telegram* column, 31 Mar. 1960.

31. See, for example, Charlotte Gower Chapman, *Milocca: A Sicilian Village* (Cambridge, Mass., 1971); Ann Cornelisen, *Women of the Shadows: A Study of the Wives and Mothers of Southern Italy* (New York, 1977); Constance Cronin, *The Sting of Change: Sicilians in Sicily and Australia* (Chicago, 1970); Donna Gabbaccia, *From Sicily to Elizabeth Street: Housing and Social Change among Italian Immigrants* (Albany, NY, 1984); Judith E. Smith, *Family Connections: A History of Italian and Jewish Immigrant Lives in Providence, Rhode Island 1900–1940* (Albany, NY, 1985); Iacovetta, *Such Hardworking People.*

32. Gabaccia and Iacovetta, 'Women, Work, and Protest in the Italian Diaspora'.

33. In 1961, Italian-speaking men in Toronto earned on average $3,016; Italian-speaking women earned on average $1,456. Anthony Richmond, *Immigrants and Ethnic Groups in Metropolitan Toronto* (Toronto, 1967), 22.

34. Interviews with author.

35. Ardis Cameron, *Radicals of the Worst Sort: Laboring Women in Lawrence, Massachusetts, 1860–1912* (Chicago, 1993). See also Steven Penfold, ' "Have You No Manhood In You?": Gender and Class in the Cape Breton Coal Towns', *Acadiensis* 23, 2 (Spring 1994): 21–44; Priscilla Long, 'The Women of the Colorado Iron and Fuel Strike, 1913–14', in Ruth Milkman, ed., *Women, Work and Protest: A Century of US Women's Labor History* (Boston, 1985).

36. Interview with author.

37. Robert Ventresca, ' "Cowering Women, Combative Men?": Femininity, Masculinity and Ethnicity on Strike in Two Southern Ontario Towns, Italians on Strike in Postwar Ontario, 1960–1980' *Labour/Le Travail* 39 (Spring 1997): 125–58.

38. For example, Columba Furio, 'The Cultural Background of the Italian Immigrant Woman and Its Impact on Her Unionization in the New York Garment Industry, 1880–1919', in George Pozzetta, ed., *Pane e Lavore: The Italian American Working Class* (Toronto, 1980); Cameron, *Radicals*; Ventresca, ' "Cowering Women, Combative Men?" '; Gabaccia and Iacovetta, 'Women, Work, and Protest in the Italian Diaspora'; Carina Silberstein, 'Becoming Visible: Italian Immigrant Women in the Garment and Textile Industries in Argentina, 1890–1930', and Jennifer

Guglielmo, 'What Have We Got to Lose? Italian American Women's Workplace Organizing Strategies, East Harlem, New York, 1930–1940', both papers presented to the Berkshire Conference on the History of Women, June 1996.

39. National Archives of Canada, MG 31, vol. 1, Marino Toppan Papers, File on Correspondence and Memoirs, 1961–8, Toppan to Thomas Murphy, Washington, 7 July 1961.

40. Rosemary Boxer, *Toronto Telegram*, 24 June, 9 July 1961; interviews with author.

41. Cited in *Toronto Telegram*, 2 Aug. 1960.

42. Interview with author.

43. On this theme, see David Roediger, *The Wages of Whiteness: Race and the Making of the American Working-class* (London, 1991); Barrett and Roediger, 'In Between Peoples'; Franca Iacovetta, 'Manly Militants, Cohesive Communities, and Defiant Domestics: Writing about Immigrants in Canadian History', *Labour/Le Travail* 36 (Fall 1995): 217–52.

44. Colantonio, *From the Ground Up*, ch. 5, 100–1.

45. *Toronto Star*, 29 Mar., 4, 7 Apr. 1960; *Toronto Telegram*, 30, 31 Mar. 1960.

46. *Globe and Mail*, 12 June 1961 (D. Allen).

47. *Toronto Telegram*, 2, 3 Aug. 1960; *Toronto Star*, 2, 3 Aug. 1960; *Globe and Mail*, 2, 3 Aug. 1960.

48. *Toronto Telegram*, 2, 3 Aug. 1960; *Toronto Star*, 2, 3 Aug. 1960.

49. *Toronto Telegram*, 3, 4 Aug. 1960; *Toronto Star*, 4 Aug. 1960; *Globe and Mail*, 4, 6 Aug 1960.

50. Colantonio, *From the Ground Up*, ch. 4, 24; interviews with author; *Toronto Telegram*, letter to editor, 2 June 1960.

51. *Toronto Telegram*, 20, 22 June 1961.

52. Interviews with author.

53. *Globe and Mail*, 22, 23 June 1961; *Toronto Telegram*, 22 June 1961; *Toronto Star*, 22 June 1961; Kenneth Bagnell, *Canadese: A Portrait of the Italian Canadians* (Toronto, 1989), 159–60.

54. *Toronto Star*, 3 June 1961; *Toronto Telegram*, 3, 6 June 1961; editorial, *Canadian Labour* 6 (Sept. 1961): 4.

55. *Globe and Mail*, 17 June 1961 (A.E. Burt); *Toronto Star*, 6, 7, 16 June 1961.

56. *Globe and Mail*, 12 June 1961 (D. Allen), 7 June 1961 (R.A. Meagan).

57. *Toronto Telegram*, 19 Mar. 1960.

58. For example, ibid., 31 Mar., 3, 5, 8, 11 Apr. 1960.

59. Cited ibid., 23 July 1961.

60. Boxer cited in Colantonio, *From the Ground Up*, ch. 6, 136–7; *Toronto Star*, 3, 7 June 1961; *Globe and Mail*, 7 June 1961.

61. *Toronto Star*, 8 July 1961; *Globe and Mail*, 16 June 1961 (H. Dust); *Toronto Telegram*, 5 July 1961 (D. Braithwaite); *Toronto Star*, 24 June 1961(sheet metal worker). See also *Star*, 3, 10 June 1961; *Telegram*, 3, 6, 7, 27 June 1961.

62. *Toronto Star*, 29 Mar., 4, 7 Apr. 1960; *Toronto Telegram*, 30, 31 Mar. 1960.

63. For some differing perspectives, see references in note 2.

64. Kirk, 'History, language, ideas and post-modernism', 239.

65. See, for example, Roper and Tosh, 'Introduction'; Joy Parr, 'Gender and Historical Practice', in Joy Parr and Mark Rosenfeld, eds, *Gender and History in Canada* (Toronto, 1996); R.W. Connell, 'The Big Picture: Masculinities in Recent World History', *Theory and Society* 22 (1993); Madge Pon, 'Like a Chinese Puzzle: The Construction of Chinese Masculinity in *Jack Canuck*', in Parr and Rosenfeld, eds, *Gender and History in Canada*.

66. An insightful look at this complex issue is Nancy Forestell, 'Historians and the Politics of Masculinity', paper presented to the Canadian Historical Association, June 1996. Also see the introduction to this volume.

67. For example, Ava Baron, 'Gender and Labour History: Learning from the Past, Looking to the Future', in Baron, ed., *Work Engendered*; Alice Kessler-Harris, *Out to Work: A History of Wage-Earning Women in the United States* (New York, 1982); Bettina Bradbury, 'Women's History and Working-Class History', *Labour/Le Travail* 19 (Spring 1987); Linda Kealey, *Enlisting Women for the Cause: Women, Labour and the Left in Canada, 1890–1920* (Toronto, 1998).

THE CANADIAN SOCIAL HISTORY SERIES

Edith Burley,
*Servants of the Honourable Company:
Work, Discipline, and Conflict in the
Hudson's Bay Company, 1770–1870,*
1997.
ISBN 0–19–541296–6

Mercedes Steedman,
*Angels of the Workplace: Women and
the Construction of Gender Relations
in the Canadian Clothing Industry,
1890–1940,* 1997.
ISBN 0–19–54308–3

**Angus McLaren and
Arlene Tigar McLaren,**
*The Bedroom and the State: The
Changing Practices and Politics of
Contraception and Abortion in Canada,
1880–1997,* 1997.
ISBN 0–19–541318–0

**Kathryn McPherson, Cecilia
Morgan, and Nancy M. Forestell,
Editors,**
*Gendered Pasts: Historical Essays in
Feminity and Masculinity in Canada,*
1999.
ISBN 0–8020–8690–X

Gillian Creese,
*Contracting Masculinity: Gender,
Class, and Race in a White-Collar
Union, 1944–1994,* 1999.
ISBN 0–19–541454–3

Geoffrey Reaume,
*Remembrance of Patients Past: Patient
Life at the Toronto Hospital for the
Insane, 1870–1940,* 2000.
ISBN 0–19–541538–8

Miriam Wright,
*A Fishery for Modern Times: The State
and the Industrialization of the Newfoundland Fishery. 1934–1968,* 2001.
ISBN 0–19–541620–1

Judy Fudge and Eric Tucker,
*Labour Before the Law: The Regulation
of Workers' Collective Action in
Canada, 1900–1948,* 2001.
ISBN 0–19–541633–3

Mark Moss,
*Manliness and Militarism: Educating
Young Boys in Ontario for War,* 2001.
ISBN 0–19–541594–9

Joan Sangster,
*Regulating Girls and Women: Sexuality,
Family, and the Law in Ontario
1920–1960,* 2001.
ISBN 0–19–541663–5

Reinhold Kramer and Tom Mitchell,
*Walk Towards the Gallows: The
Tragedy of Hilda Blake, Hanged 1899,*
2002.
ISBN 0–19–541686–4

Mark Kristmanson,
*Plateaus of Freedom: Nationality, Cul-
ture, and State Security in Canada,
1940–1960,* 2002.
ISBN 0–19–541866–2

Robin Jarvis Brownlie,
*A Fatherly Eye: Indian Agents,
Government Power, and
Aboriginal Resistance in Ontario,
1918–1939.* 2003
ISBN 0–19–541891–3